THE

ACADEMICA OF CICERO.

THE TEXT REVISED AND EXPLAINED

BY

JAMES S. REID,

M.L. CAMB. M.A. (LOND.)
ASSISTANT TUTOR AND LATE FELLOW, CHRIST'S COLLEGE, CAMBRIDGE;
ASSISTANT EXAMINER IN CLASSICS TO THE UNIVERSITY OF LONDON.

LONDON:
MACMILLAN AND CO.
1874

TO

THOSE OF HIS PUPILS

WHO HAVE READ WITH HIM

THE ACADEMICA,

THIS EDITION

IS AFFECTIONATELY DEDICATED

BY

THE EDITOR.

ISBN-13:
978-1981291380

ISBN-10:
1981291385

PREFACE.

Since the work of Davies appeared in 1725, no English scholar has edited the *Academica*. In Germany the last edition with explanatory notes is that of Goerenz, published in 1810. To the poverty and untrustworthiness of Goerenz's learning Madvig's pages bear strong evidence; while the work of Davies, though in every way far superior to that of Goerenz, is very deficient when judged by the criticism of the present time.

This edition has grown out of a course of Intercollegiate lectures given by me at Christ's College several years ago. I trust that the work in its present shape will be of use to undergraduate students of the Universities, and also to pupils and teachers alike in all schools where the philosophical works of Cicero are studied, but especially in those where an attempt is made to impart such instruction in the Ancient Philosophy as will prepare the way for the completer knowledge now required in the final Classical Examinations for Honours both at Oxford and Cambridge. My notes have been written throughout with a practical reference to the needs of junior students. During the last three or four years I have read the *Academica* with a large number of intelligent pupils, and there is scarcely a note of mine which has not been suggested by some difficulty or want of theirs. My plan has been, first, to embody in an Introduction such information concerning Cicero's philosophical views and the literary history of the *Academica* as could not be readily got from existing books; next, to provide a good text; then to aid the student in obtaining a higher knowledge of Ciceronian Latinity, and lastly, to put it in his power to learn thoroughly the philosophy with which Cicero deals.

My text may be said to be founded on that of Halm which appeared in the edition of Cicero's philosophical works published in 1861 under the editorship of Baiter and Halm as a continuation of Orelli's second edition of Cicero's works, which was interrupted by the death of that editor. I have never however allowed one of Halm's readings to pass without carefully weighing the evidence he presents; and I have also studied all original criticisms upon the text to which I could obtain access. The result is a text which lies considerably nearer the MSS. than that of Halm. My obligations other than those to Halm are sufficiently acknowledged in my notes; the chief are to Madvig's little book entitled *Emendationes ad Ciceronis libros Philosophicos*, published in 1825 at Copenhagen, but never, I believe, reprinted, and to Baiter's text in the edition of Cicero's works by himself and Kayser. In a very few passages I have introduced emendations of my own, and that only where the conjecttires of other Editors seemed to me to depart too widely from the MSS. If any apology be needed for discussing, even sparingly, in the notes, questions of textual criticism, I may say that I have done so from a conviction that the very excellence of the texts now in use is depriving a Classical training of a great deal of its old educational value. The judgment was better cultivated when the student had to fight his way through bad texts to the author's meaning and to a mastery of the Latin tongue. The acceptance of results without a knowledge of the processes by which they are obtained is worthless for the purposes of education, which is thus made to rest on memory alone. I have therefore done my best to place before the reader the arguments for and against different readings in the most important places where the text is doubtful.

My experience as a teacher and examiner has proved to me that the students for whom this edition is intended have a far smaller acquaintance than they ought to have with the peculiarities and niceties of language which the best Latin writers display. I have striven to guide them to the best teaching of Madvig, on whose foundation every succeeding editor of Cicero must build. His edition of the *De Finibus* contains more valuable material for illustrating, not merely the language, but also the subject-matter of the *Academica*, than all the professed editions of the latter work in existence. Yet, even after Madvig's labours, a great deal remains to be done in pointing out what is, and what is not, Ciceronian Latin. I have therefore added very many references from my own reading, and from other sources. Wherever a quotation would not have been given but for its appearance in some other work, I have pointed out the authority from whom it was taken. I need hardly say that I do not expect or intend readers to look out all the references given. It was necessary to provide material by means of which the student might illustrate for himself a Latin usage, if it were new to him, and might solve any linguistic difficulty that occurred. Want of space has compelled me often to substitute a mere reference for an actual quotation.

As there is no important doctrine of Ancient Philosophy which is not touched upon somewhere in the *Academica*, it is evidently impossible for an editor to give information which would be complete for a reader who is studying that subject for the first time. I have therefore tried to enable readers to find easily for themselves the information they require, and have only dwelt in my own language upon such philosophical difficulties as were in some special way bound up with the *Academica*. The two books chiefly referred to in my notes are the English translation of Zeller's *Stoics, Epicureans and Sceptics* (whenever Zeller is quoted without any further description this book is meant), and the *Historia Philosophiae* of Ritter and Preller. The *pages*, not the *sections*, of the fourth edition of this work are quoted. These books, with Madvig's *De Finibus*, all teachers ought to place in the hands of pupils who are studying a philosophical work of Cicero. Students at the Universities ought to have constantly at hand Diogenes Laertius, Stobaeus, and Sextus Empiricus, all of which have been published in cheap and convenient forms.

Although this edition is primarily intended for junior students, it is hoped that it may not be without interest for maturer scholars, as bringing together much scattered information illustrative of the *Academica*, which was before difficult of access. The present work will, I hope, prepare the way for an exhaustive edition either from my own or some more competent hand. It must be regarded as an experiment, for no English scholar of recent times has treated any portion of Cicero's philosophical works with quite the purpose which I have kept in view and have explained above. Should this attempt meet with favour, I propose to edit after the same plan some others of the less known and less edited portions of Cicero's writings.

In dealing with a subject so unusually difficult and so rarely edited I cannot hope to have escaped errors, but after submitting my views to repeated revision during four years, it seems better to publish them than to withhold from students help they so greatly need. Moreover, it is a great gain, even at the cost of some errors, to throw off that intellectual disease of over-fastidiousness which is so prevalent in this University, and causes more than anything else the unproductiveness of English scholarship as compared with that of Germany,

I have only to add that I shall be thankful for notices of errors and omissions from any who are interested in the subject.

JAMES S. REID.

CHRIST'S COLLEGE, CAMBRIDGE, *December, 1873.*

LIST OF ABBREVIATIONS USED IN THIS WORK.

Cic. = Cicero; Ac., Acad. = Academica; Ac., Acad. Post. = Academica Posteriora; D.F. = De Finibus; T.D. = Tusculan Disputations; N.D. = De Natura Deorum; De Div. = De Divinatione; Parad. = Paradoxa; Luc. = Lucullus; Hortens. = Hortensius; De Off. = De Officiis; Tim. = Timaeus; Cat. Mai. = Cato Maior; Lael. = Laelius; De Leg. = De Legibus; De Rep. = De Republica; Somn. Scip. = Somnium Scipionis; De Or. = De Oratore; Orat. = Orator; De Inv. = De Inventione; Brut. = Brutus; Ad Att. = Ad Atticum; Ad Fam. = Ad Familiares; Ad Qu. Frat. = Ad Quintum Fratrem; In Verr., Verr. = In Verrem; Div. in. Qu. Caec. = Divinatio in Quintum Caecilium; In Cat. = In Catilinam.

Plat. = Plato: Rep. = Republic; Tim. = Timaeus; Apol. = Apologia Socratis; Gorg. = Gorgias; Theaet. = Theaetetus.

Arist. = Aristotle; Nic. Eth. = Nicomachean Ethics; Mag. Mor. = Magna Moralia; De Gen. An. = De Generatione Animalium; De Gen. et Corr. = De Generatione et Corruptione; Anal. Post. = Analytica Posteriora; Met. = Metaphysica; Phys. = Physica.

Plut. = Plutarch; De Plac. Phil. = De Placitis Philosophorum; Sto. Rep. = De Stoicis Repugnantiis.

Sext. = Sextus; Sext. Emp. = Sextus Empiricus; Adv. Math. or A.M. = Adversus Mathematicos; Pyrrh. Hypotyp. or Pyrrh. Hyp. or P.H. = Pyrrhoneôn Hypotyposeôn Syntagmata.

Diog. or Diog. Laert. = Diogenes Laertius.

Stob. = Stobaeus; Phys. = Physica; Eth. = Ethica.

Galen; De Decr. Hipp. et Plat. = De Decretis Hippocratis et Platonis.

Euseb. = Eusebius; Pr. Ev. = Praeparatio Evangelii.

Aug. or August. = Augustine; Contra Ac. or C. Ac. = Contra Academicos; De Civ. Dei = De Civitate Dei.

Quintil. = Quintilian; Inst. Or. = Institutiones Oratoriae.

Seneca; Ep. = Epistles; Consol. ad Helv. = Consolatio ad Helvidium.

Epic. = Epicurus; Democr. = Democritus.

Madv. = Madvig; M.D.F. = Madvig's edition of the De Finibus; Opusc. = Opuscula; Em. = Emendationes ad Ciceronis libros Philosophicos; Em. Liv. = Emendationes Livianae; Gram. = Grammar.

Bentl. = Bentley; Bait. = Baiter; Dav. = Davies; Ern. = Ernesti; Forc. = Forcellini; Goer. = Goerenz; Herm. = Hermann; Lamb. = Lambinus; Man. or Manut. = Manutius; Turn. = Turnebus; Wes. or Wesenb. = Wesenberg.

Corss. = Corssen; Ausspr. = Aussprache, Vokalismus und Betonung.

Curt. = Curtius; Grundz. = Grundzüge der Griechischen Etymologie.

Corp. Inscr. = Corpus Inscriptionum Latinarum.

Dict. Biogr. = Dictionary of Classical Biography.

Cf. = compare; conj. = 'conjecture' or 'conjectures'; conjug. = conjugation; constr. = construction; ed. = edition; edd. = editors; em. = emendation; ex. = example; exx. = examples; exc. = except; esp. = especially; fragm. = fragment or fragments; Gr. and Gk. = Greek; Introd. = Introduction; Lat. = Latin; n. = note; nn. = notes; om. = omit, omits, or omission; prep. = preposition; qu. = quotes or quoted by; subj. = subjunctive.

R. and P. = Ritter and Preller's Historia Philosophiae ex fontium locis contexta.

THE ACADEMICA OF CICERO

INTRODUCTION.

I. *Cicero as a Student of Philosophy and Man of Letters: 90—45 B.C.*

It would seem that Cicero's love for literature was inherited from his father, who, being of infirm health, lived constantly at Arpinum, and spent the greater part of his time in study.[1] From him was probably derived that strong love for the old Latin dramatic and epic poetry which his son throughout his writings displays. He too, we may conjecture, led the young Cicero to feel the importance of a study of philosophy to serve as a corrective for the somewhat narrow rhetorical discipline of the time.[2]

Cicero's first systematic lessons in philosophy were given him by the Epicurean Phaedrus, then at Rome because of the unsettled state of Athens, whose lectures he attended at a very early age, even before he had assumed the toga virilis. The pupil seems to have been converted at once to the tenets of the [ii] master.[3] Phaedrus remained to the end of his life a friend of Cicero, who speaks warmly in praise of his teacher's amiable disposition and refined style. He is the only Epicurean, with, perhaps, the exception of Lucretius, whom the orator ever allows to possess any literary power.[4] Cicero soon abandoned Epicureanism, but his schoolfellow, T. Pomponius Atticus, received more lasting impressions from the teaching of Phaedrus. It was probably at this period of their lives that Atticus and his friend became acquainted with Patro, who succeeded Zeno of Sidon as head of the Epicurean school.[5]

At this time (i.e. before 88 B.C.) Cicero also heard the lectures of Diodotus the Stoic, with whom he studied chiefly, though not exclusively, the art of dialectic.[6] This art, which Cicero deems so important to the orator that he calls it "abbreviated eloquence," was then the monopoly of the Stoic school. For some time Cicero spent all his days with Diodotus in the severest study, but he seems never to have been much attracted by the general Stoic teaching. Still, the friendship between the two lasted till the death of Diodotus, who, according to a fashion set by the Roman Stoic circle of the time of Scipio and Laelius, became an inmate of Cicero's house, where he died in B.C. 59, leaving his pupil heir to a not inconsiderable property.[7] He seems to have been one of the most accomplished [iii] men of his time, and Cicero's feelings towards him were those of gratitude, esteem, and admiration.[8]

In the year 88 B.C. the celebrated Philo of Larissa, then head of the Academic school, came to Rome, one of a number of eminent Greeks who fled from Athens on the approach of its siege during the Mithridatic war. Philo, like Diodotus, was a man of versatile genius: unlike the Stoic philosopher, he was a perfect master both of the theory and the practice of oratory. Cicero had scarcely heard him before all inclination for Epicureanism was swept from his mind, and he surrendered himself wholly, as he tells us, to the brilliant Academic.[9] Smitten with a marvellous enthusiasm he abandoned all other studies for philosophy. His zeal was quickened by the conviction that the old judicial system of Rome was overthrown for ever, and that the great career once open to an orator was now barred.[10]

We thus see that before Cicero was twenty years of age, he had been brought into intimate connection with at least three of the most eminent philosophers of the age, who represented the three most vigorous and important Greek schools. It is fair to conclude that he must have become thoroughly acquainted with their spirit, and with the main tenets of each. His own statements, after every deduction necessitated by his egotism has been made, leave no doubt about his diligence as a student. In his later works he often dwells on his youthful devotion to philosophy.[11] It would be unwise to lay too much stress on the intimate connection [iv] which subsisted between the rhetorical and the ethical teaching of the Greeks; but there can be little doubt that from the great rhetorician Molo, then Rhodian ambassador at Rome, Cicero gained valuable information concerning the ethical part of Greek philosophy.

During the years 88—81 B.C., Cicero employed himself incessantly with the study of philosophy, law, rhetoric, and belles lettres. Many ambitious works in the last two departments mentioned were written by him at this period. On Sulla's return to the city after his conquest of the Marian party in Italy, judicial affairs once more took their regular course, and Cicero appeared as a pleader in the courts, the one philosophic orator of Rome, as he not unjustly boasts[12]. For two years he was busily engaged, and then suddenly left Rome for a tour in Eastern Hellas. It is usually supposed that he came into collision with Sulla through the freedman Chrysogonus, who was implicated in the case of Roscius. The silence of Cicero is enough to condemn this theory, which rests on no better evidence than that of Plutarch. Cicero himself, even when mentioning his speech in defence of Roscius, never assigns any other cause for his departure than his health, which was being undermined by his passionate style of oratory[13].

The whole two years 79—77 B.C. were spent in the society of Greek philosophers and rhetoricians. The first six months passed at Athens, and were almost entirely devoted to philosophy, since, with the exception [v] of Demetrius Syrus, there were no eminent rhetorical teachers at that time resident in the city[14]. By the advice of Philo himself[15], Cicero attended the lectures of that clear thinker and writer, as Diogenes calls him[16], Zeno of Sidon, now the head of the Epicurean school. In Cicero's later works there are several references to his teaching. He was biting and sarcastic in speech, and spiteful in spirit, hence in striking contrast to Patro and Phaedrus[17]. It is curious to find that Zeno is numbered by Cicero among those pupils and admirers of Carneades whom he had known[18]. Phaedrus was now at Athens, and along with Atticus who loved him beyond all other philosophers[19], Cicero spent much time in listening to his instruction, which was eagerly discussed by the two pupils[20]. Patro was probably in Athens at the same time, but this is nowhere explicitly stated. Cicero must at this time have attained an almost complete familiarity with the Epicurean doctrines.

There seem to have been no eminent representatives of the Stoic school then at Athens. Nor is any mention made of a Peripatetic teacher whose lectures Cicero might have attended, though M. Pupius Piso, a professed Peripatetic, was one of his companions in this sojourn at Athens[21]. Only three notable Peripatetics were at this time living. Of these Staseas of Naples, who lived some time in Piso's house, was not then at Athens[22]; it is probable, however, from a mention of [vi] him in the De Oratore, that Cicero knew himm through Piso. Diodorus, the pupil of Critolaus, is frequently named by Cicero, but never as an acquaintance. Cratippus was at this time unknown to him.

The philosopher from whose lessons Cicero certainly learned most at this period was Antiochus of Ascalon, now the representative of a Stoicised Academic school. Of this teacher, however, I shall have to treat later, when I shall attempt to estimate the influence he exercised over our author. It is sufficient here to say that on the main point which was in controversy between Philo and Antiochus, Cicero still continued to think with his earlier teacher. His later works, however, make it evident that he set a high value on the abilities and the learning of Antiochus, especially in dialectic, which was taught after Stoic principles. Cicero speaks of him as eminent among the philosophers of the time, both for talent and acquirement [23]; as a man of acute intellect[24]; as possessed of a pointed style[25]; in fine, as the most cultivated and keenest of the philosophers of the age[26]. A considerable friendship sprang up between Antiochus and Cicero[27], which was strengthened by the fact that many friends of the latter, such as Piso, Varro, Lucullus and Brutus, more or less adhered to the views of Antiochus. It is improbable that Cicero at this time became acquainted with Aristus the brother of Antiochus, since in the Academica[28] he is mentioned in such a way as to show that he was unknown to Cicero in B.C. 62.

[vii] The main purpose of Cicero while at Athens had been to learn philosophy; in Asia and at Rhodes he devoted himself chiefly to rhetoric, under the guidance of the most noted Greek teachers, chief of whom, was his old friend Molo, the coryphaeus of the Rhodian school[29]. Cicero, however, formed while at Rhodes one friendship which largely influenced his views of philosophy, that with Posidonius the pupil of Panaetius, the most famous Stoic of the age. To him Cicero makes reference in his works oftener than to any other instructor. He speaks of him as the greatest of the Stoics[30]; as a most notable philosopher, to visit whom Pompey, in the midst of his eastern campaigns, put himself to much trouble[31]; as a minute inquirer[32]. He is scarcely ever mentioned without some expression of affection, and Cicero tells us that he read his works more than those of any other author[33]. Posidonius was at a later time resident at Rome, and stayed in Cicero's house. Hecato the Rhodian, another pupil of Panaetius, may have been at Rhodes at this time. Mnesarchus and Dardanus, also hearers of Panaetius, belonged to an earlier time, and although Cicero was well acquainted with the works of the former, he does not seem to have known either personally.

From the year 77 to the year 68 B.C., when the series of letters begins, Cicero was doubtless too busily engaged with legal and political affairs to spend much time in systematic study. That his oratory owed much to philosophy from the first he repeatedly insists; [viii] and we know from his letters that it was his later practice to refresh his style by much study of the Greek writers, and especially the philosophers. During the period then, about which we have little or no information, we may believe that he kept up his old knowledge by converse with his many Roman friends who had a bent towards philosophy, as well as with the Greeks who from time to time came to Rome and frequented the houses of the Optimates; to this he added such reading as his leisure would allow. The letters contained in the first book of those addressed to Atticus, which range over the years 68—62 B.C., afford many proofs of the abiding strength of his passion for literary employment. In the earlier part of this time we find him entreating Atticus to let him have a library which was then for sale; expressing at the same time in the strongest language his loathing for public affairs, and his love for books, to which he looks as the support of his old age[34]. In the midst of his busiest political occupations, when he was working his hardest for the consulship, his heart was given to the adornment of his Tusculan villa in a way suited to his literary and philosophic tastes. This may be taken as a specimen of his spirit throughout his life. He was before all things a man of letters; compared with literature, politics and oratory held quite a secondary place in his affections. Public business employed his intellect, but never his heart.

The year 62 released him from the consulship and enabled him to indulge his literary tastes. To this year belong the publication of his speeches, which were [ix] crowded, he says, with the maxims of philosophy[35]; the history of his consulship, in Latin and Greek, the Greek version which he sent to Posidonius being modelled on Isocrates and Aristotle; and the poem on his consulship, of which some fragments remain. A year or two later we find him reading with enthusiasm the works of Dicaearchus, and keeping up his acquaintance with living Greek philosophers[36]. His long lack of leisure seems to have caused an almost unquenchable thirst for reading at this time. His friend Paetus had inherited a valuable library, which he presented to Cicero. It was in Greece at the time, and Cicero thus writes to Atticus: "If you love me and feel sure of my love for you, use all the endeavours of your friends, clients, acquaintances, freedmen, and even slaves to prevent a single leaf from being lost.... Every day I find greater satisfaction in study, so far as my forensic labours permit[37]." At this period of his life Cicero spent much time in study at his estates near Tusculum, Antium, Formiae, and elsewhere. I dwell with greater emphasis on these facts, because of the idea now spread abroad that Cicero was a mere dabbler in literature, and that his works were extempore paraphrases of Greek books half understood. In truth, his appetite for every kind of literature was insatiable, and his attainments in each department considerable. He was certainly the most learned Roman of his age, with the single exception of Varro. One of his letters to Atticus[38] will give a fair picture of his life at this time. He especially studied the political writings of [x] the Greeks, such as Theophrastus and Dicaearchus[39]. He also wrote historical memoirs after the fashion, of Theopompus[40].

The years from 59—57 B.C. were years in which Cicero's private cares overwhelmed all thought of other occupation. Soon after his return from exile, in the year 56, he describes himself as "devouring literature" with a marvellous man named Dionysius[41], and laughingly pronouncing that nothing is sweeter than universal knowledge. He spent great part of the year 55 at Cumae or Naples "feeding upon" the library of Faustus Sulla, the son of the Dictator[42]. Literature formed then, he tells us, his solace and support, and he would rather sit in a garden seat which Atticus had, beneath a bust of Aristotle, than in the ivory chair of office. Towards the end of the year, he was busily engaged on the *De Oratore*, a work which clearly proves his continued familiarity with Greek philosophy[43]. In the following year (54) he writes that politics must cease for him, and that he therefore returns unreservedly to the life most in accordance with nature, that of the student[44]. During this year he was again for the most part at those of his country villas where his best collections of books were. At this time was written the *De Republica*, a work to which I may appeal for evidence that his old philosophical studies had by no means been allowed to drop[45]. Aristotle is especially mentioned as one of the authors [xi] read at this time[46]. In the year 52 B.C. came the *De Legibus*, written amid many distracting occupations; a work professedly modelled on Plato and the older philosophers of the Socratic schools.

In the year 51 Cicero, then on his way to Cilicia, revisited Athens, much to his own pleasure and that of the Athenians. He stayed in the house of Aristus, the brother of Antiochus and teacher of Brutus. His acquaintance with this philosopher was lasting, if we may judge from the affectionate mention in the *Brutus*[47]. Cicero also speaks in kindly terms of Xeno, an Epicurean friend of Atticus, who was then with Patro at Athens. It was at this time that Cicero interfered to prevent Memmius, the pupil of the great Roman Epicurean Lucretius, from destroying the house in which Epicurus had lived[48]. Cicero seems to have been somewhat disappointed with the state of philosophy at Athens, Aristus being the only man of merit then resident there[49]. On the journey from Athens to his province, he made the acquaintance of Cratippus, who afterwards taught at Athens as head of the Peripatetic school[50]. At this time he was resident at Mitylene, where Cicero seems to have passed some time in his society[51]. He was by far the greatest, Cicero said, of all the Peripatetics he had himself heard, and indeed equal in merit to the most eminent of that school[52].

The care of that disordered province Cilicia enough to employ Cicero's thoughts till the end of 50. [xii] Yet he yearned for Athens and philosophy. He wished to leave some memorial of himself at the beautiful city, and anxiously asked Atticus whether it would look foolish to build a προπυλον at the Academia, as Appius, his predecessor, had done at Eleusis[53]. It seems the Athenians of the time were in the habit of adapting their ancient statues to suit the noble Romans of the day, and of placing on them fulsome inscriptions. Of this practice Cicero speaks with loathing. In one letter of this date he carefully discusses the errors Atticus had pointed out in the books *De Republica*[54]. His wishes with regard to Athens still kept their hold upon his mind, and on his way home from Cilicia he spoke of conferring on the city some signal favour[55]. Cicero was anxious to show Rhodes, with its school of eloquence, to the two boys Marcus and Quintus, who accompanied him, and they probably touched there for a few days[56]. From thence they went to Athens, where Cicero again stayed with Aristus[57], and renewed his friendship with other philosophers, among them Xeno the friend of Atticus[58].

On Cicero's return to Italy public affairs were in a very critical condition, and left little room for thoughts about literature. The letters which belong to this time are very pathetic. Cicero several times contrasts the statesmen of the time with the Scipio he had himself drawn in the *De Republica*[59]; when he thinks of Caesar, Plato's description of the tyrant is present to [xiii] his mind[60]; when, he deliberates about the course he is himself to take, he naturally recals the example of Socrates, who refused to leave Athens amid the misrule of the thirty tyrants[61]. It is curious to find Cicero, in the very midst of civil war, poring over the book of Demetrius the Magnesian concerning concord[62]; or employing his days in arguing with himself a string of abstract philosophical propositions about tyranny[63]. Nothing could more clearly show that he was really a man of books; by nothing but accident a politician. In these evil days, however, nothing was long to his taste; books, letters, study, all in their turn became unpleasant[64].

As soon as Cicero had become fully reconciled to Caesar in the year 46 he returned with desperate energy to his old literary pursuits. In a letter written to Varro in that year[65], he says "I assure you I had no sooner returned to Rome than I renewed my intimacy with my old friends, my books." These gave him real comfort, and his studies seemed to bear richer fruit than in his days of prosperity[66]. The tenor of all his letters at this time is the same: see especially the remaining letters to Varro and also to Sulpicius[67]. The *Partitiones Oratoriae*, the *Paradoxa*, the *Orator*, and the *Laudatio Catonis*, to which Caesar replied by his *Anticato*, were all finished within the year. Before the end of the year the *Hortensius* and the *De Finibus* had probably both been planned and commenced. [xiv] Early in the following year the *Academica*, the history of which I shall trace elsewhere, was written.

I have now finished the first portion of my task; I have shown Cicero as the man of letters and the student of philosophy during that portion of his life which preceded the writing of the *Academica*. Even the evidence I have produced, which does not include such indirect indications of philosophical study as might be obtained from the actual philosophical works of Cicero, is sufficient to justify his boast that at no time had he been divorced from philosophy[68]. He was entitled to repel the charge made by some people on the publication of his first book of the later period—the *Hortensius*—that he was a mere tiro in philosophy, by the assertion that on the contrary nothing had more occupied his thoughts throughout the whole of a wonderfully energetic life[69]. Did the scope of this edition allow it, I should have little difficulty in showing from a minute survey of his works, and a comparison of them with ancient authorities, that his knowledge of Greek philosophy was nearly as accurate as it was extensive. So far as the *Academica* is concerned, I have had in my notes an opportunity of defending Cicero's substantial accuracy; of the success of the defence I must leave the reader to judge. During the progress of this work I shall have to expose the groundlessness of many feelings and judgments now current which have contributed to produce a low estimate of Cicero's philosophical attainments, but there is one piece of unfairness which I shall have no better opportunity of mentioning [xv] than the present. It is this. Cicero, the philosopher, is made to suffer for the shortcomings of Cicero the politician. Scholars who have learned to despise his political weakness, vanity, and irresolution, make haste to depreciate his achievements in philosophy, without troubling themselves to inquire too closely into their intrinsic value. I am sorry to be obliged to instance the illustrious Mommsen, who speaks of the *De Legibus* as "an oasis in the desert of this dreary and voluminous writer." From political partizanship, and prejudices based on facts irrelevant to the matter in hand, I beg all students to free themselves in reading the *Academica*.

II. *The Philosophical Opinions of Cicero.*

In order to define with clearness the position of Cicero as a student of philosophy, it would be indispensable to enter into a detailed historical examination of the later Greek schools—the Stoic, Peripatetic, Epicurean and new Academic. These it would be necessary to know, not merely as they came from the hands of their founders, but as they existed in Cicero's age; Stoicism not as Zeno understood it, but as Posidonius and the other pupils of Panaetius propounded it; not merely the Epicureanism of Epicurus, but that of Zeno, Phaedrus, Patro, and Xeno; the doctrines taught in the Lyceum by Cratippus; the new Academicism of Philo as well as that of Arcesilas and Carneades; the medley of Academicism, Peripateticism, and Stoicism put forward by Antiochus in the name of the Old [xvi] Academy. A systematic attempt to distinguish between the earlier and later forms of doctrine held by these schools is still a great desideratum. Cicero's statements concerning any particular school are generally tested by comparing them with the assertions made by ancient authorities about the earlier representatives of the school. Should any discrepancy appear, it is at once concluded that Cicero is in gross error, whereas, in all probability, he is uttering opinions which would have been recognised as genuine by those who were at the head of the school in his day. The criticism of Madvig even is not free from this error, as will be seen from my notes on several passages of the *Academica*[70]. As my space forbids me to attempt the thorough inquiry I have indicated as desirable, I can but describe in rough outline the relation in which Cicero stands to the chief schools.

The two main tasks of the later Greek philosophy were, as Cicero often insists, the establishment of a criterion such as would suffice to distinguish the true from the false, and the determination of an ethical standard[71]. We have in the *Academica* Cicero's view of the first problem: that the attainment of any infallible criterion was impossible. To go more into detail here would be to anticipate the text of the *Lucullus* as well as my notes. Without further refinements, I may say that Cicero in this respect was in substantial agreement with the New Academic school, and in opposition to all other schools. As he himself says, the doctrine that absolute knowledge is impossible was the one Academic tenet against which all the other schools [xvii] were combined[72]. In that which was most distinctively New Academic, Cicero followed the New Academy.

It is easy to see what there was in such a tenet to attract Cicero. Nothing was more repulsive to his mind than dogmatism. As an orator, he was accustomed to hear arguments put forward with equal persuasiveness on both sides of a case. It seemed to him arrogant to make any proposition with a conviction of its absolute, indestructible and irrefragable truth. One requisite of a philosophy with him was that it should avoid this arrogance[73]. Philosophers of the highest respectability had held the most opposite opinions on the same subjects. To withhold absolute assent from all doctrines, while giving a qualified assent to those which seemed most probable, was the only prudent course[74]. Cicero's temperament also, apart from his experience as an orator, inclined him to charity and toleration, and repelled him from the fury of dogmatism. He repeatedly insists that the diversities of opinion which the most famous intellects display, ought to lead men to teach one another with all gentleness and meekness[75]. In positiveness of assertion there seemed to be something reckless and disgraceful, unworthy of a self-controlled character[76]. Here we have a touch of feeling thoroughly Roman. Cicero further urges arguments similar to some put forward by a long series of English thinkers from Milton to Mill, to show that the free conflict of opinion is necessary [xviii] to the progress of philosophy, which was by that very freedom brought rapidly to maturity in Greece[77]. Wherever authority has loudly raised its voice, says Cicero, there philosophy has pined. Pythagoras[78] is quoted as a warning example, and the baneful effects of authority are often depicted[79]. The true philosophic spirit requires us to find out what can be said for every view. It is a positive duty to discuss all aspects of every question, after the example of the Old Academy and Aristotle[80]. Those who demand a dogmatic statement of belief are mere busybodies[81]. The Academics glory in their freedom of judgment. They are not compelled to defend an opinion whether they will or no, merely because one of their predecessors has laid it down[82]. So far does Cicero carry this freedom, that in the fifth book of the *Tusculan Disputations*, he maintains a view entirely at variance with the whole of the fourth book of the *De Finibus*, and when the discrepancy is pointed out, refuses to be bound by his former statements, on the score that he is an Academic and a freeman[83]. "Modo hoc, modo illud probabilius videtur[84]." The Academic sips the best of every school[85]. He roams in the wide field of philosophy, while the Stoic dares not stir a foot's breadth away from Chrysippus[86]. The Academic is only anxious that people should combat his opinions; for he makes it his sole [xix] aim, with Socrates, to rid himself and others of the mists of error[87]. This spirit is even found in Lucullus the Antiochean[88]. While professing, however, this philosophic bohemianism, Cicero indignantly repels the charge that the Academy, though claiming to seek for the truth, has no truth to follow[89]. The probable is for it the true.

Another consideration which attracted Cicero to these tenets was their evident adaptability to the purposes of oratory, and the fact that eloquence was, as he puts it, the child of the Academy[90]. Orators, politicians, and stylists had ever found their best nourishment in the teaching of the Academic and Peripatetic masters[91]. The Stoics and Epicureans cared nothing for power of expression. Again, the Academic tenets were those with which the common sense of the world could have most sympathy[92]. The Academy also was the school which had the most respectable pedigree. Compared with its system, all other philosophies were plebeian[93]. The philosopher who best preserved the Socratic tradition was most estimable, *ceteris paribus*, and that man was Carneades[94].

In looking at the second great problem, that of the ethical standard, we must never forget that it was considered by nearly all the later philosophers as of overwhelming importance compared with the first. Philosophy was emphatically defined as the art of [xx] conduct (*ars vivendi*). All speculative and non-ethical doctrines were merely estimable as supplying a basis on which this practical art could be reared. This is equally true of the Pyrrhonian scepticism and of the dogmatism of Zeno and Epicurus. Their logical and physical doctrines were mere outworks or ramparts within which the ordinary life of the school was carried on. These were useful chiefly in case of attack by the enemy; in time of peace ethics held the supremacy. In this fact we shall find a key to unlock many difficulties in Cicero's philosophical writings. I may instance one passage in the beginning of the *Academica Posteriora*[95], which has given much trouble to editors. Cicero is there charged by Varro with having deserted the Old Academy for the New, and admits the charge. How is this to be reconciled with his own oft-repeated statements that he never recanted the doctrines Philo had taught him? Simply thus. Arcesilas, Carneades, and Philo had been too busy with their polemic against Zeno and his followers, maintained on logical grounds, to deal much with ethics. On the other hand, in the works which Cicero had written and published before the *Academica*, wherever he had touched philosophy, it had been on its ethical side. The works themselves, moreover, were direct imitations of early Academic and Peripatetic writers, who, in the rough popular view which regarded ethics mainly or solely, really composed a single school, denoted by the phrase "Vetus Academia." General readers, therefore, who considered ethical resemblance as of far greater moment than dialectical [xxi] difference, would naturally look upon Cicero as a supporter of their "Vetus Academia," so long as he kept clear of dialectic; when he brought dialectic to the front, and pronounced boldly for Carneades, they would naturally regard him as a deserter from the Old Academy to the New. This view is confirmed by the fact that for many years before Cicero wrote, the Academic dialectic had found no eminent expositor. So much was this the case, that when Cicero wrote the *Academica* he was charged with constituting himself the champion of an exploded and discredited school[96].

Cicero's ethics, then, stand quite apart from his dialectic. In the sphere of morals he felt the danger of the principle of doubt. Even in the *De Legibus* when the dialogue turns on a moral question, he begs the New Academy, which has introduced confusion into these subjects, to be silent[97]. Again, Antiochus, who in the dialectical dialogue is rejected, is in the *De Legibus* spoken of with considerable favour[98]. All ethical systems which seemed to afford stability to moral principles had an attraction for Cicero. He was fascinated by the Stoics almost beyond the power of resistance. In respect of their ethical and religious ideas he calls them "great and famous philosophers[99]," and he frequently speaks with something like shame of the treatment they had received at the hands of Arcesilas and Carneades. Once he gives expression to a fear lest they should be the only true philosophers [xxii] after all[100]. There was a kind of magnificence about the Stoic utterances on morality, more suited to a superhuman than a human world, which allured Cicero more than the barrenness of the Stoic dialectic repelled him[101]. On moral questions, therefore, we often find him going farther in the direction of Stoicism than even his teacher Antiochus. One great question which divided the philosophers of the time was, whether happiness was capable of degrees. The Stoics maintained that it was not, and in a remarkable passage Cicero agrees with them, explicitly rejecting the position of Antiochus, that a life enriched by virtue, but unattended by other advantages, might be happy, but could not be the happiest possible[102]. He begs the Academic and Peripatetic schools to cease from giving an uncertain sound (balbutire) and to allow that the happiness of the wise man would remain unimpaired even if he were thrust into the bull of Phalaris[103]. In another place he admits the purely Stoic doctrine that virtue is one and indivisible[104]. These opinions, however, he will not allow to be distinctively Stoic, but appeals to Socrates as his authority for them[105]. Zeno, who is merely an ignoble craftsman of words, stole them from the Old Academy. This is Cicero's general feeling with regard to Zeno, and there can be no doubt that he caught it from Antiochus who, in stealing the doctrines of Zeno, ever stoutly maintained that Zeno had stolen them before. Cicero, however, regarded chiefly the ethics of Zeno with this feeling, while Antiochus so [xxiii] regarded chiefly the dialectic. It is just in this that the difference between Antiochus and Cicero lies. To the former Zeno's dialectic was true and Socratic, while the latter treated it as un-Socratic, looking upon Socrates as the apostle of doubt[106]. On the whole Cicero was more in accord with Stoic ethics than Antiochus. Not in all points, however: for while Antiochus accepted without reserve the Stoic paradoxes, Cicero hesitatingly followed them, although he conceded that they were Socratic[107]. Again, Antiochus subscribed to the Stoic theory that all emotion was sinful; Cicero, who was very human in his joys and sorrows, refused it with horror[108]. It must be admitted that on some points Cicero was inconsistent. In the *De Finibus* he argued that the difference between the Peripatetic and Stoic ethics was merely one of terms; in the *Tusculan Disputations* he held it to be real. The most Stoic in tone of all his works are the *Tusculan Disputations* and the *De Officiis*.

With regard to physics, I may remark at the outset that a comparatively small importance was in Cicero's time attached to this branch of philosophy. Its chief importance lay in the fact that ancient theology was, as all natural theology must be, an appendage of physical science. The religious element in Cicero's nature inclined him very strongly to sympathize with the Stoic views about the grand universal operation of divine power. Piety, sanctity, and moral good, were impossible in any form, he thought, if the divine [xxiv] government of the universe were denied[109]. It went to Cicero's heart that Carneades should have found it necessary to oppose the beautiful Stoic theology, and he defends the great sceptic by the plea that his one aim was to arouse men to the investigation of the truth[110]. At the same time, while really following the Stoics in physics, Cicero often believed himself to be following Aristotle. This partly arose from the actual adoption by the late Peripatetics of many Stoic doctrines, which they gave out as Aristotelian. The discrepancy between the spurious and the genuine Aristotelian views passed undetected, owing to the strange oblivion into which the most important works of Aristotle had fallen[111]. Still, Cicero contrives to correct many of the extravagances of the Stoic physics by a study of Aristotle and Plato. For a thorough understanding of his notions about physics, the *Timaeus* of Plato, which he knew well and translated, is especially important. It must not be forgotten, also, that the Stoic physics were in the main Aristotelian, and that Cicero was well aware of the fact.

Very few words are necessary in order to characterize Cicero's estimate of the Peripatetic and Epicurean schools. The former was not very powerfully represented during his lifetime. The philosophical descendants of the author of the *Organon* were notorious for their ignorance of logic[112], and in ethics had approximated considerably to the Stoic teaching. While not much influenced by the school, Cicero generally [xxv] treats it tenderly for the sake of its great past, deeming it a worthy branch of the true Socratic family. With the Epicureans the case was different. In physics they stood absolutely alone, their system was grossly unintellectual, and they discarded mathematics. Their ethical doctrines excited in Cicero nothing but loathing, dialectic they did not use, and they crowned all their errors by a sin which the orator could never pardon, for they were completely indifferent to every adornment and beauty of language.

III. *The aim of Cicero in writing his philosophical works.*

It is usual to charge Cicero with a want of originality as a philosopher, and on that score to depreciate his works. The charge is true, but still absurd, for it rests on a misconception, not merely of Cicero's purpose in writing, but of the whole spirit of the later Greek speculation. The conclusion drawn from the charge is also quite unwarranted. If the later philosophy of the Greeks is of any value, Cicero's works are of equal value, for it is only from them that we get any full or clear view of it. Any one who attempts to reconcile the contradictions of Stobaeus, Diogenes Laertius, Sextus Empiricus, Plutarch and other authorities, will perhaps feel little inclination to cry out against the confusion of Ciceros ideas. Such outcry, now so common, is due largely to the want, which I have already noticed, of any clear exposition of the [xxvi] variations in doctrine which the late Greek schools exhibited during the last two centuries before the Christian era. But to return to the charge of want of originality. This is a virtue which Cicero never claims. There is scarcely one of his works (if we except the third book of the *De Officiis*), which he does not freely confess to be taken wholly from Greek sources. Indeed at the time when he wrote, originality would have been looked upon as a fault rather than an excellence. For two centuries, if we omit Carneades, no one had propounded anything substantially novel in philosophy: there had been simply one eclectic combination after another of pre-existing tenets. It would be hasty to conclude that the writers of these two centuries are therefore undeserving of our study, for the spirit, if not the substance of the doctrines had undergone a momentous change, which ultimately exercised no unimportant influence on society and on the Christian religion itself.

When Cicero began to write, the Latin language may be said to have been destitute of a philosophical literature. Philosophy was a sealed study to those who did not know Greek. It was his aim, by putting the best Greek speculation into the most elegant Latin form, to extend the education of his countrymen, and to enrich their literature. He wished at the same time to strike a blow at the ascendency of Epicureanism throughout Italy. The doctrines of Epicurus had alone appeared in Latin in a shape suited to catch the popular taste. There seems to have been a very large Epicurean literature in Latin, of which all but a few scanty traces is now lost. C. Amafinius, mentioned in [xxvii] the *Academica*[113], was the first to write, and his books seem to have had an enormous circulation[114]. He had a large number of imitators, who obtained such a favourable reception, that, in Cicero's strong language, they took possession of the whole of Italy[115]. Rabirius and Catius the Insubrian, possibly the epicure and friend of Horace, were two of the most noted of these writers. Cicero assigns various reasons for their extreme popularity: the easy nature of the Epicurean physics, the fact that there was no other philosophy for Latin readers, and the voluptuous blandishments of pleasure. This last cause, as indeed he in one passage seems to allow, must have been of little real importance. It is exceedingly remarkable that the whole of the Roman Epicurean literature dealt in an overwhelmingly greater degree with the physics than with the ethics of Epicurus. The explanation is to be found in the fact that the Italian races had as yet a strong practical basis for morality in the legal and social constitution of the family, and did not much feel the need of any speculative system; while the general decay among the educated classes of a belief in the supernatural, accompanied as it was by an increase of superstition among the masses, prepared the way for the acceptance of a purely mechanical explanation of the universe. But of this subject, interesting and important as it is in itself, and neglected though it has been, I can treat no farther.

These Roman Epicureans are continually reproached [xxviii] by Cicero for their uncouth style of writing[116]. He indeed confesses that he had not read them, but his estimate of them was probably correct. A curious question arises, which I cannot here discuss, as to the reasons Cicero had for omitting all mention of Lucretius when speaking of these Roman Epicureans. The most probable elucidation is, that he found it impossible to include the great poet in his sweeping condemnation, and being unwilling to allow that anything good could come from the school of Epicurus, preferred to keep silence, which nothing compelled him to break, since Lucretius was an obscure man and only slowly won his way to favour with the public.

In addition to his desire to undermine Epicureanism in Italy, Cicero had a patriotic wish to remove from the literature of his country the reproach that it was completely destitute where Greek was richest. He often tries by the most far-fetched arguments to show that philosophy had left its mark on the early Italian peoples[117]. To those who objected that philosophy was best left to the Greek language, he replies with indignation, accusing them of being untrue to their country[118]. It would be a glorious thing, he thinks, if

Romans were no longer absolutely compelled to resort to Greeks[119]. He will not even concede that the Greek is a richer tongue than the Latin[120]. As for the alleged incapacity of the Roman intellect to deal with philosophical [xxix] enquiries, he will not hear of it. It is only, he says, because the energy of the nation has been diverted into other channels that so little progress has been made. The history of Roman oratory is referred to in support of this opinion[121]. If only an impulse were given at Rome to the pursuit of philosophy, already on the wane in Greece, Cicero thought it would flourish and take the place of oratory, which he believed to be expiring amid the din of civil war[122].

There can be no doubt that Cicero was penetrated by the belief that he could thus do his country a real service. In his enforced political inaction, and amid the disorganisation of the law-courts, it was the one service he could render[123]. He is within his right when he claims praise for not abandoning himself to idleness or worse, as did so many of the most prominent men of the time[124]. For Cicero idleness was misery, and in those evil times he was spurred on to exertion by the deepest sorrow[125]. Philosophy took the place of forensic oratory, public harangues, and politics[126]. It is strange to find Cicero making such elaborate apologies as he does for devoting himself to philosophy, and a careless reader might set them down to egotism. But it must never be forgotten that at Rome such studies were merely the amusement of the wealthy; the total devotion of a life to them seemed well enough for Greeks, [xxx] but for Romans unmanly, unpractical and unstatesmanlike[127]. There were plenty of Romans who were ready to condemn such pursuits altogether, and to regard any fresh importation from Greece much in the spirit with which things French were received by English patriots immediately after the great war. Others, like the Neoptolemus of Ennius, thought a little learning in philosophy was good, but a great deal was a dangerous thing[128]. Some few preferred that Cicero should write on other subjects[129]. To these he replies by urging the pressing necessity there was for works on philosophy in Latin.

Still, amid much depreciation, sufficient interest and sympathy were roused by his first philosophical works to encourage Cicero to proceed. The elder generation, for whose approbation he most cared, praised the books, and many were incited both to read and to write philosophy[130]. Cicero now extended his design, which seems to have been at first indefinite, so as to bring within its scope every topic which Greek philosophers were accustomed to treat[131]. Individual questions in philosophy could not be thoroughly understood till the whole subject had been mastered[132]. This design then, which is not explicitly stated in the two earliest works which we possess, the *Academica* and the *De Finibus*, required the composition of a sort of philosophical encyclopaedia. Cicero never claimed to be more than an interpreter of Greek philosophy [xxxi] to the Romans. He never pretended to present new views of philosophy, or even original criticisms on its history. The only thing he proclaims to be his own is his style. Looked at in this, the true light, his work cannot be judged a failure. Those who contrive to pronounce this judgment must either insist upon trying the work by a standard to which it does not appeal, or fail to understand the Greek philosophy it copies, or perhaps make Cicero suffer for the supposed worthlessness of the philosophy of his age.

In accordance with Greek precedent, Cicero claims to have his oratorical and political writings, all or nearly all published before the *Hortensius*, included in his philosophical encyclopaedia[133]. The only two works strictly philosophical, even in the ancient view, which preceded the *Academica*, were the *De Consolatione*, founded on Crantor's book, περι πενθους, and the *Hortensius*, which was introductory to philosophy, or, as it was then called, protreptic.

For a list of the philosophical works of Cicero, and the dates of their composition, the student must be referred to the *Dict. of Biography*, Art. Cicero.

IV. *History of the Academica.*

On the death of Tullia, which happened at Tusculum in February, 45 B.C., Cicero took refuge in the solitude of his villa at Astura, which was pleasantly situated on the Latin coast between Antium and [xxxii] Circeii[134]. Here he sought to soften his deep grief by incessant toil. First the book *De Consolatione* was written. He found the mechanic exercise of composition the best solace for his pain, and wrote for whole days together[135]. At other times he would plunge at early morning into the dense woods near his villa, and remain there absorbed in study till nightfall[136]. Often exertion failed to bring relief; yet he repelled the entreaties of Atticus that he would return to the forum and the senate. A grief, which books and solitude could scarcely enable him to endure, would crush him, he felt, in the busy city[137].

It was amid such surroundings that the *Academica* was written. The first trace of an intention to write the treatise is found in a letter of Cicero to Atticus, which seems to belong to the first few weeks of his bereavement[138]. It was his wont to depend on Atticus very much for historical and biographical details, and in the letter in question he asks for just the kind of information which would be needed in writing the *Academica*. The words with which he introduces his request imply that he had determined on some new work to which our *Academica* would correspond[139]. He asks what reason brought to Rome the embassy which Carneades accompanied; who was at that time the leader of the Epicurean school; who were then the most noted πολιτικοι at Athens. The meaning of the last question is made clear by a passage in the *De Oratore*[140], [xxxiii] where Cicero speaks of the combined Academic and Peripatetic schools under that name. It may be with reference to the progress of the *Academica* that in a later letter he expresses himself satisfied with the advance he has made in his literary undertakings[141]. During the whole of the remainder of his sojourn at Astura he continued to be actively employed; but although he speaks of various other literary projects, we find no express mention in his letters to Atticus of the *Academica*[142]. He declares that however much his detractors at Rome may reproach him with inaction, they could not read the numerous difficult works on which he has been engaged within the same space of time that he has taken to write them[143].

In the beginning of June Cicero spent a few days at his villa near Antium[144], where he wrote a treatise addressed to Caesar, which he afterwards suppressed[145]. From the same place he wrote to Atticus of his intention to proceed to Tusculum or Rome by way of Lanuvium about the middle of June[146]. He had in the time immediately following Tullia's death entertained an aversion for Tusculum, where she died. This he felt now compelled to conquer, otherwise he must either abandon Tusculum altogether, or, if he returned at all, a delay of even ten years would make the effort no less painful[147]. Before setting out for Antium Cicero [xxxiv] wrote to Atticus that he had finished while at Astura *duo magna* συνταγματα, words which have given rise to much controversy[148]. Many scholars, including Madvig, have understood that the first edition of the *Academica*, along with the *De Finibus*, is intended. Against this view the reasons adduced by Krische are convincing[149]. It is clear from the letters to Atticus that the *De Finibus* was being worked out book by book long after the first edition of the *Academica* had been placed in the hands of Atticus. The *De Finibus* was indeed begun at Astura[150], but it was still in an unfinished state when Cicero began to revise the *Academica*[151]. The final arrangement of the characters in the *De Finibus* is announced later still[152]; and even at a later date Cicero complains that Balbus had managed to obtain surreptitiously a copy of the fifth book before it was properly corrected, the irrepressible Caerellia having copied the whole five books while in that state[153]. A passage in the *De Divinatione*[154] affords almost direct evidence that the *Academica* was published before the *De Finibus*. On all these grounds I hold that these two works cannot be those which Cicero describes as having been finished simultaneously at Astura.

Another view of the συνταγματα in question is that they are simply the two books, entitled *Catulus* and *Lucullus*, of the *Priora Academica*. In my opinion [xxxv] the word συνταγμα, the use of which to denote a portion of a work Madvig suspects[155], thus obtains its natural meaning. Cicero uses the word συνταξις of the whole work[156], while συνταγμα[157], and συγγραμμα[158], designate definite portions or divisions of a work. I should be quite content, then, to refer the words of Cicero to the *Catulus* and *Lucullus*. Krische, however, without giving reasons, decides that this view is unsatisfactory, and prefers to hold that the *Hortensius* (or *de Philosophia*) and the *Priora Academica* are the compositions in question. If this conjecture is correct, we have in the disputed passage the only reference to the *Hortensius* which is to be found in the letters of Cicero. We are quite certain that the book was written at Astura, and published before the *Academica*. This would be clear from the mention in the *Academica Posteriora* alone[159], but the words of Cicero in the *De Finibus*[160] place it beyond all doubt, showing as they do that the *Hortensius* had been published a sufficiently long time before the *De Finibus*, to have become known to a tolerably large circle of readers. Further, in the *Tusculan Disputations* and the *De Divinatione*[161] the *Hortensius* and the *Academica* are mentioned together in such a way as to show that the former was finished and given to the world before the latter. Nothing therefore stands in the way of Krische's conjecture, except the doubt I have expressed as to the use of the word συνταγμα, which equally affects the old view maintained by Madvig.

[xxxvi]

Whatever be the truth on this point, it cannot be disputed that the *Hortensius* and the *Academica* must have been more closely connected, in style and tone, than any two works of Cicero, excepting perhaps the *Academica* and the *De Finibus*. The interlocutors in the *Hortensius* were exactly the same as in the *Academica Priora*, for the introduction of Balbus into some editions of the fragments of the *Hortensius* is an error[162]. The discussion in the *Academica Priora* is carried on at Hortensius' villa near Bauli; in the *Hortensius* at the villa of Lucullus near Cumae. It is rather surprising that under these circumstances there should be but one direct reference to the *Hortensius* in the *Lucullus*[163].

While at his Tusculan villa, soon after the middle of June, B.C. 45, Cicero sent Atticus the *Torquatus*, as he calls the first book of the *De Finibus*[164]. He had already sent the first edition of the *Academica* to Rome[165]. We have a mention that new prooemia had been added to the *Catulus* and *Lucullus*, in which the public characters from whom the books took their names were extolled. In all probability the extant prooemium of the *Lucullus* is the one which was then affixed. Atticus, who visited Cicero at Tusculum, had doubtless pointed out the incongruity between the known attainments of Catulus and Lucullus, and the parts they were made to take in difficult philosophical discussions. It is not uncharacteristic of Cicero that his first plan for healing the incongruity should be a [xxxvii] deliberate attempt to impose upon his readers a set of statements concerning the ability and culture of these two noble Romans which he knew, and in his own letters to Atticus admitted, to be false. I may note, as of some interest in connection with the *Academica*, the fact that among the unpleasant visits received by Cicero at Tusculum was one from Varro[166].

On the 23rd July, Cicero left Home for Arpinum, in order, as he says, to arrange some business matters, and to avoid the embarrassing attentions of Brutus[167]. Before leaving Astura, however, it had been his intention to go on to Arpinum[168]. He seems to have been still unsatisfied with his choice of interlocutors for the *Academica*, for the first thing he did on his arrival was to transfer the parts of Catulus and Lucullus to Cato and Brutus[169]. This plan was speedily cast aside on the receipt of a letter from Atticus, strongly urging that the whole work should be dedicated to Varro, or if not the *Academica*, the *De Finibus*[170]. Cicero had never been very intimate with Varro: their acquaintance seems to have been chiefly maintained through Atticus, who was at all times anxious to draw them more closely together. Nine years before he had pressed Cicero to find room in his works for some mention of Varro[171]. The nature of the works on which our author was then engaged had made it difficult to comply with the request[172]. Varro had promised on his side, full two years before the *Academica* was [xxxviii] written, to dedicate to Cicero his great work *De Lingua Latino*. In answer to the later entreaty of Atticus, Cicero declared himself very much dissatisfied with Varro's failure to fulfil his promise. From this it is evident that Cicero knew nothing of the scope or magnitude of that work. His complaint that Varro had been writing for two years without making any progress[173], shows that there could have been little of anything like friendship between the two. Apart from these causes for grumbling, Cicero thought the suggestion of Atticus a "godsend[174]." Since the *De Finibus* was already "betrothed" to Brutus, he promised to transfer to Varro the *Academica*, allowing that Catulus and Lucullus, though of noble birth, had no claim to learning[175]. So little of it did they possess that they could never even have dreamed of the doctrines they had been made in the first edition of the *Academica* to maintain[176]. For them another place was to be found, and the remark was made that the *Academica* would just suit Varro, who was a follower of Antiochus, and the fittest person to expound the opinions of that philosopher[177]. It happened that continual rain fell during the first few days of Cicero's stay at Arpinum, so he employed his whole time in editing once more his *Academica*, which he now divided into four books instead of two, making the interlocutors himself, Varro and Atticus[178]. The position occupied by Atticus in the dialogue was quite an [xxxix] inferior one, but he was so pleased with it that Cicero determined to confer upon him often in the future such minor parts[179]. A suggestion of Atticus that Cotta should also be introduced was found impracticable[180].

Although the work of re-editing was vigorously pushed on, Cicero had constant doubts about the expediency of dedicating the work to Varro. He frequently throws the whole responsibility for the decision upon Atticus, but for whose importunities he would probably again have changed his plans. Nearly every letter written to Atticus during the progress of the work contains entreaties that he would consider the matter over and over again before he finally decided[181]. As no reasons had been given for these solicitations, Atticus naturally grew impatient, and Cicero was obliged to assure him that there were reasons, which he could not disclose in a letter[182]. The true reasons, however, did appear in some later letters. In one Cicero said: "I am in favour of Varro, and the more so because he wishes it, but you know he is

δεινος ανηρ, ταχα κεν και αναιτιον αιτιοωιτο.

So there often flits before me a vision of his face, as he grumbles, it may be, that my part in the treatise is more liberally sustained than his; a charge which you will perceive to be untrue[183]." Cicero, then, feared Varro's temper, and perhaps his knowledge and real critical fastidiousness. Before these explanations Atticus [xl] had concluded that Cicero was afraid of the effect the work might produce on the public. This notion Cicero assured him to be wrong; the only cause for his vacillation was his doubt as to how Varro would receive the dedication[184]. Atticus would seem to have repeatedly communicated with Varro, and to have assured Cicero that there was no cause for fear; but the latter refused to take a general assurance, and anxiously asked for a detailed account of the reasons from which it proceeded[185]. In order to stimulate his friend, Atticus affirmed that Varro was jealous of some to whom Cicero had shown more favour[186]. We find Cicero eagerly asking for more information, on this point: was it Brutus of whom Varro was jealous? It seems strange that Cicero should not have entered into correspondence with Varro himself. Etiquette seems to have required that the recipient of a dedication should be assumed ignorant of the intentions of the donor till they were on the point of being actually carried out. Thus although Cicero saw Brutus frequently while at Tusculum, he apparently did not speak to him about the *De Finibus*, but employed Atticus to ascertain his feeling about the dedication[187].

Cicero's own judgment about the completed second edition of the *Academica* is often given in the letters. He tells us that it extended, on the whole, to greater length than the first, though much had been omitted; [xli] he adds, "Unless human self love deceives me, the books have been so finished that the Greeks themselves have nothing in the same department of literature to approach them.... This edition will be more brilliant, more terse, and altogether better than the last[188]." Again: "The Antiochean portion has all the point of Antiochus combined with any polish my style may possess[189]." Also: "I have finished the book with I know not what success, but with a care which nothing could surpass[190]." The binding and adornment of the presentation copy for Varro received great attention, and the letter accompanying it was carefully elaborated[191]. Yet after everything had been done and the book had been sent to Atticus at Rome, Cicero was still uneasy as to the reception it would meet with from Varro. He wrote thus to Atticus: "I tell you again and again that the presentation will be at your own risk. So if you begin to hesitate, let us desert to Brutus, who is also a follower of Antiochus. 0 Academy, on the wing as thou wert ever wont, flitting now hither, now thither!" Atticus on his part "shuddered" at the idea of taking the responsibility[192]. After the work had passed into his hands, Cicero begged him to take all precautions to prevent it from getting into circulation until they could meet one another in Rome[193]. This warning was necessary, because Balbus and Caerellia had just managed to get access to the *De Finibus*[194]. In a letter, dated apparently a day or two later, Cicero declared his intention [xlii] to meet Atticus at Rome and send the work to Varro, should it be judged advisable to do so, after a consultation[195]. The meeting ultimately did not take place, but Cicero left the four books in Atticus' power, promising to approve any course that might be taken[196]. Atticus wrote to say that as soon as Varro came to Rome the books would be sent to him. "By this time, then," says Cicero, when he gets the letter, "you have taken the fatal step; oh dear! if you only knew at what peril to yourself! Perhaps my letter stopped you, although you had not read it when you wrote. I long to hear how the matter stands[197]." Again, a little later: "You have been bold enough, then, to give Varro the books? I await his judgment upon them, but when will he read them?" Varro probably received the books in the first fortnight of August, 45 B.C., when Cicero was hard at work on the *Tusculan Disputations*[198]. A copy of the first edition had already got into Varro's hands, as we learn from a letter, in which Cicero begs Atticus to ask Varro to make some alterations in his copy of the *Academica*, at a time when the fate of the second edition was still undecided[199]. From this fact we may conclude that Cicero had given up all hope of suppressing the first edition. If he consoles Atticus for the uselessness of his copies of the first edition, it does not contradict my supposition, for Cicero of course assumes that Atticus, whatever may be the feeling of other people, wishes to have the "Splendidiora, breviora, [xliii] meliora." Still, on every occasion which offered, the author sought to point out as his authorised edition the one in four books. He did so in a passage written immediately after the *Academica Posteriora* was completed[200], and often subsequently, when he most markedly mentioned the number of the books as four[201]. That he wished the work to bear the title *Academica* is clear[202]. The expressions *Academica quaestio*, Ακαδημικη συνταξις, and *Academia*, are merely descriptive[203]; so also is the frequent appellation *Academici libri*[204]. The title *Academicae Quaestiones*, found in many editions, is merely an imitation of the *Tusculanae Quaestiones*, which was supported by the false notion, found as early as Pliny[205], that Cicero had a villa called Academia, at which the book was written. He had indeed a Gymnasium at his Tusculan villa, which he called his Academia, but we are certain from the letters to Atticus that the work was written entirely at Astura, Antium, and Arpinum.

Quintilian seems to have known the first edition very well[206], but the second edition is the one which is most frequently quoted. The four books are expressly referred to by Nonius, Diomedes, and Lactantius, under the title *Academica*. Augustine speaks of them only as *Academici libri*, and his references show that he knew the second edition only. Lactantius also uses this name occasionally, though he generally speaks of [xliv] the *Academica*. Plutarch shows only a knowledge of the first edition[207].

I have thought it advisable to set forth in plain terms the history of the genesis of the book, as gathered from Cicero's letters to Atticus. That it was not unnecessary to do so may be seen from the astounding theories which old scholars of great repute put forward concerning the two editions. A fair summary of them may be seen in the preface of Goerenz. I now proceed to examine into the constitution and arrangement of the two editions.

a. *The lost dialogue "Catulus."*

The whole of the characters in this dialogue and the *Lucullus* are among those genuine Optimates and adherents of the senatorial party whom Cicero so loves to honour. The Catulus from whom the lost dialogue was named was son of the illustrious colleague of Marius. With the political career of father and son we shall have little to do. I merely inquire what was their position with respect to the philosophy of the time, and the nature of their connection with Cicero.

Catulus the younger need not detain us long. It is clear from the *Lucullus*[208] that he did little more than put forward opinions he had received from his father. Cicero would, doubtless, have preferred to introduce the elder man as speaking for himself, but in that case, as in the *De Oratore*, the author would have been [xlv] compelled to exclude himself from the conversation[209]. The son, therefore, is merely the mouthpiece of the father, just as Lucullus, in the dialogue which bears his name, does nothing but render literally a speech of Antiochus, which he professes to have heard[210]. For the arrangement in the case of both a reason is to be found in their ατριψια with respect to philosophy[211]. This ατριψια did not amount to απαιδευσια, or else Cicero could not have made Catulus the younger the advocate of philosophy in the *Hortensius*[212]. Though Cicero sometimes classes the father and son together as men of literary culture and perfect masters of Latin style, it is very evident on a comparison of all the passages where the two are mentioned, that no very high value was placed on the learning of the son[213]. But however slight were the claims of Catulus the younger to be considered a philosopher, he was closely linked to Cicero by other ties. During all the most brilliant period of Cicero's life, Catulus was one of the foremost Optimates of Rome, and his character, life, and influence are often depicted in even extravagant language by the orator[214]. He is one of the pillars of the state[215], Cicero cries, and deserves to be classed with the ancient worthies of Rome[216]. When he opposes the Manilian law, and asks the people on whom they would rely if Pompey, with such gigantic power concentrated in his hands, were to die, the people answer with one [xlvi] voice "On you[217]." He alone was bold enough to rebuke the follies, on the one hand, of the mob, on the other, of the senate[218]. In him no storm of danger, no favouring breeze of fortune, could ever inspire either fear or hope, or cause to swerve from his own course[219]. His influence, though he be dead, will ever live among his countrymen[220]. He was not only glorious in his life, but fortunate in his death[221].

Apart from Cicero's general agreement with Catulus in politics, there were special causes for his enthusiasm. Catulus was one of the *viri consulares* who had given their unreserved approval to the measures taken for the suppression of the Catilinarian conspiracy, and was the first to confer on Cicero the greatest glory of his life, the title "Father of his country[222]." So closely did Cicero suppose himself to be allied to Catulus, that a friend tried to console him for the death of Tullia, by bidding him remember "Catulus and the olden times[223]." The statement of Catulus, often referred to by Cicero, that Rome had never been so unfortunate as to have two bad consuls in the same year, except when Cinna held the office, may have been intended to point a contrast between the zeal of Cicero and the lukewarmness of his colleague Antonius[224]. Archias, who wrote in honour of Cicero's consulship, lived in the house of the two Catuli[225].

[xlvii]

We have seen that when Cicero found it too late to withdraw the first edition of the *Academica* from circulation, he affixed a prooemium to each book, Catulus being lauded in the first, Lucullus in the second. From the passages above quoted, and from our knowledge of Cicero's habit in such matters, we can have no difficulty in conjecturing at least a portion of the contents of the lost prooemium to the *Catulus*. The achievements of the elder Catulus were probably extolled, as well as those of his son. The philosophical knowledge of the elder man was made to cast its lustre on the younger. Cicero's glorious consulship was once more lauded, and great stress was laid upon the patronage it received from so famous a man as the younger Catulus, whose praises were sung in the fervid language which Cicero lavishes on the same theme elsewhere. Some allusion most likely was made to the connection of Archias with the Catuli, and to the poem he had written in Cicero's honour. Then the occasion of the dialogue, its supposed date, and the place where it was held, were indicated. The place was the Cuman villa of Catulus[226]. The feigned date must fall between the year 60 B.C. in which Catulus died, and 63, the year of Cicero's consulship, which is alluded to in the *Lucullus*[227]. It is well known that in the arrangement of his dialogues Cicero took every precaution against anachronisms.

The prooemium ended, the dialogue commenced. Allusion was undoubtedly made to the *Hortensius*, in which the same speakers had been engaged; and after more compliments had been bandied about, most of [xlviii] which would fall to Cicero's share, a proposal was made to discuss the great difference between the dogmatic and sceptic schools. Catulus offered to give his father's views, at the same time commending his father's knowledge of philosophy. Before we proceed to construct in outline the speech of Catulus from indications offered by the *Lucullus*, it is necessary to speak of the character and philosophical opinions of Catulus the elder.

In the many passages where Cicero speaks of him, he seldom omits to mention his *sapientia*, which implies a certain knowledge of philosophy. He was, says Cicero, the kindest, the most upright, the wisest, the holiest of men[228]. He was a man of universal merit, of surpassing worth, a second Laelius[229]. It is easy to gather from the *De Oratore*, in which he appears as an interlocutor, a more detailed view of his accomplishments. Throughout the second and third books he is treated as the lettered man, par excellence, of the company[230]. Appeal is made to him when any question is started which touches on Greek literature and philosophy. We are especially told that even with Greeks his acquaintance with Greek, and his style of speaking it, won admiration[231]. He defends the Greeks from the attacks of Crassus[232]. He contemptuously contrasts the Latin historians with the Greek[233]. He depreciates the later Greek rhetorical teaching, while he bestows [xlix] high commendation on the early sophists[234]. The systematic rhetoric of Aristotle and Theophrastus is most to his mind[235]. An account is given by him of the history of Greek speculation in Italy[236]. The undefiled purity of his Latin style made him seem to many the only speaker of the language[237]. He had written a history of his own deeds, in the style of Xenophon, which Cicero had imitated[238], and was well known as a wit and writer of epigrams[239].

Although so much is said of his general culture, it is only from the *Academica* that we learn definitely his philosophical opinions. In the *De Oratore*, when he speaks of the visit of Carneades to Rome[240], he does not declare himself a follower of that philosopher, nor does Crassus, in his long speech about Greek philosophy, connect Catulus with any particular teacher. The only Greek especially mentioned as a friend of his, is the poet Antipater of Sidon[241]. Still it might have been concluded that he was an adherent either of the Academic or Peripatetic Schools. Cicero repeatedly asserts that from no other schools can the orator spring, and the whole tone of the *De Oratore* shows that Catulus could have had no leaning towards the Stoics or Epicureans[242]. The probability is that he had never placed himself under the instruction of Greek teachers for any length of time, but had rather gained his information [l] from books and especially from the writings of Clitomachus. If he had ever been in actual communication with any of the prominent Academics, Cicero would not have failed to tell us, as he does in the case of Antonius[243], and Crassus[244]. It is scarcely possible that any direct intercourse between Philo and Catulus can have taken place, although one passage in the *Lucullus* seems to imply it[245]. Still Philo had a brilliant reputation during the later years of Catulus, and no one at all conversant with Greek literature or society could fail to be well acquainted with his opinions[246]. No follower of Carneades and Clitomachus, such as Catulus undoubtedly was[247], could view with indifference the latest development of Academic doctrine. The famous books of Philo were probably not known to Catulus[248].

I now proceed to draw out from the references in the *Lucullus* the chief features of the speech of Catulus the younger. It was probably introduced by a mention of Philo's books[249]. Some considerable portion of the speech must have been directed against the innovations made by Philo upon the genuine Carneadean doctrine. These the elder Catulus had repudiated with great warmth, even charging Philo with wilful misrepresentation of the older Academics[250]. The most important part of the speech, however, must have consisted of a defence of Carneades and Arcesilas against [li] the dogmatic schools[251]. Catulus evidently concerned himself more with the system of the later than with that of the earlier sceptic. It is also exceedingly probable that he touched only very lightly on the negative Academic arguments, while he developed fully that positive teaching about the πιθανον which was so distinctive of Carneades. All the counter arguments of Lucullus which concern the destructive side of Academic teaching appear to be distinctly aimed at Cicero, who must have represented it in the discourse of the day before[252]. On the other hand, those parts of Lucullus' speech which deal with the constructive part of Academicism[253] seem to be intended for Catulus, to whom the maintenance of the genuine Carneadean distinction between αδηλα and ακαταληπτα would be a peculiarly congenial task. Thus the commendation bestowed by Lucullus on the way in which the *probabile* had been handled appertains to Catulus. The exposition of the sceptical criticism would naturally be reserved for the most brilliant and incisive orator of the party— Cicero himself. These conjectures have the advantage of establishing an intimate connection between the prooemium, the speech of Catulus, and the succeeding one of Hortensius. In the prooemium the innovations of Philo were mentioned; Catulus then showed that the only object aimed at by them, a satisfactory basis for επιστημη, was already attained by the Carneadean theory of the πιθανον; whereupon Hortensius showed, after the principles of Antiochus, that [lii] such a basis was provided by the older philosophy, which both Carneades and Philo had wrongly abandoned. Thus Philo becomes the central point or pivot of the discussion. With this arrangement none of the indications in the *Lucullus* clash. Even the demand made by Hortensius upon Catulus[254] need only imply such a bare statement on the part of the latter of the negative Arcesilaean doctrines as would clear the ground for the Carneadean πιθανον. One important opinion maintained by Catulus after Carneades, that the wise man would opine[255] (τον σοφον δοξασειν), seems another indication of the generally constructive character of his exposition. Everything points to the conclusion that this part of the dialogue was mainly drawn by Cicero from the writings of Clitomachus.

Catulus was followed by Hortensius, who in some way spoke in favour of Antiochean opinions, but to what extent is uncertain[256]. I think it extremely probable that he gave a résumé of the history of philosophy, corresponding to the speech of Varro in the beginning of the *Academica Posteriora*. One main reason in favour of this view is the difficulty of understanding to whom, if not to Hortensius, the substance of the speech could have been assigned in the first edition. In the *Academica Posteriora* it was necessary to make Varro speak first and not second as Hortensius did; this accounts for the disappearance in the second edition of the polemical argument of Hortensius[257], which would be appropriate only in the mouth of one [liii] who was answering a speech already made. On the view I have taken, there would be little difficulty in the fact that Hortensius now advocates a dogmatic philosophy, though in the lost dialogue which bore his name he had argued against philosophy altogether[258], and denied that philosophy and wisdom were at all the same thing[259]. Such a historical résumé as I have supposed Hortensius to give would be within the reach of any cultivated man of the time, and would only be put forward to show that the New Academic revolt against the supposed old Academico-Peripatetic school was unjustifiable. There is actual warrant for stating that his exposition of Antiochus was merely superficial[260]. We are thus relieved from the necessity of forcing the meaning of the word *commoveris*[261], from which Krische infers that the dialogue, entitled *Hortensius*, had ended in a conversion to philosophy of the orator from whom it was named. To any such conversion we have nowhere else any allusion.

The relation in which Hortensius stood to Cicero, also his character and attainments, are too well known to need mention here. He seems to have been as nearly innocent of any acquaintance with philosophy as it was possible for an educated man to be. Cicero's materials for the speech of Hortensius were, doubtless, drawn from the published works and oral teaching of Antiochus.

The speech of Hortensius was answered by Cicero himself. If my view of the preceding speech is correct, [liv] it follows that Cicero in his reply pursued the same course which he takes in his answer to Varro, part of which is preserved in the *Academica Posteriora*[262]. He justified the New Academy by showing that it was in essential harmony with the Old, and also with those ancient philosophers who preceded Plato. Lucullus, therefore, reproves him as a rebel in philosophy, who appeals to great and ancient names like a seditious tribune[263]. Unfair use had been made, according to Lucullus, of Empedocles, Anaxagoras, Democritus, Parmenides, Xenophanes, Plato, and Socrates[264]. But Cicero did not merely give a historical summary. He must have dealt with the theory of καταληπτικη φαντασια and εννοιαι (which though really Stoic had been adopted by Antiochus), since he found it necessary to "manufacture" (*fabricari*) Latin terms to represent the Greek[265]. He probably also commented on the headlong rashness with which the dogmatists gave their assent to the truth of phenomena. To this a retort is made by Lucullus[266]. That Cicero's criticism of the dogmatic schools was incomplete may be seen by the fact that he had not had occasion to Latinize the terms καταληψις (i.e. in the abstract, as opposed to the individual καταληπτικη φαντασια), εναργεια, ῾ορμη, αποδειξις, δογμα, οικειον, αδηλα, εποχη, nearly all important terms in the Stoic, and to some extent in the Antiochean system, all of which Lucullus is obliged to translate for himself[267]. The more the matter is examined the more clearly does it appear that the main purpose [lv] of Cicero in this speech was to justify from the history of philosophy the position of the New Academy, and not to advance sceptical arguments against experience, which were reserved for his answer to Lucullus. In his later speech, he expressly tells us that such sceptical paradoxes as were advanced by him in the first day's discourse were really out of place, and were merely introduced in order to disarm Lucullus, who was to speak next[268]. Yet these arguments must have occupied some considerable space in Cicero's speech, although foreign to its main intention[269]. He probably gave a summary classification of the sensations, with the reasons for refusing to assent to the truth of each class[270]. The whole constitution and tenor of the elaborate speech of Cicero in the *Lucullus* proves that no general or minute demonstration of the impossibility of επιστημη in the dogmatic sense had been attempted in his statement of the day before. Cicero's argument in the *Catulus* was allowed by Lucullus to have considerably damaged the cause of Antiochus[271]. The three speeches of Catulus, Hortensius, and Cicero had gone over nearly the whole ground marked out for the discussion[272], but only cursorily, so that there was plenty of room for a more minute examination in the *Lucullus*.

One question remains: how far did Cicero defend Philo against the attack of Catulus? Krische believes [lvi] that the argument of Catulus was answered point by point. In this opinion I cannot concur. Cicero never appears elsewhere as the defender of Philo's reactionary doctrines[273]. The expressions of Lucullus seem to imply that this part of his teaching had been dismissed by all the disputants[274]. It follows that when Cicero, in his letter of dedication to Varro, describes his own part as that of Philo (*partes mihi sumpsi Philonis*[275]), he merely attaches Philo's name to those general New Academic doctrines which had been so brilliantly supported by the pupil of Clitomachus in his earlier days. The two chief sources for Cicero's speech in the *Catulus* were, doubtless, Philo himself and Clitomachus.

In that intermediate form of the *Academica*, where Cato and Brutus appeared in the place of Hortensius and Lucullus, there can be no doubt that Brutus occupied a more prominent position than Cato. Consequently Cato must have taken the comparatively inferior part of Hortensius, while Brutus took that of Lucullus. It may perhaps seem strange that a Stoic of the Stoics like Cato should be chosen to represent Antiochus, however much that philosopher may have borrowed from Zeno. The rôle given to Hortensius, however, was in my view such as any cultivated man might sustain who had not definitely committed himself to sceptical principles. So eminent an Antiochean as Brutus cannot have been reduced to the comparatively secondary position assigned to Hortensius in the *Academica Priora*. He would naturally occupy the [lvii] place given to Varro in the second edition[276]. If this be true, Brutus would not speak at length in the first half of the work. Cato is not closely enough connected with the *Academica* to render it necessary to treat of him farther.

b. *The "Lucullus."*

The day after the discussion narrated in the *Catulus*, during which Lucullus had been merely a looker-on, the whole party left the Cuman villa of Catulus early in the morning, and came to that of Hortensius at Bauli[277]. In the evening, if the wind favoured, Lucullus was to leave for his villa at Neapolis, Cicero for his at Pompeii[278]. Bauli was a little place on the gulf of Baiae, close to Cimmerium, round which so many legends lingered[279]. The scenery in view was magnificent[280]. As the party were seated in the xystus with its polished floor and lines of statues, the waves rippled at their feet, and the sea away to the horizon glistened and quivered under the bright sun, and changed colour under the freshening breeze. Within sight lay the Cuman shore and Puteoli, thirty stadia distant[281].

Cicero strove to give vividness to the dialogue and [lviii] to keep it perfectly free from anachronisms. Diodotus is spoken of as still living, although when the words were written he had been dead for many years[282]. The surprise of Hortensius, who is but a learner in philosophy, at the wisdom of Lucullus, is very dramatic[283]. The many political and private troubles which were pressing upon Cicero when he wrote the work are kept carefully out of sight. Still we can catch here and there traces of thoughts and plans which were actively employing the author's mind at Astura. His intention to visit Tusculum has left its mark on the last section of the book, while in the last but one the *De Finibus*, the *De Natura Deorum* and other works are shadowed forth[284]. In another passage the design of the *Tusculan Disputations*, which was carried out immediately after the publication of the *Academica* and *De Finibus*, is clearly to be seen[285].

Hortensius and Catulus now sink to a secondary position in the conversation, which is resumed by Lucullus. His speech is especially acknowledged by Cicero to be drawn from the works of Antiochus[286]. Nearly all that is known of the learning of Lucullus is told in Cicero's dialogue, and the passages already quoted from the letters. He seems at least to have dallied with culture, although his chief energy, as a private citizen, was directed to the care of his fish-ponds[287]. In his train when he went to Sicily was the poet Archias, and during the whole of his residence in [lix] the East he sought to attach learned men to his person. At Alexandria he was found in the company of Antiochus, Aristus, Heraclitus Tyrius, Tetrilius Rogus and the Selii, all men of philosophic tastes[288]. He is several times mentioned by Pliny in the *Natural History* as the patron of Greek artists. Yet, as we have already seen, Cicero acknowledged in his letters to Atticus that Lucullus was no philosopher. He has to be propped up, like Catulus, by the authority of another person. All his arguments are explicitly stated to be derived from a discussion in which he had heard Antiochus engage. The speech of Lucullus was, as I have said, mainly a reply to that of Cicero in the *Catulus*. Any closer examination of its contents must be postponed till I come to annotate its actual text. The same may be said of Cicero's answer.

In the intermediate form of the *Academica*, the speech of Lucullus was no doubt transferred to Brutus, but as he has only such a slight connection with the work, I do not think it necessary to do much more than call attention to the fact. I may, however, notice the close relationship in which Brutus stood to the other persons with whom we have had to deal. He was nephew of Cato, whose half-sister Servilia was wife of Lucullus[289]. Cato was tutor to Lucullus' son, with Cicero for a sort of adviser: while Hortensius had married a divorced wife of Cato. All of them were of the Senatorial party, and Cato and Brutus lived to be present, with Cicero, during the war between Pompey [lx] and Caesar. Brutus and Cicero were both friends of Antiochus and Aristus, whose pupil Brutus was[290].

c. *The Second Edition.*

When Cicero dedicated the *Academica* to Varro, very slight alterations were necessary in the scenery and other accessories of the piece. Cicero had a villa close to the Cuman villa of Catulus and almost within sight of Hortensius' villa at Bauli[291]. Varro's villa, at which the scene was now laid, was close to the Lucrine lake[292]. With regard to the feigned date of the discourse, we may observe that at the very outset of the work it is shown to be not far distant from the actual time of composition[293]. Many allusions are made to recent events, such as the utter overthrow of the Pompeian party, the death of Tullia[294], and the publication of the *Hortensius*[295]. Between the date of Tullia's death and the writing of the *Academica*, it can be shown that Varro, Cicero and Atticus could not have met together at Cumae. Cicero therefore for once admits into his works an impossibility in fact. This impossibility would at once occur to Varro, and Cicero anticipates his wonder in the letter of dedication[296].

For the main facts of Varro's life the student must be referred to the ordinary sources of information. A short account of the points of contact between his life and that of Cicero, with a few words about his philosophical [lxi] opinions, are alone needed here. The first mention we have of Varro in any of Cicero's writings is in itself sufficient to show his character and the impossibility of anything like friendship between the two. Varro had done the orator some service in the trying time which came before the exile. In writing to Atticus Cicero had eulogised Varro; and in the letter to which I refer he begs Atticus to send Varro the eulogy to read, adding "*Mirabiliter moratus est, sicut nosti,* ελικτα και ουδεν[297]." All the references to Varro in the letters to Atticus are in the same strain. Cicero had to be pressed to write Varro a letter of thanks for supposed exertions in his behalf, during his exile[298]. Several passages show that Cicero refused to believe in Varro's zeal, as reported by Atticus[299]. On Cicero's return from exile, he and Varro remained in the same semi-friendly state. About the year 54 B.C., as we have already seen, Atticus in vain urged his friend to dedicate some work to the great polymath. After the fall of the Pompeian cause, Cicero and Varro do seem to have been drawn a little closer together. Eight letters, written mostly in the year before the *Academica* was published, testify to this approximation[300]. Still they are all cold, forced and artificial; very different from the letters Cicero addressed to his real intimates, such for instance as Sulpicius, Caelius, Paetus, Plancus, and Trebatius. They all show a fear of giving offence to the harsh temper of Varro, and a humility in presence of his vast learning which is by [lxii] no means natural to Cicero. The negotiations between Atticus and Cicero with respect to the dedication of the second edition, as detailed already, show sufficiently that this slight increase in cordiality did not lead to friendship[301].

The philosophical views of Varro can be gathered with tolerable accuracy from Augustine, who quotes considerably from, the work of Varro *De Philosophia*[302]. Beyond doubt he was a follower of Antiochus and the so-called Old Academy. How he selected this school from, among the 288 philosophies which he considered possible, by an elaborate and pedantic process of exhaustion, may be read by the curious in Augustine. My notes on the *Academica Posteriora* will show that there is no reason for accusing Cicero of having mistaken Varro's philosophical views. This supposition owes its currency to Müller, who, from Stoic phrases in the *De Lingua Latina*, concluded that Varro had passed over to the Stoics before that work was written. All that was Stoic in Varro came from Antiochus[303].

The exact specification of the changes in the arrangement of the subject-matter, necessitated by the dedication to Varro, will be more conveniently deferred till we come to the fragments of the second edition preserved by Nonius and others. Roughly speaking, the following were the contents of the four books. Book I.: the historico-philosophical exposition of Antiochus' views, formerly given by Hortensius, now by Varro; then the historical justification of the Philonian position, [lxiii] which Cicero had given in the first edition as an answer to Hortensius[304]. Book II.: an exposition by Cicero of Carneades' positive teaching, practically the same as that given by Catulus in ed. I.; to this was appended, probably, that foretaste of the negative arguments against dogmatism, which in ed. 1. had formed part of the answer made by Cicero to Hortensius. Book III.: a speech of Varro in reply to Cicero, closely corresponding to that of Lucullus in ed. 1. Book IV.: Cicero's answer, substantially the same as in ed. 1. Atticus must have been almost a κωφον προσωπον.

I may here notice a fact which might puzzle the student. In some old editions the *Lucullus* is marked throughout as *Academicorum liber IV*. This is an entire mistake, which arose from a wrong view of Nonius' quotations, which are always from the *second* edition, and can tell us nothing about the constitution of the *first*. One other thing is worth remark. Halm (as many before him had done) places the *Academica Priora* before the *Posteriora*. This seems to me an unnatural arrangement; the subject-matter of the *Varro* is certainly prior, logically, to that of the *Lucullus*.

M. TULLII CICERONIS

ACADEMICORUM POSTERIORUM

LIBER PRIMUS.

I. 1. In Cumano nuper cum mecum Atticus noster esset, nuntiatum est nobis a M. Varrone, venisse eum Roma pridie vesperi et, nisi de via fessus esset, continuo ad nos venturum fuisse. Quod cum audissemus, nullam moram interponendam putavimus quin videremus hominem nobiscum et studiis isdem et vetustate amicitiae coniunctum. Itaque confestim ad eum ire perreximus, paulumque cum *ab* eius villa abessemus, ipsum ad nos venientem vidimus: atque ilium complexi, ut mos amicorum est, satis eum longo intervallo ad suam villam reduximus. 2. Hic pauca primo, atque ea percontantibus nobis, ecquid forte Roma novi, Atticus: Omitte ista, quae nec percontari nec audire sine molestia possumus, quaeso, inquit, et quaere potius ecquid ipse novi. Silent enim diutius Musae Varronis quam solebant, nec tamen istum cessare, sed celare quae scribat existimo. Minime vero, inquit ille: intemperantis enim arbitror esse scribere quod occultari velit: sed habeo opus magnum in manibus, idque iam pridem: ad hunc enim ipsum—me autem dicebat—quaedam institui, quae et sunt magna sane et limantur a me politius. 3. Et ego: Ista quidem, inquam, Varro, iam diu exspectans, non audeo tamen flagitare: audivi enim e Libone nostro, cuius nosti studium—nihil enim eius modi celare possumus—non te ea intermittere, sed accuratius tractare nec de manibus umquam deponere. Illud autem mihi ante hoc tempus numquam in mentem venit a te requirere: sed nunc, postea quam sum ingressus res eas, quas tecum simul didici, mandare monumentis philosophiamque veterem illam a Socrate ortam Latinis litteris illustrare, quaero quid sit cur, cum multa scribas, genus hoc praetermittas, praesertim cum et ipse in eo excellas et id studium totaque ea res longe ceteris et studiis et artibus antecedat.

II. 4. Tum ille: Rem a me saepe deliberatam et multum agitatam requiris. Itaque non haesitans respondebo, sed ea dicam, quae mihi sunt in promptu, quod ista ipsa de re multum, ut dixi, et diu cogitavi. Nam cum philosophiam viderem diligentissime Graecis litteris explicatam, existimavi, si qui de nostris eius studio tenerentur, si essent Graecis doctrinis eruditi, Graeca potius quam nostra lecturos: sin a Graecorum artibus et disciplinis abhorrerent, ne haec quidem curaturos, quae sine eruditione Graeca intellegi non possunt: itaque ea nolui scribere, quae nec indocti intellegere possent nec docti legere curarent. 5. Vides autem—eadem enim ipse didicisti—non posse nos Amafinii aut Rabirii similis esse, qui nulla arte adhibita de rebus ante oculos positis volgari sermone disputant, nihil definiunt, nihil partiuntur, nihil apta interrogatione concludunt, nullam denique artem esse nec dicendi nec disserendi putant. Nos autem praeceptis dialecticorum et oratorum etiam, quoniam utramque vim virtutem esse nostri putant, sic parentes, ut legibus, verbis quoque novis cogimur uti, quae docti, ut dixi, a Graecis petere malent, indocti ne a nobis quidem accipient, ut frustra omnis suscipiatur *labor*. 6. Iam vero physica, si Epicurum, id est, si Democritum probarem, possem scribere ita plane, ut Amafinius. Quid est enim magnum, cum causas rerum efficientium sustuleris, de corpusculorum—ita enim appellat atomos—concursione fortuita loqui? Nostra tu physica nosti, quae cum contineantur ex effectione et ex materia ea, quam fingit et format effectio, adhibenda etiam geometria est, quam quibusnam quisquam enuntiare verbis aut quem ad intellegendum poterit adducere? *Quid*, haec ipsa de vita et moribus, et de expetendis fugiendisque rebus? Illi enim simpliciter pecudis et hominis idem bonum esse censent: apud nostros autem non ignoras quae sit et quanta subtilitas. 7. Sive enim Zenonem sequare, magnum est efficere ut quis intelligat quid sit illud verum et simplex bonum, quod non possit ab honestate seiungi: quod bonum quale sit negat omnino Epicurus sine voluptatibus sensum moventibus ne suspicari *quidem*. Si vero Academiam veterem persequamur, quam nos, ut scis, probamus, quam erit illa acute explicanda nobis! quam argute, quam obscure etiam contra Stoicos disserendum! Totum igitur illud philosophiae studium mihi quidem ipse sumo et ad vitae constantiam quantum possum et ad delectationem animi, nec ullum arbitror, ut apud Platonem est, maius aut melius a dis datum munus homini. 8. Sed meos amicos, in quibus est studium, in Graeciam mitto, id est, ad Graecos ire iubeo, ut ea a fontibus potius hauriant quam rivulos consectentur. Quae autem nemo adhuc docuerat nec erat unde studiosi scire possent, ea, quantum potui—nihil enim magno opere meorum miror—feci ut essent nota nostris. A Graecis enim peti non poterant ac post L. Aelii nostri occasum ne a Latinis quidem. Et tamen in illis veteribus nostris, quae Menippum imitati, non interpretati, quadam hilaritate conspersimus, multa admixta ex intima philosophia, multa dicta dialectice †quae quo facilius minus docti intelligerent, iucunditate quadam ad legendum invitati, in laudationibus, in his ipsis antiquitatum prooemiis †philosophe scribere voluimus, si modo consecuti sumus.

III. 9. Tum, ego. Sunt, inquam, ista, Varro. Nam nos in nostra urbe peregrinantis errantisque tamquam hospites tui libri quasi domum deduxerunt, ut possemus aliquando qui et ubi essemus agnoscere. Tu aetatem patriae, tu descriptiones temporum, tu sacrorum iura, tu sacerdotum, tu domesticam, tu bellicam disciplinam, tu sedem regionum locorum, tu omnium divinarum humanarumque rerum nomina, genera, officia, causas aperuisti, plurimumque poetis nostris omninoque Latinis et litteris luminis et verbis attulisti, atque ipse varium et elegans omni fere numero poema fecisti philosophiamque multis locis incohasti, ad impellendum satis, ad edocendum parum. 10. Causam autem probabilem tu quidem adfers; aut enim Graeca legere malent qui erunt eruditi aut ne haec quidem qui illa nesciunt. Sed da mihi nunc: satisne probas? Immo vero et haec qui illa non poterunt et qui Graeca poterunt non contemnent sua. Quid enim causae est cur poetas Latinos Graecis litteris eruditi legant, philosophos non legant? an quia delectat Ennius, Pacuvius, Attius, multi alii, qui non verba, sed vim Graecorum expresserunt poetarum? Quanto magis philosophi delectabunt, si, ut illi Aeschylum, Sophoclem, Euripidem, sic hi Platonem imitentur, Aristotelem, Theophrastum? Oratores quidem laudari video, si qui e nostris Hyperidem sint aut Demosthenem imitati. 11. Ego autem—dicam enim, ut res est—dum me ambitio, dum honores, dum causae, dum rei publicae non solum cura, sed quaedam etiam procuratio multis officiis implicatum et constrictum tenebat, haec inclusa habebam et, ne obsolescerent, renovabam, cum licebat, legendo. Nunc vero et fortunae gravissimo percussus volnere et administratione rei publicae liberatus, doloris medicinam a philosophia peto et otii oblectationem hanc honestissimam iudico. Aut enim huic aetati hoc maxime aptum est aut iis rebus, si quas dignas laude gessimus, hoc in primis consentaneum aut etiam ad nostros civis erudiendos nihil utilius aut, si haec ita non sunt, nihil aliud video quod agere possimus. 12. Brutus quidem noster, excellens omni genere laudis, sic philosophiam Latinis litteris persequitur, nihil ut iisdem de rebus Graecia desideret, et eandem quidem sententiam sequitur quam tu. Nam Aristum Athenis audivit aliquam diu, cuius tu fratrem Antiochum. Quam ob rem da, quaeso, te huic etiam generi litterarum.

IV. 13. Tum, ille. Istuc quidem considerabo, nec vero sine te. Sed de te ipso quid est, inquit, quod audio? Quanam, inquam, de re? Relictam a te veterem illam, inquit, tractari autem novam. Quid? ergo, inquam, Antiocho id magis licuerit, nostro familiari, remigrare in domum veterem e nova quam nobis in novam e vetere? certe enim recentissima quaeque sunt correcta et emendata maxime. Quamquam Antiochi magister Philo, magnus vir, ut tu existimas ipse, negat in libris, quod coram etiam ex ipso audiebamus, duas Academias esse erroremque eorum, qui ita putarunt, coarguit. Est, inquit, ut dicis: sed ignorare te non arbitror, quae contra *ea* Philonis Antiochus scripserit. 14. Immo vero et ista et totam veterem Academiam, a qua absum iam diu, renovari a te, nisi molestum est, velim, et simul, adsidamus, inquam, si videtur. Sane istud quidem, inquit: sum enim admodum infirmus. Sed videamus idemne Attico placeat fieri a me, quod te velle video. Mihi vero, ille: quid est enim quod malim quam ex Antiocho iam pridem audita recordari? et simul videre satisne ea commode dici possit Latine? Quae cum essent dicta, in conspectu consedimus [omnes].

15. Tum Varro ita exorsus est: Socrates mihi videtur, id quod constat inter omnis, primus a rebus occultis et ab ipsa natura involutis, in quibus omnes ante eum philosophi occupati fuerunt, avocavisse philosophiam et ad vitam communem adduxisse, ut de virtutibus et vitiis omninoque de bonis rebus et malis quaereret, caelestia autem vel procul esse a nostra cognitione censeret vel, si maxime cognita essent, nihil tamen ad bene vivendum *valere*. 16. Hic in omnibus fere sermonibus, qui ab iis qui illum audierunt perscripti varie *et* copiose sunt, ita disputat ut nihil adfirmet ipse, refellat alios: nihil se scire dicat nisi id ipsum, eoque praestare ceteris, quod illi quae nesciant scire se putent, ipse se nihil scire, id unum sciat, ob eamque rem se arbitrari ab Apolline omnium sapientissimum esse dictum, quod haec esset una omnis sapientia non arbitrari sese scire quod nesciat. Quae cum diceret constanter et in ea sententia permaneret, omnis eius oratio tamen in virtute laudanda et in hominibus ad virtutis studium cohortandis consumebatur, ut e Socraticorum libris, maximeque Platonis, intellegi potest. 17. Platonis autem auctoritate, qui varius et multiplex et copiosus fuit, una et consentiens duobus vocabulis philosophiae forma instituta est, Academicorum et Peripateticorum: qui rebus congruentes nominibus differebant. Nam cum Speusippum, sororis filium, Plato philosophiae quasi heredem reliquisset, duos autem praestantissimo studio atque doctrina, Xenocratem Chalcedonium et Aristotelem Stagiritem, qui erant cum Aristotele, Peripatetici dicti sunt, quia disputabant inambulantes in Lycio, illi autem, qui Platonis instituto in Academia, quod est alterum gymnasium, coetus erant et sermones habere soliti, e loci vocabulo nomen habuerunt. Sed utrique Platonis ubertate completi certam quandam disciplinae formulam composuerunt et eam quidem plenam ac refertam, illam autem Socraticam dubitationem de omnibus rebus et nulla adfirmatione adhibita consuetudinem disserendi reliquerunt. Ita facta est, quod minime Socrates probabat, ars quaedam philosophiae et rerum ordo et descriptio disciplinae. 18. Quae quidem erat primo duobus, ut dixi, nominibus una: nihil enim inter Peripateticos et illam veterem Academiam differebat. Abundantia quadam ingeni praestabat, ut mihi quidem videtur, Aristoteles, sed idem fons erat utrisque et eadem rerum expetendarum fugiendarumque partitio.

V. Sed quid ago? inquit, aut sumne sanus, qui haec vos doceo? nam etsi non sus Minervam, ut aiunt, tamen inepte quisquis Minervam docet. Tum Atticus: Tu vero, inquit, perge, Varro: valde enim amo nostra atque nostros, meque ista delectant, cum Latine dicuntur, et isto modo. Quid me, inquam, putas, qui philosophiam iam professus sim populo nostro exhibiturum? Pergamus igitur, inquit, quoniam placet. 19. Fuit ergo iam accepta a Platone philosophandi ratio triplex: una de vita et moribus, altera de natura et rebus occultis, tertia de disserendo et quid verum sit, quid falsum, quid rectum in oratione pravumve, quid consentiens, quid repugnans iudicando. Ac primum partem illam bene vivendi a natura petebant eique parendum esse dicebant, neque ulla alia in re nisi in natura quaerendum esse illud summum bonum quo omnia referrentur, constituebantque extremum esse rerum expetendarum et finem bonorum adeptum esse omnia e natura et animo et corpore et vita. Corporis autem alia ponebant esse in toto, alia in partibus: valetudinem, viris pulchritudinem in toto, in partibus autem sensus integros et praestantiam aliquam partium singularum, ut in pedibus celeritatem, vim in manibus, claritatem in voce, in lingua etiam explanatam vocum impressionem: 20. animi autem, quae essent ad comprehendendam ingeniis virtutem idonea, eaque ab iis in naturam et mores dividebantur. Naturae celeritatem ad discendum et memoriam dabant: quorum utrumque mentis esset proprium et ingeni. Morum autem putabant studia esse et quasi consuetudinem: quam partim exercitationis adsiduitate, partim ratione formabant, in quibus erat philosophia ipsa. In qua quod incohatum est neque absolutum, progressio quaedam ad virtutem appellatur: quod autem absolutum, id est virtus, quasi perfectio naturae omniumque rerum, quas in animis ponunt, una res optima. Ergo haec animorum. 21. Vitae autem—id enim erat tertium—adiuncta esse dicebant, quae ad virtutis usum valerent. Nam virtus animi bonis et corporis cernitur, et *in* quibusdam quae non tam naturae quam beatae vitae adiuncta sunt. Hominem esse censebant quasi partem quandam civitatis et universi generis humani, eumque esse coniunctum cum hominibus humana quadam societate. Ac de summo quidem atque naturali bono sic agunt: cetera autem pertinere ad id putant aut adaugendum aut tuendum, ut divitias, ut opes, ut gloriam, ut gratiam. Ita tripartita ab iis inducitur ratio bonorum.

VI. 22. Atque haec illa sunt tria genera, quae putant plerique Peripateticos dicere. Id quidem non falso: est enim haec partitio illorum: illud imprudenter, si alios esse Academicos, qui tum appellarentur, alios Peripateticos arbitrantur. Communis haec ratio et utrisque hic bonorum finis videbatur, adipisci quae essent prima natura quaeque ipsa per sese expetenda, aut omnia aut maxima. Ea sunt autem maxima, quae in ipso animo atque in ipsa virtute versantur. Itaque omnis illa antiqua philosophia sensit in una virtute esse positam beatam vitam, nec tamen beatissimam, nisi adiungerentur et corporis et cetera, quae supra dicta sunt, ad virtutis usum idonea. 23. Ex hac descriptione agendi quoque aliquid in vita et officii ipsius initium reperiebatur: quod erat in conservatione earum rerum, quas natura praescriberet. Hinc gignebatur fuga desidiae voluptatumque contemptio: ex quo laborum dolorumque susceptio multorum magnorumque recti honestique causa et earum rerum, quae erant congruentes cum descriptione naturae, unde et amicitia exsistebat et iustitia atque aequitas: eaeque voluptatibus et multis vitae commodis anteponebantur. Haec quidem fuit apud eos morum institutio et eius partis, quam primam posui, forma atque descriptio.

24. De natura autem—id enim sequebatur—ita dicebant, ut eam dividerent in res duas, ut altera esset efficiens, altera autem quasi huic se praebens, ea quae efficeretur aliquid. In eo, quod efficeret, vim esse censebant, in eo autem, quod efficeretur, materiam quandam: in utroque tamen utrumque: neque enim materiam ipsam cohaerere potuisse, si nulla vi contineretur, neque vim sine aliqua materia. Nihil est enim quod non alicubi esse cogatur. Sed quod ex utroque, id iam corpus et quasi qualitatem quandam nominabant: dabitis enim profecto, ut in rebus inusitatis, quod Graeci ipsi faciunt, a quibus haec iam diu tractantur, utamur verbis interdum inauditis.

VII. 25. Nos vero, inquit Atticus: quin etiam Graecis licebit utare, cum voles, si te Latina forte deficient. Bene sane facis: sed enitar ut Latine loquar, nisi in huiusce modi verbis, ut philosophiam aut rhetoricam aut physicam aut dialecticam appellem, quibus, ut aliis multis, consuetudo iam utitur pro Latinis. Qualitates igitur appellavi, quas ποιοτητας Graeci vocant, quod ipsum apud Graecos non est vulgi verbum, sed philosophorum, atque id in multis. Dialecticorum vero verba nulla sunt publica: suis utuntur. Et id quidem commune omnium fere est artium. Aut enim nova sunt rerum novarum facienda nomina aut ex aliis transferenda. Quod si Graeci faciunt, qui in his rebus tot iam saecula versantur, quanto id magis nobis concedendum est, qui haec nunc primum tractare conamur? 26. Tu vero, inquam, Varro, bene etiam meriturus mihi videris de tuis civibus, si eos non modo copia rerum auxeris, uti fecisti, sed etiam verborum. Audebimus ergo, inquit, novis verbis uti te auctore, si necesse erit. Earum igitur qualitatum sunt aliae principes, aliae ex his ortae. Principes sunt unius modi et simplices: ex his autem ortae variae sunt et quasi multiformes. Itaque aër—utimur enim pro Latino—et ignis et aqua et terra prima sunt: ex his autem ortae animantium formae earumque rerum, quae gignuntur e terra. Ergo illa initia et, ut e Graeco vertam, elementa dicuntur: e quibus aër et ignis movendi vim habent et efficiendi, reliquae partes accipiendi et quasi patiendi, aquam dico et terram. Quintum genus, e quo essent astra mentesque, singulare eorumque quattuor, quae supra dixi, dissimile Aristoteles quoddam esse rebatur. 27. Sed subiectam putant omnibus sine ulla specie atque carentem omni illa qualitate—faciamus enim tractando usitatius hoc verbum et tritius—materiam quandam, ex qua omnia expressa atque efficta sint: quae tota omnia accipere possit omnibusque modis mutari atque ex omni parte, eoque etiam interire non in nihilum, sed in suas partis, quae infinite secari ac dividi possint, cum sit nihil omnino in rerum natura minimum quod dividi nequeat: quae autem moveantur, omnia intervallis moveri, quae intervalla item infinite dividi possint. 28. Et cum ita moveatur illa vis, quam qualitatem esse diximus, et cum sic ultro citroque versetur, materiam ipsam totam penitus commutari putant et illa effici, quae appellant qualia, e quibus in omni natura cohaerente et continuata cum omnibus suis partibus effectum esse mundum, extra quem nulla pars materiae sit nullumque corpus, partis autem esse mundi omnia, quae insint in eo, quae natura sentiente teneantur, in qua ratio perfecta insit, quae sit eadem sempiterna: nihil enim valentius esse a quo intereat: 29. quam vim animum esse dicunt mundi eandemque esse mentem sapientiamque perfectam, quem deum appellant, omniumque rerum, quae sunt ei subiectae, quasi prudentiam quandam, procurantem caelestia maxime, deinde in terris ea, quae pertinent ad homines: quam interdum eandem necessitatem appellant, quia nihil aliter possit atque ab ea constitutum sit, inter quasi fatalem et immutabilem continuationem ordinis sempiterni: non numquam eandem fortunam, quod efficiat multa improvisa ac necopinata nobis propter obscuritatem ignorationemque causarum.

VIII. 30. Tertia deinde philosophiae pars, quae erat in ratione et in disserendo, sic tractabatur ab utrisque. Quamquam oriretur a sensibus, tamen non esse iudicium veritatis in sensibus. Mentem volebant rerum esse iudicem: solam censebant idoneam cui crederetur, quia sola cerneret id, quod semper esset simplex et unius modi et tale quale esset. Hanc illi ιδεαν appellabant, iam a Platone ita nominatam, nos recte speciem possumus dicere. 31. Sensus autem omnis hebetes et tardos esse arbitrabantur, nec percipere ullo modo res eas, quae subiectae sensibus viderentur, quae essent aut ita parvae, ut sub sensum cadere non possent, aut ita mobiles et concitatae, ut nihil umquam unum esset constans, ne idem quidem, quia continenter laberentur et fluerent omnia. Itaque hanc omnem partem rerum opinabilem appellabant. 32. Scientiam autem nusquam esse censebant nisi in animi notionibus atque rationibus: qua de causa definitiones rerum probabant, et has ad omnia, de quibus disceptabatur, adhibebant. Verborum etiam explicatio probabatur, id est, qua de causa quaeque essent ita nominata, quam ετυμολογιαν appellabant: post argumentis et quasi rerum notis ducibus utebantur ad probandum et ad concludendum id, quod explanari volebant: itaque tradebatur omnis dialecticae disciplina, id est, orationis ratione conclusae. Huic quasi ex altera parte oratoria vis dicendi adhibebatur, explicatrix orationis perpetuae ad persuadendum accommodatae. 33. Haec erat illis disciplina a Platone tradita: cuius quas acceperim mutationes, si voltis, exponam. Nos vero volumus, inquam, ut pro Attico etiam respondeam.

IX. Et recte, inquit, respondes: praeclare enim explicatur Peripateticorum et Academiae veteris auctoritas. Aristoteles primus species, quas paulo ante dixi, labefactavit: quas mirifice Plato erat amplexatus, ut in iis quiddam divinum esse diceret. Theophrastus autem, vir et oratione suavis et ita moratus, ut prae se probitatem quandam et ingenuitatem ferat, vehementius etiam fregit quodam modo auctoritatem veteris disciplinae: spoliavit enim virtutem suo decore imbecillamque reddidit, quod negavit in ea sola positum esse beate vivere. 34. Nam Strato, eius auditor, quamquam fuit acri ingenio, tamen ab ea disciplina omnino semovendus est: qui cum maxime necessariam partem philosophiae, quae posita est in virtute et moribus, reliquisset totumque se ad investigationem naturae contulisset, in ea ipsa plurimum dissedit a suis. Speusippus autem et Xenocrates, qui primi Platonis rationem auctoritatemque susceperant, et post eos Polemo et Crates unaque Crantor, in Academia congregati, diligenter ea, quae a superioribus acceperant, tuebantur. Iam Polemonem audiverant adsidue Zeno et Arcesilas. 35. Sed Zeno cum Arcesilam anteiret aetate valdeque subtiliter dissereret et peracute moveretur, corrigere conatus est disciplinam. Eam quoque, si videtur, correctionem explicabo, sicut solebat Antiochus. Mihi vero, inquam, videtur, quod vides idem significare Pomponium.

X. Zeno igitur nullo modo is erat, qui, ut Theophrastus, nervos virtutis inciderit, sed contra, qui omnia quae ad beatam vitam pertinerent in una virtute poneret nec quicquam aliud numeraret in bonis, idque appellaret honestum, quod esset simplex quoddam et solum et unum bonum. 36. Cetera autem etsi nec bona nec mala essent, tamen alia secundum naturam dicebat, alia naturae esse contraria. His ipsis alia interiecta et media numerabat. Quae autem secundum naturam essent, ea sumenda et quadam aestimatione dignanda docebat, contraque contraria: neutra autem in mediis relinquebat, in quibus ponebat nihil omnino esse momenti. 37. Sed quae essent sumenda, ex iis alia pluris esse aestimanda, alia minoris. Quae pluris, ea praeposita appellabat, reiecta autem quae minoris. Atque ut haec non tam rebus quam vocabulis commutaverat, sic inter recte factum atque peccatum, officium et contra officium media locabat quaedam: recte facta sola in bonis actionibus ponens, prave, id est peccata, in malis: officia autem servata praetermissaque media putabat, ut dixi. 38. Cumque superiores non omnem virtutem in ratione esse dicerent, sed quasdam virtutes natura aut more perfectas, hic omnis in ratione ponebat, cumque illi ea genera virtutum, quae supra dixi, seiungi posse arbitrarentur, hic nec id ullo modo fieri posse disserebat nec virtutis usum modo, ut superiores, sed ipsum habitum per se esse praeclarum, nec tamen virtutem cuiquam adesse quin ea semper uteretur. Cumque perturbationem animi illi ex homine non tollerent, naturaque et condolescere et concupiscere et extimescere et efferri laetitia dicerent, sed eas contraherent in angustumque deducerent, hic omnibus his quasi morbis voluit carere sapientem. 39. Cumque eas perturbationes antiqui naturalis esse dicerent et rationis expertis aliaque in parte animi cupiditatem, alia rationem collocarent, ne his quidem adsentiebatur. Nam et perturbationes voluntarias esse putabat opinionisque iudicio suscipi et omnium perturbationum arbitrabatur matrem esse immoderatam quamdam intemperantiam. Haec fere de moribus.

XI. De naturis autem sic sentiebat, primum, ut quattuor initiis rerum illis quintam hanc naturam, ex qua superiores sensus et mentem effici rebantur, non adhiberet. Statuebat enim ignem esse ipsam naturam, quae quidque gigneret, et mentem atque sensus. Discrepabat etiam ab isdem quod nullo modo arbitrabatur quicquam effici posse ab ea, quae expers esset corporis, cuius generis Xenocrates et superiores etiam animum esse dixerant, nec vero aut quod efficeret aliquid aut quod efficeretur posse esse non corpus. 40. Plurima autem in illa tertia philosophiae parte mutavit. In qua primum de sensibus ipsis quaedam dixit nova, quos iunctos esse censuit e quadam quasi impulsione oblata extrinsecus, quam ille φαντασιαν, nos visum appellemus licet, et teneamus hoc verbum quidem: erit enim utendum in reliquo sermone saepius. Sed ad haec, quae visa sunt et quasi accepta sensibus, adsensionem adiungit animorum, quam esse volt in nobis positam et voluntariam. 41. Visis non omnibus adiungebat fidem, sed iis solum, quae propriam quandam haberent declarationem earum rerum, quae viderentur: id autem visum, cum ipsum per se cerneretur, comprehendibile—feretis hoc? Nos vero, inquit. Quonam enim modo καταληπτον diceres?— Sed, cum acceptum iam et approbatum esset, comprehensionem appellabat, similem iis rebus, quae manu prehenderentur: ex quo etiam nomen hoc duxerat, cum eo verbo antea nemo tali in re usus esset, plurimisque idem novis verbis—nova enim dicebat—usus est. Quod autem erat sensu comprehensum, id ipsum sensum appellabat, et si ita erat comprehensum, ut convelli ratione non posset, scientiam: sin aliter, inscientiam nominabat: ex qua exsisteret etiam opinio, quae esset imbecilla et cum falso incognitoque communis. 42. Sed inter scientiam et inscientiam comprehensionem illam, quam dixi, collocabat, eamque neque in rectis neque in pravis numerabat, sed soli credendum esse dicebat. E quo sensibus etiam fidem tribuebat, quod, ut supra dixi, comprehensio facta sensibus et vera esse illi et fidelis videbatur, non quod omnia, quae essent in re, comprehenderet, sed quia nihil quod cadere in eam posset relinqueret quodque natura quasi normam scientiae et principium sui dedisset, unde postea notiones rerum in animis imprimerentur, e quibus non principia solum, sed latiores quaedam ad rationem inveniendam viae reperiuntur. Errorem autem et temeritatem et ignorantiam et opinationem et suspicionem et uno nomine omnia, quae essent aliena firmae et constantis adsensionis, a virtute sapientiaque removebat. Atque in his fere commutatio constitit omnis dissensioque Zenonis a superioribus.

XII. 43. Quae cum dixisset: Breviter sane minimeque obscure exposita est, inquam, a te, Varro, et veteris Academiae ratio et Stoicorum: verum esse [autem] arbitror, ut Antiocho, nostro familiari, placebat, correctionem veteris Academiae potius quam aliquam novam disciplinam putandam. Tunc Varro: Tuae sunt nunc partes, inquit, qui ab antiquorum ratione desciscis et ea, quae ab Arcesila novata sunt, probas, docere quod et qua de causa discidium factum sit, ut videamus satisne ista sit iusta defectio. 44. Tum ego: Cum Zenone, inquam, ut accepimus, Arcesilas sibi omne certamen instituit, non pertinacia aut studio vincendi, ut mihi quidem videtur, sed earum rerum obscuritate, quae ad confessionem ignorationis adduxerant Socratem et iam ante Socratem Democritum, Anaxagoram, Empedoclem, omnis paene veteres: qui nihil cognosci, nihil percipi, nihil sciri posse dixerunt: angustos sensus, imbecillos animos, brevia curricula vitae et, ut Democritus, in profundo veritatem esse demersam, opinionibus et institutis omnia teneri, nihil veritati relinqui, deinceps omnia tenebris circumfusa esse dixerunt. 45. Itaque Arcesilas negabat esse quicquam quod sciri posset, ne illud quidem ipsum, quod Socrates sibi reliquisset: sic omnia latere censebat in occulto: neque esse quicquam quod cerni aut intellegi posset: quibus de causis nihil oportere neque profiteri neque adfirmare quemquam neque adsensione approbare, cohibereque semper et ab omni lapsu continere temeritatem, quae tum esset insignis, cum aut falsa aut incognita res approbaretur, neque hoc quicquam esse turpius quam cognitioni et perceptioni adsensionem approbationemque praecurrere. Huic rationi quod erat consentaneum faciebat, ut contra omnium sententias dicens in eam plerosque deduceret, ut cum in eadem re paria contrariis in partibus momenta rationum invenirentur, facilius ab utraque parte adsensio sustineretur. 46. Hanc Academiam novam appellant, quae mihi vetus videtur, si quidem Platonem ex illa vetere numeramus, cuius in libris nihil adfirmatur et in utramque partem multa disseruntur, de omnibus quaeritur, nihil certi dicitur: sed tamen illa, quam exposui*sti*, vetus, haec nova nominetur: quae usque ad Carneadem perducta, qui quartus ab Arcesila fuit, in eadem Arcesilae ratione permansit. Carneades autem nullius philosophiae partis ignarus et, ut cognovi ex iis, qui illum audierant, maximeque ex Epicureo Zenone, qui cum ab eo plurimum dissentiret, unum tamen praeter ceteros mirabatur, incredibili quadam fuit facultate....

ACADEMICORUM POSTERIORUM FRAGMENTA.

EX LIBRO I.

1. Nonius p. 65 Merc. *Digladiari dictum est dissentire et dissidere, dictum a gladiis. Cicero Academicorum lib. I.*: quid autem stomachatur Menesarchus? quid Antipater digladiatur cum Carneade tot voluminibus?

2. Nonius s.v. *concinnare p. 43. Idem in Academicis lib. I.*: qui cum similitudine verbi concinere maxime sibi videretur.

EX LIBRO II.

3. Nonius p. 65. *Aequor ab aequo et plano Cicero Academicorum lib. II. vocabulum accepisse confirmat*: quid tam planum videtur quam mare? e quo etiam aequor illud poetae vocant.

4. Nonius p. 69. *Adamare Cicero Academicorum lib. II.*: qui enim serius honores adamaverunt vix admittuntur ad eos nec satis commendati multitudini possunt esse.

5. Nonius p. 104. *Exponere pro exempla boni ostentare. Cicero Academicis lib. II.*: frangere avaritiam, scelera ponere, vitam suam exponere ad imitandum iuventuti.

6. Nonius p. 121. *Hebes positum pro obscuro aut obtuso. Cicero Academicorum lib. II.*: quid? lunae quae liniamenta sint potesne dicere? cuius et nascentis et senescentis alias hebetiora, alias acutiora videntur cornua.

7. Nonius p. 162. *Purpurascit. Cicero Academicorum lib. II.*: quid? mare nonne caeruleum? at eius unda, cum est pulsa remis, purpurascit: et quidem aquae tinctum quodam modo et infectum....

8. Nonius p. 162. *Perpendiculi et normae. Cic. Academicorum lib. II.*: atqui si id crederemus, non egeremus perpendiculis, non normis, non regulis.

9. Nonius p. 394. *Siccum dicitur aridum et sine humore ... Siccum dicitur et sobrium, non madidum ... Cic. Academicorum lib. II.*: alius (*color*) adultis, alius adulescentibus, alius aegris, *alius sanis*, alius siccis, alius vinulentis ...

10. Nonius p. 474. *Urinantur. Cic. in Academicis lib. II.*: si quando enim nos demersimus, ut qui urinantur, aut nihil superum aut obscure admodum cernimus.

11. Nonius p. 545. *Alabaster. Cic. Academicorum lib. II.*: quibus etiam alabaster plenus unguenti puter esse videtur.

EX LIBRO III.

Cicero ad Att. XVI. 6. §4. *De gloria librum ad te misi: at in eo* prooemium *id est, quod in Academico tertio.*

12. Nonius p. 65. *Digladiari ... idem tertio:* digladiari autem semper, depugnare cum facinorosis et audacibus, quis non cum miserrimum, tum etiam stultissimum dixerit?

13. Nonius p. 65. *Exultare dictum est exilire. Cic. Academicorum lib. III.*: et ut nos nunc sedemus ad Lucrinum pisciculosque exultantes videmus ...

14. Nonius p. 123. *Ingeneraretur ut innasceretur. Cic. Academicorum lib. III.*: in tanta animantium varietate, homini ut soli cupiditas ingeneraretur cognitionis et scientiae.

15. Nonius p. 419. *Vindicare, trahere, liberare ... Cicero Academicorum lib. III.*: aliqua potestas sit, vindicet se in libertatem.

16. Lactantius Inst. div. VI. 24. *Cicero ... cuius haec in Academico tertio verba sunt:* quod si liceret, ut iis qui in itinere deerravissent, sic vitam deviam secutis corrigere errorem paenitendo, facilior esset emendatio temeritatis.

17. Diomedes p. 373, ed. Putsch.: p. 377, ed. Keil. *Varro ad Ciceronem tertio* fixum *et Cicero Academicorum tertio* (= *Lucullus* §27): †malcho in opera adfixa.

18. Nonius p. 139. *Mordicibus et mordicus pro morsu, pro morsibus ... Cic. Academicorum lib. III.*: perspicuitatem, quam mordicus tenere debemus, abesse dicemus. = *Lucullus* §51.

19. Nonius p. 117. *Gallinas. Cic. Academicorum lib. III.*: qui gallinas alere permultas quaestus causa solerent: ii cum ovum inspexerant, quae gallina peperisset dicere solebant. = *Lucullus* §57.

EX LIBRO IIII.

20. Nonius p. 69, *Adstipulari positum est adsentiri. Cic. in Academicis lib. IIII.*: falsum esse.... Antiochus. = *Lucullus* §67.

21. Nonius p. 65. *Maeniana ab inventore eorum Maenio dicta sunt; unde et columna Maenia. Cic. Academicorum lib. IIII.*: item ille cum aestuaret, veterum ut Maenianorum, sic Academicorum viam secutus est. = *Lucullus* §70.

22. Nonius p. 99. *Dolitum, quod dolatum usu dicitur, quod est percaesum vel abrasum vel effossum ... Cicero dolatum Academicorum lib. IIII.*: non enim est e saxo sculptus aut e robore dolatus. = *Lucullus* §100.

23. Nonius p. 164. *Ravum fulvum. Cic. Academicorum lib. IIII.*: quia nobismet ipsis tum caeruleum, tum ravum videtur, quodque nunc a sole conlucet.... = *Lucullus* §105.

24. Nonius p. 107. *Exanclare est perpeti vel superare. Cic. Academicorum lib. IIII.*: credoque Clitomacho ita scribenti ut Herculi quendam laborem exanclatum. = *Lucullus* §108.

25. Nonius p. 163. *Pingue positum pro impedito et inepto. Cic. Academicorum lib. IIII.*: quod ipsi ... contrarium. = *Lucullus* §109.

26. Nonius p. 122. *Infinitatem. Cic. Academicorum lib. IIII.*: at hoc Anaximandro infinitatem. = *Lucullus* §118.

27. Nonius p. 65. *Natrices dicuntur angues natantes Cic. Academicorum lib. IIII.*: sic enim voltis ... fecerit. = *Lucullus* §120.

28. Nonius p. 189. *Uncinatum ab unco. Cic. Academicorum lib. IIII.*: nec ut ille qui asperis et hamatis uncinatisque corpusculis concreta haec esse dicat. = *Lucullus* §121.

29. Martianus Capella V. §517, p. 444, ed. Kopp. *Cicero ... in Academicis*: latent ista omnia, Varro, magnis obscurata et circumfusa tenebris. = *Lucullus* §122.

30. Nonius p. 102. *E regione positum est ex adverso. Cic. Academicorum lib. IIII.*: nec ego non ita ... vos etiam dicitis e regione nobis in contraria parte terrae qui adversis vestigiis stent contra nostra vestigia. = *Lucullus* §123.

31. Nonius p. 80. *Balbuttire est cum quadam linguae haesitatione et confusione trepidare, Cic. Academicorum lib. IIII.*: plane, ut supra dictus, Stoicus perpauca balbuttiens. = *Lucullus* §135.

Ex LIBRIS INCERTIS.

32. Lactantius Inst. div. III. 14. *Haec tua verba sunt (sc. Cicero!)*: mihi autem non modo ad sapientiam caeci videmur, sed ad ea ipsa quae aliqua ex parte cerni videantur, hebetes et obtusi.

33. August. contra Academicos II. §26.: *id probabile vel veri simile Academici vacant, quod nos ad agendum sine adsensione potent invitare. ... Talia, inquit Academicus, mihi videntur omnia quae probabilia vel veri similia putavi nominanda: quae tu si alio nomine vis vocare, nihil repugno. Satis enim mihi est te iam bene accepisse quid dicam, id est, quibus rebus haec nomina imponam; non enim vocabulorum opificem, sed rerum inquisitorem decet esse sapientem. [Proximis post hunc locum verbis perspicue asseverat Augustinus haec ipsius esse Ciceronis verba.]*

34. Augustin. c. Acad. III. §15. *Est in libris Ciceronis quae in huius causae (i.e. Academicorum) patrocinium scripsit, locus quidam.... Academico sapienti ab omnibus ceterarum sectarum, qui sibi sapientes videntur, secundas partes dari; cum primas sibi quemque vindicare necesse sit; ex quo posse probabiliter confici eum recte primum esse iudicio suo, qui omnium ceterorum judicio sit secundus.*

35. Augustin. c. Acad. III. §43. *Ait enim Cicero* illis (*i.e. Academicis*) morem fuisse occultandi sententiam suam nec eam cuiquam, nisi qui secum ad senectutem usque vixissent, aperire consuesse.

36. Augustin. De Civit. Dei VI. 2. *Denique et ipse Tullius huic (i.e. M.T. Varroni) tale testimonium perhibet, ut in libris Academicis eam quae ibi versatur disputationem se habuisse cum M. Varrone,* homine, *inquit,* omnium facile acutissimo et sine ulla dubitatione doctissimo.

ACADEMICORUM PRIORUM

LIBER II.

I. 1. Magnum ingenium Luci Luculli magnumque optimarum artium studium, tum omnis liberalis et digna homine nobili ab eo percepta doctrina, quibus temporibus florere in foro maxime potuit, caruit omnino rebus urbanis. Ut enim admodum adolescens cum fratre pari pietate et industria praedito paternas inimicitias magna cum gloria est persecutus, in Asiam quaestor profectus, ibi permultos annos admirabili quadam laude provinciae praefuit; deinde absens factus aedilis, continuo praetor—licebat enim celerius legis praemio—, post in Africam, inde ad consulatum, quem ita gessit ut diligentiam admirarentur omnes, ingenium cognoscerent. Post ad Mithridaticum bellum missus a senatu non modo opinionem vicit omnium, quae de virtute eius erat, sed etiam gloriam superiorum. 2. Idque eo fuit mirabilius, quod ab eo laus imperatoria non admodum exspectabatur, qui adolescentiam in forensi opera, quaesturae diuturnum tempus Murena bellum in Ponto gerente in Asia pace consumpserat. Sed incredibilis quaedam ingeni magnitudo non desideravit indocilem usus disciplinam. Itaque cum totum iter et navigationem consumpsisset partim in percontando a peritis, partim in rebus gestis legendis, in Asiam factus imperator venit, cum esset Roma profectus rei militaris rudis. Habuit enim divinam quandam memoriam rerum, verborum maiorem Hortensius, sed quo plus in negotiis gerendis res quam verba prosunt, hoc erat memoria illa praestantior, quam fuisse in Themistocle, quem facile Graeciae principem ponimus, singularem ferunt: qui quidem etiam pollicenti cuidam se artem ei memoriae, quae tum primum proferebatur, traditurum respondisse dicitur oblivisci se malle discere, credo, quod haerebant in memoria quaecumque audierat et viderat. Tali ingenio praeditus Lucullus adiunxerat etiam illam, quam Themistocles spreverat, disciplinam. Itaque ut litteris consignamus quae monumentis mandare volumus, sic ille in animo res insculptas habebat. 3. Tantus ergo imperator in omni genere belli fuit, proeliis, oppugnationibus, navalibus pugnis totiusque belli instrumento et apparatu, ut ille rex post Alexandrum maximus hunc a se maiorem ducem cognitum quam quemquam eorum, quos legisset, fateretur. In eodem tanta prudentia fuit in constituendis temperandisque civitatibus, tanta aequitas, ut hodie stet Asia Luculli institutis servandis et quasi vestigiis persequendis. Sed etsi magna cum utilitate rei publicae, tamen diutius quam vellem tanta vis virtutis atque ingeni peregrinata afuit ab oculis et fori et curiae. Quin etiam, cum victor a Mithridatico bello revertisset, inimicorum calumnia triennio tardius quam debuerat triumphavit. Nos enim consules introduximus paene in urbem currum clarissimi viri: cuius mihi consilium et auctoritas quid tum in maximis rebus profuisset dicerem, nisi de me ipso dicendum esset: quod hoc tempore non est necesse. Itaque privabo illum potius debito testimonio quam id cum mea laude communicem.

II. 4. Sed quae populari gloria decorari in Lucullo debuerunt, ea fere sunt et Graecis litteris celebrata et Latinis. Nos autem illa externa cum multis, haec interiora cum paucis ex ipso saepe cognovimus. Maiore enim studio Lucullus cum omni litterarum generi tum philosophiae deditus fuit quam qui illum ignorabant arbitrabantur, nec vero ineunte aetate solum, sed et pro quaestore aliquot annos et in ipso bello, in quo ita magna rei militaris esse occupatio solet, ut non multum imperatori sub ipsis pellibus otii relinquatur. Cum autem e philosophis ingenio scientiaque putaretur Antiochus, Philonis auditor, excellere, eum secum et quaestor habuit et post aliquot annos imperator, cumque esset ea memoria, quam ante dixi, ea saepe audiendo facile cognovit, quae vel semel audita meminisse potuisset. Delectabatur autem mirifice lectione librorum, de quibus audiebat.

5. Ac vereor interdum ne talium personarum cum amplificare velim, minuam etiam gloriam. Sunt enim multi qui omnino Graecas non ament litteras, plures qui philosophiam, reliqui, etiam si haec non improbent, tamen earum rerum disputationem principibus civitatis non ita decoram putant. Ego autem, cum Graecas litteras M. Catonem in senectute didicisse acceperim, P. autem Africani historiae loquantur in legatione illa nobili, quam ante censuram obiit, Panaetium unum omnino comitem fuisse, nec litterarum Graecarum nec philosophiae iam ullum auctorem requiro. 6. Restat ut iis respondeam, qui sermonibus eius modi nolint personas tam gravis illigari. Quasi vero clarorum virorum aut tacitos congressus esse oporteat aut ludicros sermones aut rerum colloquia leviorum! Etenim, si quodam in libro vere est a nobis philosophia laudata, profecto eius tractatio optimo atque amplissimo quoque dignissima est, nec quicquam aliud videndum est nobis, quos populus Romanus hoc in gradu collocavit, nisi ne quid privatis studiis de opera publica detrahamus. Quod si, cum fungi munere debebamus, non modo operam nostram numquam a populari coetu removimus, sed ne litteram quidem ullam fecimus nisi forensem, quis reprehendet nostrum otium, qui in eo non modo nosmet ipsos hebescere et languere nolumus, sed etiam ut plurimis prosimus enitimur? Gloriam vero non modo non minui, sed etiam augeri arbitramur eorum, quorum ad populariis illustrisque laudes has etiam minus notas minusque pervolgatas adiungimus. 7. Sunt etiam qui negent in iis, qui in nostris libris disputent, fuisse earum rerum, de quibus disputatur, scientiam: qui mihi videntur non solum vivis, sed etiam mortuis invidere.

III. Restat unum genus reprehensorum, quibus Academiae ratio non probatur. Quod gravius ferremus, si quisquam ullam disciplinam philosophiae probaret praeter eam, quam ipse sequeretur. Nos autem, quoniam contra omnis dicere quae videntur solemus, non possumus quin alii a nobis dissentiant recusare: quamquam nostra quidem causa facilis est, qui verum invenire sine ulla contentione volumus, idque summa cura studioque conquirimus. Etsi enim omnis cognitio multis est obstructa difficultatibus eaque est et in ipsis rebus obscuritas et in iudiciis nostris infirmitas, ut non sine causa antiquissimi et doctissimi invenire se posse quod cuperent diffisi sint, tamen nec illi defecerunt neque nos studium exquirendi defetigati relinquemus, neque nostrae disputationes quicquam aliud agunt nisi ut in utramque partem dicendo eliciant et tamquam exprimant aliquid, quod aut verum sit aut ad id quam proxime accedat. 8. Neque inter nos et eos, qui se scire arbitrantur, quicquam interest, nisi quod illi non dubitant quin ea vera sint, quae defendunt: nos probabilia multa habemus, quae sequi facile, adfirmare vix possumus. Hoc autem liberiores et solutiores sumus, quod integra nobis est iudicandi potestas, nec ut omnia, quae praescripta et quasi imperata sint, defendamus necessitate ulla cogimur. Nam ceteri primum ante tenentur adstricti quam quid esset optimum iudicare potuerunt: deinde infirmissimo tempore aetatis aut obsecuti amico cuidam aut una alicuius, quem primum audierunt, oratione capti de rebus incognitis iudicant et, ad quamcumque sunt disciplinam quasi tempestate delati, ad eam tamquam ad saxum adhaerescunt. 9. Nam, quod dicunt omnino se credere ei, quem iudicent fuisse sapientem, probarem, si id ipsum rudes et indocti iudicare potuissent—statuere enim qui sit sapiens vel maxime videtur esse sapientis—, sed ut potuerint, potuerunt omnibus rebus auditis, cognitis etiam reliquorum sententiis, iudicaverunt autem re semel audita atque ad unius se auctoritatem contulerunt. Sed nescio quo modo plerique errare malunt eamque sententiam, quam adamaverunt, pugnacissime defendere quam sine pertinacia quid constantissime dicatur exquirere. Quibus de rebus et alias saepe multa quaesita et disputata sunt et quondam in Hortensii villa, quae est ad Baulos, cum eo Catulus et Lucullus nosque ipsi postridie venissemus, quam apud Catulum fuissemus. Quo quidem etiam maturius venimus, quod erat constitutum, si ventus esset, Lucullo in Neapolitanum, mihi in Pompeianum navigare. Cum igitur pauca in xysto locuti essemus, tum eodem in spatio consedimus.

IV. 10. Hic Catulus: Etsi heri, inquit, id, quod quaerebatur, paene explicatum est, ut tota fere quaestio tractata videatur, tamen exspecto ea, quae te pollicitus es, Luculle, ab Antiocho audita dicturum. Equidem, inquit Hortensius, feci plus quam vellem: totam enim rem Lucullo integram servatam oportuit. Et tamen fortasse servata est: a me enim ea, quae in promptu erant, dicta sunt, a Lucullo autem reconditiora desidero. Tum ille: Non sane, inquit, Hortensi, conturbat me exspectatio tua, etsi nihil est iis, qui placere volunt, tam adversarium, sed quia non laboro quam valde ea, quae dico, probaturus sim, eo minus conturbor. Dicam enim nec mea nec ea, in quibus, si non fuerint, *non* vinci me malim quam vincere. Sed mehercule, ut quidem nunc se causa habet, etsi hesterno sermone labefactata est, mihi tamen videtur esse verissima. Agam igitur, sicut Antiochus agebat: nota enim mihi res est. Nam et vacuo animo illum audiebam et magno studio, eadem de re etiam saepius, ut etiam maiorem exspectationem mei faciam quam modo fecit Hortensius. Cum ita esset exorsus, ad audiendum animos ereximus. 11. At ille: Cum Alexandriae pro quaestore, inquit, essem, fuit Antiochus mecum et erat iam antea Alexandriae familiaris Antiochi Heraclitus Tyrius, qui et Clitomachum multos annos et Philonem audierat, homo sane in ista philosophia, quae nunc prope dimissa revocatur, probatus et nobilis: cum quo Antiochum saepe disputantem audiebam, sed utrumque leniter. Et quidem isti libri duo Philonis, de quibus heri dictum a Catulo est, tum erant adlati Alexandriam tumque primum in Antiochi manus venerant: et homo natura lenissimus—nihil enim poterat fieri illo mitius—stomachari tamen coepit. Mirabar: nec enim umquam ante videram. At ille, Heracliti memoriam implorans, quaerere ex eo viderenturne illa Philonis aut ea num vel e Philone vel ex ullo Academico audivisset aliquando? Negabat. Philonis tamen scriptum agnoscebat: nec id quidem dubitari poterat: nam aderant mei familiares, docti homines, P. et C. Selii et Tetrilius Rogus, qui se illa audivisse Romae de Philone et ab eo ipso illos duos libros dicerent descripsisse. 12. Tum et illa dixit Antiochus, quae heri Catulus commemoravit a patre suo dicta Philoni, et alia plura, nec se tenuit quin contra suum doctorem librum etiam ederet, qui Sosus inscribitur. Tum igitur et cum Heraclitum studiose audirem contra Antiochum disserentem et item Antiochum contra Academicos, dedi Antiocho operam diligentius, ut causam ex eo totam cognoscerem. Itaque compluris dies adhibito Heraclito doctisque compluribus et in iis Antiochi fratre, Aristo, et praeterea Aristone et Dione, quibus ille secundum fratrem plurimum tribuebat, multum temporis in ista una disputatione consumpsimus. Sed ea pars, quae contra Philonem erat, praetermittenda est: minus enim acer est adversarius is, qui ista, quae sunt heri defensa, negat Academicos omnino dicere. Etsi enim mentitur, tamen est adversarius lenior. Ad Arcesilam Carneademque veniamus.

V. 13. Quae cum dixisset, sic rursus exorsus est: Primum mihi videmini—me autem nomine appellabat, cum veteres physicos nominatis, facere idem, quod seditiosi cives solent, cum aliquos ex antiquis claros viros proferunt, quos dicant fuisse popularis, ut eorum ipsi similes esse videantur. Repetunt ii a P. Valerio, qui exactis regibus primo anno consul fuit, commemorant reliquos, qui leges popularis de provocationibus tulerint, cum consules essent; tum ad hos notiores, C. Flaminium, qui legem agrariam aliquot annis ante secundum Punicum bellum tribunus plebis tulerit invito senatu et postea bis consul factus sit, L. Cassium, Q. Pompeium: illi quidem etiam P. Africanum referre in eundem numerum solent. Duos vero sapientissimos et clarissimos fratres, P. Crassum et P. Scaevolam, aiunt Ti. Graccho auctores legum fuisse, alterum quidem, ut videmus, palam, alterum, ut suspicantur, obscurius. Addunt etiam C. Marium. Et de hoc quidem nihil mentiuntur. Horum nominibus tot virorum atque tantorum expositis eorum se institutum sequi dicunt. 14. Similiter vos, cum perturbare, ut illi rem publicam, sic vos philosophiam bene iam constitutam velitis, Empedoclem, Anaxagoram, Democritum, Parmenidem, Xenophanem, Platonem etiam et Socratem profertis. Sed neque Saturninus, ut nostrum inimicum potissimum nominem, simile quicquam habuit veterum illorum nec Arcesilae calumnia conferenda est cum Democriti verecundia. Et tamen isti physici raro admodum, cum haerent aliquo loco, exclamant quasi mente incitati, Empedocles quidem, ut interdum mihi furere videatur, abstrusa esse omnia, nihil nos sentire, nihil cernere, nihil omnino quale sit posse reperire: maiorem autem partem mihi quidem omnes isti videntur nimis etiam quaedam adfirmare plusque profiteri se scire quam sciant. 15. Quod si illi tum in novis rebus quasi modo nascentes haesitaverunt, nihilne tot saeculis, summis ingeniis, maximis studiis explicatum putamus? nonne, cum iam philosophorum disciplinae gravissimae constitissent, tum exortus est ut in optima re publica Ti. Gracchus qui otium perturbaret, sic Arcesilas qui constitutam philosophiam everteret et in eorum auctoritate delitisceret, qui negavissent quicquam sciri aut percipi posse? quorum e numero tollendus est et Plato et Socrates: alter, quia reliquit perfectissimam disciplinam, Peripateticos et Academicos, nominibus differentis, re congruentis, a quibus Stoici ipsi verbis magis quam sententiis dissenserunt. Socrates autem de se ipse detrahens in disputatione plus tribuebat iis, quos volebat refellere. Ita, cum aliud agnosceret atque sentiret, libenter uti solitus est ea dissimulatione, quam Graeci ειρωνειαν vocant: quam ait etiam in Africano fuisse Fannius, idque propterea vitiosum in illo non putandum, quod idem fuerit in Socrate.

VI. 16. Sed fuerint illa veteribus, si voltis, incognita. Nihilne est igitur actum, quod investigata sunt, postea quam Arcesilas Zenoni, ut putatur, obtrectans nihil novi reperienti, sed emendanti superiores immutatione verborum, dum huius definitiones labefactare volt, conatus est clarissimis rebus tenebras obducere? Cuius primo non admodum probata ratio, quamquam floruit cum acumine ingeni tum admirabili quodam lepore dicendi, proxime a Lacyde solo retenta est: post autem confecta a Carneade, qui est quartus ab Arcesila: audivit enim Hegesinum, qui Euandrum audierat, Lacydi discipulum, cum Arcesilae Lacydes fuisset. Sed ipse Carneades diu tenuit: nam nonaginta vixit annos, et qui illum audierant, admodum floruerunt: e quibus industriae plurimum in Clitomacho fuit—declarat multitudo librorum—ingeni non minus in [Aeschine], in Charmada eloquentiae, in Melanthio Rhodio suavitatis. Bene autem nosse Carneadem Stratoniceus Metrodorus putabatur. 17. Iam Clitomacho Philo vester operam multos annos dedit. Philone autem vivo patrocinium Academiae non defuit. Sed, quod nos facere nunc ingredimur, ut contra Academicos disseramus, id quidam e philosophis et ii quidem non mediocres faciendum omnino non putabant: nec vero esse ullam rationem disputare cum iis, qui nihil probarent, Antipatrumque Stoicum, qui multus in eo fuisset, reprehendebant, nec definiri aiebant necesse esse quid esset cognitio aut perceptio aut, si verbum e verbo volumus, comprehensio, quam καταληψιν illi vocant, eosque, qui persuadere vellent, esse aliquid quod comprehendi et percipi posset, inscienter facere dicebant, propterea quod nihil esset clarius εναργειαι, ut Graeci: perspicuitatem aut evidentiam nos, si placet, nominemus fabricemurque, si opus erit, verba, ne hic sibi—me appellabat iocans—hoc licere putet soli: sed tamen orationem nullam putabant illustriorem ipsa evidentia reperiri posse nec ea, quae tam clara essent, definienda censebant. Alii autem negabant se pro hac evidentia quicquam priores fuisse dicturos, sed ad ea, quae contra dicerentur, dici oportere putabant, ne qui fallerentur. 18. Plerique tamen et definitiones ipsarum etiam evidentium rerum non improbant et rem idoneam, de qua quaeratur, et homines dignos, quibuscum disseratur, putant. Philo autem, dum nova quaedam commovet, quod ea sustinere vix poterat, quae contra Academicorum pertinaciam dicebantur, et aperte mentitur, ut est reprehensus a patre Catulo, et, ut docuit Antiochus, in id ipsum se induit, quod timebat. Cum enim ita negaret, quicquam esse, quod comprehendi posset—id enim volumus esse ακαταληπτον—, si illud esset, sicut Zeno definiret, tale visum—iam enim hoc pro φαντασιαι verbum satis hesterno sermone trivimus— visum igitur impressum effictumque ex eo, unde esset, quale esse non posset, ex eo, unde non esset, id nos a Zenone definitum rectissime dicimus: qui enim potest quicquam comprehendi, ut plane confidas perceptum id cognitumque esse, quod est tale, quale vel falsum esse possit? hoc cum infirmat tollitque Philo, iudicium tollit incogniti et cogniti: ex quo efficitur nihil posse comprehendi. Ita imprudens eo, quo minime volt, revolvitur. Qua re omnis oratio contra Academiam suscipitur a nobis, ut retineamus eam definitionem, quam Philo voluit evertere. Quam nisi obtinemus, percipi nihil posse concedimus.

VII. 19. Ordiamur igitur a sensibus: quorum ita clara iudicia et certa sunt, ut, si optio naturae nostrae detur, et ab ea deus aliqui requirat contentane sit suis integris incorruptisque sensibus an postulet melius aliquid, non videam quid quaerat amplius. Nec vero hoc loco exspectandum est, dum de remo inflexo aut de collo columbae respondeam: non enim is sum, qui quidquid videtur tale dicam esse quale videatur. Epicurus hoc viderit et alia multa. Meo autem iudicio ita est maxima in sensibus veritas, si et sani sunt ac valentes et omnia removentur, quae obstant et impediunt. Itaque et lumen mutari saepe volumus et situs earum rerum, quas intuemur, et intervalla aut contrahimus aut diducimus, multaque facimus usque eo, dum adspectus ipse fidem faciat sui iudicii. Quod idem fit in vocibus, in odore, in sapore, ut nemo sit nostrum qui in sensibus sui cuiusque generis iudicium requirat acrius. 20. Adhibita vero exercitatione et arte, ut oculi pictura teneantur, aures cantibus, quis est quin cernat quanta vis sit in sensibus? Quam multa vident pictores in umbris et in eminentia, quae nos non videmus! quam multa, quae nos fugiunt in cantu, exaudiunt in eo genere exercitati! qui primo inflatu tibicinis Antiopam esse aiunt aut Andromacham, quum id nos ne suspicemur quidem. Nihil necesse est de gustatu et odoratu loqui, in quibus intellegentia, etsi vitiosa, est quaedam tamen. Quid de tactu, et eo quidem, quem philosophi interiorem vocant, aut doloris aut voluptatis? in quo Cyrenaici solo putant veri esse iudicium, quia sentiatur:—potestne igitur quisquam dicere inter eum, qui doleat, et inter eum, qui in voluptate sit, nihil interesse? aut, ita qui sentiet non apertissime insaniat? 21. Atqui qualia sunt haec, quae sensibus percipi dicimus, talia secuntur ea, quae non sensibus ipsis percipi dicuntur, sed quodam modo sensibus, ut haec: 'illud est album, hoc dulce, canorum illud, hoc bene olens, hoc asperum.' Animo iam haec tenemus comprehensa, non sensibus. 'Ille' deinceps 'equus est, ille canis.' Cetera series deinde sequitur, maiora nectens, ut haec, quae quasi expletam rerum comprehensionem amplectuntur: 'si homo est, animal est mortale, rationis particeps.' Quo e genere nobis notitiae rerum imprimuntur, sine quibus nec intellegi quicquam nec quaeri disputarive potest. 22. Quod si essent falsae notitiae—εννοιας enim notitias appellare tu videbare—, si igitur essent hae falsae aut eius modi visis impressae, qualia visa a falsis discerni non possent, quo tandem his modo uteremur? quo modo autem quid cuique rei consentaneum esset, quid repugnaret videremus? Memoriae quidem certe, quae non modo philosophiam, sed omnis vitae usus omnisque artis una maxime continet, nihil omnino loci relinquitur. Quae potest enim esse memoria falsorum? aut quid quisquam meminit, quod non animo comprehendit et tenet? Ars vero quae potest esse nisi quae non ex una aut duabus, sed ex multis animi perceptionibus constat? Quam si subtraxeris, qui distingues artificem ab inscio? Non enim fortuito hunc artificem dicemus esse, illum negabimus, sed cum alterum percepta et comprehensa tenere videmus, alterum non item. Cumque artium aliud eius modi genus sit, ut tantum modo animo rem cernat, aliud, ut moliatur aliquid et faciat, quo modo aut geometres cernere ea potest, quae aut nulla sunt aut internosci a falsis non possunt, aut is, qui fidibus utitur, explere numeros et conficere versus? Quod idem in similibus quoque artibus continget, quarum omne opus est in faciendo atque agendo. Quid enim est quod arte effici possit, nisi is, qui artem tractabit, multa perceperit?

VIII. 23. Maxime vero virtutum cognitio confirmat percipi et comprehendi multa posse. In quibus solis inesse etiam scientiam dicimus, quam nos non comprehensionem modo rerum, sed eam stabilem quoque et immutabilem esse censemus, itemque sapientiam, artem vivendi, quae ipsa ex sese habeat constantiam. Ea autem constantia si nihil habeat percepti et cogniti, quaero unde nata sit aut quo modo? Quaero etiam, ille vir bonus, qui statuit omnem cruciatum perferre, intolerabili dolore lacerari potius quam aut officium prodat aut fidem, cur has igitur sibi tam gravis leges imposuerit, cum quam ob rem ita oporteret nihil haberet comprehensi, percepti, cogniti, constituti? Nullo igitur modo fieri potest ut quisquam tanti aestimet aequitatem et fidem, ut eius conservandae causa nullum supplicium recuset, nisi iis rebus adsensus sit, quae falsae esse non possint. 24. Ipsa vero sapientia, si se ignorabit sapientia sit necne, quo modo primum obtinebit nomen sapientiae? deinde quo modo suscipere aliquam rem aut agere fidenter audebit, cum certi nihil erit quod sequatur? cum vero dubitabit quid sit extremum et ultimum bonorum, ignorans quo omnia referantur, qui poterit esse sapientia? Atque etiam illud perspicuum est, constitui necesse esse initium, quod sapientia, cum quid agere incipiat, sequatur, idque initium esse naturae accommodatum. Nam aliter appetitio—eam enim volumus esse ʽορμην—, qua ad agendum impellimur, et id appetimus, quod est visum, moveri non potest. 25. Illud autem, quod movet, prius oportet videri eique credi: quod fieri non potest, si id, quod visum erit, discerni non poterit a falso. Quo modo autem moveri animus ad appetendum potest, si id, quod videtur, non percipitur accommodatumne naturae sit an alienum? Itemque, si quid offici sui sit non occurrit animo, nihil umquam omnino aget, ad nullam rem umquam impelletur, numquam movebitur. Quod si aliquid aliquando acturus est, necesse est id ei verum, quod occurrit, videri. 26. Quid quod, si ista vera sunt, ratio omnis tollitur, quasi quaedam lux lumenque vitae, tamenne in ista pravitate perstabitis? Nam quaerendi initium ratio attulit, quae perfecit virtutem, cum esset ipsa ratio confirmata quaerendo. Quaestio autem est appetitio cognitionis quaestionisque finis inventio. At nemo invenit falsa, nec ea, quae incerta permanent, inventa esse possunt, sed, cum ea, quae quasi involuta fuerunt, aperta sunt, tum inventa dicuntur. Sic et initium quaerendi et exitus percipiendi et comprehendendi tenet*ur*. Itaque argumenti conclusio, quae est Graece ἀποδειξις, ita definitur: 'ratio, quae ex rebus perceptis ad id, quod non percipiebatur, adducit.'

IX. 27. Quod si omnia visa eius modi essent, qualia isti dicunt, ut ea vel falsa esse possent, neque ea posset ulla notio discernere, quo modo quemquam aut conclusisse aliquid aut invenisse diceremus aut quae esset conclusi argumenti fides? Ipsa autem philosophia, quae rationibus progredi debet, quem habebit exitum? Sapientiae vero quid futurum est? quae neque de se ipsa dubitare debet neque de suis decretis, quae philosophi vocant δογματα, quorum nullum sine scelere prodi poterit. Cum enim decretum proditur, lex veri rectique proditur, quo e vitio et amicitiarum proditiones et rerum publicarum nasci solent. Non potest igitur dubitari quin decretum nullum falsum possit esse sapientique satis non sit non esse falsum, sed etiam stabile, fixum, ratum esse debeat, quod movere nulla ratio queat. Talia autem neque esse neque videri possunt eorum ratione, qui illa visa, e quibus omnia decreta sunt nata, negant quicquam a falsis interesse. 28. Ex hoc illud est natum, quod postulabat Hortensius, ut id ipsum saltem perceptum a sapiente diceretis, nihil posse percipi. Sed Antipatro hoc idem postulanti, cum diceret ei, qui adfirmaret nihil posse percipi, consentaneum esse unum tamen illud dicere percipi posse, ut alia non possent, Carneades acutius resistebat. Nam tantum abesse dicebat, ut id consentaneum esset, ut maxime etiam repugnaret. Qui enim negaret quicquam esse quod perciperetur, eum nihil excipere: ita necesse esse, ne id ipsum quidem, quod exceptum non esset, comprehendi et percipi ullo modo posse. 29. Antiochus ad istum locum pressius videbatur accedere. Quoniam enim id haberent Academici decretum,—sentitis enim iam hoc me δογμα dicere—, nihil posse percipi, non debere eos in suo decreto, sicut in ceteris rebus, fluctuare, praesertim cum in eo summa consisteret: hanc enim esse regulam totius philosophiae, constitutionem veri falsi, cogniti incogniti: quam rationem quoniam susciperent docereque vellent quae vis*a* accipi oporteret et quae repudiari, certe hoc ipsum, ex quo omne veri falsique iudicium esset, percipere eos debuisse: etenim duo esse haec maxima in philosophia, iudicium veri et finem bonorum, nec sapientem posse esse, qui aut cognoscendi esse initium ignoret aut extremum expetendi, ut aut unde proficiscatur aut quo perveniendum sit nesciat: haec autem habere dubia neque iis ita confidere, ut moveri non possint, abhorrere a sapientia plurimum. Hoc igitur modo potius erat ab his postulandum, ut hoc unum saltem, percipi nihil posse, perceptum esse dicerent. Sed de inconstantia totius illorum sententiae, si ulla sententia cuiusquam esse potest nihil approbantis, sit, ut opinor, dictum satis.

X. 30. Sequitur disputatio copiosa illa quidem, sed paulo abstrusior—habet enim aliquantum a physicis—, ut verear ne maiorem largiar ei, qui contra dicturus est, libertatem et licentiam. Nam quid eum facturum putem de abditis rebus et obscuris, qui lucem eripere conetur? Sed disputari poterat subtiliter, quanto quasi artificio natura fabricata esset primum animal omne, deinde hominem maxime, quae vis esset in sensibus, quem ad modum primum visa nos pellerent, deinde appetitio ab his pulsa sequeretur, tum ut sensus ad res percipiendas intenderemus. Mens enim ipsa, quae sensuum fons est atque etiam ipsa sensus est, naturalem vim habet, quam intendit ad ea, quibus movetur. Itaque alia visa sic adripit, ut iis statim utatur, alia quasi recondit, e quibus memoria oritur. Cetera autem similitudinibus construit, ex quibus efficiuntur notitiae rerum, quas Graeci tum εννοιας, tum προληψεις vocant. Eo cum accessit ratio argumentique conclusio rerumque innumerabilium multitudo, tum et perceptio eorum omnium apparet et eadem ratio perfecta his gradibus ad sapientiam pervenit. 31. Ad rerum igitur scientiam vitaeque constantiam aptissima cum sit mens hominis, amplectitur maxime cognitionem, et istam καταληψιν, quam, ut dixi, verbum e verbo exprimentes comprehensionem dicemus, cum ipsam per se amat—nihil est enim ei veritatis luce dulcius—tum etiam propter usum. Quocirca et sensibus utitur et artis efficit, quasi sensus alteros, et usque eo philosophiam ipsam corroborat, ut virtutem efficiat, ex qua re una vita omnis apta sit. Ergo ii, qui negant quicquam posse comprehendi, haec ipsa eripiunt vel instrumenta vel ornamenta vitae vel potius etiam totam vitam evertunt funditus ipsumque animal orbant animo, ut difficile sit de temeritate eorum, perinde ut causa postulat, dicere.

32. Nec vero satis constituere possum quod sit eorum consilium aut quid velint. Interdum enim cum adhibemus ad eos orationem eius modi: 'Si ea, quae disputentur, vera sint, tum omnia fore incerta,' respondent: 'Quid ergo istud ad nos? num nostra culpa est? naturam accusa, quae in profundo veritatem, ut ait Democritus, penitus abstruserit.' Alii autem elegantius, qui etiam queruntur, quod eos insimulemus omnia incerta dicere, quantumque intersit inter incertum et id, quod percipi non possit, docere conantur eaque distinguere. Cum his igitur agamus, qui haec distinguunt: illos, qui omnia sic incerta dicunt, ut stellarum numerus par an impar sit, quasi desperatos aliquos relinquamus. Volunt enim—et hoc quidem vel maxime vos animadvertebam moveri—probabile aliquid esse et quasi veri simile, eaque se uti regula et in agenda vita et in quaerendo ac disserendo.

XI. 33. Quae ista regula est veri et falsi, si notionem veri et falsi, propterea quod ea non possunt internosci, nullam habemus? Nam si habemus, interesse oportet ut inter rectum et pravum, sic inter verum et falsum. Si nihil interest, nulla regula est nec potest is, cui est visio veri falsique communis, ullum habere iudicium aut ullam omnino veritatis notam. Nam cum dicunt hoc se unum tollere, ut quicquam possit ita videri, ut non eodem modo falsum etiam possit videri, cetera autem concedere, faciunt pueriliter. Quo enim omnia iudicantur sublato reliqua se negant tollere: ut si quis quem oculis privaverit, dicat ea, quae cerni possent, se ei non ademisse. Ut enim illa oculis modo agnoscuntur, sic reliqua visis, sed propria veri, non communi veri et falsi nota. Quam ob rem, sive tu probabilem visionem sive probabilem et quae non impediatur, ut Carneades volebat, sive aliud quid proferes quod sequare, ad visum illud, de quo agimus, tibi erit revertendum. 34. In eo autem, si erit communitas cum falso, nullum erit iudicium, quia proprium in communi signo notari non potest. Sin autem commune nihil erit, habeo quod volo: id enim quaero, quod ita mihi videatur verum, ut non possit item falsum videri. Simili in errore versantur, cum convicio veritatis coacti perspicua a perceptis volunt distinguere et conantur ostendere esse aliquid perspicui, verum illud quidem impressum in animo atque mente, neque tamen id percipi atque comprehendi posse. Quo enim modo perspicue dixeris album esse aliquid, cum possit accidere ut id, quod nigrum sit, album esse videatur? aut quo modo ista aut perspicua dicemus aut impressa subtiliter, cum sit incertum vere inaniterne moveatur? Ita neque color neque corpus nec veritas nec argumentum nec sensus neque perspicuum ullum relinquitur. 35. Ex hoc illud iis usu venire solet, ut, quidquid dixerint, a quibusdam interrogentur: 'Ergo istuc quidem percipis?' Sed qui ita interrogant, ab iis irridentur. Non enim urguent, ut coarguant neminem ulla de re posse contendere neque adseverare sine aliqua eius rei, quam sibi quisque placere dicit, certa et propria nota. Quod est igitur istuc vestrum probabile? Nam si, quod cuique occurrit et primo quasi adspectu probabile videtur, id confirmatur, quid eo levius? 36. Sin ex circumspectione aliqua et accurata consideratione, quod visum sit, id se dicent sequi, tamen exitum non habebunt: primum quia iis visis, inter quae nihil interest, aequaliter omnibus abrogatur fides: deinde, cum dicant posse accidere sapienti ut, cum omnia fecerit diligentissimeque circumspexerit, exsistat aliquid quod et veri simile videatur et absit longissime a vero, ne si magnam partem quidem, ut solent dicere, ad verum ipsum aut quam proxime accedant, confidere sibi poterunt. Ut enim confidant, notum iis esse debebit insigne veri, quo obscurato et oppresso quod tandem verum sibi videbuntur attingere? Quid autem tam absurde dici potest quam cum ita locuntur: 'Est hoc quidem illius rei signum aut argumentum et ea re id sequor, sed fieri potest ut id, quod significatur, aut falsum sit aut nihil sit omnino.' Sed de perceptione hactenus. Si quis enim ea, quae dicta sunt, labefactare volet, facile etiam absentibus nobis veritas se ipsa defendet.

XII. 37. His satis cognitis, quae iam explicata sunt, nunc de adsensione atque approbatione, quam Graeci συγκαταθεσιν vocant, pauca dicemus, non quo non latus locus sit, sed paulo ante iacta sunt fundamenta. Nam cum vim, quae esset in sensibus, explicabamus, simul illud aperiebatur, comprehendi multa et percipi sensibus, quod fieri sine adsensione non potest. Deinde cum inter inanimum et animal hoc maxime intersit, quod animal agit aliquid—nihil enim agens ne cogitari quidem potest quale sit—, aut ei sensus adimendus est aut ea, quae est in nostra potestate sita, reddenda adsensio. 38. At vero animus quodam modo eripitur iis, quos neque sentire neque adsentiri volunt. Ut enim necesse est lancem in libra ponderibus impositis deprimi, sic animum perspicuis cedere. Nam quo modo non potest animal ullum non appetere id, quod accommodatum ad naturam appareat—Graeci id οικειον appellant—, sic non potest obiectam rem perspicuam non approbare. Quamquam, si illa, de quibus disputatum est, vera sunt, nihil attinet de adsensione omnino loqui. Qui enim quid percipit, adsentitur statim. Sed haec etiam secuntur, nec memoriam sine adsensione posse constare nec notitias rerum nec artis, idque, quod maximum est, ut sit aliquid in nostra potestate, in eo, qui rei nulli adsentietur, non erit. 39. Ubi igitur virtus, si nihil situm est in ipsis nobis? Maxime autem absurdum vitia in ipsorum esse potestate neque peccare quemquam nisi adsensione: hoc idem in virtute non esse, cuius omnis constantia et firmitas ex iis rebus constat, quibus adsensa est et quas approbavit, omninoque ante videri aliquid quam agamus necesse est, eique, quod visum sit, adsentiatur. Qua re qui aut visum aut adsensum tollit, is omnem actionem tollit e vita.

XIII. 40. Nunc ea videamus, quae contra ab his disputari solent. Sed prius potestis totius eorum rationis quasi fundamenta cognoscere. Componunt igitur primum artem quandam de iis, quae visa dicimus, eorumque et vim et genera definiunt, in his, quale sit id, quod percipi et comprehendi possit, totidem verbis quot Stoici. Deinde illa exponunt duo, quae quasi contineant omnem hanc quaestionem: quae ita videantur, ut etiam alia eodem modo videri possint nec in iis quicquam intersit, non posse eorum alia percipi, alia non percipi: nihil interesse autem, non modo si omni ex parte eiusdem modi sint, sed etiam si discerni non possint. Quibus positis unius argumenti conclusione tota ab his causa comprehenditur. Composita ea conclusio sic est: 'Eorum, quae videntur, alia vera sunt, alia falsa, et quod falsum est, id percipi non potest: quod autem verum visum est, id omne tale est, ut eiusdem modi etiam falsum possit videri.' Et, 'quae visa sint eius modi, ut in iis nihil intersit, non posse accidere ut eorum alia percipi possint, alia non possint. 41. Nullum igitur est visum quod percipi possit.' Quae autem sumunt, ut concludant id, quod volunt, ex his duo sibi putant concedi: neque enim quisquam repugnat. Ea sunt haec: 'Quae visa falsa sint, ea percipi non posse,' et alterum: 'Inter quae visa nihil intersit, ex iis non posse alia talia esse, ut percipi possint, alia ut non possint:' reliqua vero multa et varia oratione defendunt, quae sunt item duo, unum: 'quae videantur, eorum alia vera esse, alia falsa,' alterum: 'omne visum, quod sit a vero, tale esse, quale etiam a falso possit esse.' 42. Haec duo proposita non praetervolant, sed ita dilatant, ut non mediocrem curam adhibeant et diligentiam. Dividunt enim in partis et eas quidem magnas: primum in sensus, deinde in ea, quae ducuntur a sensibus et ab omni consuetudine, quam obscurari volunt. Tum perveniunt ad eam partem, ut ne ratione quidem et coniectura ulla res percipi possit. Haec autem universa concidunt etiam minutius. Ut enim de sensibus hesterno sermone vidistis, item faciunt de reliquis, in singulisque rebus, quas in minima dispertiunt, volunt efficere iis omnibus, quae visa sint, veris adiuncta esse falsa, quae a veris nihil differant: ea cum talia sint, non posse comprehendi.

XIV. 43. Hanc ego subtilitatem philosophia quidem dignissimam iudico, sed ab eorum causa, qui ita disserunt, remotissimam. Definitiones enim et partitiones et horum luminibus utens oratio, tum similitudines dissimilitudinesque et earum tenuis et acuta distinctio fidentium est hominum illa vera et firma et certa esse quae tutentur, non eorum qui clament nihilo magis vera illa esse quam falsa. Quid enim agant, si, cum aliquid definierint, roget eos quispiam, num illa definitio possit in aliam rem transferri quamlubet? Si posse dixerint, quid dicere habeant cur illa vera definitio sit? sin negaverint, fatendum sit, quoniam vel illa vera definitio transferri non possit in falsum, quod ea definitione explicetur, id percipi posse: quod minime illi volunt. Eadem dici poterunt in omnibus partibus. 44. Si enim dicent ea, de quibus disserent, se dilucide perspicere nec ulla communione visorum impediri, comprehendere ea se fatebuntur. Sin autem negabunt vera visa a falsis posse distingui, qui poterunt longius progredi? Occurretur enim, sicut occursum est. Nam concludi argumentum non potest nisi iis, quae ad concludendum sumpta erunt, ita probatis, ut falsa eiusdem modi nulla possint esse. Ergo si rebus comprehensis et perceptis nisa et progressa ratio hoc efficiet, nihil posse comprehendi, quid potest reperiri quod ipsum sibi repugnet magis? cumque ipsa natura accuratae orationis hoc profiteatur, se aliquid patefacturam quod non appareat et, quo id facilius adsequatur, adhibituram et sensus et ea, quae perspicua sint, qualis est istorum oratio, qui omnia non tam esse quam videri volunt? Maxime autem convincuntur, cum haec duo pro congruentibus sumunt tam vehementer repugnantia: primum esse quaedam falsa visa: quod cum volunt, declarant quaedam esse vera: deinde ibidem, inter falsa visa et vera nihil interesse. At primum sumpseras, tamquam interesset: ita priori posterius, posteriori superius non iungitur.

45. Sed progrediamur longius et ita agamus, ut nihil nobis adsentati esse videamur, quaeque ab iis dicuntur, sic persequamur, ut nihil in praeteritis relinquamus. Primum igitur perspicuitas illa, quam diximus, satis magnam habet vim, ut ipsa per sese ea, quae sint, nobis ita ut sint indicet. Sed tamen, ut maneamus in perspicuis firmius et constantius, maiore quadam opus est vel arte vel diligentia, ne ab iis, quae clara sint ipsa per sese, quasi praestigiis quibusdam et captionibus depellamur. Nam qui voluit subvenire erroribus Epicurus iis, qui videntur conturbare veri cognitionem, dixitque sapientis esse opinionem a perspicuitate seiungere, nihil profecit: ipsius enim opinionis errorem nullo modo sustulit.

XV. 46. Quam ob rem cum duae causae perspicuis et evidentibus rebus adversentur, auxilia totidem sunt contra comparanda. Adversatur enim primum, quod parum defigunt animos et intendunt in ea, quae perspicua sunt, ut quanta luce ea circumfusa sint possint agnoscere; alterum est, quod fallacibus et captiosis interrogationibus circumscripti atque decepti quidam, cum eas dissolvere non possunt, desciscunt a veritate. Oportet igitur et ea, quae pro perspicuitate responderi possunt, in promptu habere, de quibus iam diximus, et esse armatos, ut occurrere possimus interrogationibus eorum captionesque discutere: quod deinceps facere constitui. 47. Exponam igitur generatim argumenta eorum, quoniam ipsi etiam illi solent non confuse loqui. Primum conantur ostendere multa posse videri esse, quae omnino nulla sint, cum animi inaniter moveantur eodem modo rebus iis, quae nullae sint, ut iis, quae sint. Nam cum dicatis, inquiunt, visa quaedam mitti a deo, velut ea, quae in somnis videantur quaeque oraculis, auspiciis, extis declarentur—haec enim aiunt probari Stoicis, quos contra disputant—, quaerunt quonam modo, falsa visa quae sint, ea deus efficere possit probabilia: quae autem plane proxime ad verum accedant, efficere non possit? aut, si ea quoque possit, cur illa non possit, quae perdifficiliter, internoscantur tamen? et, si haec, cur non inter quae nihil sit omnino? 48. Deinde, cum mens moveatur ipsa per sese, ut et ea declarant, quae cogitatione depingimus, et ea, quae vel dormientibus vel furiosis videntur non numquam, veri simile est sic etiam mentem moveri, ut non modo non internoscat vera visa illa sint anne falsa, sed ut in iis nihil intersit omnino: ut si qui tremerent et exalbescerent vel ipsi per se motu mentis aliquo vel obiecta terribili re extrinsecus, nihil ut esset, qui distingueretur tremor ille et pallor, neque ut quicquam interesset inter intestinum et oblatum. Postremo si nulla visa sunt probabilia, quae falsa sint, alia ratio est. Sin autem sunt, cur non etiam quae non facile internoscantur? cur non ut plane nihil intersit? praesertim cum ipsi dicatis sapientem in furore sustinere se ab omni adsensu, quia nulla in visis distinctio appareat.

XVI. 49. Ad has omnis visiones inanis Antiochus quidem et permulta dicebat et erat de hac una re unius diei disputatio. Mihi autem non idem faciendum puto, sed ipsa capita dicenda. Et primum quidem hoc reprehendendum, quod captiosissimo genere interrogationis utuntur, quod genus minime in philosophia probari solet, cum aliquid minutatim et gradatim additur aut demitur. Soritas hoc vocant, quia acervum efficiunt uno addito grano. Vitiosum sane et captiosum genus! Sic enim adscenditis: Si tale visum obiectum est a deo dormienti, ut probabile sit, cur non etiam ut valde veri simile? cur deinde non ut difficiliter a vero internoscatur? deinde ut ne internoscatur quidem? postremo ut nihil inter hoc et illud intersit? Huc si perveneris, me tibi primum quidque concedente, meum vitium fuerit: sin ipse tua sponte processeris, tuum. 50. Quis enim tibi dederit aut omnia deum posse aut ita facturum esse, si possit? quo modo autem sumis, ut, si quid cui simile esse possit, sequatur ut etiam difficiliter internosci possit? deinde ut ne internosci quidem? postremo ut eadem sint? ut, si lupi canibus similes *sunt*, eosdem dices ad extremum. Et quidem honestis similia sunt quaedam non honesta et bonis non bona et artificiosis minime artificiosa: quid dubitamus igitur adfirmare nihil inter haec interesse? Ne repugnantia quidem videmus? Nihil est enim quod de suo genere in aliud genus transferri possit. At si efficeretur, ut inter visa differentium generum nihil interesset, reperirentur quae et in suo genere essent et in alieno. 51. Quod fieri qui potest? Omnium deinde inanium visorum una depulsio est, sive illa cogitatione informantur, quod fieri solere concedimus, sive in quiete sive per vinum sive per insaniam. Nam ab omnibus eiusdem modi visis perspicuitatem, quam mordicus tenere debemus, abesse dicemus. Quis enim, cum sibi fingit aliquid et cogitatione depingit, non simul ac se ipse commovit atque ad se revocavit, sentit quid intersit inter perspicua et inania? Eadem ratio est somniorum. Num censes Ennium, cum in hortis cum Ser. Galba vicino suo ambulavisset, dixisse: 'Visus sum mihi cum Galba ambulare?' At, cum somniavit, ita narravit:

'visus Homerus adesse poeta.'

Idemque in Epicharmo:

'Nam videbar somniare med ego esse mortuum.'

Itaque, simul ut experrecti sumus, visa illa contemnimus neque ita habemus, ut ea, quae in foro gessimus.

XVII. 52. At enim dum videntur, eadem est in somnis species eorum*que*, quae vigilantes videmus! Primum interest: sed id omittamus. Illud enim dicimus, non eandem esse vim neque integritatem dormientium et vigilantium nec mente nec sensu. Ne vinolenti quidem quae faciunt, eadem approbatione faciunt qua sobrii: dubitant, haesitant, revocant se interdum iisque, quae videntur, imbecillius adsentiuntur, cumque edormiverunt, illa visa quam levia fuerint intellegunt. Quod idem contingit insanis, ut et incipientes furere sentiant et dicant aliquid, quod non sit, id videri sibi, et, cum relaxentur, sentiant atque illa dicant Alcmaeonis:

'Sed mihi ne utiquam cor consentit cum oculorum

adspectu' ...

53. At enim ipse sapiens sustinet se in furore, ne approbet falsa pro veris. Et alias quidem saepe, si aut in sensibus ipsius est aliqua forte gravitas aut tarditas aut obscuriora sunt quae videntur aut a perspiciendo temporis brevitate excluditur. Quamquam totum hoc, sapientem aliquando sustinere adsensionem, contra vos est. Si enim inter visa nihil interesset, aut semper sustineret aut numquam. Sed ex hoc genere toto perspici potest levitas orationis eorum, qui omnia cupiunt confundere. Quaerimus gravitatis, constantiae, firmitatis, sapientiae iudicium: utimur exemplis somniantium, furiosorum, ebriosorum. Illud attendimus in hoc omni genere quam inconstanter loquamur? Non enim proferremus vino aut somno oppressos aut mente captos tam absurde, ut tum diceremus interesse inter vigilantium visa et sobriorum et sanorum et eorum, qui essent aliter adfecti, tum nihil interesse. 54. Ne hoc quidem cernunt, omnia se reddere incerta, quod nolunt, ea dico incerta, quae αδηλα Graeci. Si enim res se ita habeant, ut nihil intersit, utrum ita cui videatur, ut insano, an sano, cui possit exploratum esse de sua sanitate? quod velle efficere non mediocris insaniae est. Similitudines vero aut geminorum aut signorum anulis impressorum pueriliter consectantur. Quis enim nostrum similitudines negat esse, cum eae plurimis in rebus appareant? Sed, si satis est ad tollendam cognitionem similia esse multa multorum, cur eo non estis contenti, praesertim concedentibus nobis? et cur id potius contenditis, quod rerum natura non patitur, ut non suo quidque genere sit tale, quale est, nec sit in duobus aut pluribus nulla re differens ulla communitas? ut [sibi] sint et ova ovorum et apes apium simillimae: quid pugnas igitur? aut quid tibi vis in geminis? Conceditur enim similis esse, quo contentus esse potueras: tu autem vis eosdem plane esse, non similis: quod fieri nullo modo potest. 55. Dein confugis ad physicos eos, qui maxime in Academia irridentur, a quibus ne tu quidem iam te abstinebis, et ais Democritum dicere innumerabilis esse mundos et quidem sic quosdam inter sese non solum similis, sed undique perfecte et absolute ita pares, ut inter eos nihil prorsus intersit [et eos quidem innumerabiles], itemque homines. Deinde postulas, ut, si mundus ita sit par alteri mundo, ut inter eos ne minimum quidem intersit, concedatur tibi ut in hoc quoque nostro mundo aliquid alicui sic sit par, ut nihil differat, nihil intersit. Cur enim, inquies, ex illis individuis, unde omnia Democritus gigni adfirmat, in

reliquis mundis et in iis quidem innumerabilibus innumerabiles Q. Lutatii Catuli non modo possint esse, sed etiam sint, in hoc tanto mundo Catulus alter non possit effici?

XVIII. 56. Primum quidem me ad Democritum vocas, cui non adsentior potiusque refello propter id, quod dilucide docetur a politioribus physicis singularum rerum singulas proprietates esse. Fac enim antiquos illos Servilios, qui gemini fuerunt, tam similis quam dicuntur, num censes etiam eosdem fuisse? Non cognoscebantur foris, at domi: non ab alienis, at a suis. An non videmus hoc usu venire, ut, quos numquam putassemus a nobis internosci posse, eos consuetudine adhibita tam facile internosceremus, uti ne minimum quidem similes viderentur? 57. Hic, pugnes licet, non repugnabo: quin etiam concedam illum ipsum sapientem, de quo omnis hic sermo est, cum ei res similes occurrant, quas non habeat dinotatas, retenturum adsensum nec umquam ulli viso adsensurum, nisi quod tale fuerit, quale falsum esse non possit. Sed et ad ceteras res habet quandam artem, qua vera a falsis possit distinguere, et ad similitudines istas usus adhibendus est. Ut mater geminos internoscit consuetudine oculorum, sic tu internosces, si adsueveris. Videsne ut in proverbio sit ovorum inter se similitudo? Tamen hoc accepimus, Deli fuisse compluris salvis rebus illis, qui gallinas alere permultas quaestus causa solerent: ii cum ovum inspexerant, quae id gallina peperisset dicere solebant. 58. Neque id est contra nos: nam nobis satis est ova illa non internoscere: nihil enim magis adsentiri par est, hoc illud esse, quasi inter illa omnino nihil interesset: habeo enim regulam, ut talia visa vera iudicem, qualia falsa esse non possint: ab hac mihi non licet transversum, ut aiunt, digitum discedere, ne confundam omnia. Veri enim et falsi non modo cognitio, sed etiam natura tolletur, si nihil erit quod intersit: ut etiam illud absurdum sit, quod interdum soletis dicere, cum visa in animos imprimantur, non vos id dicere, inter ipsas impressiones nihil interesse, sed inter species et quasdam formas eorum. Quasi vero non specie visa iudicentur! quae fidem nullam habebunt sublata veri et falsi nota. 59. Illud vero perabsurdum, quod dicitis, probabilia vos sequi, si re nulla impediamini. Primum qui potestis non impediri, cum a veris falsa non distent? deinde quod iudicium est veri, cum sit commune falsi? Ex his illa necessario nata est ἐποχή, id est adsensionis retentio, in qua melius sibi constitit Arcesilas, si vera sunt quae de Carneade non nulli existimant. Si enim percipi nihil potest, quod utrique visum est, tollendus adsensus est. Quid enim est tam futile quam quicquam approbare non cognitum? Carneadem autem etiam heri audiebamus solitum esse *eo* delabi interdum, ut diceret opinaturum, id est peccaturum esse sapientem. Mihi porro non tam certum est esse aliquid, quod comprehendi possit, de quo iam nimium etiam diu disputo, quam sapientem nihil opinari, id est, numquam adsentiri rei vel falsae vel incognitae. 60. Restat illud, quod dicunt, veri inveniendi causa contra omnia dici oportere et pro omnibus. Volo igitur videre quid invenerint. Non solemus, inquit, ostendere. Quae sunt tandem ista mysteria? aut cur celatis, quasi turpe aliquid, sententiam vestram? Ut, qui audient, inquit, ratione potius quam auctoritate ducantur. Quid, si utroque? num peius est? Unum tamen illud non celant, nihil esse quod percipi possit. An in eo auctoritas nihil obest? Mihi quidem videtur vel plurimum. Quis enim ista tam aperte perspicueque et perversa et falsa secutus esset, nisi tanta in Arcesila, multo etiam maior in Carneade et copia rerum et dicendi vis fuisset?

XIX. 61. Haec Antiochus fere et Alexandreae tum et multis annis post, multo etiam adseverantius, in Syria cum esset mecum, paulo ante quam est mortuus. Sed iam confirmata causa te, hominem amicissimum—me autem appellabat—et aliquot annis minorem natu, non dubitabo monere: Tune, cum tantis laudibus philosophiam extuleris Hortensiumque nostrum dissentientem commoveris, eam philosophiam sequere quae confundit vera cum falsis, spoliat nos iudicio, privat approbatione, omnibus orbat sensibus? Et Cimmeriis quidem, quibus adspectum solis sive deus aliquis sive natura ademerat sive eius loci, quem incolebant, situs, ignes tamen aderant, quorum illis uti lumine licebat, isti autem, quos tu probas, tantis offusis tenebris ne scintillam quidem ullam nobis ad dispiciendum reliquerunt: quos si sequamur, iis vinculis simus adstricti, ut nos commovere nequeamus. 62. Sublata enim adsensione omnem et motum animorum et actionem rerum sustulerunt: quod non modo recte fieri, sed omnino fieri non potest. Provide etiam ne uni tibi istam sententiam minime liceat defendere. An tu, cum res occultissimas aperueris in lucemque protuleris iuratusque dixeris ea te comperisse, quod mihi quoque licebat, qui ex te illa cognoveram, negabis esse rem ullam quae cognosci, comprehendi, percipi possit?

Vide, quaeso, etiam atque etiam ne illarum quoque rerum pulcherrimarum a te ipso minuatur auctoritas. Quae cum dixisset ille, finem fecit. 63. Hortensius autem vehementer admirans, quod quidem perpetuo Lucullo loquente fecerat, ut etiam manus saepe tolleret, nec mirum: nam numquam arbitror contra Academiam dictum esse subtilius, me quoque, iocansne an ita sentiens—non enim satis intellegebam—, coepit hortari, ut sententia desisterem. Tum mihi Catulus: Si te, inquit, Luculli oratio flexit, quae est habita memoriter, accurate, copiose, taceo neque te quo minus, si tibi ita videatur, sententiam mutes deterrendum puto. Illud vero non censuerim, ut eius auctoritate moveare. Tantum enim non te modo monuit, inquit adridens, ut caveres ne quis improbus tribunus plebis, quorum vides quanta copia semper futura sit, adriperet te et in contione quaereret qui tibi constares, cum idem negares quicquam certi posse reperiri, idem te comperisse dixisses. Hoc, quaeso, cave ne te terreat. De causa autem ipsa malim quidem te ab hoc dissentire. Sin cesseris, non magno opere mirabor. Memini enim Antiochum ipsum, cum annos multos alia sensisset, simul ac visum sit, sententia destitisse. Haec cum dixisset Catulus, me omnes intueri.

XX. 64. Tum ego non minus commotus quam soleo in causis maioribus, huius modi quadam oratione sum exorsus: Me, Catule, oratio Luculli de ipsa re ita movit, ut docti hominis et copiosi et parati et nihil praetereuntis eorum, quae pro illa causa dici possent, non tamen ut ei respondere posse diffiderem. Auctoritas autem tanta plane me movebat, nisi tu opposuisses non minorem tuam. Adgrediar igitur, si pauca ante quasi de fama mea dixero. 65. Ego enim si aut ostentatione aliqua adductus aut studio certandi ad hanc potissimum philosophiam me applicavi, non modo stultitiam meam, sed etiam mores et naturam condemnandam puto. Nam, si in minimis rebus pertinacia reprehenditur, calumnia etiam coercetur, ego de omni statu consilioque totius vitae aut certare cum aliis pugnaciter aut frustrari cum alios tum etiam me ipsum velim? Itaque, nisi ineptum putarem in tali disputatione id facere, quod, cum de re publica disceptatur, fieri interdum solet, iurarem per Iovem deosque penates me et ardere studio veri reperiendi et ea sentire, quae dicerem. 66. Qui enim possum non cupere verum invenire, cum gaudeam, si simile veri quid invenerim? Sed, ut hoc pulcherrimum esse iudico, vera videre, sic pro veris probare falsa turpissimum est. Nec tamen ego is sum, qui nihil umquam falsi approbem, qui numquam adsentiar, qui nihil opiner, sed quaerimus de sapiente. Ego vero ipse et magnus quidem sum opinator—non enim sum sapiens—et meas cogitationes sic dirigo, non ad illam parvulam Cynosuram,

'Qua fidunt duce nocturna Phoenices in alto,'

ut ait Aratus, eoque directius gubernant, quod eam tenent,

'Quae cursu interiore, brevi convertitur orbe,'

sed Helicen et clarissimos Septemtriones, id est, rationes has latiore specie, non ad tenue elimatas. Eo fit ut errem et vager latius. Sed non de me, ut dixi, sed de sapiente quaeritur. Visa enim ista cum acriter mentem sensumve pepulerunt, accipio iisque interdum etiam adsentior, nec percipio tamen; nihil enim arbitror posse percipi. Non sum sapiens; itaque visis cedo nec possum resistere. Sapientis autem hanc censet Arcesilas vim esse maximam, Zenoni adsentiens, cavere ne capiatur, ne fallatur videre. Nihil est enim ab ea cogitatione, quam habemus de gravitate sapientis, errore, levitate, temeritate diiunctius. Quid igitur loquar de firmitate sapientis? quem quidem nihil opinari tu quoque, Luculle, concedis. Quod quoniam a te probatur—ut praepostere tecum agam, mox referam me ad ordinem—haec primum conclusio quam habeat vim considera.

XXI. 67. Si ulli rei sapiens adsentietur umquam, aliquando etiam opinabitur: numquam autem opinabitur: nulli igitur rei adsentietur. Hanc conclusionem Arcesilas probabat: confirmabat enim et primum et secundum. Carneades non numquam secundum illud dabat: adsentiri aliquando. Ita sequebatur etiam opinari, quod tu non vis et recte, ut mihi videris. Sed illud primum, sapientem, si adsensurus esset, etiam opinaturum, falsum esse et Stoici dicunt et eorum adstipulator Antiochus: posse enim eum falsa a veris et quae non possint percipi ab iis, quae possint, distinguere. 68. Nobis autem primum, etiam si quid percipi possit, tamen ipsa consuetudo adsentiendi periculosa esse videtur et lubrica. Quam ob rem cum tam vitiosum esse constet adsentiri quicquam aut falsum aut incognitum, sustinenda est potius omnis adsensio, ne praecipitet, si temere processerit. Ita enim finitima sunt falsa veris, eaque, quae percipi non possunt, *iis quae possunt*—si modo ea sunt quaedam: iam enim videbimus—, ut tam in praecipitem locum non debeat se sapiens committere. Sin autem omnino nihil esse quod percipi possit a me sumpsero et, quod tu mihi das, accepero, sapientem nihil opinari, effectum illud erit, sapientem adsensus omnes cohibiturum, ut videndum tibi sit, idne malis an aliquid opinaturum esse sapientem. Neutrum, inquies, illorum. Nitamur igitur, nihil posse percipi: etenim de eo omnis est controversia.

XXII. 69. Sed prius pauca cum Antiocho, qui haec ipsa, quae a me defenduntur, et didicit apud Philonem tam diu, ut constaret diutius didicisse neminem, et scripsit de his rebus acutissime, et idem haec non acrius accusavit in senectute quam antea defensitaverat. Quamvis igitur fuerit acutus, ut fuit, tamen inconstantia levatur auctoritas. Quis enim iste dies illuxerit quaero, qui illi ostenderit eam, quam multos annos esse negitavisset, veri et falsi notam. Excogitavit aliquid? Eadem dicit quae Stoici. Poenituit illa sensisse? Cur non se transtulit ad alios et maxime ad Stoicos? eorum enim erat propria ista dissensio. Quid? eum Mnesarchi poenitebat? quid? Dardani? qui erant Athenis tum principes Stoicorum. Numquam a Philone discessit, nisi postea quam ipse coepit qui se audirent habere. 70. Unde autem subito vetus Academia revocata est? Nominis dignitatem videtur, cum a re ipsa desciceret, retinere voluisse, quod erant qui illum gloriae causa facere dicerent, sperare etiam fore ut ii, qui se sequerentur, Antiochii vocarentur. Mihi autem magis videtur non potuisse sustinere concursum omnium philosophorum. Etenim de ceteris sunt inter illos non nulla communia: haec Academicorum est una sententia, quam reliquorum philosophorum nemo probet. Itaque cessit, et ut ii, qui sub Novis solem non ferunt, item ille, cum aestuaret, veterum, ut Maenianorum, sic Academicorum umbram secutus est. 71. Quoque solebat uti argumento tum, cum ei placebat nihil posse percipi, cum quaereret, Dionysius ille Heracleotes utrum comprehendisset certa illa nota, qua adsentiri dicitis oportere, illudne, quod multos annos tenuisset Zenonique magistro credidisset, honestum quod esset, id bonum solum esse, an quod postea defensitavisset, honesti inane nomen esse, voluptatem esse summum bonum: qui ex illius commutata sententia docere vellet nihil ita signari in animis nostris a vero posse, quod non eodem modo possit a falso, is curavit *ut* quod argumentum ex Dionysio ipse sumpsisset, ex eo ceteri sumerent. Sed cum hoc alio loco plura, nunc ad ea, quae a te, Luculle, dicta sunt.

XXIII. 72. Et primum quod initio dixisti videamus quale sit: similiter a nobis de antiquis philosophis commemorari atque seditiosi solerent claros viros, sed tamen popularis aliquos nominare. Illi cum res *non* bonas tractent, similes bonorum videri volunt. Nos autem dicimus ea nobis videri, quae vosmet ipsi nobilissimis philosophis placuisse conceditis. Anaxagoras nivem nigram dixit esse. Ferres me, si ego idem dicerem? Tu, ne si dubitarem quidem. At quis est? num hic sophistes?—sic enim appellabantur ii, qui ostentationis aut quaestus causa philosophabantur—: maxima fuit et gravitatis et ingeni gloria. 73. Quid loquar de Democrito? Quem cum eo conferre possumus non modo ingeni magnitudine, sed etiam animi? qui ita sit ausus ordiri: 'Haec loquor de universis.' Nihil excipit de quo non profiteatur. Quid enim esse potest extra universa? quis hunc philosophum non anteponit Cleanthi, Chrysippo, reliquis inferioris aetatis? qui mihi cum illo collati quintae classis videntur. Atque is non hoc dicit, quod nos, qui veri esse aliquid non negamus, percipi posse negamus; ille verum plane negat esse: sensus quidem non obscuros dicit, sed tenebricosos: sic enim appellat [eos]. Is, qui hunc maxime est admiratus, Chius Metrodorus initio libri, qui est de natura: 'Nego,' inquit, 'scire nos sciamusne aliquid an nihil sciamus, ne id ipsum quidem, nescire aut scire, scire nos, nec omnino sitne aliquid an nihil sit.' 74. Furere tibi Empedocles videtur: at mihi dignissimum rebus iis, de quibus loquitur, sonum fundere. Num ergo is excaecat nos aut orbat sensibus, si parum magnam vim censet in iis esse ad ea, quae sub eos subiecta sunt, iudicanda? Parmenides, Xenophanes, minus bonis quamquam versibus, sed tamen illi versibus increpant eorum adrogantiam quasi irati, qui, cum sciri nihil possit, audeant se scire dicere. Et ab iis aiebas removendum

Socratem et Platonem. Cur? an de ullis certius possum dicere? Vixisse cum iis equidem videor: ita multi sermones perscripti sunt, e quibus dubitari non possit quin Socrati nihil sit visum sciri posse. Excepit unum tantum, 'scire se nihil se scire,' nihil amplius. Quid dicam de Platone? qui certe tam multis libris haec persecutus non esset, nisi probavisset. Ironiam enim alterius, perpetuam praesertim, nulla fuit ratio persequi.

XXIV. 75. Videorne tibi, non ut Saturninus, nominare modo illustris homines, sed imitari numquam nisi clarum, nisi nobilem? Atqui habebam molestos vobis, sed minutos, Stilponem, Diodorum, Alexinum, quorum sunt contorta et aculeata quaedam σοφισματα; sic enim appellantur fallaces conclusiunculae. Sed quid eos colligam, cum habeam Chrysippum, qui fulcire putatur porticum Stoicorum? Quam multa ille contra sensus, quam multa contra omnia, quae in consuetudine probantur! At dissolvit idem. Mihi quidem non videtur: sed dissolverit sane. Certe tam multa non collegisset, quae nos fallerent probabilitate magna, nisi videret iis resisti non facile posse. 76. Quid Cyrenaici *tibi* videntur, minime contempti philosophi? Qui negant esse quicquam quod percipi possit extrinsecus: ea se sola percipere, quae tactu intimo sentiant, ut dolorem, ut voluptatem: neque se quo quid colore aut quo sono sit scire, sed tantum sentire adfici se quodam modo.

Satis multa de auctoribus. Quamquam ex me quaesieras nonne putarem post illos veteres tot saeculis inveniri verum potuisse tot ingeniis tantisque studiis quaerentibus. Quid inventum sit paulo post videro, te ipso quidem iudice. Arcesilam vero non obtrectandi causa cum Zenone pugnavisse, sed verum invenire voluisse sic intellegitur. 77. Nemo, inquam, superiorum non modo expresserat, sed ne dixerat quidem posse hominem nihil opinari, nec solum posse, sed ita necesse esse sapienti. Visa est Arcesilae cum vera sententia tum honesta et digna sapiente. Quaesivit de Zenone fortasse quid futurum esset, si nec percipere quicquam posset sapiens nec opinari sapientis esset. Ille, credo, nihil opinaturum, quoniam esset, quod percipi posset. Quid ergo id esset? Visum, credo. Quale igitur visum? tum illum ita definisse, ex eo, quod esset, sicut esset, impressum et signatum et effictum. Post requisitum etiamne, si eiusdem modi esset visum verum, quale vel falsum. Hic Zenonem vidisse acute nullum esse visum quod percipi posset, si id tale esset ab eo, quod est, ut eiusdem modi ab eo, quod non est, posset esse. Recte consensit Arcesilas; ad definitionem additum: neque enim falsum percipi posse neque verum, si esset tale, quale vel falsum. Incubuit autem in eas disputationes, ut doceret nullum tale esse visum a vero, ut non eiusdem modi etiam a falso possit esse. 78. Haec est una contentio, quae adhuc permanserit. Nam illud, nulli rei adsensurum esse sapientem, nihil ad hanc controversiam pertinebat. Licebat enim nihil percipere et tamen opinari, quod a Carneade dicitur probatum: equidem Clitomacho plus quam Philoni aut Metrodoro credens, hoc magis ab eo disputatum quam probatum puto. Sed id omittamus. Illud certe opinatione et perceptione sublata sequitur, omnium adsensionum retentio, ut, si ostendero nihil posse percipi, tu concedas numquam adsensurum esse.

XXV. 79. Quid ergo est quod percipi possit, si ne sensus quidem vera nuntiant? quos tu, Luculle, communi loco defendis: quod ne [id] facere posses, idcirco heri non necessario loco contra sensus tam multa dixeram. Tu autem te negas infracto remo neque columbae collo commoveri. Primum cur? Nam et in remo sentio non esse id, quod videatur, et in columba pluris videri colores nec esse plus uno. Deinde nihilne praeterea diximus?—Manent illa omnia, iacet ista causa: veracis suos esse sensus dicit.—Igitur semper auctorem habes eum, qui magno suo periculo causam agat! Eo enim rem demittit Epicurus, si unus sensus semel in vita mentitus sit, nulli umquam esse credendum. 80. Hoc est verum esse, confidere suis testibus et importune insistere! Itaque Timagoras Epicureus negat sibi umquam, cum oculum torsisset, duas ex lucerna flammulas esse visas: opinionis enim esse mendacium, non oculorum. Quasi quaeratur quid sit, non quid videatur. Sed hic quidem maiorum similis: tu vero, qui visa sensibus alia vera dicas esse, alia falsa, qui ea distinguis? Desine, quaeso, communibus locis: domi nobis ista nascuntur. Si, inquis, deus te interroget: Sanis modo et integris sensibus, num amplius quid desideras? quid respondeas?—Utinam quidem roget? Audiret quam nobiscum male ageret. Ut enim vera videamus, quam longe videmus? Ego Catuli Cumanum ex hoc loco video, Pompeianum non cerno, neque quicquam interiectum est quod obstet, sed intendi acies longius non potest. O praeclarum prospectum! Puteolos videmus: at familiarem nostrum C. Avianium, fortasse in porticu Neptuni ambulantem, non videmus. 81. At ille nescio qui, qui in scholis nominari solet, mille et octingenta stadia quod abesset videbat: quaedam volucres longius. Responderem igitur audacter isti vestro deo me plane his oculis non esse contentum. Dicet me acrius videre quam illos pisces fortasse qui neque videntur a nobis et nunc quidem sub oculis sunt neque ipsi nos suspicere possunt. Ergo ut illis aqua, sic nobis aër crassus offunditur. At amplius non desideramus. Quid? talpam num desiderare lumen putas? Neque tam quererer cum deo, quod parum longe quam quod falsum viderem. Videsne navem illam? Stare nobis videtur: at iis, qui in nave sunt, moveri haec villa. Quaere rationem cur ita videatur: quam ut maxime inveneris, quod haud scio an non possis, non tu verum testem habere, sed eum non sine causa falsum testimonium dicere ostenderis.

XXVI. 82. Quid ego de nave? Vidi enim a te remum contemni. Maiora fortasse quaeris. Quid potest esse sole maius? quem mathematici amplius duodeviginti partibus confirmant maiorem esse quam terram. Quantulus nobis videtur! Mihi quidem quasi pedalis. Epicurus autem posse putat etiam minorem esse eum quam videatur, sed non multo: ne maiorem quidem multo putat esse vel tantum esse, quantus videatur, ut oculi aut nihil mentiantur aut non multum. Ubi igitur illud est semel? Sed ab hoc credulo, qui numquam sensus mentiri putat, discedamus: qui ne nunc quidem, cum ille sol, qui tanta incitatione fertur, ut celeritas eius quanta sit ne cogitari quidem possit, tamen nobis stare videtur. 83. Sed, ut minuam controversiam, videte, quaeso, quam in parvo lis sit. Quattuor sunt capita, quae concludant nihil esse quod nosci, percipi, comprehendi possit, de quo haec tota quaestio est. E quibus primum est esse aliquod visum falsum, secundum non posse id percipi, tertium, inter quae visa nihil intersit, fieri non posse ut eorum alia percipi possint, alia non possint, quartum nullum esse visum verum a sensu profectum, cui non appositum sit visum aliud, quod ab eo nihil intersit quodque percipi non possit. Horum quattuor capitum secundum et tertium omnes concedunt. Primum Epicurus non dat; vos, quibuscum res est, id quoque conceditis. Omnis pugna de quarto est. 84. Qui igitur P. Servilium Geminum videbat, si Quintum se videre putabat, incidebat in eius modi visum, quod percipi non posset, quia nulla nota verum distinguebatur a falso: qua distinctione sublata quam haberet in C. Cotta, qui bis cum Gemino consul fuit, agnoscendo eius modi notam, quae falsa esse non posset? Negas tantam similitudinem in rerum natura esse. Pugnas omnino, sed cum adversario facili. Ne sit sane: videri certe potest. Fallet igitur sensum, et si una fefellerit similitudo, dubia omnia reddiderit. Sublato enim iudicio illo, quo oportet agnosci, etiam si ipse erit, quem videris, qui tibi videbitur, tamen non ea nota iudicabis, qua dicis oportere, ut non possit esse eiusdem modi falsa. 85. Quando igitur potest tibi P. Geminus Quintus videri, quid habes explorati cur non possit tibi Cotta videri qui non sit, quoniam aliquid videtur esse, quod non est? Omnia dicis sui generis esse, nihil esse idem, quod sit aliud. Stoicum est quidem nec admodum credibile 'nullum esse pilum omnibus rebus talem, qualis sit pilus alius, nullum granum.' Haec refelli possunt, sed pugnare nolo. Ad id enim, quod agitur, nihil interest omnibusne partibus visa res nihil differat an internosci non possit, etiam si differat. Sed, si hominum similitudo tanta esse non potest, ne signorum quidem? Dic mihi, Lysippus eodem aere, eadem temperatione, eodem caelo atque ceteris omnibus, centum Alexandros eiusdem modi facere non posset? Qua igitur notione discerneres? 86. Quid? si in eius*dem* modi cera centum sigilla hoc anulo impressero, ecquae poterit in agnoscendo esse distinctio? an tibi erit quaerendus anularius aliqui, quoniam gallinarium invenisti Deliacum illum, qui ova cognosceret?

XXVII. Sed adhibes artem advocatam etiam sensibus. Pictor videt quae nos non videmus et, simul inflavit tibicen, a perito carmen agnoscitur. Quid? hoc nonne videtur contra te valere, si sine magnis artificiis, ad quae pauci accedunt, nostri quidem generis admodum, nec videre nec audire possimus? Iam illa praeclara, quanto artificio esset sensus nostros mentemque et totam constructionem hominis fabricata natura! 87. Cur non extimescam opinandi temeritatem? Etiamne hoc adfirmare potes, Luculle, esse aliquam vim, cum prudentia et consilio scilicet, quae finxerit vel, ut tuo verbo utar, quae fabricata sit hominem? Qualis ista fabrica est? ubi adhibita? quando? cur? quo modo? Tractantur ista ingeniose: disputantur etiam eleganter. Denique videantur sane, ne adfirmentur modo. Sed de physicis mox et quidem ob eam causam, ne tu, qui idem me facturum paulo ante dixeris, videare mentitus. Sed ut ad ea, quae clariora sunt, veniam, res iam universas profundam, de quibus volumina impleta sunt non a nostris solum, sed etiam a Chrysippo:—de quo queri solent Stoici, dum studiose omnia conquisierit contra sensus et perspicuitatem contraque omnem consuetudinem contraque rationem, ipsum sibi respondentem inferiorem fuisse, itaque ab eo armatum esse Carneadem.—88. Ea sunt eius modi, quae a te diligentissime tractata sunt. Dormientium et vinolentorum et furiosorum visa imbecilliora esse dicebas quam vigilantium, siccorum, sanorum. Quo modo? quia, cum experrectus esset Ennius, non diceret 'se vidisse Homerum, sed visum esse,' Alcmaeo autem:

'Sed mihi ne utiquam cor consentit ...'

Similia de vinolentis. Quasi quisquam neget et qui experrectus sit, eum somnia *reri* et cuius furor consederit, putare non fuisse ea vera, quae essent sibi visa in furore. Sed non id agitur: tum, cum videbantur, quo modo viderentur, id quaeritur. Nisi vero Ennium non putamus ita totum illud audivisse,

'O pietas animi ...',

si modo id somniavit, ut si vigilans audiret. Experrectus enim potuit illa visa putare, ut erant, somnia: dormienti vero aeque ac vigilanti probabantur. Quid? Iliona somno illo:

'Mater, te appello ...'

nonne ita credit filium locutum, ut experrecta etiam crederet? Unde enim illa:

'Age adsta: mane, audi: iterandum eadem istaec mihi!' num videtur minorem habere visis quam vigilantes fidem?

XXVIII. 89. Quid loquar de insanis? qualis tandem fuit adfinis tuus, Catule, Tuditanus? quisquam sanissimus tam certa putat quae videt quam is putabat quae videbantur? Quid ille, qui:

'Video, video te. Vive, Ulixes, dum licet,'

nonne etiam bis exclamavit se videre, cum omnino non videret? Quid? apud Euripidem Hercules, cum, ut Eurysthei filios, ita suos configebat sagittis, cum uxorem interemebat, cum conabatur etiam patrem, non perinde movebatur falsis, ut veris moveretur? Quid? ipse Alcmaeo tuus, qui negat 'cor sibi cum oculis consentire,' nonne ibidem incitato furore:

'unde haec flamma oritur?'

et illa deinceps:

'Incedunt, incedunt: adsunt, *adsunt*, me expetunt:'

Quid? cum virginis fidem implorat:

'Fer mi auxilium, pestem abige a me, flammiferam

hanc vim, quae me excruciat!

Caerulea incinctae angui incedunt, circumstant

cum ardentibus taedis.'

Num dubitas quin sibi haec videre videatur? Itemque cetera:

'Intendit crinitus Apollo

arcum auratum, luna innixus:

Diana facem iacit a laeva.'

90. Qui magis haec crederet, si essent, quam credebat, quia videbantur? Apparet enim iam 'cor cum oculis consentire.' Omnia autem haec proferuntur, ut illud efficiatur, quo certius nihil potest esse, inter visa vera et falsa ad animi adsensum nihil interesse. Vos autem nihil agitis, cum illa falsa vel furiosorum vel somniantium recordatione ipsorum refellitis. Non enim id quaeritur, qualis recordatio fieri soleat eorum, qui experrecti sint, aut eorum, qui furere destiterint, sed qualis visio fuerit aut furentium aut somniantium tum cum movebantur. Sed abeo a sensibus.

91. Quid est quod ratione percipi possit? Dialecticam inventam esse dicitis, veri et falsi quasi disceptatricem et iudicem. Cuius veri et falsi? et in qua re? In geometriane quid sit verum aut falsum dialecticus iudicabit an in litteris an in musicis? At ea non novit. In philosophia igitur. Sol quantus sit quid ad illum? Quod sit summum bonum quid habet ut queat iudicare? Quid igitur iudicabit? quae coniunctio, quae diiunctio vera sit, quid ambigue dictum sit, quid sequatur quamque rem, quid repugnet? Si haec et horum similia iudicat, de se ipsa iudicat. Plus autem pollicebatur. Nam haec quidem iudicare ad ceteras res, quae sunt in philosophia multae atque magnae, non est satis. 92. Sed quoniam tantum in ea arte ponitis, videte ne contra vos tota nata sit: quae primo progressu festive tradit elementa loquendi et ambiguorum intellegentiam concludendique rationem, tum paucis additis venit ad soritas, lubricum sane et periculosum locum, quod tu modo dicebas esse vitiosum interrogandi genus.

XXIX. Quid ergo? istius vitii num nostra culpa est? Rerum natura nullam nobis dedit cognitionem finium, ut ulla in re statuere possimus quatenus. Nec hoc in acervo tritici solum, unde nomen est, sed nulla omnino in re minutatim interrogati, dives pauper, clarus obscurus sit, multa pauca, magna parva, longa brevia, lata angusta, quanto aut addito aut dempto certum respondeamus [non] habemus.—93. At vitiosi sunt soritae.—Frangite igitur eos, si potestis, ne molesti sint. Erunt enim, nisi cavetis. Cautum est, inquit. Placet enim Chrysippo, cum gradatim interrogetur, verbi causa, tria pauca sint anne multa, aliquanto prius quam ad multa perveniat quiescere, id est, quod ab his dicitur, ἡσυχάζειν. Per me vel stertas licet, inquit Carneades, non modo quiescas. Sed quid proficit? Sequitur enim, qui te ex somno excitet et eodem modo interroget. Quo in numero conticuisti, si ad eum numerum unum addidero, multane erunt? Progrediere rursus, quoad videbitur. Quid plura? hoc enim fateris, neque ultimum te paucorum neque primum multorum respondere posse. Cuius generis error ita manat, ut non videam quo non possit accedere. 94. Nihil me laedit, inquit: ego enim, ut agitator callidus, prius quam ad finem veniam, equos sustinebo, eoque magis, si locus is, quo ferentur equi, praeceps erit. Sic me, inquit, ante sustineo nec diutius captiose interroganti respondeo. Si habes quod liqueat neque respondes, superbus es: si non habes, ne tu quidem percipis. Si, quia obscura, concedo. Sed negas te usque ad obscura progredi. Illustribus igitur rebus insistis. Si id tantum modo, ut taceas, nihil adsequeris. Quid enim ad illum, qui te captare volt, utrum tacentem irretiat te an loquentem? Sin autem usque ad novem, verbi gratia, sine dubitatione respondes pauca esse, in decimo insistis: etiam a certis et illustrioribus cohibes adsensum. Hoc idem me in obscuris facere non sinis. Nihil igitur te contra soritas ars ista adiuvat, quae nec augentis nec minuentis quid aut primum sit aut postremum docet. 95. Quid? quod eadem illa ars, quasi Penelope telam retexens, tollit ad extremum superiora. Utrum ea vestra an nostra culpa est? Nempe fundamentum dialecticae est, quidquid enuntietur—id autem appellant αξιωμα, quod est quasi effatum—, aut verum esse aut falsum. Quid igitur? haec vera an falsa sunt? Si te mentiri dicis idque verum dicis, mentiris *an* verum dicis? Haec scilicet inexplicabilia esse dicitis. Quod est odiosius quam illa, quae nos non comprehensa et non percepta dicimus.

XXX. Sed hoc omitto. Illud quaero, si ista explicari non possunt, nec eorum ullum iudicium invenitur, ut respondere possitis verane an falsa sint, ubi est illa definitio: 'effatum esse id, quod aut verum aut falsum sit'? Rebus sumptis adiungam ex his sequendas esse alias, alias improbandas, quae sint in genere contrario. 96. Quo modo igitur hoc conclusum esse iudicas? 'Si dicis *nunc lucere et verum dicis, lucet; dicis autem* nunc lucere et verum dicis: lucet igitur.' Probatis certe genus et rectissime conclusum dicitis. Itaque in docendo eum primum concludendi modum traditis. Aut quidquid igitur eodem modo concluditur probabitis aut ars ista nulla est. Vide ergo hanc conclusionem probaturusne sis: 'Si dicis te mentiri verumque dicis, mentiris; dicis autem te mentiri verumque dicis, mentiris igitur.' Qui potes hanc non probare, cum probaveris eiusdem generis superiorem? Haec Chrysippea sunt, ne ab ipso quidem dissoluta. Quid enim faceret huic conclusioni? 'Si lucet, lucet; lucet autem: lucet igitur.' Cederet scilicet. Ipsa enim ratio conexi, cum concesseris superius, cogit inferius concedere. Quid ergo haec ab illa conclusione differt? 'Si mentiris, mentiris: mentiris autem: mentiris igitur.' Hoc negas te posse nec approbare nec improbare. 97. Qui igitur magis illud? Si ars, si ratio, si via, si vis denique conclusionis valet, eadem est in utroque. Sed hoc extremum eorum est: postulant ut excipiantur haec inexplicabilia. Tribunum aliquem censeo adeant: a me istam exceptionem numquam impetrabunt. Etenim cum ab Epicuro, qui totam dialecticam et contemnit et irridet, non impetrent ut verum esse concedat quod ita effabimur, 'aut vivet cras Hermarchus aut non vivet' cum dialectici sic statuant, omne, quod ita diiunctum sit, quasi 'aut etiam aut non,' non modo verum esse, sed etiam necessarium: vide quam sit catus is, quem isti tardum putant. Si enim, inquit, alterutrum concessero necessarium esse, necesse erit cras Hermarchum aut vivere aut non vivere; nulla autem est in natura rerum talis necessitas. Cum hoc igitur dialectici pugnent, id est, Antiochus et Stoici: totam enim evertit dialecticam. Nam si e contrariis diiunctio—contraria autem ea dico, cum alterum aiat, alterum neget, si talis diiunctio falsa potest esse, nulla vera est. 98. Mecum vero quid habent litium, qui ipsorum disciplinam sequor? Cum aliquid huius modi inciderat, sic ludere Carneades solebat: 'Si recte conclusi, teneo: sin vitiose, minam Diogenes reddet.' Ab eo enim Stoico dialecticam didicerat: haec autem merces erat dialecticorum. Sequor igitur eas vias, quas didici ab Antiocho, nec reperio quo modo iudicem 'si lucet, lucet,' verum esse ob eam causam, quod ita didici, omne, quod ipsum ex se conexum sit, verum esse, non iudicem 'si mentiris, mentiris,' eodem modo [esse] conexum. Aut igitur hoc et illud aut, nisi hoc, ne illud quidem iudicabo.

XXXI. Sed, ut omnes istos aculeos et totum tortuosum genus disputandi relinquamus ostendamusque qui simus, iam explicata tota Carneadis sententia Antiochea ista corruent universa. Nec vero quicquam ita dicam, ut quisquam id fingi suspicetur: a Clitomacho sumam, qui usque ad senectutem cum Carneade fuit, homo et acutus, ut Poenus, et valde studiosus ac diligens. Et quattuor eius libri sunt de sustinendis adsensionibus. Haec autem, quae iam dicam, sunt sumpta de primo. 99. Duo placet esse Carneadi genera visorum, in uno hanc divisionem: 'alia visa esse quae percipi possint, alia quae non possint,' in altero autem: 'alia visa esse probabilia; alia non probabilia.' Itaque, quae contra sensus contraque perspicuitatem dicantur, ea pertinere ad superiorem divisionem: contra posteriorem nihil dici oportere: qua re ita placere: tale visum nullum esse, ut perceptio consequeretur, ut autem probatio, multa. Etenim contra naturam esset, si probabile nihil esset. Et sequitur omnis vitae ea, quam tu, Luculle, commemorabas, eversio. Itaque et sensibus probanda multa sunt, teneatur modo illud, non inesse in iis quicquam tale, quale non etiam falsum nihil ab eo differens esse possit. Sic, quidquid acciderit specie probabile, si nihil se offeret quod sit probabilitati illi contrarium, utetur eo sapiens ac sic omnis ratio vitae gubernabitur. Etenim is quoque, qui a vobis sapiens inducitur, multa sequitur probabilia, non comprehensa neque percepta neque adsensa, sed similia veri: quae nisi probet, omnis vita tollatur. 100. Quid enim? conscendens navem sapiens num comprehensum animo habet atque perceptum se ex sententia navigaturum? Qui potest? Sed si iam ex hoc loco proficiscatur Puteolos stadia triginta, probo navigio, bono gubernatore, hac tranquillitate, probabile videatur se illuc venturum esse salvum. Huius modi igitur visis consilia capiet et agendi et non agendi, faciliorque erit, ut albam esse nivem probet, quam erat Anaxagoras, qui id non modo ita esse negabat, sed sibi, quia sciret aquam nigram esse, unde illa concreta esset, albam ipsam esse, ne videri quidem. 101. Et quaecumque res eum sic attinget, ut sit visum illud probabile neque ulla re impeditum, movebitur. Non enim est e saxo sculptus aut e robore dolatus, habet corpus, habet animum, movetur mente, movetur sensibus, ut ei multa vera videantur, neque tamen habere insignem illam et propriam percipiendi notam: eoque sapientem non adsentiri, quia possit eiusdem modi exsistere falsum aliquod, cuius modi hoc verum. Neque nos contra sensus aliter dicimus ac Stoici, qui multa falsa esse dicunt, longeque aliter se habere ac sensibus videantur.

XXXII. Hoc autem si ita sit, ut unum modo sensibus falsum videatur, praesto est qui neget rem ullam percipi posse sensibus. Ita nobis tacentibus ex uno Epicuri capite, altero vestro perceptio et comprehensio tollitur. Quod est caput Epicuri? 'Si ullum sensus visum falsum est, nihil percipi potest.' Quod vestrum? 'Sunt falsa sensus visa.' Quid sequitur? ut taceam, conclusio ipsa loquitur: 'nihil posse percipi.' Non concedo, inquit, Epicuro. Certa igitur cum illo, qui a te totus diversus est: noli mecum, qui hoc quidem certe, falsi esse aliquid in sensibus, tibi adsentior. 102. Quamquam nihil mihi tam mirum videtur quam ista dici, ab Antiocho quidem maxime, cui erant ea, quae paulo ante dixi, notissima. Licet enim haec quivis arbitratu suo reprehendat, quod negemus rem ullam percipi posse, certe levior reprehensio est: quod tamen dicimus esse quaedam probabilia, non videtur hoc satis esse vobis. Ne sit: illa certe debemus effugere, quae a te vel maxime agitata sunt: 'nihil igitur cernis? nihil audis? nihil tibi est perspicuum?' Explicavi paulo ante Clitomacho auctore quo modo ista Carneades diceret. Accipe quem ad modum eadem dicantur a Clitomacho in eo libro, quem ad C. Lucilium scripsit poëtam, cum scripsisset isdem de rebus ad L. Censorinum, eum, qui consul cum M. Manilio fuit. Scripsit igitur his fere verbis—sunt enim mihi nota, propterea quod earum ipsarum rerum, de quibus agimus, prima institutio et quasi disciplina illo libro continetur—, sed scriptum est ita: 103. 'Academicis placere esse rerum eius modi dissimilitudines, ut aliae probabiles videantur, aliae contra: id autem non esse satis cur alia posse percipi dicas, alia non posse, propterea quod multa falsa probabilia sint, nihil autem falsi perceptum et cognitum possit esse.' Itaque ait vehementer errare eos, qui dicant ab Academia sensus eripi, a quibus numquam dictum sit aut colorem aut saporem aut sonum nullum esse, illud sit disputatum, non inesse in his propriam, quae nusquam alibi esset, veri et certi notam. 104. Quae cum exposuisset, adiungit dupliciter dici adsensus sustinere sapientem: uno modo, cum hoc intelligatur, omnino eum rei nulli adsentiri: altero, cum se a respondendo, ut aut approbet quid aut improbet, sustineat, ut neque neget aliquid neque aiat. Id cum ita sit, alterum placere, ut numquam adsentiatur, alterum tenere, ut sequens probabilitatem, ubicumque haec aut occurrat aut deficiat, aut 'etiam' aut 'non' respondere possit. †Nec, ut placeat, eum, qui de omnibus rebus contineat se ab adsentiendo, moveri tamen et agere aliquid, reliquit eius modi visa, quibus ad actionem excitemur: item ea, quae interrogati in utramque partem respondere possimus, sequentes tantum modo, quod ita visum sit, dum sine adsensu: neque tamen omnia eius modi visa approbari, sed ea, quae nulla re impedirentur. 105. Haec si vobis non probamus, sint falsa sane, invidiosa certe non sunt. Non enim lucem eripimus, sed ea, quae vos percipi comprehendique, eadem nos, si modo probabilia sint, videri dicimus.

XXXIII. Sic igitur inducto et constituto probabili, et eo quidem expedito, soluto, libero, nulla re implicato, vides profecto, Luculle, iacere iam illud tuum perspicuitatis patrocinium. Isdem enim hic sapiens, de quo loquor, oculis quibus iste vester caelum, terram, mare intuebitur, isdem sensibus reliqua, quae sub quemque sensum cadunt, sentiet. Mare illud, quod nunc Favonio nascente purpureum videtur, idem huic nostro videbitur, nec tamen adsentietur, quia nobismet ipsis modo caeruleum videbatur, mane ravum, quodque nunc, qua a sole collucet, albescit et vibrat dissimileque est proximo et continenti, ut, etiam si possis rationem reddere cur id eveniat, tamen non possis id verum esse, quod videbatur oculis, defendere. 106. Unde memoria, si nihil percipimus? Sic enim quaerebas. Quid? meminisse visa nisi comprehensa non possumus? Quid? Polyaenus, qui magnus mathematicus fuisse dicitur, is postea quam

Epicuro adsentiens totam geometriam falsam esse credidit, num illa etiam, quae sciebat, oblitus est? Atqui, falsum quod est, id percipi non potest, ut vobismet ipsis placet. Si igitur memoria perceptarum comprehensarumque rerum est, omnia, quae quisque meminit, habet ea comprehensa atque percepta. Falsi autem comprehendi nihil potest, et omnia meminit Siron Epicuri dogmata. Vera igitur illa sunt nunc omnia. Hoc per me licet: sed tibi aut concedendum est ita esse, quod minime vis, aut memoriam mihi remittas oportet et fateare esse ei locum, etiam si comprehensio perceptioque nulla sit. 107. Quid fiet artibus? Quibus? Iisne, quae ipsae fatentur coniectura se plus uti quam scientia, an iis, quae tantum id, quod videtur, secuntur nec habent istam artem vestram, qua vera et falsa diiudicent?

Sed illa sunt lumina duo, quae maxime causam istam continent. Primum enim negatis fieri posse ut quisquam nulli rei adsentiatur. At id quidem perspicuum est. Cum Panaetius, princeps prope meo quidem iudicio Stoicorum, ea de re dubitare se dicat, quam omnes praeter eum Stoici certissimam putant, vera esse haruspicum [*responsa*], auspicia, oracula, somnia, vaticinationes, seque ab adsensu sustineat: quod is potest facere vel de iis rebus, quas illi, a quibus ipse didicit, certas habuerint, cur id sapiens de reliquis rebus facere non possit? An est aliquid, quod positum vel improbare vel approbare possit, dubitare non possit? an tu in soritis poteris hoc, cum voles: ille in reliquis rebus non poterit eodem modo insistere, praesertim cum possit sine adsensione ipsam veri similitudinem non impeditam sequi? 108. Alterum est, quod negatis actionem ullius rei posse in eo esse, qui nullam rem adsensu suo comprobet. Primum enim videri oportet in quo sit etiam adsensus. Dicunt enim Stoici sensus ipsos adsensus esse, quos quoniam appetitio consequatur, actionem sequi: tolli autem omnia, si visa tollantur.

XXXIV. Hac de re in utramque partem et dicta sunt et scripta multa, sed brevi res potest tota confici. Ego enim etsi maximam actionem puto repugnare visis, obsistere opinionibus, adsensus lubricos sustinere, credoque Clitomacho ita scribenti, Herculi quendam laborem exanclatum a Carneade, quod, ut feram et immanem beluam, sic ex animis nostris adsensionem, id est, opinationem et temeritatem extraxisset, tamen, ut ea pars defensionis relinquatur, quid impediet actionem eius, qui probabilia sequitur, nulla re impediente? 109. Hoc, inquit, ipsum impediet, quod statuet, ne id quidem, quod probet, posse percipi. Iam istuc te quoque impediet in navigando, in conserendo, in uxore ducenda, in liberis procreandis plurimisque in rebus, in quibus nihil sequere praeter probabile.

Et tamen illud usitatum et saepe repudiatum refers, non ut Antipater, sed, ut ais, 'pressius.' Nam Antipatrum reprehensum, quod diceret consentaneum esse ei, qui adfirmaret nihil posse comprehendi, id ipsum saltem dicere posse comprehendi, quod ipsi Antiocho pingue videbatur et sibi ipsum contrarium. Non enim potest convenienter dici nihil comprehendi posse, si quicquam comprehendi posse dicatur. Illo modo potius putat urguendum fuisse Carneadem: cum sapientis nullum decretum esse possit nisi comprehensum, perceptum, cognitum, ut hoc ipsum decretum, quod sapientis esset, nihil posse percipi, fateretur esse perceptum. Proinde quasi nullum sapiens aliud decretum habeat et sine decretis vitam agere possit! 110. Sed ut illa habet probabilia non percepta, sic hoc ipsum, nihil posse percipi. Nam si in hoc haberet cognitionis notam, eadem uteretur in ceteris. Quam quoniam non habet, utitur probabilibus. Itaque non metuit ne confundere omnia videatur et incerta reddere. Non enim, quem ad modum, si quaesitum ex eo sit, stellarum numerus par an impar sit, item, si de officio multisque aliis de rebus, in quibus versatus exercitatusque sit, nescire se dicat. In incertis enim nihil probabile est, in quibus autem est, in iis non deerit sapienti nec quid faciat nec quid respondeat. 111. Ne illam quidem praetermisisti, Luculle, reprehensionem Antiochi—nec mirum: in primis enim est nobilis—, qua solebat dicere Antiochus Philonem maxime perturbatum. Cum enim sumeretur, unum, esse quaedam falsa visa, alterum nihil ea differre a veris, non adtendere, superius illud ea re a se esse concessum, quod videretur esse quaedam in vivis differentia, eam tolli altero, quo neget visa a falsis vera differre; nihil tam repugnare. Id ita esset, si nos verum omnino tolleremus. Non facimus. Nam tam vera quam falsa cernimus. Sed probandi species est: percipiendi signum nullum habemus.

XXXV. 112. Ac mihi videor nimis etiam nunc agere ieiune. Cum sit enim campus in quo exsultare possit oratio, cur eam tantas in angustias et in Stoicorum dumeta compellimus? si enim mihi cum Peripatetico res esset, qui id percipi posse diceret, 'quod impressum esset e vero,' neque adhiberet illam magnam accessionem, 'quo modo imprimi non posset a falso,' cum simplici homine simpliciter agerem nec magno opere contenderem atque etiam, si, cum ego nihil dicerem posse comprehendi, diceret ille sapientem interdum opinari, non repugnarem, praesertim ne Carneade quidem huic loco valde repugnante: nunc quid facere possum? 113. Quaero enim quid sit quod comprehendi possit. Respondet mihi non Aristoteles aut Theophrastus, ne Xenocrates quidem aut Polemo, sed qui his minor est: 'tale verum quale falsum esse non possit.' Nihil eius modo invenio. Itaque incognito nimirum adsentiar, id est, opinabor. Hoc mihi et Peripatetici et vetus Academia concedit: vos negatis, Antiochus in primis, qui me valde movet, vel quod amavi hominem, sicut ille me, vel quod ita iudico, politissimum et acutissimum omnium nostrae memoriae philosophorum. A quo primum quaero quo tandem modo sit eius Academiae, cuius esse se profiteatur? Ut omittam alia, haec duo, de quibus agitur, quis umquam dixit aut veteris Academiae aut Peripateticorum, vel id solum percipi posse, quod esset verum tale, quale falsum esse non posset, vel sapientem nihil opinari? Certe nemo. Horum neutrum ante Zenonem magno opere defensum est. Ego tamen utrumque verum puto, nec dico temporis causa, sed ita plane probo.

XXXVI. 114. Illud ferre non possum. Tu cum me incognito adsentiri vetes idque turpissimum esse dicas et plenissimum temeritatis, tantum tibi adroges, ut exponas disciplinam sapientiae, naturam rerum omnium evolvas, mores fingas, finis bonorum malorumque constituas, officia describas, quam vitam ingrediar definias, idemque etiam disputandi et intellegendi iudicium dicas te et artificium traditurum, perficies ut ego ista innumerabilia complectens nusquam labar, nihil opiner? Quae tandem ea est disciplina, ad quam me deducas, si ab hac abstraxeris? Vereor ne subadroganter facias, si dixeris tuam. Atqui ita dicas necesse est. 115. Neque vero tu solus, sed ad suam quisque rapiet. Age, restitero Peripateticis, qui sibi cum oratoribus cognationem esse, qui claros viros a se instructos dicant rem publicam saepe rexisse, sustinuero Epicureos, tot meos familiaris, tam bonos, tam inter se amantis viros, Diodoto quid faciam Stoico, quem a puero audivi? qui mecum vivit tot annos? qui habitat apud me? quem et admiror et diligo? qui ista Antiochea contemnit? Nostra, inquies, sola vera sunt. Certe sola, si vera: plura enim vera discrepantia esse non possunt. Utrum igitur nos impudentes, qui labi nolumus, an illi adrogantes, qui sibi persuaserint scire se solos omnia? Non me quidem, inquit, sed sapientem dico scire. Optime: nempe ista scire, quae sunt in tua disciplina. Hoc primum quale est, a non sapiente explicari sapientiam? Sed discedamus a nobismet ipsis, de sapiente loquamur, de quo, ut saepe iam dixi, omnis haec quaestio est.

116. In tres igitur partis et a plerisque et a vobismet ipsis distributa sapientia est. Primum ergo, si placet, quae de natura rerum sint quaesita, videamus: at illud ante. Estne quisquam tanto inflatus errore, ut sibi se illa scire persuaserit? Non quaero rationes eas, quae ex coniectura pendent, quae disputationibus huc et illuc trahuntur, nullam adhibent persuadendi necessitatem. Geometrae provideant, qui se profitentur non persuadere, sed cogere, et qui omnia vobis, quae describunt, probant. Non quaero ex his illa initia mathematicorum, quibus non concessis digitum progredi non possunt. Punctum esse quod magnitudinem nullam habeat: extremitatem et quasi libramentum in quo nulla omnino crassitudo sit: liniamentum sine ulla latitudine [carentem]. Haec cum vera esse concessero, si adigam ius iurandum sapientem, nec prius quam Archimedes eo inspectante rationes omnis descripserit eas, quibus efficitur multis partibus solem maiorem esse quam terram, iuraturum putas? Si fecerit, solem ipsum, quem deum censet esse, contempserit. 117. Quod si geometricis rationibus non est crediturus, quae vim adferunt in docendo, vos ipsi ut dicitis, ne ille longe aberit ut argumentis credat philosophorum, aut, si est crediturus, quorum potissimum? Omnia enim physicorum licet explicare; sed longum est: quaero tamen quem sequatur. Finge aliquem nunc fieri sapientem, nondum esse, quam potissimum sententiam eliget *et* disciplinam? Etsi quamcumque eliget, insipiens eliget. Sed sit ingenio divino, quem unum e physicis potissimum probabit? Nec plus uno poterit. Non persequor quaestiones infinitas: tantum de principiis rerum, e quibus omnia constant, videamus quem probet: est enim inter magnos homines summa dissensio.

XXXVII. 118. Princeps Thales, unus e septem, cui sex reliquos concessisse primas ferunt, ex aqua dixit constare omnia. At hoc Anaximandro, populari et sodali suo, non persuasit: is enim infinitatem naturae dixit esse, e qua omnia gignerentur. Post eius auditor Anaximenes infinitum aëra, sed ea, quae ex eo orirentur, definita: gigni autem terram, aquam, ignem, tum ex his omnia. Anaxagoras materiam infinitam, sed ex ea particulas, similis inter se, minutas, eas primum confusas, postea in ordinem adductas a mente divina. Xenophanes, paulo etiam antiquior, unum esse omnia neque id esse mutabile et id esse deum neque natum umquam et sempiternum, conglobata figura: Parmenides ignem, qui moveat terram, quae ab eo formetur: Leucippus, plenum et inane: Democritus huic in hoc similis, uberior in ceteris: Empedocles haec pervolgata et nota quattuor: Heraclitus ignem: Melissus hoc, quod esset infinitum et immutabile, et fuisse semper et fore. Plato ex materia in se omnia recipiente mundum factum esse censet a deo sempiternum. Pythagorei ex numeris et mathematicorum initiis proficisci volunt omnia. Ex his eliget vester sapiens unum aliquem, credo, quem sequatur: ceteri tot viri et tanti repudiati ab eo condemnatique discedent. 119. Quamcumque vero sententiam probaverit, eam sic animo comprehensam habebit, ut ea, quae sensibus, nec magis approbabit nunc lucere, quam, quoniam Stoicus est, hunc mundum esse sapientem, habere mentem, quae et se et ipsum fabricata sit et omnia moderetur, moveat, regat. Erit ei persuasum etiam solem, lunam, stellas omnis, terram, mare deos esse, quod quaedam animalis intellegentia per omnia ea permanet et transeat, fore tamen aliquando ut omnis hic mundus ardore deflagret.

XXXVIII. Sint ista vera—vides enim iam me fateri aliquid esse veri—, comprehendi ea tamen et percipi nego. Cum enim tuus iste Stoicus sapiens syllabatim tibi ista dixerit, veniet flumen orationis aureum fundens Aristoteles, qui illum desipere dicat: neque enim ortum esse umquam mundum, quod nulla fuerit novo consilio inito tam praeclari operis inceptio, et ita esse eum undique aptum, ut nulla vis tantos queat motus mutationemque moliri, nulla senectus diuturnitate temporum exsistere, ut hic ornatus umquam dilapsus occidat. Tibi hoc repudiare, illud autem superius sicut caput et famam tuam defendere necesse erit, cum mihi ne ut dubitem quidem relinquatur. 120. Ut omittam levitatem temere adsentientium, quanti libertas ipsa aestimanda est non mihi necesse esse quod tibi est? Cur deus, omnia nostra causa cum faceret—sic enim voltis—, tantam vim natricum viperarumque fecerit? cur mortifera tam multa *ac* perniciosa terra marique disperserit? Negatis haec tam polite tamque subtiliter effici potuisse sine divina aliqua sollertia. Cuius quidem vos maiestatem deducitis usque ad apium formicarumque perfectionem, ut etiam inter deos Myrmecides aliquis minutorum opusculorum fabricator fuisse videatur. 121. Negas sine deo posse quicquam. Ecce tibi e transverso Lampsacenus Strato, qui det isti deo immunitatem magni quidem muneris: sed cum sacerdotes deorum vacationem habeant, quanto est aequius habere ipsos deos! Negat opera deorum se uti ad fabricandum mundum. Quaecumque sint, docet omnia effecta esse natura, nec, ut ille, qui asperis et levibus et hamatis uncinatisque corporibus concreta haec esse dicat interiecto inani. Somnia censet haec esse Democriti non docentis, sed optantis. Ipse autem singulas mundi partis persequens, quidquid aut sit aut fiat, naturalibus fieri aut factum esse docet ponderibus et motibus. Ne ille et deum opere magno liberat et me timore. Quis enim potest, cum existimet curari se a deo, non et dies et noctes divinum numen horrere et, si quid adversi acciderit—quod cui non accidit?—extimescere ne id iure evenerit? Nec Stratoni tamen adsentior, nec vero tibi. Modo hoc, modo illud probabilius videtur.

XXXIX. 122. Latent ista omnia, Luculle, crassis occultata et circumfusa tenebris, ut nulla acies humani ingeni tanta sit, quae penetrare in caelum, terram intrare possit: corpora nostra non novimus: qui sint situs partium, quam vim quaeque pars habeat ignoramus. Itaque medici ipsi, quorum intererat ea nosse, aperuerunt, ut viderentur. Nec eo tamen aiunt empirici notiora esse illa, quia possit fieri ut patefacta et detecta mutentur. Sed ecquid nos eodem modo rerum naturas persecare, aperire, dividere possumus, ut videamus terra penitusne defixa sit et quasi radicibus suis haereat an media pendeat? 123. Habitari ait Xenophanes in luna eamque esse terram multarum urbium et montium. Portenta videntur, sed tamen neque ille, qui dixit, iurare posset, ita se rem habere, neque ego non ita. Vos etiam dicitis esse e regione nobis, e contraria parte terrae, qui adversis vestigiis stent contra nostra vestigia, quos αντιποδας vocatis: cur mihi magis suscensetis, qui ista non aspernor, quam iis, qui, cum audiunt, desipere vos arbitrantur?

Hicetas Syracusius, ut ait Theophrastus, caelum, solem, lunam, stellas, supera denique omnia stare censet neque praeter terram rem ullam in mundo moveri: quae cum circum axem se summa celeritate convertat et torqueat, eadem effici omnia, quae, si stante terra caelum moveretur. Atque hoc etiam Platonem in Timaeo dicere quidam arbitrantur, sed paulo obscurius. Quid tu, Epicure? loquere. Putas solem esse tantulum? Egone? ne bis quidem tantum! Et vos ab illo irridemini et ipsi illum vicissim eluditis. Liber igitur a tali irrisione Socrates, liber Aristo Chius, qui nihil istorum sciri putat posse. 124. Sed redeo ad animum et corpus. Satisne tandem ea nota sunt nobis, quae nervorum natura sit, quae venarum? tenemusne quid sit animus, ubi sit? denique sitne an, ut Dicaearcho visum est, ne sit quidem ullus? Si est, tresne partis habeat, ut Platoni placuit, rationis, irae, cupiditatis, an simplex unusque sit? si simplex, utrum sit ignis an anima an sanguis an, ut Xenocrates, numerus nullo corpore—quod intellegi quale sit vix potest—et, quidquid est, mortale sit an aeternum? nam utramque in partem multa dicuntur. Horum aliquid vestro sapienti certum videtur, nostro ne quid maxime quidem probabile sit occurrit: ita sunt in plerisque contrariarum rationum paria momenta.

XL. 125. Sin agis verecundius et me accusas, non quod tuis rationibus non adsentiar, sed quod nullis, vincam animum cuique adsentiar deligam ... quem potissimum? quem? Democritum: semper enim, ut scitis, studiosus nobilitatis fui. Urguebor iam omnium vestrum convicio. Tune aut inane quicquam putes esse, cum ita completa et conferta sint omnia, ut et quod movebitur corporum cedat et qua quidque cesserit aliud ilico subsequatur? aut atomos ullas, e quibus quidquid efficiatur, illarum sit dissimillimum? aut sine aliqua mente rem ullam effici posse praeclaram? et cum in uno mundo ornatus hic tam sit mirabilis, innumerabilis supra infra, dextra sinistra, ante post, alios dissimilis, alios eiusdem modi mundos esse? et, ut nos nunc simus ad Baulos Puteolosque videamus, sic innumerabilis paribus in locis isdem esse nominibus, honoribus, rebus gestis, ingeniis, formis, aetatibus, isdem de rebus disputantis? et, si nunc aut si etiam dormientes aliquid animo videre videamur, imagines extrinsecus in animos nostros per corpus irrumpere? Tu vero ista ne asciveris neve fueris commenticiis rebus adsensus. Nihil sentire est melius quam tam prava sentire. 126. Non ergo id agitur, ut aliquid adsensu meo comprobem; quae tu, vide ne impudenter etiam postules, non solum adroganter, praesertim cum ista tua mihi ne probabilia quidem videantur. Nec enim divinationem, quam probatis, ullam esse arbitror, fatumque illud, quo omnia contineri dicitis, contemno. Ne exaedificatum quidem hunc mundum divino consilio existimo, atque haud scio an ita sit.

XLI. Sed cur rapior in invidiam? licetne per vos nescire quod nescio? an Stoicis ipsis inter se disceptare, cum his non licebit? Zenoni et reliquis fere Stoicis aether videtur summus deus, mente praeditus, qua omnia regantur. Cleanthes, qui quasi maiorum est gentium Stoicus, Zenonis auditor, solem dominari et rerum potiri putat. Ita cogimur dissensione sapientium dominum nostrum ignorare, quippe qui nesciamus soli an aetheri serviamus. Solis autem magnitudinem—ipse enim hic radiatus me intueri videtur ac monet ut crebro faciam mentionem sui—vos ergo huius magnitudinem quasi decempeda permensi refertis: huic me quasi malis architectis mensurae vestrae nego credere. Ergo dubium est uter nostrum sit, leniter ut dicam, verecundior? 127. Neque tamen istas quaestiones physicorum exterminandas puto. Est enim animorum ingeniorumque naturale quoddam quasi pabulum consideratio contemplatioque naturae. Erigimur, elatiores fieri videmur, humana despicimus, cogitantesque supera atque caelestia haec nostra ut exigua et minima contemnimus. Indagatio ipsa rerum cum maximarum tum etiam occultissimarum habet oblectationem. Si vero aliquid occurrit, quod veri simile videatur, humanissima completur animus voluptate. 128. Quaeret igitur haec et vester sapiens et hic noster, sed vester, ut adsentiatur, credat, adfirmet, noster, ut vereatur temere opinari praeclareque agi secum putet, si in eius modi rebus veri simile quod sit invenerit. Veniamus nunc ad bonorum malorumque notionem: at paulum ante dicendum est. Non mihi videntur considerare, cum physica ista valde adfirmant, earum etiam rerum auctoritatem, si quae illustriores videantur, amittere. Non enim magis adsentiuntur neque approbant lucere nunc, quam, cum cornix cecinerit, tum aliquid eam aut iubere aut vetare, nec magis adfirmabunt signum illud, si erunt mensi, sex pedum esse quam solem, quem metiri non possunt, plus quam duodeviginti partibus maiorem esse quam terram. Ex quo illa conclusio nascitur: si sol quantus sit percipi non potest, qui ceteras res eodem modo quo magnitudinem solis approbat, is eas res non percipit. Magnitudo autem solis percipi non potest. Qui igitur id approbat, quasi percipiat, nullam rem percipit. Responderint posse percipi quantus sol sit. Non repugnabo, dum modo eodem pacto cetera percipi comprehendique dicant. Nec enim possunt dicere aliud alio magis minusve comprehendi, quoniam omnium rerum una est definitio comprehendendi.

XLII. 129. Sed quod coeperam: Quid habemus in rebus bonis et malis explorati? nempe fines constituendi sunt ad quos et bonorum et malorum summa referatur: qua de re est igitur inter summos viros maior dissensio? Omitto illa, quae relicta iam videntur, ut Herillum, qui in cognitione et scientia summum bonum ponit: qui cum Zenonis auditor esset, vides quantum ab eo dissenserit et quam non multum a Platone. Megaricorum fuit nobilis disciplina, cuius, ut scriptum video, princeps Xenophanes, quem modo nominavi, deinde eum secuti Parmenides et Zeno, itaque ab his Eleatici philosophi nominabantur. Post Euclides, Socratis discipulus, Megareus, a quo iidem illi Megarici dicti, qui id bonum solum esse dicebant, quod esset unum et simile et idem semper. Hic quoque multa a Platone. A Menedemo autem, quod is Eretria fuit, Eretriaci appellati, quorum omne bonum in mente positum et mentis acie, qua verum cerneretur, Herilli similia, sed, opinor, explicata uberius et ornatius. 130. Hos si contemnimus et iam abiectos putamus, illos certe minus despicere debemus, Aristonem, qui cum Zenonis fuisset auditor, re probavit ea quae ille verbis, nihil esse bonum nisi virtutem, nec malum nisi quod virtuti esset contrarium: in mediis ea momenta, quae Zeno voluit, nulla esse censuit. Huic summum bonum est in his rebus neutram in partem moveri, quae αδιαφορια ab ipso dicitur. Pyrrho autem ea ne sentire quidem sapientem, quae απαθεια nominatur. Has igitur tot sententias ut omittamus, haec nunc videamus, quae diu multumque defensa sunt. 131. Alii voluptatem finem esse voluerunt: quorum princeps Aristippus, qui Socratem audierat, unde Cyrenaici. Post Epicurus, cuius est disciplina nunc notior, neque tamen cum Cyrenaicis de ipsa voluptate consentiens. Voluptatem autem et honestatem finem esse Callipho censuit: vacare omni molestia Hieronymus: hoc idem cum honestate Diodorus: ambo hi Peripatetici. Honeste autem vivere fruentem rebus iis, quas primas homini natura conciliet, et vetus Academia censuit, ut indicant scripta Polemonis, quem Antiochus probat maxime, et Aristoteles eiusque amici nunc proxime videntur accedere. Introducebat etiam Carneades, non quo probaret, sed ut opponeret Stoicis, summum bonum esse frui rebus iis, quas primas natura conciliavisset. Honeste autem vivere, quod ducatur a conciliatione naturae, Zeno statuit finem esse bonorum, qui inventor et princeps Stoicorum fuit.

XLIII. 132. Iam illud perspicuum est, omnibus iis finibus bonorum, quos exposui, malorum finis esse contrarios. Ad vos nunc refero quem sequar: modo ne quis illud tam ineruditum absurdumque respondeat: 'Quemlibet, modo aliquem.' Nihil potest dici inconsideratius. Cupio sequi Stoicos. Licetne—omitto per Aristotelem, meo iudicio in philosophia prope singularem—per ipsum Antiochum? qui appellabatur Academicus, erat quidem, si perpauca mutavisset, germanissimus Stoicus. Erit igitur res iam in discrimine. Nam aut Stoicus constituatur sapiens aut veteris Academiae. Utrumque non potest. Est enim inter eos non de terminis, sed de tota possessione contentio. Nam omnis ratio vitae definitione summi boni continetur, de qua qui dissident, de omni vitae ratione dissident. Non potest igitur uterque sapiens esse, quoniam tanto opere dissentiunt, sed alter. Si Polemoneus, peccat Stoicus, rei falsae adsentiens— nam vos quidem nihil esse dicitis a sapiente tam alienum—: sin vera sunt Zenonis, eadem in veteres Academicos *et* Peripateticos dicenda. Hic igitur neutri adsentietur? Sin, inquam, uter est prudentior? 133. Quid? cum ipse Antiochus dissentit quibusdam in rebus ab his, quos amat, Stoicis, nonne indicat non posse illa probanda esse sapienti? Placet Stoicis omnia peccata esse paria. At hoc Antiocho vehementissime displicet. Liceat tandem mihi considerare utram sententiam sequar. Praecide, inquit: statue aliquando quidlibet. Quid, quod quae dicuntur et acuta mihi videntur in utramque partem et paria? nonne caveam ne scelus faciam? Scelus enim dicebas esse, Luculle, dogma prodere. Contineo igitur me, ne incognito assentiar: quod mihi tecum est dogma commune. 134. Ecce multo maior etiam dissensio. Zeno in una virtute positam beatam vitam putat. Quid Antiochus? Etiam, inquit, beatam, sed non beatissimam. Deus ille, qui nihil censuit deesse virtuti, homuncio hic, qui multa putat praeter virtutem homini partim cara esse, partim etiam necessaria. Sed ille vereor ne virtuti plus tribuat quam natura patiatur, praesertim Theophrasto multa diserte copioseque dicente. Et hic metuo ne vix sibi constet, qui cum dicat esse quaedam et corporis et fortunae mala, tamen eum, qui in his omnibus sit, beatum fore censeat, si sapiens sit. Distrahor: tum hoc mihi probabilius, tum illud videtur, et tamen, nisi alterutrum sit, virtutem iacere plane puto. Verum in his discrepant.

XLIV. 135. Quid? illa, in quibus consentiunt, num pro veris probare possumus? Sapientis animum numquam nec cupiditate moveri nec laetitia efferri. Age, haec probabilia sane sint: num etiam illa, numquam timere, numquam dolere? Sapiensne non timeat, si patria deleatur? non doleat, si deleta sit? Durum, sed Zenoni necessarium, cui praeter honestum nihil est in bonis, tibi vero, Antioche, minime, cui praeter honestatem multa bona, praeter turpitudinem multa mala videntur, quae et venientia metuat sapiens necesse est et venisse doleat. Sed quaero quando ista fuerint *ab* Academia vetere decreta, ut animum sapientis commoveri et conturbari negarent? Mediocritates illi probabant et in omni permotione naturalem volebant esse quendam modum. Legimus omnes Crantoris veteris Academici de luctu. Est enim non magnus, verum aureolus et, ut Tuberoni Panaetius praecipit, ad verbum ediscendus libellus. Atque illi quidem etiam utiliter a natura dicebant permotiones istas animis nostris datas: metum cavendi causa, misericordiam aegritudinemque clementiae, ipsam iracundiam fortitudinis quasi cotem esse dicebant, recte secusne alias viderimus. 136. Atrocitas quidem ista tua quo modo in veterem Academiam irruperit nescio: illa vero ferre non possum, non quo mihi displiceant: sunt enim Socratica pleraque mirabilia Stoicorum, quae παραδοξα nominantur, sed ubi Xenocrates, ubi Aristoteles ista tetigit? hos enim quasi eosdem esse voltis. Illi umquam dicerent sapientis solos reges, solos divites, solos formosos? omnia, quae ubique essent, sapientis esse? neminem consulem, praetorem, imperatorem, nescio an ne quinquevirum quidem quemquam nisi sapientem? postremo, solum civem, solum liberum? insipientis omnis peregrinos, exsules, servos, furiosos? denique scripta Lycurgi, Solonis, duodecim tabulas nostras non esse leges? ne urbis quidem aut civitatis, nisi quae essent sapientium? 137. Haec tibi, Luculle, si es adsensus Antiocho, familiari tuo, tam sunt defendenda quam moenia: mihi autem bono modo, tantum quantum videbitur.

XLV. Legi apud Clitomachum, cum Carneades et Stoicus Diogenes ad senatum in Capitolio starent, A. Albinum, qui tum P. Scipione et M. Marcello coss. praetor esset, eum, qui cum avo tuo, Luculle, consul fuit, doctum sane hominem, ut indicat ipsius historia scripta Graece, iocantem dixisse Carneadi: 'Ego tibi, Carneade, praetor esse non videor, quia sapiens non sum: nec haec urbs nec in ea civitas.' Tum ille: 'Huic Stoico non videris.' Aristoteles aut Xenocrates, quos Antiochus sequi volebat, non dubitavisset quin et praetor ille esset et Roma urbs et eam civitas incoleret. Sed ille noster est plane, ut supra dixi, Stoicus, perpauca balbutiens. 138. Vos autem mihi veremini ne labar ad opinionem et aliquid asciscam et comprobem incognitum, quod minime voltis. Quid consilii datis? Testatur saepe Chrysippus tres solas esse sententias, quae defendi possint, de finibus bonorum: circumcidit et amputat multitudinem: aut enim honestatem esse finem aut voluptatem aut utrumque: nam qui summum bonum dicant id esse, si vacemus omni molestia, eos invidiosum nomen voluptatis fugere, sed in vicinitate versari, quod facere eos etiam, qui illud idem cum honestate coniungerent, nec multo secus eos, qui ad honestatem prima naturae commoda adiungerent: ita tres relinquit sententias, quas putat probabiliter posse defendi. 139. Sit sane ita—quamquam a Polemonis et Peripateticorum et Antiochi finibus non facile divellor, nec quicquam habeo adhuc probabilius—, verum tamen video quam suaviter voluptas sensibus nostris blandiatur. Labor eo, ut adsentiar Epicuro aut Aristippo. Revocat virtus vel potius reprehendit manu: pecudum illos motus esse dicit, hominem iungit deo. Possum esse medius, ut, quoniam Aristippus, quasi animum nullum habeamus, corpus solum tuetur, Zeno, quasi corporis simus expertes, animum solum complectitur, ut Calliphontem sequar, cuius quidem sententiam Carneades ita studiose defensitabat, ut eam probare etiam videretur. Quamquam Clitomachus adfirmabat numquam se intellegere potuisse quid Carneadi probaretur. Sed, si istum finem velim sequi, nonne ipsa veritas et gravis et recta ratio mihi obversetur? Tu, cum honestas in voluptate contemnenda consistat, honestatem cum voluptate tamquam hominem cum belua copulabis?

XLVI. 140. Unum igitur par quod depugnet reliquum est, voluptas cum honestate. De quo Chrysippo fuit, quantum ego sentio, non magna contentio. Alteram si sequare, multa ruunt et maxime communitas cum hominum genere, caritas, amicitia, iustitia, reliquae virtutes: quarum esse nulla potest, nisi erit gratuita. Nam quae voluptate quasi mercede aliqua ad officium impellitur, ea non est virtus, sed fallax imitatio simulatioque virtutis. Audi contra illos, qui nomen honestatis a se ne intellegi quidem dicant, nisi forte, quod gloriosum sit in volgus, id honestum velimus dicere: fontem omnium bonorum in corpore esse, hanc normam, hanc regulam, hanc praescriptionem esse naturae, a qua qui aberravisset, eum numquam quid in vita sequeretur habiturum. 141. Nihil igitur me putatis, haec et alia innumerabilia cum audiam, moveri? Tam moveor quam tu, Luculle, neque me minus hominem quam te putaveris. Tantum interest, quod tu, cum es commotus, adquiescis, adsentiris, approbas, verum illud certum, comprehensum, perceptum, ratum, firmum, fixum esse vis, deque eo nulla ratione neque pelli neque moveri potes: ego nihil eius modi esse arbitror, cui si adsensus sim, non adsentiar saepe falso, quoniam vera a falsis nullo discrimine separantur, praesertim cum iudicia ista dialecticae nulla sint.

142. Venio enim iam ad tertiam partem philosophiae. Aliud iudicium Protagorae est, qui putet id cuique verum esse, quod cuique videatur: aliud Cyrenaicorum, qui praeter permotiones intimas nihil putant esse iudicii: aliud Epicuri, qui omne iudicium in sensibus et in rerum notitiis et in voluptate constituit. Plato autem omne iudicium veritatis veritatemque ipsam abductam ab opinionibus et a sensibus cogitationis ipsius et mentis esse voluit. 143. Num quid horum probat noster Antiochus? Ille vero ne maiorum quidem suorum. Ubi enim aut Xenocratem sequitur, cuius libri sunt de ratione loquendi multi et multum probati, aut ipsum Aristotelem, quo profecto nihil est acutius, nihil politius? A Chrysippo pedem nusquam.

XLVII. Quid ergo Academici appellamur? an abutimur gloria nominis? aut cur cogimur eos sequi, qui inter se dissident? In hoc ipso, quod in elementis dialectici docent, quo modo iudicare oporteat verum falsumne sit, si quid ita conexum est, ut hoc, 'si dies est, lucet,' quanta contentio est! Aliter Diodoro, aliter Philoni, Chrysippo aliter placet. Quid? cum Cleanthe doctore suo quam multis rebus Chrysippus dissidet! quid? duo vel principes dialecticorum, Antipater et Archidemus, opiniosissimi homines, nonne multis in rebus dissentiunt? 144. Quid me igitur, Luculle, in invidiam et tamquam in contionem vocas? et quidem, ut seditiosi tribuni solent, occludi tabernas iubes? quo enim spectat illud, cum artificia tolli quereris a nobis, nisi ut opifices concitentur? qui si undique omnes convenerint, facile contra vos incitabuntur. Expromam primum illa invidiosa, quod eos omnis, qui in contione stabunt, exsules, servos, insanos esse dicatis: deinde ad illa veniam, quae iam non ad multitudinem, sed ad vosmet ipsos, qui adestis, pertinent. Negat enim vos Zeno, negat Antiochus scire quicquam. Quo modo? inquies: nos enim defendimus etiam insipientem multa comprehendere. 145. At scire negatis quemquam rem ullam nisi sapientem. Et hoc quidem Zeno gestu conficiebat. Nam, cum extensis digitis adversam manum ostenderat, 'visum,' inquiebat, 'huius modi est.' Deinde, cum paulum digitos contraxerat, 'adsensus huius modi.' Tum cum plane compresserat pugnumque fecerat, comprehensionem illam esse dicebat: qua ex similitudine etiam nomen ei rei, quod ante non fuerat, κατάληψιν imposuit. Cum autem laevam manum adverterat et illum pugnum arte vehementerque compresserat, scientiam talem esse dicebat, cuius compotem nisi sapientem esse neminem. Sed qui sapientes sint aut fuerint ne ipsi quidem solent dicere. Ita tu nunc, Catule, lucere nescis nec tu, Hortensi, in tua villa nos esse. 146. Num minus haec invidiose dicuntur? nec tamen nimis eleganter: illa subtilius. Sed quo modo tu, si nihil comprehendi posset, artificia concidere dicebas neque mihi dabas id, quod probabile esset, satis magnam vim habere ad artis, sic ego nunc tibi refero artem sine scientia esse non posse. An pateretur hoc Zeuxis aut Phidias aut Polyclitus, nihil se scire, cum in iis esset tanta sollertia? Quod si eos docuisset aliquis quam vim habere diceretur scientia, desinerent irasci: ne nobis quidem suscenserent, cum didicissent id tollere nos, quod nusquam esset, quod autem satis esset ipsis relinquere. Quam rationem maiorum etiam comprobat diligentia, qui primum iurare 'ex sui animi sententia' quemque voluerunt, deinde ita teneri 'si sciens falleret,' quod inscientia multa versaretur in vita, tum, qui testimonium diceret, ut 'arbitrari' se diceret etiam quod ipse vidisset, quaeque iurati iudices cognovissent, ea non ut esse facta, sed ut 'videri' pronuntiarentur.

XLVIII. 147. Verum, quoniam non solum nauta significat, sed etiam Favonius ipse insusurrat navigandi nobis, Luculle, tempus esse et quoniam satis multa dixi, est mihi perorandum. Posthac tamen, cum haec quaeremus, potius de dissensionibus tantis summorum virorum disseramus, de obscuritate naturae deque errore tot philosophorum, qui de bonis contrariisque rebus tanto opere discrepant, ut, cum plus uno verum esse non possit, iacere necesse sit tot tam nobilis disciplinas, quam de oculorum sensuumque reliquorum mendaciis et de sorite aut pseudomeno, quas plagas ipsi contra se Stoici texuerunt. 148. Tum Lucullus: Non moleste, inquit, fero nos haec contulisse. Saepius enim congredientes nos, et maxime in Tusculanis nostris, si quae videbuntur, requiremus. Optime, inquam, sed quid Catulus sentit? quid Hortensius? Tum Catulus: Egone? inquit, ad patris revolvor sententiam, quam quidem ille Carneadeam esse dicebat, ut percipi nihil putem posse, adsensurum autem non percepto, id est, opinaturum sapientem existimem, sed ita, ut intellegat se opinari sciatque nihil esse quod comprehendi et percipi possit: qua re εποχην illam omnium rerum non probans, illi alteri sententiae, nihil esse quod percipi possit, vehementer adsentior. Habeo, inquam, sententiam tuam nec eam admodum aspernor. Sed tibi quid tandem videtur, Hortensi? Tum ille ridens: Tollendum. Teneo te, inquam: nam ista Academiae est propria sententia. Ita sermone confecto Catulus remansit: nos ad naviculas nostras descendimus.

NOTES.

BOOK I.

§§1—14. Summary. Cic., Varro and Atticus meet at Cumae (1). Cic., after adroitly reminding Varro that the promised dedication of the *De Lingua Latina* is too long delayed, turns the conversation towards philosophy, by asking Varro why he leaves this subject untouched (2, 3). Varro thinks philosophy written in Latin can serve no useful purpose, and points to the failures of the Roman Epicureans (4—6). He greatly believes in philosophy, but prefers to send his friends to Greece for it, while he devotes himself to subjects which the Greeks have not treated (7, 8). Cic. lauds this devotion, but demurs to the theory that philosophy written in Latin is useless. Latins may surely imitate Greek philosophers as well as Greek poets and orators. He gives reasons why he should himself make the attempt, and instancing the success of Brutus, again begs Varro to write on philosophy (9—12). Varro putting the request on one side charges Cic. with deserting the Old Academy for the New. Cic. defends himself, and appeals to Philo for the statement that the New Academy is in harmony with the Old. Varro refers to Antiochus as an authority on the other side. This leads to a proposal on the part of Cic. to discuss thoroughly the difference between Antiochus and Philo. Varro agrees, and promises an exposition of the principles of Antiochus (13, 14).

§1. *Noster*: our common friend. Varro was much more the friend of Atticus than of Cic., see Introd. p. 37. *Nuntiatum*: the spelling *nunciatum* is a mistake, cf. Corssen, *Ausspr.* I. p. 51. *A M. Varrone: from M. Varro's house* news came. *Audissemus*: Cic. uses the contracted forms of such subjunctives, as well as the full forms, but not intermediate forms like *audiissemus*. *Confestim*: note how artfully Cic. uses the dramatic form of the dialogue in order to magnify his attachment for Varro. *Ab eius villa*: the prep is absent from the MSS., but Wesenberg (*Em. M.T. Cic. Epistolarum*, p. 62) shows that it must be inserted. Cic. writes *abesse Roma* (*Ad Fam.* V. 15, 4), *patria* (*T.D.* V. 106) etc., but not *abesse officio* (*De Off.* I. 43, where Wes. alters it) or the like. *Satis eum longo intervallo*: so all the MSS.; but Halm, after Davies, reads *se visentum* for *satis eum*, quoting *Ad Att.* I. 4, Madv. *tum* for *eum* (Baiter and Halm's ed. of 1861, p. 854). The text is sound; the repetition of pronouns (*illum, eum*) is quite Ciceronian. The emphatic *ille* is often repeated by the unemphatic *is*, cf. *T.D.* III. 71, and *M.D.F.* V. 22. I may note that the separation of *satis* from *longo* by the word *eum* is quite in Cicero's style (see my note on 25 *quanta id magis*). Some editors stumble (Goerenz miserably) by taking *intervallo* of distance in space, instead of duration in time, while others wrongly press *satis*, which only means "tolerably," to mean "sufficiently." The words *satis longo intervallo* simply = "after a tolerably long halt." For the clause *ut mos*, etc., cf. *De Or.* II. 13.

§2. *Hic pauca primo*: for the omission of *locuti*, cf. the very similar passages in *D.F.* I. 14, III. 8, also my note on 14. *Atque ea*: Halm brackets *ea*, quite needlessly, for its insertion is like Cic. *Ecquid forte Roma novi*: *Roma* is the ablative, and some verb like *attulisset* is omitted. (So Turnebus.) To take it as nom., understanding *faciat*, is clearly wrong. *Percontari*: the spelling *percunctari* rests on false derivation (Corss. I. 36). *Ecquid ipse novi*: cf. *De Or.* II. 13. The MSS. have *et si quid*, bad Latin altered by Manutius. *Istum*: some edd. *ipsum*, but Cic. often makes a speaker use *iste* of a person who is present. Goer. qu. *Brut.* 125, *De Or.* II. 228. *Velit*: Walker reads *velis* with St Jerome. For *quod velit = quod quis velit*, cf. *De Or.* I. 30. *In manibus*: so often, cf. *Cat. Mai.* 38. *Idque*: MSS. have in the place of this *quod* with variants *que, quae, qui, quo*. Dav. gave *quia*, which was the vulgate reading down to Halm, who reads *idque*, after Christ. *Ad hunc enim ipsum*: MSS. have *eum* for *enim* (exc. Halm's G). Such a combination of pronouns is vainly defended by Goer.; for expressions like *me illum ipsum* (*Ad Att.* II. 1, 11) are not in point. Of course if *quia* be read above, *eum* must be ejected altogether. *Quaedam institui*: the *De Lingua Latina*; see *Ad. Att* XIII. 12.

§3. *E Libone*: the father-in-law of Sext. Pompeius; see Cæsar *B. Civ.* III. 5, 16, 24. *Nihil enim eius modi* again all MSS. except Halm's G. have *eum* for *enim*. Christ conj. *enim eum*; so Baiter. *Illud ... requirere*:

i.e. the question which follows; cf. *requiris* in 4. *Tecum simul*: Halm's G om. *tecum*; but cf. *De Or.* III. 330. *Mandare monumentis—letteris illustrare*: common phrases in Cic., e.g. *D.F.* I. 1, *T.D.* I. 1, *De Div.* II. 4. *Monumentis*: this, and not *monimentis* (Halm) or *monementis*, is probably the right spelling; cf. Corss. II. 314. *Ortam a*: Cic. *always* writes the prep. after *ortus*; cf. *M.D.F.* V. 69. *Genus*: regularly used by Cic. as *opus* by Quintilian to mean "department of literature." *Ea res*: one of Halm's MSS. followed by Baiter has *ars*; on the other hand Bentley (if the *amicus* so often quoted in Davies' notes be really he) reads *artibus* for *rebus* below. The slight variation, however, from *res* to *artibus* is such as Cic. loves. *Ceteris*: the spelling *caeteris* (Klotz) is absolutely wrong, cf. Corss. I. 325. *Antecedat*: some MSS. give *antecellat*. a frequent variant, cf. *De Off.* I. 105

§4. *Deliberatam—agitatam*: Cic. as usual exaggerates the knowledge possessed by the *personae* of the dialogue; cf. Introd. p. 38, *De Or.* II. 1. *In promptu*: so II. 10. *Quod ista ipsa ... cogitavi*: Goer., who half a page back had made merry over the gloss hunters, here himself scented a miserable gloss; Schutz, Goerenz's echo expels the words. Yet they are thoroughly like Cic. (cf. *De Div.* II. 1, *Cat. Mai.* 38), and moreover nothing is more Ciceronian than the repetition of words and clauses in slightly altered forms. The reason here is partly the intense desire to flatter Varro. *Si qui ... si essent*: the first *si* has really no conditional force, *si qui* like ειτινες merely means "all who," for a strong instance see *Ad Fam.* I. 9, 13, ed Nobbe, *si accusandi sunt, si qui pertimuerunt*. *Ea nolui scribere*, etc.: very similar expressions occur in the prologue to *D.F.* I., which should be compared with this prologue throughout.

§5. *Vides ... didicisti*: MSS. have *vides autem eadem ipse didicisti enim*. My reading is that of Dav. followed by Baiter. Halm, after Christ, has *vides autem ipse—didicisti enim eadem—non posse*, etc. *Similis*: Halm, in deference to MSS., makes Cic. write *i* and *e* indiscriminately in the acc. plur. of i stems. I shall write *i* everywhere, we shall thus, I believe, be far nearer Cicero's real writing. Though I do not presume to say that his usage did not vary, he must in the vast majority of instances have written *i*, see Corss. I. 738—744. *Amafinii aut Rabirii*: cf. Introd. p. 26. *Definiunt ... partiuntur*: n. on 32. *Interrogatione*: Faber saw this to be right, but a number of later scholars alter it, e.g. Bentl. *argumentatione*, Ernesti *ratione*. But the word as it stands has exactly the meaning these alterations are intended to secure. *Interrogatio* is merely the *conclusio* or syllogism put as a series of questions. Cf. *Paradoxa* 2, with *T.D.* II. 42 which will show that *interrogatiuncula* and *conclusiuncula* are almost convertible terms. See also *M.D.F.* I. 39. *Nec dicendi nec disserendi*: Cic.'s constant mode of denoting the Greek ῾ρητορικη and διαλεκτικη; note on 32. *Et oratorum etiam*: Man., Lamb. om. *etiam*, needlessly. In *Ad Fam.* IX. 25, 3, the two words even occur without any other word to separate them. For *oratorum* Pearce conj. *rhetorum*. *Rhetor*, however is not thus used in Cic.'s phil. works. *Utramque vim virtutem*: strange that Baiter (esp. after Halm's note) should take Manutius' far-fetched conj. *unam* for *virtutem*. Any power or faculty (vis, δυναμις) may be called in Gk. αρετη, in Lat *virtus*. Two passages, *D.F.* III. 72, *De Or.* III. 65, will remove all suspicion from the text. *Verbis quoque novis*: MSS. have *quanquam* which however is impossible in such a place in Cic. (cf. *M.D.F.* V. 68). *Ne a nobis quidem*: so all the MSS., but Orelli (after Ernesti) thinking the phrase "*arrogantius dictum*" places *quidem* after *accipient*. The text is quite right, *ne quidem*, as Halm remarks, implies no more than the Germ. *auch nicht*, cf. also Gk. ουδε. *Suscipiatur labor*: MSS. om. the noun, but it is added by a later hand in G.

§6. *Epicurum, id est si Democritum*: for the charge see *D.F.* I. 17, IV. 13, *N.D.* I. 73. *Id est* often introduces in Cic. a clause which intensifies and does not merely explain the first clause, exx. in *M.D.F.* I. 33. *Cum causas rerum efficientium sustuleris*: cf. *D.F.* I. 18, the same charge is brought by Aristotle against the Atomists, *Met.* A, 2. Many editors from Lamb. to Halm and Baiter read *efficientis*, which would then govern *rerum* (cf. *D.F.* V. 81, *De Fato*, 33, also Gk. ποιητικος). But the genitive is merely one of definition, the *causae* are the *res efficientes*, for which cf. 24 and *Topica*, 58, *proximus locus est rerum efficientium, quae causae appellantur*. So Faber, though less fully. *Appellat*: i.e. Amafinius, who first so translated ατομος. *Quae cum contineantur*: this reading has far the best MSS. authority, it must be kept, and *adhibenda etiam* begins the *apodosis*. Madvig (*Emendationes ad Ciceronis Libros Philosophicos*, Hauniae, 1825, p. 108) tacitly reads *continentur* without *cum*, so Orelli and Klotz. Goer. absurdly tries to prop up the subj. without *cum*. *Quam quibusnam*: Durand's em. for *quoniam quibusnam* of the MSS., given by Halm and also Baiter. Madv. (*Em.* p. 108) made a forced defence of *quoniam*, as marking a rapid transition from one subject to another (here from physics to ethics) like the Gk. επει, only one parallel instance, however, was adduced (*T.D.* III. 14) and the usage probably is not Latin. *Adducere?*: The note of interrogation is Halm's; thus the whole sentence, so far, explains the difficulty of setting forth the true system of physics. If *quoniam* is read and no break made at *adducere*, all after *quoniam* will refer to ethics, in that case there will be a strange change of subject in passing from *quisquam* to *haec ipsa*, both which expressions will be nominatives to *poterit*, further, there will be the almost impossible ellipse of *ars*, *scientia*, or something of the kind after *haec ipsa*. On every ground the reading of Madv. is insupportable. *Quid, haec ipsa*: I have added *quid* to fill up the lacuna left by Halm, who supposes much more to have fallen out. [The technical philosophical terms contained in this section will be elucidated later. For the Epicurean ignorance of geometry see note on II. 123] *Illi enim simpliciter*: "frankly," cf. *Ad Fam.* VIII. 6, 1 *Pecudis et hominis*: note on II. 139.

§7. *Sive sequare ... magnum est*: for the constr. cf. II. 140. *Magnum est*: cf. *quid est magnum*, 6. *Verum et simplex bonum*: cf. 35. *Quod bonum ... ne suspicari quidem* an opinion often denounced by Cic., see esp *T.D.* III. 41, where Cic.'s Latin agrees very closely with the Greek preserved by Diog. Laert. X. 6 (qu. Zeller, 451), and less accurately by Athenaeus, VII. 279 (qu. R. and P. 353). *Ne suspicari quidem*: for this MSS. give *nec suspicari*, but Madv. (*D.F.*, Excursus III.) has conclusively shown that *nec* for *ne ... quidem* is post Augustan Latin. Christ supposes some thing like *sentire* to have fallen out before *nec suspicari*; that this is wrong is clear from the fact that in *D.F.* II. 20, 30, *T.D.* III. 46, *N.D.* I. 111, where the same opinion of Epicurus is dealt with, we have either *ne suspicari quidem* or *ne intellegere quidem* (cf. also *In Pisonem* 69). Further, *ne ... quidem* is esp frequent with *suspicari* (*D.F.* II. 20), and verbs of the kind (*cogitari* II. 82), and especially, as Durand remarked, at the end of sentences eg *Verr.* II. 1, 155. Notice *negat ... ne suspicari quidem* without *se*, which however Baiter inserts, in spite of the numerous passages produced from Cic. by Madv. (*Em.* 111), in which not only *se*, but *me*, *nos*, and other accusatives of pronouns are omitted before the infinitive, after verbs like *negat*. Cf. also the omission of *sibi* in *Paradoxa* 40. *Si vero*: this, following *sive enim* above, is a departure from Cic.'s rule which is to write *sive—sive* or *si—sin*, but not *si—sive* or *sive—si*. This and two or three other similar passages in Cic. are explained as anacolutha by Madv. in a most important and exhaustive excursus to his *D.F.* (p. 785, ed. 2), and are connected with other instances of broken sequence. There is no need therefore to read *sive* here, as did Turn. Lamb. Dav. and others. *Quam nos ... probamus*: cf. Introd. p. 62. *Erit explicanda*: for the separation of these words by other words interposed, which is characteristic of Cic., see 11, 17. I am surprised that Halm and Baiter both follow Ernesti in his hypercritical objection to the phrase *explicare Academiam*, and read *erunt* against the MSS., making *illa* plural. If *erunt* is read, *erit* must be supplied from it to go with *disserendum*, which is harsh. *Quam argute, quam obscure*: at first sight an oxymoron, but *argute* need not only imply *clearness*, it means merely "acutely". *Quantum possum*: some MSS. have *quantam*, which is scarcely Latin, since in Cic. an accusative only follows *nequeo*, *volo*, *malo*, *possum*, and such verbs when an infinitive can be readily supplied to govern it. For *velle* see a good instance in *D.F.* III. 68, where consult Madv. *Constantiam*: the notions of firmness, consistency, and clearness of mind are bound up in this word, cf. II. 53. *Apud Platonem*: *Timaeus*, 47 B, often quoted or imitated by Cic., cf. *De Leg.* I. 58, *Laelius* 20, 47, *T.D.* I. 64.

§8. *Id est ... jubeo*: these words have been naturally supposed a gloss. But Cicero is nothing if not tautological; he is fond of placing slight variations in phrase side by side. See some remarkable instances of slightly varied phrases connected by *id est* in *D.F.* I. 72, II. 6, 90. I therefore hold Halm and Baiter to be wrong in bracketing the words. *Ea a*: Lamb., objecting to the sound (which is indeed not like Cic.), would read *e* for *a*, which Halm would also prefer. *De*, *ab*, and *ex* follow *haurire* indifferently in Cic. *Rivulos consectentur*: so Wordsworth, "to hunt the waterfalls". The metaphor involved in *fontibus*—

rivulos is often applied by Cic. to philosophy, see esp. a sarcastic passage about Epicurus in *N.D.* I. 120. *Nihil enim magno opere*: *magno opere* should be written in two words, not as *magnopere*, cf. the phrases *maximo opere*, *nimio opere*, the same holds good of *tanto opere*, *quanto opere*. *L. Aelii*: MSS. *Laelii*. The person meant is L. Aelius Stilo or Praeconinus, the master of Varro, and the earliest systematic grammarian of Rome. See Quintil. *Inst. Or.* X. 1, 99, Gellius X. 21, Sueton. *Gramm.* 3. *Occasum*: an unusual metaphor. *Menippum*: a Cynic satirist, see *Dict. Biogr.* Considerable fragments of Varro's Menippean Satires remain, and have often been edited—most recently by Riese (published by Teubner). *Imitati non interpretati*: Cic. *D.F.* I. 7, gives his opinion as to the right use to be made of Greek models. †*Quae quo*: these words are evidently wrong. Halm after Faber ejects *quae*, and is followed by Baiter. Varro is thus made to say that he stated many things dialectically, *in order that* the populace might be enticed to read. To my mind the fault lies in the word *quo*, for which I should prefer to read *cum* (=*quom*, which would be written *quō* in the MSS.) The general sense would then be "Having introduced philosophy into that kind of literature which the unlearned read, I proceeded to introduce it into that which the learned read." *Laudationibus*: λογοις επιταφιοις, cf. *Ad Att.* XIII. 48 where Varro's are mentioned. †*Philosophe scribere*: the MSS. all give *philosophie*. Klotz has *philosophiam*, which is demonstrably wrong, *physica, musica* etc. *scribere* may be said, but not *physicam, musicam* etc. *scribere*. The one passage formerly quoted to justify the phrase *philosophiam scribere* is now altered in the best texts (*T.D.* V. 121, where see Tischer). Goer. reads *philosophiae scribere*; his explanation is, as Orelli gently says, "vix Latina." I can scarcely think Halm's *philosophe* to be right, the word occurs nowhere else, and Cic. almost condemns it by his use of the Greek φιλοσοφως (*Ad Att.* XIII. 20). In older Greek the adverb does not appear, nor is φιλοσοφος used as an adjective much, yet Cic. uses *philosophus* adjectivally in *T.D.* V. 121, *Cat. Mai.* 22, *N.D.* III. 23, just as he uses *tyrannus* (*De Rep.* III. 45), and *anapaestus* (*T.D.* III. 57) Might we not read *philosophis*, in the dative, which only requires the alteration of a single letter from the MSS. reading? The meaning would then be "to write *for* philosophers," which would agree with my emendation *cum* for *quo* above. *Philosophice* would be a tempting alteration, but that the word φιλοσοφικος is not Greek, nor do *philosophicus, philosophice* occur till very late Latin times. *Si modo id consecuti sumus*: cf. *Brut.* 316.

§9. *Sunt ista*: = εστι ταυτα, so often, e.g. *Lael.* 6. Some edd. have *sint*, which is unlikely to be right. *Nos in nostra*: Augustine (*De Civ. Dei* VI. 2) quotes this with the reading *reduxerunt* for *deduxerunt*, which is taken by Baiter and by Halm; who quotes with approval Durand's remark, "*deducimus honoris causa sed errantes reducimus humanitatis.*" The words, however, are almost convertible; see *Cat. Mai.* 63. In *Lael.* 12, *Brut.* 86, we have *reducere*, where Durand's rule requires *deducere*, on the other hand cf. *Ad Herennium* IV. 64, *hospites domum deducere. Aetatem patriae* etc., August. (*De Civ. Dei* VI. 3) describes Varro's "*Libri Antiquitatum*" (referred to in 8), in which most of the subjects here mentioned were treated of. *Descriptiones temporum*: lists of dates, so χρονοι is technically used for dates, Thuc. V. 20, etc. *Tu sacerdotum*: after this Lamb. inserts *munera* to keep the balance of the clauses. Cic. however is quite as fond of variety as of formal accuracy. *Domesticam—bellicam*: opposed like *domi bellique*, cf. *Brut.* 49, *De Off.* I. 74. Augustine's reading *publicam* shows him to have been quoting from memory. *Sedem*: so the best MSS. of Aug., some edd. here give *sedium*. The argument for *sedem* is the awkwardness of making the three genitives, *sedium, regionum, locorum*, dependent on the accusatives, *nomina, genera, officia, causas*. Cic. is fond of using *sedes, locus, regio* together, see *Pro Murena*, 85, *Pro Cluentio*, 171, quoted by Goer. *Omnium divinarum humanarumque rerum*: from the frequent references of Aug. it appears that the "*Libri Antiquitatum*" were divided into two parts, one treating of *res humanae*, the other of *res divinae* (*De Civ. Dei*, IV. 1, 27, VI. 3). *Et litteris luminis*: for *luminis*, cf. *T.D.* I. 5. *Et verbis*: Manut. reads *rebus* from 26. Varro's researches into the Latin tongue are meant. *Multis locis incohasti*: Varro's book "*De Philosophia*" had apparently not yet been written.

§10. *Causa*: = προφασις. *Probabilem*: = specious. *Nesciunt*: Halm with his one MS. G, which is the work of a clever emendator, gives *nescient* to suit *malent* above, and is followed by Baiter. It is not necessary to force on Cic. this formally accurate sequence of tenses, which Halm himself allows to be broken in two similar passages, II. 20, 105. *Sed da mihi nunc, satisne probas?*: So all MSS. except G, which has the evident conj. *sed ea (eam) mihi non sane probas*. This last Baiter gives, while Halm after Durand reads *sed eam mihi non satis probas*, which is too far from the MSS. to please me. The text as it stands is not intolerable, though *da mihi* for *dic mihi* is certainly poetic. *Da te mihi* (Manut., Goer., Orelli) is far too strong for the passage, and cannot be supported by 12, *Brut.* 306, *Ad Fam.* II. 8, or such like passages. *Attius*: the old spelling *Accius* is wrong. *Si qui ... imitati*: note the collocation, and cf. 17. Halm needlessly writes *sint* for MSS. *sunt*. For this section throughout cf. the prologues to *D.F.* I., *T.D.* I. and II.

§11. *Procuratio*: for the proper meaning of *procurator* and *procuratio* see Jordan on *Pro Caecina* 55. *Implacatum et constrictum*: the conjunction introduces the intenser word, as usual; cf. 17 *plenam ac refertam*, II. 127 *exigua et minima*, so και in Greek. *Inclusa habebam*: cf. *T.D.* I. 1. *Obsolescerent*, used of *individual* memory, is noteworthy. *Percussus volnere*: many edd. give the frequent variant *perculsus*. The *volnus*, which Goer. finds so mysterious, is the death of Tullia, cf. *N.D.* I. 9, *De Consolatione*, fragment 7, ed. Nobbe, and Introd. p. 32. *Aut ... aut ... aut ... aut*: This casting about for an excuse shows how low philosophy stood in public estimation at Rome. See Introd. p. 29. The same elaborate apologies often recur, cf. esp the exordium of *N.D.* I.

§12. *Brutus*: the same praise often recurs in *D.F.* and the *Brutus Graecia desideret* so all Halm's MSS., except G, which has *Graeca*. Halm (and after him Baiter) adopts the conj. of Aldus the younger, *Graeca desideres*. A reviewer of Halm, in Schneidewin's *Philologus* XXIV. 483, approves the reading on the curious ground that Brutus was not anxious to satisfy Greek requirements, but rather to render it unnecessary for Romans to have recourse to Greece for philosophy. I keep the MSS. reading, for Greece with Cicero is the supreme arbiter of performance in philosophy, if she is satisfied the philosophic world is tranquil. Cf. *Ad Att.* I. 20, 6, *D.F.* I. 8, *Ad Qu. Fr.* II. 16, 5. I just note the em. of Turnebus, *a Graecia desideres*, and that of Dav. *Graecia desideretur*. *Eandem sententiam*: cf. Introd. p. 56. *Aristum*: cf. II. 11, and *M.D.F.* V. 8.

§13. *Sine te*: = σου διχα. *Relictam*: Cic. very rarely omits *esse*, see note on II. 77, for Cicero's supposed conversion see Introd. p. 20. *Veterem illam*: MSS. have *iam* for *illam*. The position of *iam* would be strange, in the passage which used to be compared, *Pro Cluentio* 16, Classen and Baiter now om. the word. Further, *vetus* and *nova* can scarcely be so barely used to denote the Old and the New Academy. The reading *illam* is from Madv. (*Em.* 115), and is supported by *illam veterem* (18), *illa antiqua* (22), *istius veteris* (*D.F.* V. 8), and similar uses. Bentl. (followed by Halm and Bait.) thinks *iam* comprises the last two syllables of *Academiam*, which he reads. *Correcta et emendata*: a fine sentiment to come from a conservative like Cic. The words often occur together and illustrate Cic.'s love for small diversities of expression, cf. *De Leg.* III. 30, *D.F.* IV. 21, also Tac. *Hist.* I. 37. *Negat*: MSS. have *negaret*, but Cic. never writes the subj. after *quamquam* in *oratio recta*, as Tac. does, unless there is some conditional or potential force in the sentence; see *M.D.F.* III. 70. Nothing is commoner in the MSS. than the substitution of the imp. subj. for the pres. ind. of verbs of the first conjug. and *vice versa*. *In libris*: see II. 11. *Duas Academias*: for the various modes of dividing the Academy refer to R. and P. 404. *Contra ea Philonis*: MSS. have *contra Philonis* merely, exc. Halm's V., which gives *Philonem*, as does the ed. Rom. (1471). I have added *ea*. Orelli quotes *Ad Att.* XII. 23, 2, *ex Apollodori*. Possibly the MSS. may be right, and *libros* may be supplied from *libris* above, so in *Ad Att.* XIII. 32, 2, *Dicaearchi* περι ψυχης *utrosque*, the word *libros* has to be supplied from the preceding letter, cf. a similar ellipse of *bona* in 19, 22. Madvig's *Philonia* is improbable from its non-appearance elsewhere, while the companion adjective *Antiochius* is frequent. Halm inserts *sententiam*, a heroic remedy. To make *contra* an adv. and construe *Philonis Antiochus* together, supplying *auditor*, as is done by some unknown commentators who probably only exist in Goerenz's note, is wild, and cannot be justified by *D.F.* V. 13.

§14. *A qua absum iam diu*: MSS. have strangely *aqua absumtam diu*, changed by Manut. *Renovari*: the vulg. *revocari* is a curious instance of oversight. It crept into the text of Goer. by mistake, for in his note he gave *renovari*. Orelli—who speaks of Goerenz's "*praestantissima recensio*," and founds his own text upon it two years after Madvig's crushing exposure in his *Em.* often quoted by me—not only reads *revocari*, but quotes *renovari* as an em. of the ed. Victoriana of 1536. From Orelli, Klotz, whose text has no independent value, took it. *Renovare* in Cic. often means "to refresh the memory," e.g. 11, *Brut.* 315. *Nisi molestum est*: like *nisi alienum putas*, a variation on the common *si placet, si videtur*. *Adsidamus*: some MSS. have *adsideamus*, which would be wrong here. *Sane istud*: Halm *istuc* from G. *Inquit*: for the late position of this word, which is often caused by its affinity for *quoniam, quidem*, etc., cf. *M.D.F.* III. 20 *Quae cum essent dicta, in conspectu consedimus (omnes)*: most edd. since Gulielmus print this without *essent* as a hexameter, and suppose it a quotation. But firstly, a verse so commonplace, if familiar, would occur elsewhere in Cic. as others do, if not familiar, would not be given without the name of its author. Secondly, most MSS. have *sint* or *essent* before *dicta*. It is more probable therefore that *omnes* was added from an involuntary desire to make up the hexameter rhythm. Phrases like *quae cum essent dicta consedimus* often occur in similar places in Cic.'s dialogues cf. *De Div.* II. 150, and Augustine, the imitator of Cic., *Contra Academicos*, I. 25, also *consedimus* at the end of a clause in *Brut.* 24, and *considitur* in *De Or.* III. 18. *Mihi vero*: the omission of *inquit*, which is strange to Goer., is well illustrated in *M.D.F.* I. 9. There is an odd ellipse of *laudasti* in *D.F.* V. 81.

§§15—42. Antiochus' view of the history of Philosophy. First part of Varro's Exposition, 15—18. Summary. Socrates rejected physics and made ethics supreme in philosophy (15). He had no fixed tenets, his one doctrine being that wisdom consists in a consciousness of ignorance. Moral exhortation was his task (16). Plato added to and enriched the teaching of his master, from him sprang two schools which abandoned the negative position of Socrates and adopted definite tenets, yet remained in essential agreement with one another—the Peripatetic and the Academic (17, 18).

§15. *A rebus ... involutis*: physical phenomena are often spoken of in these words by Cic., cf. 19, *Timaeus* c. 1, *D.F.* I. 64, IV. 18, V. 10, *N.D.* I. 49. Ursinus rejected *ab* here, but the insertion or omission of *ab* after the passive verb depends on the degree to which *natura* is personified, if 28 be compared with *Tim.* c. 1, this will be clear. *Involutis* = veiled; cf. *involucrum*. Cic. shows his feeling of the metaphor by adding *quasi* in II. 26, and often. *Avocavisse philosophiam*: this, the Xenophontic view of Socrates, was the popular one in Cicero's time, cf. II. 123, *T.D.* V. 10, *D.F.* V. 87, 88, also Varro in Aug. *De Civ. Dei*, VIII. 3. Objections to it, however occurred to Cic., and were curiously answered in *De Rep.* I. 16 (cf. also Varro in Aug. *De Civ. Dei*, VIII. 4). The same view is supposed to be found in Aristotle, see the passages quoted by R. and P. 141. To form an opinion on this difficult question the student should read Schleiermacher's *Essay on the Worth of Socrates as a Philosopher* (trans. by Thirlwall), and Zeller's *Socrates and the Socratic Schools*, Eng. Trans., pp. 112—116 [I dissent from his view of Aristotle's evidence], also Schwegler's *Handbook*, so far as it relates to Socrates and Plato. *Nihil tamen ad bene vivendum valere*: *valere* is absent from MSS., and is inserted by Halm, its use in 21 makes it more probable than *conferre*, which is in ed. Rom. (1471). Gronovius vainly tries to justify the MSS. reading by such passages as *D.F.* I. 39, *T.D.* I. 70. The strangest ellipse with *nihil ad* elsewhere in Cic. is in *De Leg.* I. 6.

§16. *Hic ... illum*: for this repetition of pronouns see *M.D.F.* IV. 43. *Varie et copiose*: MSS. omit *et*, but it may be doubted whether Cic. would let two *adverbs* stand together without *et*, though three may (cf. II. 63), and though with pairs of *nouns* and *adjectives, et* often is left out, as in the passages quoted here by Manut. *Ad Att.* IV. 3, 3, *Ad Fam.* XIII. 24, XIII. 28, cf. also the learned note of Wesenberg, reprinted in Baiter and Halm's edition, of Cic.'s philosophical works (1861), on *T.D.* III. 6. *Varie et copiose* is also in *De Or.* II. 240. Cf. the omission of *que* in 23, also II. 63. *Perscripti*: Cic. like Aristotle often speaks of Plato's dialogues as though they were authentic reports of Socratic conversations, cf. II. 74. *Nihil* *adfirmet*: so *T.D.* I. 99. "*Eoque praestare ceteris*" this is evidently from Plato *Apol.* p. 21, as to the proper understanding of which see note on II. 74. *Ab Apolline*, Plato *Apol.* 21 A, *Omnium*: Dav. conj. *hominum* needlessly. *Dictum*: Lamb., followed by Schutz, reads *iudicatum*, it is remarkable that in four passages where Cic. speaks of this very oracle (*Cato Mai.* 78, *Lael.* 7, 9, 13) he uses the verb *iudicare. Una omnis*: Lamb. *hominis*, Baiter also. *Omnis eius oratio tamen*: notwithstanding his negative dialectic he gave positive teaching in morals. *Tamen*: for MSS. *tam* or *tum* is due to Gruter, Halm has *tantum. Tam, tum* and *tamen* are often confused in MSS., e.g. *In Veri (Act* II.) I. 3, 65, II. 55, 112, V. 78, where see Zumpt. Goer. abuses edd. for not knowing that *tum ... et, tum ... que, et ... tum*, correspond in Cic. like *tum ... cum, tum ... tum.* His proofs of this new Latin may be sampled by *Ac.* II. 1, 43. *Ad virtutis studium cohortandis*: this broad assertion is distinctly untrue; see Zeller's *Socrates* 88, with footnote.

§17. *Varius et multiplex, et copiosus*: these characteristics are named to account for the branching off from Plato of the later schools. For *multiplex* "many sided," cf. *T.D.* V. 11. *Una et consentiens*: this is an opinion of Antiochus often adopted by Cic. in his own person, as in *D.F.* IV. 5 *De Leg.* I. 38, *De Or.* III. 67. Five ancient philosophers are generally included in this supposed harmonious Academico-Peripatetic school, viz. Aristotle, Theophrastus, Speusippus, Xenocrates, Polemo (cf. *D.F.* IV. 2), sometimes Crantor is added. The harmony was supposed to have been first broken by Polemo's pupils; so Varro says (from Antiochus) in Aug. *De Civ. Dei* XIX. 1, cf. also 34. Antiochus doubtless rested his theory almost entirely on the ethical resemblances of the two schools. In *D.F.* V. 21, which is taken direct from Antiochus, this appears, as also in Varro (in Aug. as above) who often spoke as though ethics were the whole of philosophy (cf. also *De Off.* III. 20). Antiochus probably made light of such dialectical controversies between the two schools as that about ιδεαι, which had long ceased. Krische *Uber Cicero's Akademika* p. 51, has some good remarks. *Nominibus*: the same as *vocabulis* above. Cic. does not observe Varro's distinction (*De L. L.* IX. 1) which confines *nomen* to proper nouns, *vocabulum* to common nouns, though he would not use *vocabulum* as Tac. does, for the name of a person (*Annals* XII. 66, etc.). *Quasi heredem ... duos autem*: the conj. of Ciaconus "*ex asse heredem, secundos autem*" is as acute as it is absurd. *Duos*: it is difficult to decide whether this or *duo* is right in Cic., he can scarcely have been so inconsistent as the MSS. and edd. make him (cf. Baiter and Halm's ed., *Ac.* II. 11, 13 with *De Div.* I. 6). The older inscr. in the *Corpus* vol. I. have *duo*, but only in *duoviros*, two near the time of Cic. (*C.I.* vol. I. nos. 571 and 1007) give *duos*, which Cic. probably wrote. *Duo* is in old Latin poets and Virgil. *Chalcedonium*: not *Calchedonium* as Klotz, cf. Gk. Χαλκηδονιον. *Praestantissimos*: Halm wrongly, cf. *Brut.* 125. *Stagiritem*: not *Stagiritam* as Lamb., for Cic., exc. in a few nouns like *Persa, pirata*, etc., which came down from antiquity, did not make Greek nouns in -ης into Latin nouns in -*a*. See *M.D.F.* II. 94. *Coetus ... soliti*: cf. 10. *Platonis ubertate*: cf. Quintilian's "*illa Livii lactea ubertas*." *Plenum ac refertam*: n. on 11. *Dubitationem*: Halm with one MS., G, gives *dubitantem*, Baiter *dubitanter*, Why alter? *Ars quaedam philosophiae*: before these words all Halm's MSS., exc G, insert *disserendi*, probably from the line above, Lipsius keeps it and ejects *philosophiae*, while Lamb., Day read *philosophia* in the nom. Varro, however, would never say that philosophy became entirely dialectical in the hands of the old Academics and Peripatetics. *Ars* = τεχνη, a set of definite rules, so Varro in Aug. (as above) speaks of the *certa dogmata* of this old school as opposed to the incertitude of the New Academy. *Descriptio*: so Halm here, but often *discriptio.* The *Corp. Inscr.*, vol. I. nos. 198 and 200, has thrice *discriptos* or *discriptum*, the other spelling never.

§18. *Ut mihi quidem videtur*: MSS. transpose *quidem* and *videtur*, as in 44. *Quidem*, however nearly always comes closely after the pronoun, see *M.D.F.* IV. 43, cf. also I. 71, III. 28, *Opusc.* I. 406. *Expetendarum fugiendarumque*: ᾱιρετων και φευκτων, about which more in n. on 36. The Platonic and Aristotelian ethics have indeed an external resemblance, but the ultimate bases of the two are quite different. In rejecting the Idea of the Good, Aristotle did away with what Plato would have considered most valuable in his system. The ideal theory, however, was practically defunct in the time of Antiochus, so that the similarity between the two schools seemed much greater than it was. *Non sus Minervam*: a Greek proverb, cf. Theocr. *Id.* V. 23, *De Or.* II. 233, *Ad Fam.* IX. 18, 3. Binder, in his German translation of the *Academica*, also quotes Plutarch *Præc. Polit.* 7. *Inepte ... docet*: elliptic for *inepte docet, quisquis docet*. *Nostra atque nostros*: few of the editors have understood this. Atticus affects everything Athenian, and speaks as though he were one of them; in Cic.'s letters to him the words *"tui cives,"* meaning the Athenians, often occur. *Quid me putas*: i.e. *velle*. *Exhibiturum*: Halm inserts *me* before this from his one MS. G, evidently emended here by its copyist. For the omission of *me*, cf. note on 7.

§§19—23. Part II. of Varro's Exposition: Antiochus' *Ethics*. Summary. The threefold division of philosophy into ηθικη, φυσικη, διαλεκτικη. Goodness means obedience to nature, happiness the acquisition of natural advantages. These are of three kinds, mental, bodily, and external. The bodily are described (19); then the mental, which fall into two classes, congenital and acquired, virtue being the chief of the acquired (20), then the external, which form with the bodily advantages a kind of exercise-ground for virtue (21). The ethical standard is then succinctly stated, in which virtue has chief part, and is capable in itself of producing happiness, though not the greatest happiness possible, which requires the possession of all three classes of advantages (22). With this ethical standard, it is possible to give an intelligent account of action and duty (23).

§19. *Ratio triplex*: Plato has not this division, either consciously or unconsciously, though it was generally attributed to him in Cicero's time, so by Varro himself (from Antiochus) in Aug. *De Civ. Dei* VIII. 4, and by Diog. Laert. III. 56 (see R. and P., p. 195). The division itself cannot be traced farther back than Xenocrates and the post-Aristotelian Peripatetics, to whom it is assigned by Sext. Emp. *Adv. Math.* VII. 16. It was probably first brought into strong prominence by the Stoics, whom it enabled more sharply and decisively to subordinate to Ethics all else in philosophy. Cf. esp. *M.D.F.* IV. 3. *Quid verum ... repugnans iudicando*: MSS. exc. G have *et* before *quid falsum*, whence Klotz conj. *sit* in order to obviate the awkwardness of *repugnet* which MSS. have for *repugnans*. Krische wishes to read *consequens* for *consentiens*, comparing *Orator* 115, *T.D.* V. 68, *De Div.* II. 150, to which add *T.D.* V. 21 On the other hand cf. II. 22, 91. Notice the double translations of the Greek terms, *de vita et moribus* for ηθικη, etc. This is very characteristic of Cic., as we shall see later. *Ac primum*: many MSS. and edd. *primam*, cf. 23, 30. *A natura petebant*: how Antiochus could have found this in Plato and Aristotle is difficult to see; that he did so, however, is indubitable; see *D.F.* V. 24—27, which should be closely compared with our passage, and Varro in Aug. XIX. 3. The root of Plato's system is the ιδεα of the Good, while so far is Aristotle from founding his system on the abstract φυσις, that he scarcely appeals even incidentally to φυσις in his ethical works. The abstract conception of nature in relation to ethics is first strongly apparent in Polemo, from whom it passed into Stoic hands and then into those of Antiochus. *Adeptum esse omnia*: put rather differently in *D.F.* V. 24, 26, cf. also *D.F.* II. 33, 34, *Ac.* II. 131. *Et animo et corpore et vita*: this is the τριας or τριλογια των αγαθων, which belongs in this form to late Peripateticism (cf. *M.D.F.* III. 43), the third division is a development from the βιος τελειος of Aristotle. The τριας in this distinct shape is foreign both to Plato and Arist, though Stobaeus, *Ethica* II. 6, 4, tries hard to point it out in Plato; Varro seems to merge the two last divisions into one in Aug. *De Civ. Dei* XIX 3. This agrees better with *D.F.* V. 34—36, cf. also Aug. VIII. 8. On the Antiochean *finis* see more in note on 22. *Corporis alia*: for ellipse of *bona*, see n. on 13. *Ponebant esse*: n. on 36. *In toto in partibus*: the same distinction is in Stob. *Eth.* II. 6, 7; cf. also *D.F.* V. 35. *Pulchritudinem*: Cic. *Orator* 160, puts the spelling *pulcher* beyond a doubt; it often appears in inscr. of the Republic. On the other hand only *pulcrai, pulcrum*, etc., occur in inscr., exc. *pulchre*, which is found once (*Corp. Inscr.* I. no 1019). *Sepulchrum*, however, is frequent at an early time. On the tendency to aspirate even native Latin words see Boscher in Curtius' *Studien* II. 1, p. 145. In the case of *pulcher* the false derivation from πολυχροος may have aided the corruption. Similarly in modern times J.C. Scaliger derived it from πολυ χειρ (Curtius' *Grundz* ed. 3, p. 8) For *valetudinem viris pulchritudinem*, cf. the ʽυγιεια ισχυς καλλος of Stob. *Eth.* II. 6, 7, and *T.D.* V. 22. *Sensus integros* ευαισθησια in Stob., cf. also *D.F.* V. 36 (*in sensibus est sua cuiusque virtus*). *Celeritatem*: so ποδωκεια in Stob., *bene currere* in Aug. XIX. 3. *Claritatem in voce*: cf. *De Off.* I. 133. *Impressionem*: al. *expressionem*. For the former cf. *De Or.* III. 185, which will show the meaning to be the distinct marking of each sound; for the latter *De Or.* III. 41, which will disprove Klotz's remark "*imprimit lingua voces,* *non exprimit.*" See also *De Off.* I. 133. One old ed. has *pressionem*, which, though not itself Ciceronian, recalls *presse loqui*, and *N.D.* II. 149. Pliny, *Panegyric*, c. 64, has *expressit explanavitque verba*; he and Quintilian often so use *exprimere*.

§20. *Ingeniis*: rejected by many (so Halm), but cf. *T.D.* III. 2, and *animis* below and in *N.D.* II. 58. *In naturam et mores*: for *in ea quae natura et moribus fiunt*. A similar inaccuracy of expression is found in II. 42. The division is practically Aristotle's, who severs αρεται into διανοητικαι and ηθικαι (*Nic. Eth.* I. c. 13, *Magna Mor.* I. c. 5). In *D.F.* V. 38 the διανοητικαι are called *non voluntariae*, the ηθικαι *voluntariae*. *Celeritatem ad discendum et memoriam*: cf. the ευμαθεια, μνημη of Arist. (who adds αγχινοια σοφια φρονησις), and the *docilitas, memoria* of *D.F.* V. 36. *Quasi consuetudinem*: the *quasi* marks a translation from the Greek, as frequently, here probably of εθισμος (*Nic. Eth.* II. c. 1). *Partim ratione formabant*: the relation which reason bears to virtue is set forth in *Nic. Eth.* VI. c. 2. *In quibus*: i.e. *in moribus*. All the late schools held that ethics formed the sole ultimate aim of philosophy. *Erat*: note the change from *oratio obliqua* to *recta*, and cf. the opposite change in II. 40. *Progressio*: this, like the whole of the sentence in which it stands, is intensely Stoic. For the Stoic προκορη, προκοπτειν εις αρετην, cf. *M.D.F.* IV. 64, 66, R. and P. 392, sq., Zeller, *Stoics* 258, 276. The phrases are sometimes said to be Peripatetic, if so, they must belong only to the late Stoicised Peripateticism of which we find so much in Stobaeus. *Perfectio naturae*: cf. esp. *De Leg.* I. 25. More Stoic still is the definition of virtue as the perfection of the *reason*, cf. II. 26, *D.F.* IV. 35, V. 38, and Madvig's note on *D.F.* II. 88. Faber quotes Galen *De Decr. Hipp. et Plat.* c. 5, ῾η αρετη τελειοτης εστι της ῾εκαστου φυσεος. *Una res optima*: the supremacy of virtue is also asserted by Varro in Aug. XIX. 3, cf. also *D.F.* V. 36, 38.

§21. *Virtutis usum*: so the Stoics speak of their αδιαφορα as the practising ground for virtue (*D.F.* III. 50), cf. *virtutis usum* in Aug. XIX. 1. *Nam virtus*: most MSS. have *iam*, which is out of place here. *Animi bonis et corporis cernitur et in quibusdam*: MSS. omit *et* between *cernitur* and *in*, exc. Halm's G which has *in* before *animi* and also before *corporis*. These last insertions are not necessary, as may be seen from *Topica* 80, *causa certis personis locis temporibus actionibus negotiis cernitur aut* in *omnibus aut* in *plerisque*, also *T.D.* V. 22. In Stob. II. 6, 8, the τελος of the Peripatetics is stated to be το κατ' αρετην ζην εν τοις περι σωμα και τοις εξωθεν αγαθοις, here *quibusdam quae* etc., denote the εξωθεν or εκτος αγαθα, the third class in 19. *Hominem ... societate*: all this is strongly Stoic, though also attributed to the Peripatetics by Stob. II. 6, 7 (κοινη φιλανθρωπια), etc., doubtless the humanitarianism of the Stoics readily united with the φυσει ανθρωπος πολιτικον ζωον theory of Aristotle. For Cic. cf. *D.F.* III. 66, *De Leg.* I. 23, for the Stoics, Zeller 293—296. The repetitions *hominem, humani, hominibus, humana* are striking. For the last, Bentley (i.e. Davies' anonymous friend) proposed *mundana* from *T.D.* V. 108, Varro, however, has *humana societas* in Aug. XIX. 3. *Cetera autem*: what are these *cetera*? They form portion of the εκτος αγαθα, and although not strictly contained within the *summum bonum* are necessary to enrich it and preserve it. Of the things enumerated in Stob. II. 6, 8, 13, φιλια, φιλοι would belong to the *quaedam* of Cicero, while πλουτος αρχη ευτυχια ευγενεια δυναστεια would be included in *cetera*. The same distinction is drawn in Aug. VIII. 8. *Tuendum*: most MSS. *tenendum*, but *tuendum* corresponds best with the division of αγαθα into ποιητικα and φυλακτικα, Stob. II. 6, 13. For the word *pertinere* see *M.D.F.* III. 54.

§22. *Plerique*: Antiochus believes it also Academic. *Qui tum appellarentur*: MSS. *dum*, the subj. is strange, and was felt to be so by the writer of Halm's G, which has *appellantur*. *Videbatur*: Goer. and Orelli stumble over this, not perceiving that it has the strong meaning of the Gr. εδοκει, "it was their dogma," so often. *Adipisci*: cf. *adeptum esse*, 19. *Quae essent prima natura*: MSS. have *in natura*. For the various modes of denoting the πρωτα κατα φυσιν in Latin see Madvig's *Fourth Excursus to the D.F.*, which the student of Cic.'s philosophy ought to know by heart. The phrase *prima natura* (abl.) could not stand alone, for τα πρωτα τη φυσει is one of Goerenz's numerous forgeries. The ablative is always conditioned by some verb, see Madv. A comparison of this statement of the ethical *finis* with that in 19

71

and the passages quoted in my note there, will show that Cic. drew little distinction between the Stoic τα πρωτα κατα φυσιν and the Peripatetic τριλογια. That this is historically absurd Madvig shows in his *Excursus*, but he does not sufficiently recognise the fact that Cicero has perfectly correctly reported Antiochus. At all events, Varro's report (Aug. *De Civ. Dei* XIX. 3) coincides with Cic.'s in every particular. Even the *inexplicabilis perversitas* of which Madv. complains (p. 821) is traceable to Antiochus, who, as will be seen from Augustine XIX. 1, 3, included even *virtus* among the *prima naturae*. A little reflection will show that in no other way could Antiochus have maintained the practical identity of the Stoic and Peripatetic views of the *finis*. I regret that my space does not allow me to pursue this difficult subject farther. For the Stoic πρωτα κατα φυσιν see Zeller, chap XI. *Ipsa per sese expetenda*: Gk. ʽαιρετα, which is applied to all things contained within the *summum bonum*. As the Stoic *finis* was αρετη only, that alone to them was ʽαιρετον, their πρωτα κατα φυσιν were not ʽαιρετα, (cf. *D.F.* III. 21). Antiochus' *prima naturae* were ʽαιρετα to him, cf. Aug. XIX. 3, *prima illa naturae propter se ipsa existimat expetenda* so Stob., II. 6, 7, demonstrates each branch of the τριλογια to be καθʼ ʽαυτο ʽαιρετον. *Aut omnia aut maxima*: so frequently in Cic., e.g. *D.F.* IV. 27, so Stob. II. 6, 8, τα πλειστα και κυριωτατα. *Ea sunt maxima*: so Stob., Varro in Aug. *passim*. *Sensit*: much misunderstood by edd., here = *iudicavit* not *animadvertit* cf. *M.D.F.* II. 6. *Reperiebatur*: for change of constr. cf. *D.F.* IV. 26 *Nec tamen beatissimam*: the question whether αρετη was αυταρκες προς ευδαιμονιαν was one of the most important to the late Greek philosophy. As to Antiochus, consult *M.D.F.* V. 67.

§23. *Agendi aliquid*: Gk. πραξεως, the usual translation, cf. II. 24, 37. *Officii ipsius initium*: του καθηκοντος αρχην, Stob. II. 6, 7. This sentence is covertly aimed at the New Academics, whose scepticism, according to the dogmatists, cut away the ground from action and duty, see II. 24. *Recti honestique*: these words are redolent of the Stoa. *Earum rerum*: Halm thinks something like *appetitio* has fallen out, *susceptio* however, above, is quite enough for both clauses; a similar use of it is found in *D.F.* III. 32. *Descriptione naturae*: Halm with one MS. (G) gives *praescriptione*, which is in II. 140, cf. also *praescriberet* above. The phrase is Antiochean; cf. *prima constitutio naturae* in *D.F.* IV. 15. *Aequitas*: not in the Roman legal sense, but as a translation of επιεικεια. *Eaeque*: so Halm for MSS. *haeque, haecque*. Of course *haecque*, like *hicque, sicque*, would be un-Ciceronian. *Voluptatibus*: a side blow at the Epicureans. *Forma* see n. on 33.

§§24—29. Part III of Varro's Exposition. Antiochus' *Physics*. Summary. All that is consists of force and matter, which are never actually found apart, though they are thought of as separate. When force impresses form on the formless matter, it becomes a formed entity (ποιον τι or *quale*)—(24). These formed entities are either *primary* or *secondary*. Air, fire, water, earth are primary, the two first having an active, the two last a passive function. Aristotle added a fifth (26). Underlying all formed entities is the formless matter, matter and space are infinitely subdivisible (27). Force or form acts on the formless matter and so produces the ordered universe, outside which no matter exists. Reason permeates the universe and makes it eternal. This Reason has various names—Soul of the Universe, Mind, Wisdom, Providence, Fate, Fortune are only different titles for the same thing (28, 29).

§24. *Natura*: this word, it is important to observe, has to serve as a translation both of φυσις and ουσια. Here it is ουσια in the broadest sense, all that exists. *In res duas*: the distinction between Force and Matter, the active and passive agencies in the universe, is of course Aristotelian and Platonic. Antiochus however probably apprehended the distinction as modified by the Stoics, for this read carefully Zeller, 135 sq., with the footnotes. The clearest view of Aristotle's doctrine is to be got from Schwegler, *Handbook*, pp 99—105. R. and P. 273 sq. should be consulted for the important coincidence of Force with logical *genus* (ειδος), and of Matter (ʽυλη) with logical *differentia* (διαφορα). For the *duae res*, cf. *D.F.* I. 18. *Efficiens ... huic se praebens*: an attempt to translate το ποιουν and το πασχον of the *Theaetetus*, το οθεν and το δεχομενον of the *Timaeus* (50 D). Cic. in *Tim.* has *efficere* and *pati*, Lucretius I. 440 *facere* and *fungi*. *Ea quae*: so Gruter, Halm for MSS. *eaque*. The meaning is this; passive matter when worked upon by an active generative form results in an *aliquid*, a τοδε τι as Aristotle calls it. Passive matter ῾υλη is only potentially τοδε τι, passing into actual τοδε τι, when affected by the form. (Cf. τοδε, τουτο, Plato *Tim.* 49 E, 50 A, also Arist. *Metaph* H, 1, R. and P. 270—274). A figurative description of the process is given in *Timaeus*, 50 D. *In eo quod efficeret ... materiam quandam*: Cic. is hampered by the *patrii sermonis egestas*, which compels him to render simple Greek terms by laboured periphrases. *Id quod efficit* is not distinct from, but *equivalent* to *vis, id quod efficitur* to *materia. Materiam quandam*: it is extraordinary how edd. (esp Goer.) could have so stumbled over *quandam* and *quasi* used in this fashion. Both words (which are joined below) simply mark the unfamiliarity of the Latin word in its philosophical use, in the Greek ῾υλη the strangeness had had time to wear off. *In utroque*: for *in eo quod ex utroque* (sc. *vi et materia*) *fit*, the meaning is clearly given by the next clause, viz. that Force and Matter cannot actually exist apart, but only in the compound of the two, the formed entity, which doctrine is quite Aristotelian. See the reff. given above. *Nihil enim est quod non alicubi esse cogatur*: the meaning of this is clear, that nothing can *exist* except in space *(alicubi)*, it is more difficult to see why it should be introduced here. Unless *est* be taken of merely phenomenal existence (the only existence the Stoics and Antiochus would allow), the sentence does not represent the belief of Aristotle and Plato. The ιδεαι for instance, though to Plato in the highest sense existent, do not exist in space. (Aristotle explicitly says this, *Phys.* III. 4). Aristotle also recognised much as existent which did not exist in space, as in *Phys.* IV. 5 (qu. R. and P. 289). Cic. perhaps translates here from *Tim.* 52 B, φαμεν αναγκαιον ειναι που το ῾ον ῾απαν εν τινι τοπω. For ancient theories about space the student must be referred to the histories of philosophy. A fair summary is given by Stob. *Phys.* περι κενου και τοπου και χωρας, ch. XVIII. 1. *Corpus et quasi qualitatem*: note that *corpus* is *formed*, as contrasted with *materia, unformed* matter. *Qualitas* is here wrongly used for *quale*; it ought to be used of Force only, not of the product of Force and Matter, cf. 28. The Greeks themselves sometimes confuse ποιοτης and ποιον, the confusion is aided by the ambiguity of the phrase το ποιον in Greek, which may either denote the τοδε τι as ποιον, or the Force which makes it ποιον, hence Arist. calls one of his categories το ποιον and ποιοτης indifferently For the Stoic view of ποιοτης, see Zeller, 96—103, with footnotes.

§25. *Bene facis: passim* in comedy, whence Cic. takes it; cf. *D.F.* III. 16, a passage in other respects exceedingly like this. *Rhetoricam*: Hülsemann conj. *ethicam*, which however is *not* Latin. The words have no philosophical significance here, but are simply specimens of words once foreign, now naturalised. *D.F.* III. 5 is very similar. Cic.'s words make it clear that these nouns ought to be treated as Latin first declension nouns; the MSS. often give, however, a Gk. accus. in *en. Non est vulgi verbum*: it first appears in *Theaet.* 182 A, where it is called αλλοκοτον ονομα. *Nova ... facienda*: = *imponenda* in *D.F.* III. 5. *Suis utuntur*: so *D.F.* III. 4. *Transferenda: transferre* = μεταφερειν, which is technically used as early as Isocrates. See Cic. on metaphor, *De Or.* III. 153 sq., where *necessitas* is assigned as one cause of it (159) just as here; cf. also *De Or.* III. 149. *Saecula*: the spelling *secula* is wrong; Corss. I. 325, 377. The diphthong bars the old derivations from *secare*, and *sequi. Quanto id magis*: Cic. is exceedingly fond of separating *tam quam ita tantus quantus*, etc., from the words with which they are syntactically connected, by just one small word, e.g. *Lael.* 53 *quam id recte, Acad.* II. 125 *tam sit mirabilis*, II. 68 *tam in praecipitem*; also *D.F.* III. 5 *quanto id nobis magis est concedendum qui ea nunc primum audemus attingere.*

§26. *Non modo rerum sed verborum*: cf. 9. *Igitur* picks up the broken thread of the exposition; so 35, and frequently. *Principes ... ex his ortae*: the Greek terms are ῾απλα and συνθετα, see Arist. *De Coelo*, I. 2 (R. and P. 294). The distinction puzzled Plutarch (quoted in R. and P. 382). It was both Aristotelian and Stoic. The Stoics (Zeller, 187 sq.) followed partly Heraclitus, and cast aside many refinements of Aristotle which will be found in R. and P. 297. *Quasi multiformes*: evidently a trans. of πολυειδεις, which is opposed to ῾απλους in Plat. *Phaedr.* 238 A, and often. Plato uses also μονοειδης for *unius modi*; cf. Cic. *Tim.* ch. VII., a transl. of Plat. *Tim.* 35 A. *Prima sunt: primae* (sc. *qualitates*) is the needless em. of Walker, followed by Halm. *Formae* = *genera*, ειδη. The word is applied to the four elements themselves, *N.D.* I. 19; cf. also *quintum genus* below, and *Topica*, 11—13. A good view of the history of the doctrine of the four elements may be gained from the section of Stob. *Phys.*, entitled περι αρχων και στοιχειων και του παντος. It will be there seen that Cic. is wrong in making *initia* and *elementa* here and in 39 (αρχαι and στοιχεια) convertible terms. The Greeks would call the four elements στοιχεια but *not* αρχαι, which term would be reserved for the primary Matter and Force. *Aër et ignis*: this is Stoic but *not* Aristotelian. Aristot., starting with the four necessary properties of matter, viz. heat, cold, dryness, moisture, marks the two former as active, the two latter as passive. He then assigns *two* of these properties, *one* active and *one* passive, to each of the four elements; each therefore is to him *both* active and passive. The Stoics assign only *one* property to each element; heat to fire, cold to air (cf. *N.D.* II. 26), moisture to water, dryness to earth. The doctrine of the text follows at once. Cf. Zeller, pp. 155, 187 sq., with footnotes, R. and P. 297 sq. *Accipiendi ... patiendi*: δεχεσθαι often comes in Plat. *Tim. Quintum genus*: the note on this, referred to in Introd. p. 16, is postponed to 39. *Dissimile ... quoddam*: so MSS.; one would expect *quiddam*, which Orelli gives. *Rebatur*: an old poetical word revived by Cic. *De Or.* III. 153; cf. Quintil. *Inst. Or.* VIII. 3, 26.

§27. *Subiectam ... materiam*: the ῾υποκειμενη ῾υλη of Aristotle, from which our word subject-matter is descended. *Sine ulla specie*: *species* here = *forma* above, the ειδος or μορφη of Arist. *Omnibus* without *rebus* is rare. The ambiguity is sometimes avoided by the immediate succession of a neuter relative pronoun, as in 21 in *quibusdam, quae. Expressa*: chiselled as by a sculptor (cf. *expressa effigies De Off.* III. 69); *efficta*, moulded as by a potter (see II. 77); the word was given by Turnebus for MSS. *effecta*. So Matter is called an εκμαγειον in Plat. *Tim. Quae tota omnia*: these words have given rise to needless doubts; Bentl., Dav., Halm suspect them. *Tota* is feminine sing.; cf. *materiam totam ipsam* in 28; "which matter throughout its whole extent can suffer all changes." For the word *omnia* cf. II. 118, and Plat. *Tim.* 50 B (δεχεται γαρ ηι τα παντα), 51 A (ειδος πανδεχες). The word πανδεχες is also quoted from Okellus in Stob. I. 20, 3. Binder is certainly wrong in taking *tota* and *omnia* both as neut.—"*alles und jedes.*" Cic. knew the *Tim.* well and imitated it here. The student should read Grote's comments on the passages referred to. I cannot here point out the difference between Plato's ῾υλη and that of Aristotle. *Eoque interire*: so MSS.; Halm after Dav. *eaque*. Faber was right in supposing that Cic. has said loosely of the *materia* what he ought to have said of the *qualia*. Of course the προτε ῾υλη, whether Platonic or Aristotelian, is imperishable (cf. *Tim.* 52 A. φθοραν ου προσδεχομενον). *Non in nihilum*: this is aimed at the Atomists, who maintained that infinite subdivision logically led to the passing of things into nothing and their reparation out of nothing again. See Lucr. I. 215—264, and elsewhere. *Infinite secari*: through the authority of Aristotle, the doctrine of the infinite subdivisibility of matter had become so thoroughly the orthodox one that the Atom was scouted as a silly absurdity. Cf. *D.F.* I. 20 *ne illud quidem physici credere esse minimum*, Arist. *Physica*, I. 1 ουκ εστιν ελαχιστον μεγεθος. The history of ancient opinion on this subject is important, but does not lie close enough to our author for comment. The student should at least learn Plato's opinions from *Tim.* 35 A sq. It is notable that Xenocrates, tripping over the old αντιφασις of the One and the Many, denied παν μεγεθος διαιρετον ειναι και μερος εχειν (R. and P. 245). Chrysippus followed Aristotle very closely (R. and P. 377, 378). *Intervallis moveri*: this is the theory of motion without void which Lucr. I. 370 sq. disproves, where see Munro. Cf. also Sext. Emp. *Adv. Math.* VII. 214. Aristotle denied the existence of void either within or without the universe, Strato allowed its possibility within, while denying its existence without (Stob. I. 18, 1), the Stoics did the exact opposite affirming its existence without, and denying it within the universe (Zeller 186, with footnotes). *Quae intervalla ... possint*: there is no ultimate space atom, just as there is no matter atom. As regards space, the Stoics and Antiochus closely followed Aristotle, whose ideas may be gathered from R. and P. 288, 9, and especially from M. Saint Hilaire's explanation of the *Physica*.

§28. *Ultro citroque*: this is the common reading, but I doubt its correctness. MSS. have *ultro introque*, whence *ed. Rom.* (1471) has *ultro in utroque*. I think that *in utroque*, simply, was the reading, and that *ultro* is a dittographia from *utro*. The meaning would be "since force plays this part in the compound," *utroque* being as in 24 for *eo quod ex utroque fit*. If the vulg. is kept, translate "since force has this motion and is ever thus on the move." *Ultro citroque* is an odd expression to apply to universal Force, Cic. would have qualified it with a *quasi*. Indeed if it is kept I suggest *quasi* for *cum sic*. The use of *versetur* is also strange. *E quibus in omni natura*: most edd. since Dav. (Halm included) eject *in*. It is perfectly sound if *natura* be taken as ουσια = existence substance. The meaning is "out of which *qualia*, themselves existing in (being co-extensive with) universal substance (cf. *totam commutari* above), which is coherent and continuous, the world was formed." For the *in* cf. *N.D.* II. 35, *in omni natura necesse est absolvi aliquid*, also a similar use *ib.* II. 80, and *Ac.* II. 42. If *in utroque* be read above, *in omni natura* will form an exact contrast, substance as a whole being opposed to the individual *quale*. *Cohaerente et continuata*: the Stoics made the universe much more of a unity than any other school, the expressions here and the striking parallels in *N.D.* II. 19, 84, 119, *De Div.* II. 33, *De Leg.* fragm. 1. (at the end of Bait. and Halm's ed.) all come ultimately from Stoic sources, even if they be got at second hand through Antiochus. Cf. Zeller 137, Stob. I. 22, 3. The *partes mundi* are spoken of in most of the passages just quoted, also in *N.D.* II. 22, 28, 30, 32, 75, 86, 115, 116, all from Stoic sources. *Effectum esse mundum*: Halm adds *unum* from his favourite MS. (G). *Natura sentiente*: a clumsy trans. of αισθητη ουσια = substance which can affect the senses. The same expression is in *N.D.* II. 75. It should not be forgotten, however, that to the Stoics the universe was itself sentient, cf. *N.D.* II. 22, 47, 87. *Teneantur*: for *contineantur*; cf. *N.D.* II. 29 with II. 31 *In qua ratio perfecta insit*: this is thorough going Stoicism. Reason, God, Matter, Universe, are interchangeable terms with the Stoics. See Zeller 145—150 By an inevitable inconsistency, while believing that Reason *is* the Universe, they sometimes speak of it as being *in* the Universe, as here (cf. Diog. Laert. VII. 138, *N.D.* II. 34) In a curious passage (*N.D.* I. 33), Cic. charges Aristotle with the same inconsistency. For the Pantheistic idea cf. Pope "lives through all life, extends through all extent". *Sempiterna*: Aristotle held this: see II. 119 and *N.D.* II. 118, Stob. I. 21, 6. The Stoics while believing that our world would be destroyed by fire (Diog. Laert. VII. 141, R. and P. 378, Stob. I. 20, 1) regarded the destruction as merely an absorption into the Universal World God, who will recreate the world out of himself, since he is beyond the reach of harm (Diog. Laert. VII. 147, R. and P. 386, Zeller 159) Some Stoics however denied the εκπυρωσις. *Nihil enim valentius*: this is an argument often urged, as in *N.D.* II. 31 (*quid potest esse mundo valentius?*), Boethus quoted in Zeller 159. *A quo intereat*: *interire* here replaces the passive of *perdere* cf. αναστηναι, εκπιπτειν ʿυπο τινος.

§29. *Quam vim animum*: there is no need to read *animam*, as some edd. do. The Stoics give their World God, according to his different attributes, the names God, Soul, Reason, Providence, Fate, Fortune, Universal Substance, Fire, Ether, All pervading Air-Current, etc. See Zeller, ch. VI. *passim.* Nearly all these names occur in *N.D.* II. The whole of this section is undilutedly Stoic, one can only marvel how Antiochus contrived to fit it all in with the known opinions of old Academics and Peripatetics. *Sapientiam*: cf. *N.D.* II. 36 with III. 23, in which latter passage the Stoic opinion is severely criticised. *Deum*: Cic. in *N.D.* I. 30 remarks that Plato in his *Timaeus* had already made the *mundus* a God. *Quasi prudentium quandam*: the Greek προνοια is translated both by *prudentia* and *providentia* in the same passage, *N.D.* II. 58, also in *N.D.* II. 77—80. *Procurantem ... quae pertinent ad homines*: the World God is perfectly beneficent, see *Ac.* II. 120, *N.D.* I. 23, II. 160 (where there is a quaint jest on the subject), Zeller 167 sq. *Necessitatem*: αναγκην, which is ειρμος αιτιων, *causarum series sempiterna* (*De Fato* 20, cf. *N.D.* I. 55, *De Div.* I. 125, 127, Diog. VII. 149, and Zeller as before). This is merely the World God apprehended as regulating the orderly sequence of cause upon cause. When the World God is called Fortune, all that is expressed is human inability to see this orderly sequence. Τυχη therefore is defined as αιτια αδηλος ανθρωπινωι λογισμωι (Stob. I. 7, 9, where the same definition is ascribed to Anaxagoras— see also *Topica*, 58—66). This identification of Fate with Fortune (which sadly puzzles Faber and excites his wrath) seems to have first been brought prominently forward by Heraclitus, if we may trust Stob. I. 5, 15. *Nihil aliter possit*: on *posse* for *posse fieri* see *M.D.F.* IV. 48, also *Ac.* II. 121. For the sense of Cleanthes' hymn to Zeus (i.e. the Stoic World-God), ουδε τι γιγνεται εργον επι χθονι σου διχα δαιμον. *Inter quasi fatalem*: a trans. of the Gk. κατηναγκασμενον. I see no reason for suspecting *inter*, as Halm does. *Ignorationemque causarum*: the same words in *De Div.* II. 49; cf. also August. *Contra Academicos* I. 1. In addition to studying the reff. given above, the student might with advantage read Aristotle's *Physica* II. ch. 4—6, with M. Saint Hilaire's explanation, for the views of Aristotle about τυχη and το αυτοματον, also ch. 8—9 for αναγκη. Plato's doctrine of αναγκη, which is diametrically opposed to that of the Stoics, is to be found in *Timaeus* p. 47, 48, Grote's *Plato*, III. 249—59.

§§30—32. Part iv. of Varro's Exposition: Antiochus' *Ethics*. Summary. Although the old Academics and Peripatetics based knowledge on the senses, they did not make the senses the criterion of truth, but the mind, because it alone saw the permanently real and true (30). The senses they thought heavy and clogged and unable to gain knowledge of such things as were either too small to come into the domain of sense, or so changing and fleeting that no part of their being remained constant or even the same, seeing that all parts were in a continuous flux. Knowledge based *only* on sense was therefore mere opinion (31). Real knowledge only came through the reasonings of the mind, hence they *defined* everything about which they argued, and also used verbal explanations, from which they drew proofs. In these two processes consisted their dialectic, to which they added persuasive rhetoric (32).

§30. *Quae erat*: the Platonic ην, = was, as we said. *In ratione et disserendo*: an instance of Cicero's fondness for tautology, cf. *D.F.* I. 22 *quaerendi ac disserendi*. *Quamquam oriretur*: the sentence is inexact, it is *knowledge* which takes its rise in the senses, not the criterion of truth, which is the mind itself; cf. however II. 30 and n. *Iudicium*: the constant translation of κριτηριον, a word foreign to the older philosophy. *Mentem volebant rerum esse iudicem*: Halm with his pet MS. writes *esse rerum*, thus giving an almost perfect iambic, strongly stopped off before and after, so that there is no possibility of avoiding it in reading. I venture to say that no real parallel can be found to this in Cic., it stands in glaring contradiction to his own rules about admitting metre in prose, *Orator* 194 sq., *De Or.* III. 182 sq. *Solam censebant ... tale quale esset*: probably from Plato's *Tim.* 35 A thus translated by Cic., *Tim.* c. 7 *ex ea materia quae individua est et unius modi* (αει κατα ταυτα εχουσης cf. 28 A. το κατα ταυτα εχον) *et sui simile*, cf. also *T.D.* I. 58 *id solum esse quod semper tale sit quale sit, quam* ιδεαν *appellat ille, nos speciem*, and *Ac.* II. 129. *Illi* ιδεαν, etc.: there is more than one difficulty here. The words *iam a Platone ita nom* seem to exclude Plato from the supposed old Academico-Peripatetic school. This may be an oversight, but to say first that the school (*illi*, cf. *sic tractabatur ab utrisque*) which included Aristotle held the doctrine of ιδεαι, and next, in 33, that Aristotle crushed the same doctrine, appears very absurd. We may reflect, however, that the difference between Plato's ιδεαι and Aristotle's τα καθαλου would naturally seem microscopic to Antiochus. Both theories were practically as dead in his time as those of Thales or Anaxagoras. The confusion must not be laid at Cicero's door, for Antiochus in reconciling his own dialectics with Plato's must have been driven to desperate shifts. Cicero's very knowledge of Plato has, however, probably led him to intensify what inconsistency there was in Antiochus, who would have glided over Plato's opinions with a much more cautious step.

§31. *Sensus omnis hebetes*: this stands in contradiction to the whole Antiochean view as given in II. 12—64, cf. esp. 19 *sensibus quorum ita clara et certa iudicia sunt*, etc.: Antiochus would probably defend his agreement with Plato by asserting that though sense is naturally dull, reason may sift out the certain from the uncertain. *Res eas ... quae essent aut ita*: Halm by following his pet MS. without regard to the meaning of Cic. has greatly increased the difficulty of the passage. He reads *res ullas ... quod aut ita essent*; thus making Antiochus assert that *no* true information can be got from sensation, whereas, as we shall see in the *Lucullus*, he really divided sensations into true and false. I believe that we have a mixture here of Antiochus' real view with Cicero's reminiscences of the *Theaetetus* and of Xenocrates; see below. *Nec percipere*: for this see *Lucullus* passim. Christ's conj. *percipi, quod perceptio sit mentis non sensuum*, which Halm seems to approve, is a wanton corruption of the text, cf. II. 101 *neget rem ullam percipi posse sensibus*, so 21, 119 (just like *ratione percipi* 91), also I. 41 *sensu comprehensum*. *Subiectae sensibus*: cf. II. 74 and Sext. Emp. *Adv. Math.* VIII. 9, τα 'υποπιπτοντα τη αισθησει. *Aut ita mobiles*, etc.: this strongly reminds one of the *Theaetetus*, esp. 160 D sq. For *constans* cf. εστηκος, which so often occurs there and in the *Sophistes*. *Ne idem*: Manut. for MSS. *eidem*. In the *Theaetetus*, Heraclitus' theory of flux is carried to such an extent as to destroy the self-identity of things; even the word εμε is stated to be an absurdity, since it implies a permanent subject, whereas the subject is changing from moment to moment; the expression therefore ought to be τους εμε. *Continenter*: ουνεχως; cf. Simplicius quoted in Grote's Plato, I. p. 37, about Heraclitus, εν μεταβολη γαρ συνεχει τα οντα. *Laberentur et fluerent*: cf. the phrases ‘ροη, παντα ‘ρει, ‘οιον ‘ρευματα κινεισθαι τα παντα, etc., which are scattered thickly over the *Theaet.* and the ancient texts about Heraclitus; also a very similar passage in *Orator* 10. *Opinabilem*: δοξαστην, so *opinabile* = δοξαστον in Cic. *Tim* ch. II. The term was largely used by Xenocrates (R. and P. 243—247), Arist. too distinguishes between the δοξαστον and the επιστητον, e.g *Analyt. Post.* I. 33 (qu. R. and P. 264).

§32. For this cf. *D.F.* IV. 8—10. *Notionibus*: so one MS. for *motionibus* which the rest have. *Notio* is Cicero's regular translation for εννοια, which is Stoic. This statement might have been made both by Aristotle and Plato, though each would put a separate meaning on the word *notio*. Επιστημη in Plato is of the ιδεαι only, while in Aristotle it is τον καθολου; cf. *Anal. Post.* I. 33 (R. and P. 264), λεγω νουν αρχην επιστημης. *Definitiones rerum*: these must be carefully distinguished fiom *definitiones nominum*, see the distinction drawn after Aristotle in R. and P. 265, note b. The *definitio rei* really involves the whole of philosophy with Plato and Aristotle (one might almost add, with moderns too). Its importance to Plato may be seen from the *Politicus* and *Sophistes*, to Aristotle from the passages quoted in R. and P. pp. 265, 271, whose notes will make the subject as clear as it can be made to any one who has not a knowledge of the whole of Aristotle's philosophy. *Verborum explicatio*: this is quite a different thing from those *definitiones nominum* just referred to; it is *derivation*, which does not necessitate definition. ετυμολογιαν: this is almost entirely Stoic. The word is foreign to the Classic Greek Prose, as are ετυμος and all its derivatives. (Ετυμως means "etymologically" in the *De Mundo*, which however is not Aristotle's). The word ετυμολογια is itself not frequent in the older Stoics, who use rather ονοματων ορθοτης (Diog. Laert. VII. 83), the title of their books on the subject preserved by Diog. is generally "περι των ετυμολογικων" The systematic pursuit of etymology was not earlier than Chrysippus, when it became distinctive of the Stoic school, though Zeno and Cleanthes had given the first impulse (*N.D.* III. 63). Specimens of Stoic etymology are given in *N.D.* II. and ridiculed in *N.D.* III. (cf. esp. 62 *in enodandis nominibus quod miserandum sit laboratis*). *Post argumentis et quasi rerum notis ducibus*: the use of etymology in rhetoric in order to prove something about the thing denoted by the word is well illustrated in *Topica* 10, 35. In this rhetorical sense Cic. rejects the translation *veriloquium* of ετυμολογια and adopts *notatio*, the *rerum nota* (Greek συμβολον) being the name so explained (*Top.* 35). Varro translated ετυμολογια by *originatio* (Quintil. I. 6, 28). Aristotle had already laid down rules for this rhetorical use of etymology, and Plato also incidentally adopts it, so it may speciously be said to belong to the old Academico-Peripatetic school. A closer examination of authorities would have led Halm to retract his bad em. *notationibus* for *notas ducibus*, the word *notatio* is used for the whole science of etymology, and not for particular derivations, while Cic. in numerous passages (e.g. *D.F.* V. 74) describes *verba* or *nomina* as *rerum notae*. Berkley's *nodis* for *notis* has no support, (*enodatio nominum* in *N.D.* III. 62 is quite different). One more remark, and I conclude this wearisome note. The *quasi* marks *rerum nota* as an unfamiliar trans. of συμβολον. Davies therefore ought not to have placed it before *ducibus*, which word, strong as the metaphor is, requires no qualification, see a good instance in *T.D.* I. 27. *Itaque tradebatur*: so Halm improves on Madvig's *ita* for *in qua* of the MSS., which cannot be defended. Orelli's reference to 30 *pars* for an antecedent to *qua* (*in ea parte in qua*) is violent, while Goerenz's resort to *partem rerum opinabilem* is simply silly. Manut. conj. *in quo*, Cic. does often use the neut. pronoun, as in *Orator* 3, but not quite thus. I have sometimes thought that Cic. wrote *haec, inquam* (cf. *huic* below). *Dialecticae*: as λογικη had not been Latinised, Cic. is obliged to use this word to denote λογικη, of which διαλεκτικη is really one subdivision with the Stoics and Antiochus, ‘ρητορικη which is mentioned in the next sentence being the other; see Zeller 69, 70. *Orationis ratione conclusae*: speech drawn up in a syllogistic form which becomes *oratio perpetua* under the influence of ‘ρητορικη. *Quasi ex altera parte*: a trans. of Aristotle's αντιστροφος in the beginning of the *Rhetoric*. *Oratoria*: Halm brackets this word; cf. however a close parallel in *Brut.* 261 *oratorio ornamenta dicendi*. The construction is simply a variation of Cic.'s favourite double genitive (*T.D.* III. 39), *oratoria* being put for *oratoris*. *Ad persuadendum*: το πιθανον is with Arist. and all ancient authorities the one aim of ‘ρητορικη.

§§33—42. Part v. of Varro's exposition: the departures from the old Academico-Peripatetic school. Summary. Arist. crushed the ιδεαι of Plato, Theophrastus weakened the power of virtue (33). Strato abandoned ethics for physics, Speusippus, Xenocrates, Polemo, Crates, Crantor faithfully kept the old tradition, to which Zeno and Arcesilas, pupils of Polemo, were both disloyal (34). Zeno maintained that nothing but virtue could influence happiness, and would allow the name *good* to nothing else (35). All other things he divided into three classes, some were in accordance with nature, some at discord with nature, and some were neutral. To the first class he assigned a positive value, and called them *preferred* to the second a negative value and called them *rejected*, to the third no value whatever—mere verbal alterations on the old scheme (36, 37). Though the terms *right action* and *sin* belong only to virtue and vice, he thought there was an appropriate action (*officium*) and an inappropriate, which concerned things *preferred* and things *rejected* (37). He made *all* virtue reside in the reason, and considered not the *practice* but the mere *possession* of virtue to be the important thing, although the possession could not but lead to the practice (38). All emotion he regarded as unnatural and immoral (38, 39). In physics he discarded the fifth element, and believed fire to be the universal substance, while he would not allow the existence of anything incorporeal (39). In dialectic he analysed sensation into two parts, an impulse from without, and a succeeding judgment of the mind, in passing which the will was entirely free (40). Sensations (*visa*) he divided into the true and the untrue; if the examination gone through by the mind proved irrefragably the truth of a sensation he called it *Knowledge*, if otherwise, *Ignorance* (41). *Perception*, thus defined, he regarded as morally neither right nor wrong but as the sole ultimate basis of truth. Rashness in giving assent to phenomena, and all other defects in the application to them of the reason he thought could not coexist with virtue and perfect wisdom (42).

§33. *Haec erat illis forma*: so Madv. *Em.* 118 for MSS. *prima*, comparing *formulam* in 17, also *D.F.* IV. 19, V. 9, *T.D.* III. 38, to which add *Ac.* I. 23. See other em. in Halm. Goer. proposes to keep the MSS. reading and supply *pars*, as usual. His power of *supplying* is unlimited. There is a curious similarity between the difficulties involved in the MSS. readings in 6, 15, 32 and here. *Immutationes*: so Dav. for *disputationes*, approved by Madv. *Em.* 119 who remarks that the phrase *disputationes philosophiae* would not be Latin. The em. is rendered almost certain by *mutavit* in 40, *commutatio* in 42, and *De Leg.* I. 38. Halm's odd em. *dissupationes*, so much admired by his reviewer in Schneidewin's *Philologus*, needs support, which it certainly does not receive from the one passage Halm quotes, *De Or.* III. 207. *Et recte*: for the *et* cf. *et merito*, which begins one of Propertius' elegies. *Auctoritas*: "system". *Inquit*: sc. Atticus of course. Goer., on account of the omission of *igitur* after Aristoteles, supposes Varro's speech to begin here. To the objection that Varro (who in 8 says *nihil enim meorum magno opere miror*) would not eulogise himself quite so unblushingly, Goer. feebly replies that the eulogy is meant for Antiochus, whom Varro is copying. *Aristoteles*: after this the copyist of Halm's G. alone, and evidently on his own conjecture, inserts *igitur*, which H. adopts. Varro's resumption of his exposition is certainly abrupt, but if chapter IX. ought to begin here, as Halm supposes, a reader would not be much incommoded. *Labefactavit*, that Antiochus still continued to include Aristotle in the supposed old Academico-Peripatetic school can only be explained by the fact that he considered ethical resemblances as of supreme importance, cf. the strong statement of Varro in Aug. XIX. 1 *nulla est causa philosophandi nisi finis boni.* *Divinum*: see R. and P. 210 for a full examination of the relation in which Plato's ιδεαι stand to his notion of the deity. *Suavis*: his constant epithet, see Gellius qu. R. and P. 327. His real name was not Theophrastus, he was called so from his style (cf. *loquendi nitor ille divinus*, Quint. X. 1, 83). For *suavis* of style cf. *Orat.* 161, *Brut.* 120. *Negavit*: for his various offences see *D.F.* V. 12 sq., *T.D.* V. 25, 85. There is no reason to suppose that he departed very widely from the Aristotelian ethics; we have here a Stoic view of him transmitted through Antiochus. In II. 134 Cic. speaks very differently of him. Between the particular tenet here mentioned and that of Antiochus in 22 the difference is merely verbal. *Beate* *vivere*: the only translation of ευδαιμονιαν. Cic. *N.D.* I. 95 suggests *beatitas* and *beatitudo* but does not elsewhere employ them.

§34. *Strato*: see II. 121. The statement in the text is not quite true for Diog. V. 58, 59 preserves the titles of at least seven ethical works, while Stob. II. 6, 4 quotes his definition of the αγαθον. *Diligenter ... tuebantur*: far from true as it stands, Polemo was an inchoate Stoic, cf. Diog. Laert. IV. 18, *Ac.* II. 131, *D.F.* II. 34, and R. and P. *Congregati*: "*all* in the Academic fold," cf. *Lael.* 69, *in nostro, ut ita dicam, grege.* Of Crates and Crantor little is known. *Polemonem ... Zeno et Arcesilas*: scarcely true, for Polemo was merely one of Zeno's many teachers (Diog. VII. 2, 3), while he is not mentioned by Diog. at all among the teachers of Arcesilas. The fact is that we have a mere theory, which accounts for the split of Stoicism from Academicism by the rivalry of two fellow pupils. Cf. Numenius in Euseb. *Praep. Ev.* XIV. 5, συμφοιτωντες παρα Πολεμωνι εφιλο τιμηθησαν. Dates are against the theory, see Zeller 500.

§35. *Anteiret aetate*: Arcesilas was born about 315, Zeno about 350, though the dates are uncertain. *Dissereret*: was a deep reasoner. Bentl. missing the meaning conj. *definiret. Peracute moveretur*: Bentl. *partiretur*; this with *definiret* above well illustrates his licence in emendations. Halm ought not to have doubted the soundness of the text, the words refer not to the emotional, but to the intellectual side of Zeno's nature. The very expression occurs *Ad Fam.* XV. 21, 4, see other close parallels in n. on II. 37. *Nervos ... inciderit*: same metaphor in *Philipp.* XII. 8, cf. also *T.D.* II. 27 *nervos virtutis elidere,* III. 83 *stirpis aegritudinis elidere.* (In both these passages Madv. *Em. Liv.* 135 reads *elegere* for *elidere,* I cannot believe that he is right). Plato uses νευρα εκτεμνειν metaphorically. Notice *inciderit* but *poneret.* There is no need to alter (as Manut., Lamb., Dav.) for the sequence is not uncommon in Cic., e.g. *D.F.* III. 33. *Omnia, quae*: MSS. *quaeque,* which edd. used to take for *quaecunque.* Cf. Goerenz's statement "*negari omnino nequit hac vi saepius pronomen illud reperiri*" with Madvig's utter refutation in the sixth Excursus to his *D.F. Solum et unum bonum*: for the Stoic ethics the student must in general consult R. and P. and Zeller for himself. I can only treat such points as are involved in the special difficulties of the *Academica*.

§36. *Cetera*: Stoic αδιαφορα, the presence or absence of which cannot affect happiness. The Stoics loudly protested against their being called either *bona* or *mala,* and this question was one of the great battle grounds of the later Greek philosophy. *Secundum naturam ... contraria*: Gr. κατα φυσιν, παρα φυσιν. *His ipsis ... numerabat*: I see no reason for placing this sentence after the words *quae minoris* below (with Christ) or for suspecting its genuineness (with Halm). The word *media* is the Gk. μεσα, which word however is not usually applied to *things,* but to *actions. Sumenda*: Gk. ληπτα. *Aestimatione*: αξια, positive value. *Contraque contraria*: Cic. here as in *D.F.* III. 50 feels the need of a word to express απαξια (negative value). (Madv. in his note on that passage coins the word *inaestimatio.*) *Ponebat esse*: cf. 19, *M.D.F.* V. 73.

§37. To cope thoroughly with the extraordinary difficulties of this section the student must read the whole of the chapters on Stoic ethics in Zeller and Ritter and Preller. There is no royal road to the knowledge, which it would be absurd to attempt to convey in these notes. Assuming a general acquaintance with Stoic ethics, I set out the difficulties thus: Cic. appears at first sight to have made the αποπροηγμενα a subdivision of the ληπτα (*sumenda*), the two being utterly different. I admit, with Madv. (*D.F.* III. 50), that there is no reason for suspecting the text to be corrupt, the heroic remedy of Dav., therefore, who reads *media* in the place of *sumenda,* must be rejected. Nor can anything be said for Goerenz's plan, who distorts the Stoic philosophy in order to save Cicero's consistency. On the other hand, I do not believe that Cic. could so utterly misunderstand one of the cardinal and best known doctrines of Stoicism, as to think even for a moment that the αποπροηγμενα formed a branch of the ληπτα. This view of Madvig's is strongly opposed to the fact that Cic. in 36 had explained with perfect correctness the Stoic theory of the αδιαφορα, nor is there anywhere in the numerous passages where he touches on the theory any trace of the same error. My explanation is that Cic. began with the intention to speak of the *sumenda* only and then rapidly extended his thought so as to embrace the whole class of αδιαφορα, which he accordingly dealt with in the latter part of the same sentence and in the succeeding sentence. (The remainder has its own difficulties, which I defer for the present.) Cic. therefore is chargeable not with ignorance of Stoicism but with careless writing. A striking parallel occurs in *D.F.* III. 52, *quae secundum locum obtinent,* προηγμενα *id est producta nominentur, quae vel ita appellemus, vel promota et remota.* If this language be closely pressed, the αποπροηγμενα are made of a subdivision of the προηγμενα, though no sensible reader would suppose Cic. to have had that intention. So if his words in *D.F.* V. 90 be pressed, the *sumenda* are made to include both *producta* and *reducta*, in *D.F.* III. 16 *appeterent* includes *fugerent, ibid.* II. 86 the opposite of *beata vita* is abruptly introduced. So *D.F.* II. 88 *frui dolore* must be construed together, and *ibid.* II. 73 *pudor modestia pudicitia* are said *coerceri*, the writer's thoughts having drifted on rapidly to the vices which are opposite to these virtues.

I now pass on to a second class of difficulties. Supposing that by *ex iis* Cic. means *mediis*, and not *sumendis*, about which he had intended to talk when he began the sentence; I believe that *pluris aestimanda* and *minoris aestimanda* simply indicate the αξια and απαξια of the Greek, *not* different degrees of αξια (positive value). That *minor aestimatio* should mean απαξια need not surprise us when we reflect (1) on the excessive difficulty there was in expressing this απαξια or negative value in Latin, a difficulty I have already observed on 36; (2) on the strong negative meaning which *minor* bears in Latin, e.g. *sin minus* in Cic. means "but if not." Even the Greeks fall victims to the task of expressing απαξια. Stobaeus, in a passage closely resembling ours makes ελαττων αξια equivalent to πολλη απαξια (II. 6, 6), while Sext. Emp. after rightly defining αποπροηγμενα as τα ῾ικανην απαξιαν εχοντα (*Adv. Math.* XI. 62— 64) again speaks of them as τα μη ῾ικανην εχοντα αξιαν (*Pyrrhon. Hypot.* III. 191) words which usually have an opposite meaning. Now I contend that Cicero's words *minoris aestimanda* bear quite as strong a negative meaning as the phrase of Sextus, τα μη ῾ικανην αξιαν εχοντα. I therefore conclude that Cicero has striven, so far as the Latin language allowed, to express the Stoic doctrine that, of the αδιαφορα, some have αξια while others have απαξια. He may fairly claim to have applied to his words the rule "*re intellecta in verborum usu faciles esse debemus*" (*D.F.* III. 52). There is quite as good ground for accusing Sextus and Stobaeus of misunderstanding the Stoics as there is for accusing Cicero. There are difficulties connected with the terms ῾ικανη αξια and ῾ικανη απαξια which are not satisfactorily treated in the ordinary sources of information; I regret that my space forbids me to attempt the elucidation of them. The student will find valuable aid in the notes of Madv. on the passages of the *D.F.* quoted in this note. *Non tam rebus quam vocabulis*: Cic. frequently repeats this assertion of Antiochus, who, having stolen the clothes of the Stoics, proceeded to prove that they had never properly belonged to the Stoics at all. *Inter recte factum atque peccatum*: Stob. speaks II. 6, 6 of τα μεταξυ αρετης και κακιας. (This does not contradict his words a little earlier, II. 6, 5, αρετης δε και κακιας ουδεν μεταξυ, which have regard to divisions of men, not of actions. Diog. Laert., however, VII. 127, distinctly contradicts Cic. and Stob., see R. and P. 393.) *Recte factum* = κατορθωμα, *peccatum* = ῾αμαρτημα, *officium* = καθηκον (cf. R. and P. 388—394, Zeller 238—248, 268—272). *Servata praetermissaque*: MSS. have *et* before *servata*, which all edd. since Lamb. eject. Where *et* and *que* correspond in Cic., the *que* is always an afterthought, added in oblivion of the *et*. With two nouns, adjectives, adverbs, or participles, this oblivion is barely possible, but when the conjunctions go with separate *clauses* it is possible. Cf. 43 and *M.D.F.* V. 64.

§38. *Sed quasdam virtutes*: see 20. This passage requires careful construing: after *quasdam virtutes* not the whole phrase *in ratione esse dicerent* must be repeated but *dicerent* merely, since only the *virtutes natura perfectae*, the διανοητικαι αρεται of Arist., could be said to belong to the reason, while the *virtutes more perfectae* are Aristotle's ηθικαι αρεται. Trans. "but spoke of certain excellences as perfected by the reason, or (as the case might be) by habit." *Ea genera virtutum*: both Plato and Arist. roughly divided the nature of man into two parts, the intellectual and the emotional, the former being made to govern, the latter to obey (cf. *T.D.* II. 47, and Arist. το μεν ῾ως λογον εχον, το δε επιπειθες λογωι); Zeno however asserted the nature of man to be one and indivisible and to consist solely of Reason, to which he gave the name ʽηγεμονικον (Zeller 203 sq.). Virtue also became for him one and indivisible (Zeller 248, *D.F.* III. *passim*). When the ʽηγεμονικον was in a perfect state, there was virtue, when it became disordered there was vice or emotion. The battle between virtue and vice therefore did not resemble a war between two separate powers, as in Plato and Aristotle, but a civil war carried on in one and the same country. *Virtutis usum*: cf. the description of Aristotle's *finis* in *D.F.* II. 19. *Ipsum habitum*: the mere possession. So Plato, *Theaetet.* 197 B, uses the word ʽεξις, a use which must be clearly distinguished from the later sense found in the *Ethics* of Arist. In this sense virtue is *not* a ʽεξις, according to the Stoics, but a διαθεσις (Stob. II. 6, 5, Diog. VII. 89; yet Diog. sometimes speaks of virtue loosely as a ʽεξις, VII. 92, 93; cf. Zeller 249, with footnotes). *Nec virtutem cuiquam adesse ... uteretur*: cf. Stob. II. 6, 6 δυο γενη των ανθρωπων ειναι το μεν των σπουδαιων, το δε των φαυλων, και το μεν των σπουδαιων δια παντος του βιου χρησθαι ταις αρεταις, το δε των φαυλων ταις κακιαις. *Perturbationem*: I am surprised that Halm after the fine note of Wesenberg, printed on p. 324 of the same volume in which Halm's text of the *Acad.* appears, should read the plural *perturbationes*, a conj. of Walker. *Perturbationem* means emotion in the abstract; *perturbationes* below, particular emotions. There is exactly the same transition in *T.D.* III. 23, 24, IV. 59, 65, V. 43, while *perturbatio* is used, in the same sense as here, in at least five other passages of the *T.D.*, i.e. IV. 8, 11, 24, 57, 82. *Quasi mortis*: a trans. of Stoic παθεσι, which Cic. rejects in *D.F.* III. 35. *Voluit carere sapientem*: emotion being a disturbance of equilibrium in the reason, and perfect reason being virtue (20), it follows that the Stoic sapiens must be emotionless (Zeller 228 sq.). All emotions are reasonless; ʽηδονη or *laetitia* for instance is αλογος επαρσις. (*T.D.* Books III. and IV. treat largely of the Stoic view of emotions.) Wesenberg, *Em.* to the *T.D.* III. p. 8, says Cic. always uses *efferri laetitia* but *ferri libidine*.

§39. *Aliaque in parte*: so Plato, *Tim.* 69 C, *Rep.* 436, 441, Arist. *De Anima* II. 3, etc.; cf. *T.D.* I. 20. *Voluntarias*: the whole aim of the Stoic theory of the emotions was to bring them under the predominance of the will. How the moral freedom of the will was reconciled with the general Stoic fatalism we are not told. *Opinionisque iudicio suscipi*: all emotion arose, said the Stoics, from a false judgment about some external object; cf. Diog. VII. 111. τα παθη κρισεις ειναι. Instances of each in Zeller 233. For *iudicio* cf. *D.F.* III. 35, *T.D.* III. 61, IV. 14, 15, 18. *Intemperantiam*: the same in *T.D.* IV. 22, Gk. ακολασια, see Zeller 232. *Quintam naturam*: the πεμπτη ουσια or πεμπτον σωμα of Aristotle, who proves its existence in *De Coelo* I. 2, in a curious and recondite fashion. Cic. is certainly wrong in stating that Arist. derived *mind* from this fifth element, though the finest and highest of material substances. He always guards himself from assigning a material origin to mind. Cic. repeats the error in *T.D.* I. 22, 41, 65, *D.F.* IV. 12. On this last passage Madv. has an important note, but he fails to recognise the essential fact, which is clear from Stob. I. 41, 33, that the Peripatetics of the time were in the habit of deriving the mind from αιθηρ, which is the very name that Aristotle gives to the fifth element (σωμα αιθεριον in the *De Coelo*), and of giving this out to be Aristotle's opinion. The error once made, no one could correct it, for there were a hundred influences at work to confirm it, while the works of Aristotle had fallen into a strange oblivion. I cannot here give an exhaustive account of these influences, but will mention a few. Stoicism had at the time succeeded in powerfully influencing every other sect, and it placed νους εν αιθερι (see Plutarch, qu. R. and P. 375). It had destroyed the belief in immaterial existence The notion that νους or ψυχη came from αιθηρ was also fostered by the language of Plato. He had spoken of the soul as αεικινητος in passages which were well known to Cic. and had taken great hold on his mind One from the *Phaedrus* 245 C is translated twice, in *Somnium Scipionis* (*De Rep.* VI.), and *T.D.* I. 53 sq. Now the only thing with Aristotle which is αεικινητος in eternal perfect circular motion (for to the ancients circular motion is alone perfect and eternal), is the αιθηρ or πεμπτον σωμα, that fiery external rim of the universe of which the stars are mere nodes, and with which they revolve. How natural then, in the absence of Aristotle's works, to conclude that the αεικινητος ψυχη of Plato came from the αεικινητος αιθηρ of Aristotle! Arist. had guarded himself by saying that the soul as an αρχη κινησεως must be ακινητος, but Cic. had no means of knowing this (see Stob. I. 41, 36). Again, Plato had often spoken of souls at death flying away to the outer circle of the universe, as though to their natural home, just where Arist. placed his πεμπτον σωμα Any one who will compare *T.D.* I. 43 with the *Somn. Scipionis* will see what power this had over Cicero. Further, Cic. would naturally link the mind in its origin with the stars which both Plato and Arist. looked on as divine (cf. *Somn. Scip.* 15) These considerations will be enough to show that neither Cic. nor Antiochus, whom Madv. considers responsible for the error, could have escaped it in any way not superhuman except by the recovery of Aristotle's lost works, which did not happen till too late. *Sensus*: we seem here to have a remnant of the distinction drawn by Arist. between animal heat and other heat, the former being αναλογον τω των αστρων στοιχειω (*De Gen. An.* II. 3, qu. R. and P. 299). *Ignem*: the Stoics made no difference, except one of degree, between αιθηρ and πυρ, see Zeller 189, 190. *Ipsam naturam*: πυρ is κατ' εξοχην στοιχειον (Stob. I. 10, 16), and is the first thing generated from the απoιος 'υλη; from it comes air, from air water, from water earth (Diog. Laert. VII. 136, 137) The fire is λογικον, from it comes the 'ηγεμονικον of man, which comprises within it all powers of sensation and thought. These notions came from Heraclitus who was a great hero of the Stoics (Zeller ch. VIII. with notes) For his view of sensation and thought see Sextus *Adv. Math.* VII. 127—129, qu. by R. and P. 21. The Stoics probably misunderstood him; cf. R. and P. "Heraclitus," and Grote's *Plato* I. 34 sq. *Expers corporis*: for Stoic materialism see Zeller, pp. 120 sq. The necessity of a connection between the perceiving mind and the things perceived followed from old physical principles such as that of Democritus (ου γαρ εγχωρειν τα 'ετερα και διαφεροντα πασχειν 'υπ' αλληλων, qu. from Arist. *De Gen. et Corr.* I. 7, by R. and P. 43), the same is affirmed loosely of all the old φυσικοι, (Sextus *Adv. Math.* VII. 116), and by Empedocles in his lines γαιαι μεν γαιαν οπωπαμεν, etc. Plato in the *Timaeus* fosters the same notion, though in a different way. The Stoics simply followed out boldly that line of thought. *Xenocrates*: see II. 124, n. *Superiores*: merely the supposed old Academico-Peripatetic school. *Posse esse non corpus*: there is no ultimate difference between Force and Matter in the Stoic scheme, see Zeller, pp. 134, 135.

§40. *Iunctos*: how can anything be a *compound* of one thing? The notion that *iunctos* could mean *aptos* (R. and P. 366) is untenable. I entirely agree with Madv. (first Excursus to his *D.F.*) that we have here an anacoluthon. Cic. meant to say *iunctos e quadam impulsione et ex assensu animorum*, but having to explain φαντασια was obliged to break off and resume at *sed ad haec*. The explanation of a Greek term causes a very similar anacoluthon in *De Off.* I. 153. Schuppe, *De Anacoluthis Ciceronianis* p. 9, agrees with Madv. For the expression cf. *D.F.* II. 44 *e duplici genere voluptatis coniunctus* Ernesti em. *cunctos*, Dav. *punctos, ingeniose ille quidem* says Halm, *pessime* I should say. Φαντασιαν: a full and clear account of Stoic theories of sensation is given by Zeller, ch. V., R. and P. 365 sq. *Nos appellemus licet*: the same turn of expression occurs *D.F.* III. 21, IV. 74. *Hoc verbum quidem hoc quidem* probably ought to be read, see 18. *Adsensionem* = συγκαταθεσιν. *In nobis positam*: the usual expression for freedom of the will, cf. II. 37, *De Fato*, 42, 43 (a very important passage). The actual sensation is involuntary (ακουσιον Sext. Emp. *Adv. Math.* VIII. 397). *Tironum causa* I note that the Stoics sometimes speak of the assent of the mind as *involuntary,* while the καταληπτικη φαντασια *compels* assent (see II. 38). This is, however, only true of the healthy reason, the unhealthy may refuse assent.

§41. *Visis non omnibus*: while Epicurus defended the truth of all sensations, Zeno abandoned the weak positions to the sceptic and retired to the inner citadel of the καταληπτικη φαντασια. *Declarationem*: εναργειαν, a term alike Stoic, Epicurean, and Academic, see n. on II. 17. *Earum rerum*: only this class of sensations gives correct information of the *things* lying behind. *Ipsum per se*: i.e. its whole truth lies in its own εναργεια, which requires no corroboration from without. *Comprehendibile*: this form has better MSS. authority than the vulg *comprehensibile*. Goerenz's note on these words is worth reading as a philological curiosity *Nos vero, inquit*: Halm with Manut. writes *inquam*. Why change? Atticus answers as in 14, 25, 33. Καταληπτον: strictly the *thing* which emits the *visum* is said to be καταληπτον, but, as we shall see in the *Lucullus*, the sensation and the thing from which it proceeds are often confused. *Comprehensionem*: this word properly denotes the process of perception in the abstract, not the individual perception. The Greeks, however, themselves use καταληψις for καταληπτικη φαντασια very often. *Quae manu prehenderentur*: see II. 145. *Nova enim dicebat*: an admission not often made by Cic., who usually contends, with Antiochus, that Zeno merely renamed old doctrines (cf. 43). *Sensum*: so Stob., I. 41, 25 applies the term αισθησις to the φαντασια. *Scientiam*: the word επιστημη is used in two ways by the

Stoics, (1) to denote a number of coordinated or systematised perceptions (καταληψεις or καταληπτικαι φαντασιαι) sometimes also called τεχνη (cf. Sext. *Pyrrh. Hyp.* III. 188 τεχνην δε ειναι συστημα εκ καταληψεων συγγεγυμνασμενων); (2) to denote a single perception, which use is copied by Cic. and may be seen in several passages quoted by Zeller 80. *Ut convelli ratione non posset*: here is a trace of later Stoicism. To Zeno all καταληπτικαι φαντασιαι were ασφαλεις, αμεταπτωτοι ΄υπο λογου. Later Stoics, however, allowed that some of them were not impervious to logical tests; see Sext. *Adv. Math.* VII. 253, qu. Zeller 88. Thus every καταληπτικη φαντασια, instead of carrying with it its own evidence, had to pass through the fire of sceptical criticism before it could be believed. This was, as Zeller remarks, equivalent to giving up all that was valuable in the Stoic theory. *Inscientiam: ex qua exsisteret*: I know nothing like this in the Stoic texts; αμαθια is very seldom talked of there. *Opinio*: δοξα, see Zeller and cf. *Ac.* II. 52, *T.D.* II. 52, IV. 15, 26.

§42. *Inter scientiam*: so Sextus *Adv. Math.* VII. 151 speaks of επιστημην και δοξαν και την εν μεθοπιαι τουτων καταληψιν. *Soli*: Halm, I know not why, suspects this and Christ gives *solum ei*. *Non quod omnia*: the meaning is that the reason must generalize on separate sensations and combine them before we can know thoroughly any one *thing*. This will appear if the whole sentence be read *uno haustu*; Zeller p. 78 seems to take the same view, but I have not come across anything exactly like this in the Greek. *Quasi*: this points out *normam* as a trans. of some Gk. word, κριτηριον perhaps, or γνωμων or κανων. *Notiones rerum*: Stoic εννοιαι; Zeller 81—84, R. and P. 367, 368. *Quodque natura*: the omission of *eam* is strange; Faber supplies it. *Imprimerentur*: the terms εναπεσφραγισμενη, εναπομεμαγμενη, εντετυπωμενη occur constantly, but generally in relation to φαντασιαι, not to εννοιαι. *Non principia solum*: there seems to be a ref. to those αρχαι της αποδειξεως of Arist. which, induced from experience and incapable of proof, are the bases of all proof. (See Grote's *Essay on the Origin of Knowledge*, first printed in Bain's *Mental and Moral Science*, now re-published in Grote's *Aristotle*.) Zeno's εννοιαι were all this and more. *Reperiuntur*: two things vex the edd. (1) the change from *oratio obliqua* to *recta*, which however has repeatedly taken place during Varro's exposition, and for which see *M.D.F.* I. 30, III. 49; (2) the phrase *reperire viam*, which seems to me sound enough. Dav., Halm give *aperirentur*. There is no MSS. variant. *Aliena*: cf. *alienatos D.F.* III. 18. *A virtute sapientiaque removebat*: cf. *sapiens numquam fallitur in iudicando D.F.* III. 59. The *firma adsensia* is opposed to *imbecilla* 41. For the *adsensio* of the *sapiens* see Zeller 87. More information on the subject-matter of this section will be found in my notes on the first part of the *Lucullus*. *In his constitit*: cf. II. 134.

§§43—end. Cicero's historical justification of the New Academy. Summary. Arcesilas' philosophy was due to no mere passion for victory in argument, but to the obscurity of phenomena, which had led the ancients to despair of knowledge (44). He even abandoned the one tenet held by Socrates to be certain; and maintained that since arguments of equal strength could be urged in favour of the truth or falsehood of phenomena, the proper course to take was to suspend judgment entirely (45). His views were really in harmony with those of Plato, and were carried on by Carneades (46).

§43. *Breviter*: MSS. *et breviter;* see 37. *Tunc*: rare before a consonant; see Munro on *Lucr.* I. 130. *Verum esse [autem] arbitror*: in deference to Halm I bracket *autem*, but I still think the MSS. reading defensible, if *verum* be taken as the neut. adj. and not as meaning *but*. Translate: "Yet I think the truth to be ... that it is to be thought," etc. The edd. seem to have thought that *esse* was needed to go with *putandam*. This is a total mistake; cf. *ait ... putandam*, without *esse* II. 15, *aiebas removendum* II. 74; a hundred other passages might be quoted from Cic.

§44. *Non pertinacia aut studio vincendi*: for these words see n. on II. 14. The sincerity of Arcesilas is defended also in II. 76. *Obscuritate*: a side-blow at *declaratio* 41. *Confessionem ignorationis*: see 16. Socrates was far from being a sceptic, as Cic. supposes; see note on II. 74. *Et iam ante Socratem*: MSS. *veluti amantes Socratem;* Democritus (460—357 B.C.) was really very little older than Socrates (468—

399) who died nearly sixty years before him. *Omnis paene veteres*: the statement is audaciously inexact, and is criticised II. 14. None of these were sceptics; for Democritus see my note on II. 73, for Empedocles on II. 74, for Anaxagoras on II. 72. *Nihil cognosci, nihil penipi, nihil sciri*: the verbs are all equivalent; cf. *D.F.* III. 15 *equidem soleo etiam quod uno Graeci ... idem pluribus verbis exponere. Angustos sensus*: Cic. is thinking of the famous lines of Empedocles στεινοποι μεν γαρ παλαμαι κ.τ.λ. R. and P. 107. *Brevia curricula vitae*: cf. Empedocles' παυρον δε ζωης αβιου μερος. Is there an allusion in *curricula* to Lucretius' *lampada vitai tradunt*, etc.? *In profundo*: Dem. εν βυθω, cf. II. 32. The common trans. "well" is weak, "abyss" would suit better. *Institutis*: νομω of Democritus, see R. and P. 50. Goerenz's note here is an extraordinary display of ignorance. *Deinceps omnia*: παντα εφεξης there is no need to read *denique* for *deinceps* as Bentl., Halm. *Circumfusa tenebris*: an allusion to the σκοτιη γνωσις of Democr., see II. 73. *Dixerunt*: Halm brackets this because of *dixerunt* above, parts of the verb *dicere* are however often thus repeated by Cic.

§45. *Ne illud quidem*: cf. 16. *Latere censebat* Goer. omitted *censebat* though in most MSS. Orelli and Klotz followed as usual. For the sense II. 122. *Cohibereque*: Gk. επεχειν, which we shall have to explain in the *Lucullus*. *Temeritatem ... turpius*: for these expressions, see II. 66, note. *Praecurrere*: as was the case with the dogmatists. *Paria momenta*: this is undiluted scepticism, and excludes even the possibility of the *probabile* which Carneades put forward. For the doctrine cf. II. 124, for the expression Euseb. *Praep. Evan.* XIV. c. 4 (from Numenius) of Arcesilas, ειναι γαρ παντα ακαταληπτα και τους εις εκατερα λογους ισοκρατεις αλληλοις, Sextus *Adv. Math.* IX. 207 ισοσθενεις λογοι; in the latter writer the word ισοσθενεια very frequently occurs in the same sense, e g *Pyrrhon. Hyp.* I. 8 (add *N.D.* I. 10, *rationis momenta*)

§46. *Platonem*: to his works both dogmatists and sceptics appealed, Sextus *Pyrrhon. Hyp.* I. 221 τον Πλατωνα οιν ῾οι μεν δογματικον εφασαν ειναι, ῾οι δε απο ητικον, ῾οι δε κατα μεν τι απορητικον, κατα δε τι δογματικον. Stobaeus II. 6, 4 neatly slips out of the difficulty; Πλατων πολυφωνος ων, ουχ ῾ως τινες οιονται πολυδοξος. *Exposuisti*: Durand's necessary em., approved by Krische, Halm, etc. for MSS. *exposui*. *Zenone*: see Introd. p. 5.

NOTES ON THE FRAGMENTS.

BOOK I.

1. *Mnesarchus*: see II. 69, *De Or.* I. 45, and *Dict. Biogr.* 'Antipater'; cf. II. 143, *De Off.* III. 50. Evidently this fragment belongs to that historical justification of the New Academy with which I suppose Cicero to have concluded the first book.

2. The word *concinere* occurs *D.F.* IV. 60, *N.D.* I. 16, in both which places it is used of the Stoics, who are said *re concinere, verbis discrepare* with the other schools. This opinion of Antiochus Cic. had already mentioned 43, and probably repeated in this fragment. Krische remarks that Augustine, *Cont. Acad.* II. 14, 15, seems to have imitated that part of Cicero's exposition to which this fragment belongs. If so Cic. must have condemned the unwarrantable verbal innovations of Zeno in order to excuse the extreme scepticism of Arcesilas (Krische, p. 58).

BOOK II.

3. This fragm. clearly forms part of those anticipatory sceptical arguments which Cic. in the first edition had included in his answer to Hortensius, see Introd. p. 55. The argument probably ran thus: What seems so level as the sea? Yet it is easy to prove that it is really not level.

4. On this I have nothing to remark.

5. There is nothing distinctive about this which might enable us to determine its connection with the dialogue. Probably Zeno is the person who *serius adamavit honores*.

6. The changing aspects of the same thing are pointed to here as invalidating the evidence of the senses.

7. This passage has the same aim as the last and closely resembles *Lucullus* 105.

8. The fact that the eye and hand need such guides shows how untrustworthy the senses are. A similar argument occurs in *Luc.* 86. *Perpendiculum* is a plumb line, *norma* a mason's square, the word being probably a corruption of the Greek γνωμων (Curt. *Grundz* p. 169, ed. 3), *regula*, a rule.

9. The different colours which the same persons show in different conditions, when young and when old, when sick and when healthy, when sober and when drunken, are brought forward to prove how little of permanence there is even in the least fleeting of the objects of sense.

10. *Urinari* is to dive; for the derivation see Curt. *Grundz* p. 326. A diver would be in exactly the position of the fish noticed in *Luc.* 81, which are unable to see that which lies immediately above them and so illustrate the narrow limits of the power of vision.

11. Evidently an attempt to prove the sense of smell untrustworthy. Different people pass different judgments on one and the same odour. The student will observe that the above extracts formed part of an argument intended to show the deceptive character of the senses. To these should probably be added fragm. 32. Fr. 19 shows that the impossibility of distinguishing eggs one from another, which had been brought forward in the *Catulus*, was allowed to stand in the second edition, other difficulties of the kind, such as those connected with the bent oar, the pigeon's neck, the twins, the impressions of seals (*Luc.* 19, 54), would also appear in both editions. The result of these assaults on the senses must have been summed up in the phrase *cuncta dubitanda esse* which Augustine quotes from the *Academica Posteriora* (see fragm. 36).

BOOK III.

12. This forms part of Varro's answer to Cicero, which corresponded in substance to Lucullus' speech in the *Academica Priora* The drift of this extract was most likely this: just as there is a limit beyond which the battle against criminals cannot be maintained, so after a certain point we must cease to fight against perverse sceptics and let them take their own way. See another view in Krische, p. 62.

13. Krische believes that this fragment formed part of an attempt to show that the senses were trustworthy, in the course of which the clearness with which the fishes were seen leaping from the water was brought up as evidence. (In *Luc.* 81, on the other hand, Cic. drew an argument hostile to the senses from the consideration of the fish.) The explanation seems to me very improbable. The words bear such a striking resemblance to those in *Luc.* 125 (*ut nos nunc simus ad Baulos Puteolosque videmus, sic innumerabilis paribus in locis esse isdem de rebus disputantis*) that I am inclined to think that the reference in Nonius ought to be to Book IV. and not Book III., and that Cic., when he changed the scene from Bauli to the Lucrine lake, also changed *Puteolosque* into *pisciculosque exultantes* for the sufficient reason that Puteoli was not visible from Varro's villa on the Lucrine.

14. The passion for knowledge in the human heart was doubtless used by Varro as an argument in favour of assuming absolute knowledge to be attainable. The same line is taken in *Luc.* 31, *D.F.* III. 17, and elsewhere.

15. It is so much easier to find parallels to this in Cicero's speech than in that of Lucullus in the *Academica Priora* that I think the reference in Nonius must be wrong. The talk about freedom suits a sceptic better than a dogmatist (see *Luc.* 105, 120, and Cic.'s words in 8 of the same). If my conjecture is right this fragment belongs to Book IV. Krische gives a different opinion, but very hesitatingly, p. 63.

16. This may well have formed part of Varro's explanation of the κατάληψις, *temeritas* being as much deprecated by the Antiocheans and Stoics as by the Academics cf. I. 42.

17. I conjecture *malleo* (a hammer) for the corrupt *malcho*, and think that in the second ed. some comparison from building operations to illustrate the fixity of knowledge gained through the καταλήψεις was added to a passage which would correspond in substance with 27 of the *Lucullus*. I note in Vitruvius, quoted by Forc. s.v. *malleolus*, a similar expression (*naves malleolis confixae*) and in Pliny *Nat. Hist.* XXXIV. 14 *navis fixa malleo*. *Adfixa* therefore in this passage must have agreed with some lost noun either in the neut. plur. or fem. sing.

18. This and fragm. 19 evidently hang very closely together. As Krische notes, the Stoic ενάργεια had evidently been translated earlier in the book by *perspicuitas* as in *Luc.* 17.

19. See on *Luc.* 57.

BOOK IV.

Further information on all these passages will be found in my notes on the parallel passages of the *Lucullus*.

21. *Viam* evidently a mistake for the *umbram* of *Luc.* 70.

23. The best MS. of Nonius points to *flavum* for *ravum* (*Luc.* 105). Most likely an alteration was made in the second edition, as Krische supposes, p. 64.

28. *Corpusculis*: *Luc.* 121 has *corporibus*. Krische's opinion that this latter word was in the second edition changed into the former may be supported from I. 6, which he does not notice. The conj. is confirmed by Aug. *Contr. Ac.* III. 23.

29. *Magnis obscurata*: in *Luc.* 122 it is *crassis occultata*, so that we have another alteration, see Krische, p. 64.

30. Only slight differences appear in the MSS. of the *Luc.* 123, viz. *contraria*, for *in c.*, *ad vestigia* for *contra v.*

31. *Luc.* 137 has *dixi* for *dictus*. As Cic. does not often leave out *est* with the passive verb, Nonius has probably quoted wrongly. It will be noted that the fragments of Book III. correspond to the first half of the *Luc.*, those of Book IV. to the second half. Cic. therefore divided the *Luc.* into two portions at or about 63.

UNCERTAIN BOOKS.

32. I have already said that this most likely belonged to the preliminary assault on the senses made by Cic. in the second book.

33. In the Introd. p. 55 I have given my opinion that the substance of Catulus' speech which unfolded the doctrine of the *probabile* was incorporated with Cicero's speech in the second book of this edition. To that part this fragment must probably be referred.

34. This important fragment clearly belongs to Book II., and is a jocular application of the Carneadean *probabile*, as may be seen from the words *probabiliter posse confici*.

35. Krische assigns this to the end of Varro's speech in the third Book. With this opinion I find it quite impossible to agree. A passage in the *Lucullus* (60) proves to demonstration that in the first edition this allusion to the esoteric teaching of the Academy could only have occurred either in the speech of Catulus or in that of Cicero. As no reason whatever appears to account for its transference to Varro I prefer to regard it as belonging to Cic.'s exposition of the positive side of Academic doctrine in the second book. Cic. repeatedly insists that the Academic school must not be supposed to have no truths to maintain, see *Luc.* 119, also 66 and *N.D.* I. 12. Also Aug. *Contra. Ac.* II. 29.

36. It is difficult to see where this passage could have been included if not in that prooemium to the third book which is mentioned *Ad. Att.* XVI. 6, 4. I may here add that Krische seems to me wrong in holding that the whole four books formed one discussion, finished within the limits of a single day. Why interrupt the discussion by the insertion of a prologue of so general a nature as to be taken from a stock which Cic. kept on hand ready made? (Cf. *Ad Att.* as above.)

Besides the actual fragments of the second edition, many indications of its contents are preserved in the work of Augustine entitled *Contra Academicos*, which, though written in support of dogmatic opinions, imitated throughout the second edition of the *Academica* of Cic. No writings of the Classical period had so great an influence on the culture and opinions of Augustine as the *Academica* and the lost *Hortensius*. I give, partly from Krische, the scattered indications of the contents of the former which are to be gathered from the bishop's works. In Aug. *Contr. Ac.* II. 14, 15, we have what appears to be a summary of the lost part of Book I. to the following effect. The New Academy must not be regarded as having revolted against the Old, all that it did was to discuss that new doctrine of κατάληψις advanced by Zeno. The doctrine of ἀκαταληψία though present to the minds of the ancients had never taken distinct shape, because it had met with no opposition. The Old Academy was rather enriched than attacked by the New. Antiochus, in adopting Stoicism under the name of the Old Academy, made it appear that there was a strife between it and the New. With Antiochus the historical exposition of Cic. must have ended. From this portion of the first book, Aug. derived his opinion (*Contra. Ac.* II. 1) that New Academicism was excusable from the necessities of the age in which it appeared. Indications of Book II. in Aug. are scarce, but to it I refer *Contra. Ac.* I. 7 *placuit Ciceroni nostro beatum esse qui verum investigat etiam si ad eius inventionem non valeat pervenire*, also *ibid.* III. 10 *illis (Academicis) placuit esse posse hominem sapientem, et tamen in hominem scientiam cadere non posse.* These I refer to Cicero's development of the *probabile* in Book II., although I ought to say that Krische, p. 65, maintains that the substance of Catulus' exposition in the *Ac. Priora* transferred to Book IV. of the *Ac. Posteriora.* As this would leave very meagre material for Book II., nothing indeed excepting the provisional proof of the deceptiveness of the senses, I cannot accede to his arrangement; mine, I may remark, involves a much smaller departure from the first edition. Allusions in Aug. to the attack on the senses by Cic. in Book II. are difficult to fix, as they apply equally well to the later attack in Book IV. As to Books III. and IV., I do not think it necessary here to prove from Aug. the points of agreement between them and the *Lucullus*, which will find a better place in my notes on the latter, but merely give the divergences which appear from other sources. These are the translation of σοφισματα by *cavillationes* in *Luc.* 75 (Seneca *Ep.* III.), and the insertion in 118 of *essentia* as a translation of ουσια.

BOOK II.

ENTITLED *LUCULLUS*.

§§1—12. Summary. Lucullus, though an able and cultivated man, was absent from Rome on public service too long during his earlier years to attain to glory in the forum (1). He unexpectedly proved a great general. This was due to his untiring study and his marvellous memory (2). He had to wait long for the reward of his merits as a commander and civil administrator, and was allowed no triumph till just before my consulship. What I owed to him in those troublous times I cannot now tell (3). He was not merely a general; he was also a philosopher, having learned much from Antiochus and read much for himself (4). Those enemies of Greek culture who think a Roman noble ought not to know philosophy, must be referred to the examples of Cato and Africanus (5). Others think that famous men should not be introduced into dialogues of the kind. Are they then, when they meet, to be silent or to talk about trifles? I, in applying myself to philosophy, have neglected no public duty, nor do I think the fame of illustrious citizens diminished, but enriched, by a reputation for philosophical knowledge (6). Those who hold that the interlocutors in these dialogues had no such knowledge show that they can make their envy reach beyond the grave. Some critics do not approve the particular philosophy which I follow—the Academic. This is natural, but they must know that Academicism puts no stop to inquiry (7). My school is free from the fetters of dogma; other schools are enslaved to authority (8). The dogmatists say they bow to the authority of the wise man. How can they find out the wise man without hearing all opinions? This subject was discussed by myself, Catulus, Lucullus, and Hortensius, the day after the discussion reported in the *Catulus* (9). Catulus called on Lucullus to defend the doctrines of Antiochus. This Lucullus believed himself able to do, although the doctrines had suffered in the discussion of the day before (10). He spoke thus: At Alexandria I heard discussions between Heraclitus Tyrius the pupil of Clitomachus and Philo, and Antiochus. At that very time the books mentioned by Catulus yesterday came into the hands of Antiochus, who was so angry that he wrote a book against his old teacher (11 and 12). I will now give the substance of the disputes between Heraclitus and Antiochus, omitting the remarks made by the latter against Philo (12).

§1. *Luculli*: see Introd. p. 58, and *Dict. Biog. Digna homini nobili*: a good deal of learning would have been considered *unworthy* of a man like Lucullus, see Introd. p. 30. *Percepta*: "gained," "won;" cf. *percipere fruges*, "to reap," *Cat. Mai.* 24. *Caruit*: "was cut off from;" *carere* comes from a root *skar* meaning to divide, see Corss. I. 403. For the three nouns with a singular verb see Madv. *Gram.* 213 A, who confines the usage to nouns denoting things and impersonal ideas. If the common reading *dissensit* in *De Or.* III. 68 is right, the restriction does not hold. *Admodum*: "to a degree." *Fratre*: this brother was adopted by a M. Terentius Varro, and was a man of distinction also; see *Dict. Biog. Magna cum gloria*: a ref. to *Dict. Biog.* will show that the whole affair was discreditable to the father; to our notions, the sons would have gained greater glory by letting it drop. *Quaestor*: to Sulla, who employed him chiefly in the civil administration of Asia. *Continuo*: without any interval. *Legis praemio*: this seems to mean "by the favour of a special law," passed of course by Sulla, who had restored the old *lex annalis* in all its rigour, and yet excepted his own officers from its operation. *Prooemio*, which has been proposed, would not be Latin, see *De Leg.* II. 16. *Consulatum*: he seems to have been absent during the years 84—74, in the East. *Superiorum*: scarcely that of Sulla.

§2. *Laus*: "merit," as often, so *praemium*, Virg. *Aen.* XII. 437, means a deed worthy of reward. *Non admodum exspectabatur*: Cic. forgets that Luc. had served with distinction in the Social War and the first Mithridatic war. *In Asia pace*: three good MSS. have *Asiae*; Baiter ejects *Asia*; Guilelmus read *in Asia in pace* (which Davies conjectures, though he prints *Asiae*). *Consumere* followed by an ablative without *in* is excessively rare in Cic. Madv. *D.F.* V. 53 denies the use altogether. In addition, however, to our passage, I note *hoc loco consumitur* in *T.D.* IV. 23, where Baiter's two texts (1861 and 1863) give no variants.

Pace here perhaps ought to be taken adverbially, like *tranqullo*. *Indocilem*: this is simply passive, = "untaught," as in Prop. I. 2, 12, Ov. *Fast*. III. 119 (the last qu. by Dav.). Forc. s.v. is wrong in making it active. *Factus*: = *perfectus*; cf. Hor. *Sat*. I. 5, 33 *homo factus ad unguem*, Cic. *De Or*. III. 184, *In Verr*. IV. 126. So *effectus* in silver Latin. *Rebus gestis*: military history, so often. *Divinam quandam memoriam*: the same phrase in *De Or*. II. 360. *Rerum, verborum*: same distinction in *De Or*. II. 359. *Oblivisci se malle*: the same story is told *D.F*. II. 104, *De Or*. II. 299. The ancient art of memory was begun by Simonides (who is the person denoted here by *cuidam*) and completed by Metrodorus of Scepsis, for whom see *De Or*. II. 360. *Consignamus*: cf. *consignatae in animis notiones* in *T.D*. I. 57. *litteris* must be an ablative of the instrument. *Mandare monum*.: cf. I. 3. *Insculptas*: rare in the metaphorical use, cf. *N.D*. I. 45.

§3. *Genere*: "department" cf. I. 3. *Navalibus pugnis*: ναυμαχιαις. *Instrumento et adparatu*: κατασκευη και παρασκευη. *Rex*: Mithridates. *Quos legisset*: = *de quibus l.*; cf. the use of the passive verb so common in Ovid, e.g. *Trist*. IV. 4, 14. I take of course *rex* to be nom. to *legisset*, the suggestion of a friend that Lucullus is nom. and that *quos legisset = quorum commentarios legisset* I think improbable. *Hodie*: Drakenborch on Livy V. 27 wants to read *hodieque*, which however, is not Ciceronian. In passages like *De Or*. I. 103 and *Verr*. V. 64, the *que* connects clauses and does not modify *hodie*. On this subject see Madv. *Opuscula* I. 390. *Etsi*: *M.D.F*. V. 68, shows that in Cic. a parenthetic clause with *etsi* always has a common verb with its principal clause; a rule not observed by the silver writers. The same holds of *quamquam*, see n. on I. 5. *Calumnia*: properly a fraudulent use of litigation, συκοφαντια. The chief enemy was the infamous Memmius who prosecuted him. *In urbem*: until his triumph Luc. would remain outside the city. *Profuisset*: this ought properly to be *profuerit*, but the conditional *dicerem* changes it. *Potius ... quam ... communicem*: n. on 23.

§4. *Sunt ... celebrata*: cf. I. 11, 17 for the collocation of the words. *Externa ... interiora*: cf. *De Div*. II. 124 *sed haec quoque in promptu, nunc interiora videamus*. *Pro quaestore*: for this Faber wrote *quaestor*, arguing that as Luc. was Sulla's *quaestor* and Sulla sent him to Egypt, he could not be *pro quaestor*. But surely after the first year he would be *pro quaestor*. Dav. reads *quaestor* here and 11, saying "*veterem lectionem iugulavit Faber*". *Ea memoria ... quam*: Bentl., Halm, Baiter give *qua*, Halm refers to Bentl. on Hor. *Sat*. I. 6, 15. A passage like ours is *D.F*. I. 29, *ista sis aequitate, quam ostendis*, where one MS. has *qua*. Read Madvig's lucid note there. *De quibus audiebat*: Madv. *Em*. 121 makes this equivalent to *de eis rebus de quibus*, the necessity of which explanation, though approved by Halm, I fail to see. The form of expression is very common in Cic., and the relative always refers to an actually expressed antecedent, cf. e.g. *Cat. Mai*. 83. I take *quibus* as simply = *libris*.

§5. *Ac*: strong, as often, = και μην. *Personarum*: public characters, προσωπων πολεως (*Ad. Fam*. XV. 17, 2), so *personas* 6. *Multi ... plures*: cf. Introd. p. 30. *Reliqui*: many MSS. insert *qui* by *dittographia*, as I think, though Halm, as well as Bait., retains it. On the retention or omission of this *qui* will depend the choice of *putant* or *putent* below. *Earum rerum disputationem*: for *disp*. followed by genitive see n. on I. 33. *Non ita decoram*: for this feeling see Introd. p. 30. For *non ita* cf. the Lowland Scottish "no just sae". *Historiae loquantur*: *hist*. means in Cic. rather "memoirs" than "history," which is better expressed by *res gestae*. Note that the verb *loqui* not *dicere* is used, and cf. n. on 101. *Legatione*: to the kings in Egypt and the East in alliance with Rome. The censorship was in 199 B.C. About the embassy see *Dict. Biogr*. art. 'Panactius'. *Auctorem*: one would think this simple and sound enough, Bentl. however read *fautorem*, Dav. *auditorem*.

§6. *Illigari*: "entangled" as though in something bad. For this use Forc. qu. Liv. XXXIII. 21, Tac. *Ann*. XIII. 40. *Aut ludicros sermones*: = *aut clar. vir. serm. ludic. esse oporteat*. *Rerum leviorum*: a similar argument in *D.F*. I. 12. *Quodam in libro*: the *Hortensius*. *Gradu*: so the word "degree" was once used, e.g. "a squire of low degree" in the ballad. *De opera publica detrahamus*: the dative often follows this verb, as in *D.F*. III. 7 *nihil operae reipublicae detrahens*, a passage often wrongly taken. *Operae* is the dat. after the verb, not the gen. after *nihil, reip.* the gen. after *operae,* like *opera publica* here, not the dat. after *detrahens. Nisi forensem*: the early oratorical works may fairly be said to have this character; scarcely, however, the *De Republica* or the *De Leg.* both of which fall within the period spoken of. *Ut plurimis prosimus*: cf. Introd. p. 29. *Non modo non minui, sed*: notice *non modo ... sed* thrice over in two sentences.

§7. *Sunt ... qui negent*: and truly, see Introd. p. 38. In *Cat. Mai.* §3 Cic. actually apologises for making Cato more learned than he really was. *Mortuis*: Catulus died in 60, Lucullus about 57, Hortensius 50. *Contra omnis dicere quae videntur*: MSS. mostly insert *qui* between *dicere* and *quae,* one of the best however has *dicere quae aliis* as a correction, while another has the marginal reading *qui scire sibi videntur.* The omission of *qui,* which I conjectured, but now see occurs in a MS. (Pal. 2) referred to by Halm, gives admirable sense. *Verum invenire*: cf. 60. *Contentione*: = φιλονεικια as usual. *In ... rebus obscuritas*: cf. I. 44 *rerum obscuritate. Infirmitas*: cf. I. 44 *imbecillos animos. Antiquissimi et doctissimi*: on the other hand *recentissima quaeque sunt correcta et emendata maxime* I. 13. *Diffisi*: one of the best MSS. has *diffissi,* which reminds one of the spelling *divisssiones,* asserted to be Ciceronian in Quint. *Inst. Or.* I. 7, 20. *In utramque partem*: επ' αμφοτερα, cf. I. 45. *Exprimant*: "embody," cf. n. on I. 19.

§8. *Probabilia*: πιθανα, for which see 33. *Sequi*: "act upon," cf. 99-101. *Liberiores et solutiores*: these two words frequently occur together in Cic. and illustrate his love for petty variations; see 105, also *T.D.* V. 43, *De Div.* I. 4, *De Rep.* IV. 4, *N.D.* I. 56, *Orat.* 64. *Integra*: "untrammelled," cf. the phrase "*non mihi integrum est*"—"I have committed my self." *Et quasi*: MSS. have *et quibus et quasi. Cogimur*: for this Academic freedom see Introd. p. 18. *Amico cuidam*: Orelli after Lamb. *cuipiam;* for the difference see Madv. *Gram.* 493 *b, c.*

§9. *Ut potuerint, potuerunt*: thus Lamb. corrected the MSS. reading which was simply *ut potuerunt,* "granting that they had the ability, they gained it by hearing all things, now as a matter of fact they *did* decide on a single hearing," etc. *Iudicaverunt autem*: so Lamb. for MSS. *aut.* Muretus, by what Dav. calls an "*arguta hariolatio,*" read *an* for *aut* and put a note of interrogation at *contulerunt.* C.F. Hermann (Schneidewin's *Philologus* VII. 466) introduces by conj. a sad confusion into the text, but no other good critic since Madvig's remarks in *Em.* 125 has impugned Lambinus' reading. Goerenz indeed, followed by the faithful Schutz, kept the MSS. reading with the insertion of *aut* between *sed* and *ut* at the beginning; of this Madv. says "*non solum Latina non est, sed sanae menti repugnat.*" For the proceeding which Cic. deprecates, cf. *N.D.* I. 10, *De Leg.* I. 36. *Quam adamaverunt*: "which they have learned to love;" the *ad* has the same force as προ in προμανθανειν, which means "to learn *on and on,* to learn by degrees" (cf. προυμαθον στεργειν κακοις), not, as the lexica absurdly say, "to learn beforehand, i.e. to learn thoroughly." *Constantissime*: "most consistently". *Quae est ad Baulos*: cf. Introd. p. 57. *In spatio*: this *xystus* was a colonnade with one side open to the sea, called ξυστος from its polished floor and pillars. *Consedimus*: n. on I. 14.

§10. *Servatam oportuit*: a construction very characteristic of Terence, found, but rarely, in Cic. and Livy. *In promptu ... reconditiora*: cf. *in promptu ... interiora* in *De Div.* II. 124, also *Ac.* I. 4. *Quae dico*: Goer. is exceedingly troubled by the pres. tense and wishes to read *dixero.* But the substitution of the pres. for the future is common enough in all languages cf. Iuv. IV. 130 with Mayor's copious note. *Si non fuerint*: so all Halm's best MSS. Two, however, of Davies' have *si vera* etc. In support of the text, see I. 9 (*sunt ista*) and note. *Labefactata*: this is only found as an alteration in the best MSS. and in *Ed. Rom.* (1471); the others have *labefacta.* Orelli's statement (note to his separate text of the *Academica* 1827) that Cic. commonly uses the perfect *labefeci* and the part. *labefactus* is quite wrong. The former is indeed the vulg. reading in *Pro Sestio* 101, the latter in *De Haruspicum Responsis* 60, but the last of these two passages is doubtful. Cic. as a rule prefers long forms like *sustentatus,* which occurs with *labefactatus* in *Cat. Mai.*

20. For the perfect *labefactavit* cf. I. 33. *Agam igitur*: Cic. rather overdoes the attempt to force on his readers a belief in the learning of Lucullus.

§11. *Pro quaestore*: cf. 4. *Essem*: MSS. *issem*, whence Goer. conj. *Alexandriam issem*. *Heraclitus Tyrius*: scarcely known except from this passage. *Clitomachum*: for this philosopher see Zeller 532. *Quae nunc prope dimissa revocatur*: sc. *a Cicerone*. Philo's only notable pupils had combined to form the so called "Old Academy," and when Cic. wrote the *Academica* the New Academic dialectic had been without a representative for many years. Cf. Introd. p. 21. *Libri duo*: cf. I. 13. *Heri* for this indication of the contents of the lost *Catulus*, see Introd. p. 50. *Implorans*: "appealing to," the true meaning being "to appeal to with tears," see Corss. I. 361. *Philonis*: sc. *esse*. *Scriptum agnoscebat*: i.e. it was an actual work of Ph. *Tetrilius*: some MSS. are said to have Tetrinius, and the name *Tertinius* is found on Inscr. One good MS. has *Tretilius*, which may be a mistake for *Tertilius*, a name formed like *Pompilius, Quintilius, Sextilius*. Qy, should *Petrilius*, a derivative from the word for four, be read? *Petrilius* and *Pompilius* would then agree like *Petronius* and *Pomponius*, *Petreius* and *Pompeius*. For the formation of these names see Corss. I. 116. *Rogus*: an ill omened and unknown name. *Rocus*, as Ursinus pointed out, occurs on *denarii* of the *gens Creperia*. *De Philone ... ab eo ipso*: note the change of prep. "from Philo's lips," "from his copy." *De* and *ex* are common in Cic. after *audire*, while *ab* is rather rarer. See *M.D.F.* I. 39, and for *describere ab aliquo* cf. *a te* in *Ad Att.* XIII. 22, 3.

§12. *Dicta Philoni*: for this see Introd. p. 50. It cannot mean what Goer. makes it mean, "*coram Philone*." I think it probable that *Philoni* is a marginal explanation foisted on the text. As to the statements of Catulus the elder, they are made clear by 18. *Academicos*: i.e. *novos*, who are here treated as the true Academics, though Antiochus himself claimed the title. *Aristo*: see Introd. p. 11. *Aristone*: Diog. VII. 164 mentions an Aristo of Alexandria, a Peripatetic, who may be the same. Dio seems unknown. *Negat*: see n. on 18. *Lenior*: some MSS. *levior*, as is usual with these two words. In 11 one of the earliest editions has *leviter* for *leniter*.

§§13—18. Summary. Cicero seems to me to have acted like a seditious tribune, in appealing to famous old philosophers as supporters of scepticism (13), Those very philosophers, with the exception of Empedocles, seem to me, if anything, too dogmatic (14). Even if they were often in doubt, do you suppose that no advance has been made during so many centuries by the investigations of so many men of ability? Arcesilas was a rebel against a good philosophy, just as Ti. Gracchus was a rebel against a good government (15). Has nothing really been learned since the time of Arcesilas? His opinions have had scanty, though brilliant support (16). Now many dogmatists think that no argument ought to be held with a sceptic, since argument can add nothing to the innate clearness of true sensations (17). Most however do allow of discussion with sceptics. Philo in his innovations was induced to state falsehoods, and incurred all the evils he wished to avoid, his rejection of Zeno's definition of the καταληπτικη φαντασια really led him back to that utter scepticism from which he was fleeing. We then must either maintain Zeno's definition or give in to the sceptics (18).

§13. *Rursus exorsus est*: cf. *exorsus* in 10. *Popularis*: δημοτικους. *Ii a*: so Dav. for MSS. *iam*. *Tum ad hos*: so MSS., Dav. *aut hos*. The omission of the verb *venire* is very common in Cic.'s letters. *C. Flaminium*: the general at lake Trasimene. *Aliquot annis*: one good MS. has *annos*, cf. *T.D.* I. 4, where all the best MSS. have *annos*. The ablative is always used to express point of time, and indeed it may be doubted whether the best writers *ever* use any accusative in that sense, though they do occasionally use the ablative to express duration (cf. Prop. I. 6, 7 and Madv. *Gram.* 235, 2). *L. Cassium*: this is L. Cassius Longinus Ravilla, a man of good family, who carried a ballot bill (*De Leg.* III. 35), he was the author of the *cui bono* principle and so severe a judge as to be called *scopulus reorum*. Pompeium: apparently the man who made the disgraceful treaty with Numantia repudiated by home in 139 B.C. *P. Africanum*: i.e. the younger, who supported the ballot bill of Cassius, but seems to have done nothing else for the democrats. *Fratres*: Lamb. *viros*, but cf. *Brut.* 98. *P. Scaevolam*: the pontifex, consul in the year Tib. Gracchus was killed, when he refused to use violence against the tribunes. The only connection these brothers had with the schemes of Gracchus seems to be that they were consulted by him as lawyers, about the legal effect the bills would have. *Ut videmus ... ut suspicantur*: Halm with Gruter brackets these words on the ground that the statement about Marius implies that the demagogues lie about all but him. Those words need not imply so much, and if they did, Cic. may be allowed the inconsistency.

§14. *Similiter*: it is noticeable that five MSS. of Halm have *simile*. *Xenophanem*: so Victorius for the MSS. *Xenoplatonem. Ed. Rom.* (1471) has *Cenonem*, which would point to *Zenonem*, but Cic. does not often name Zeno of Elea. *Saturninus*: of the question why he was an enemy of Lucullus, Goer. says *frustra quaeritur*. Saturninus was the persistent enemy of Metellus Numidicus, who was the uncle of Lucullus by marriage. *Arcesilae calumnia*: this was a common charge, cf. *Academicorum calumnia* in *N.D.* II. 20 and *calumnia* in 18 and 65 of this book. So August. *Contra Acad.* II. 1 speaks of *Academicorum vel calumnia vel pertinacia vel pericacia. Democriti verecundia*: Cic. always has a kind of tenderness for Democritus, as Madv. on *D.F.* I. 20 remarks, cf. *De Div.* II. 30 where Democr. is made an exception to the general *arrogantia* of the *physici. Empedocles quidem ... videatur*: cf. 74. The exordium of his poem is meant, though there is nothing in it so strong as the words of the text, see R. and P. 108. *Quale sit*: the emphasis is on *sit*, the sceptic regards only phenomenal, not essential existence. *Quasi modo nascentes*: Ciacconus thought this spurious, cf. however *T.D.* II. 5 *ut oratorum laus ... senescat ... , philosophia nascatur*.

§15. *haesitaverunt*: Goer. cf. *De Or.* I. 40. *Constitutam*: so in 14. *Delitisceret*: this is the right spelling, not *delitesceret*, which one good MS. has here, see Corssen II. 285. *Negavissent*: "had denied, as they said." *Tollendus est*: a statement which is criticised in 74. *Nominibus differentis ... dissenserunt*: genuine Antiochean opinions, see the *Academica Posteriora* 17, 43. *De se ipse*: very frequent in Cic. (cf. Madv. *Gram.* 487 *b*). *Diceret*: this is omitted by the MSS., but one has *agnosceret* on the margin; see n. on 88. *Fannius*: in his "Annals." The same statement is quoted in *De Or.* II. 270, *Brutus* 299. Brutus had written an epitome of this work of Fannius (*Ad Att.* XII. 5, 3).

§16. *Veteribus*: Bentley's em. of MSS. *vetera*: C.F. Hermann (Schneid *Philol.* VII. 457), thinking the departure from the MSS. too great, keeps *vetera* and changes *incognita* into *incondita*, comparing *De Or.* I. 197, III. 173. A glance, however, at the exx. in Forc. will show that the word always means merely "disordered, confused" in Cic. The difference here is not one between order and no order, but between knowledge and no knowledge, so that *incognita* is far better. I am not at all certain that the MSS. reading needs alteration. If kept the sense would be: "but let us suppose, for sake of argument, that the doctrines of the ancients were not *knowledge*, but mere *opinion*." The conj. of Kayser *veri nota* for *vetera* (cf. 76) and *investigatum* below, is fanciful and improbable. *Quod investigata sunt*: "in that an investigation was made." Herm. again disturbs the text which since Madv. *Em.* 127 supported it (quoting *T.D.* V. 15, Liv. XXXV. 16) had been settled. Holding that *illa* in the former sentence cannot be the subj. of the verb, he rashly ejects *nihilne est igitur actum* as a dittographia (!) from 15 *nihilne explicatum*, and reads *quot* for *quod* with Bentl. For the meaning cf. *T.D.* III. 69 and Arist. on the progress of philosophy as there quoted. *Arcesilas Zenoni ... obtrectans*: see n. on I. 34. These charges were brought by each school against the other. In Plutarch *Adv. Colotem* p. 1121 F, want of novelty is charged against Arcesilas, and the charge is at once joyfully accepted by Plut. The scepticism of Arcesilas was often excused by the provocation Zeno gave, see Aug. *Contra Acad.* II. 14, 15 and notes on fragm. 2 and 35 of the *Academica Posteriora*. *Immutatione verborum*: n. on I. 33. This phrase has also technical meanings; it translates the Greek τροποι (*Brut.* 69) and αλληγορια in *De Or.* II. 261, where an ex. is given. *Definitiones*: n. on 18. *Tenebras obducere*: such expressions abound in Cic. where the New Academy is mentioned, cf. 30 (*lucem eripere*), *N.D.* I. 6 (*noctem offundere*) Aug. *Contra Ac.* III. 14 (*quasdam nebulas offundere*), also the joke of Aug. II. 29 *tenebrae quae patronae Academicorum solent esse. Non admodum probata*: cf. the passage of

Polybius qu. by Zeller 533. *Lacyde*: the most important passages in ancient authorities concerning him are quoted by Zeller 506. It is important to note that Arcesilas left no writings so that Lacydes became the source of information about his teacher's doctrines. *Tenuit*: cf. the use of *obtinere* in *De Or.* I. 45. *In Aeschine*: so Dav. for the confused MSS. reading. For this philosopher see Zeller 533. As two MSS. have *hac nonne* Christ conj. *Hagnone* which Halm, as well as Baiter takes; Zeller 533 seems to adopt this and at once confuses the supposed philosopher with one Agnon just mentioned in Quint. II. 17, 15. There is not the slightest reason for this, Agnon and Hagnon being known, if known at all, from these two passages only.

§17. *Patrocinium*: for the word cf. *N.D.* I. 6. *Non defuit*: such patronage *was* wanting in the time of Arcesilas (16). *Faciendum omnino non putabant*: "Epictetus (Arrian, *Diss.* I. 27, 15) quietly suppresses a sceptic by saying ουκ αγω σχολην προς ταυτα" (Zeller 85, n.). In another passage (Arrian, I. 5) Epict. says it is no more use arguing with a sceptic than with a corpse. *Ullam rationem disputare*: the same constr. occurs in 74 and *Pro Caecina* 15, *Verr. Act.* I. 24. *Antipatrum*: cf. fragm. 1 of Book I. *Verbum e verbo*: so 31, *D.F.* III. 15, *T.D.* III. 7, not *verbum de verbo*, which Goer. asserts to be the usual form. *Comprehensio*: cf. I. 41. *Ut Graeci*: for the ellipse of the verb cf. I. 44 *ut Democritus*. *Evidentiam*: other translations proposed by Cic. were *illustratio* (Quint. VI. 2, 32) and *perspicientia* (*De Off.* I. 15). *Fabricemur*: cf. 87, 119, 121. *Me appellabat*: Cic. was the great advocate for the Latinisation of Greek terms (*D.F.* III. 15). *Sed tamen*: this often resumes the interrupted narrative, see Madv. *Gram.* 480. *Ipsa evidentia*: note that the verb *evidere* is not Latin.

§18. *Sustinere*: cf. 70. *Pertinaciam*: the exact meaning of this may be seen from *D.F.* II. 107, III. 1. It denotes the character which cannot recognise a defeat in argument and refuses to see the force of an opponent's reasoning. For the application of the term to the Academics, cf. n. on 14, 66, also I. 44 and *D.F.* V. 94, *N.D.* I. 13, in the last of which passages the Academy is called *procax*. *Mentitur*: cf. 12. *Ita negaret*: this *ita* corresponds to *si* below,—a common sequence of particles in Cic., cf. 19. Ακαταληπτον: the conj. of Turnebus καταληπτον is unnecessary, on account of the negative contained in *negaret*. *Visum*: cf. I. 40. *Trivimus*: cf. I. 27. *Visum igitur*: the Greek of this definition will be found in Zeller 86. The words *impressum effictumque* are equivalent to εναπεσφραγισμενη και εναπομεμαγμενη in the Gk. It must not be forgotten that the Stoics held a sensation to be a real alteration (ἑτεροιωσις) of the material substance of the soul through the action of some external thing, which impresses its image on the soul as a seal does on wax, cf. Zeller 76 and 77 with footnotes. *Ex eo unde esset ... unde non esset*: this translation corresponds closely to the definition given by Sextus in four out of the six passages referred to by Zeller (in *Adv. Math.* VIII. 86 *Pyrrh. Hypotyp.* III. 242, the definition is clipt), and in Diog. Laert. VII. 50 (in 46 he gives a clipt form like that of Sextus in the two passages just referred to). It is worth remarking (as Petrus Valentia did, p. 290 of Orelli's reprint of his *Academica*) that Cic. omits to represent the words κατ' αυτο το ὑπαρχον. Sextus *Adv. Math.* VII. 249 considers them essential to the definition and instances Orestes who looking at Electra, mistook her for an Erinys. The φαντασια therefore which he had although απο ὑπαρχοντος (proceeding from an actually existent thing) was not κατα το ὑπαρχον, i.e. did not truly represent that existent thing. Aug. *Cont. Acad.* II. 11 quotes Cicero's definition and condenses it thus; *his signis verum posse comprehendi quae signa non potest habere quod falsum est.* *Iudicium*: κριτηριον, a test to distinguish between the unknown and the known. *Eo, quo minime volt*: several things are clear, (1) that Philo headed a reaction towards dogmatism, (2) that he based the possibility of knowledge on a ground quite different from the καταληπτικη φαντασια, which he pronounced impossible, (3) that he distorted the views of Carneades to suit his own. As to (1) all ancient testimony is clear, cf. 11, Sextus *Pyrr. Hyp.* I. 235, who tells us that while the Carneadeans believed all things to be ακαταληπτα, Philo held them to be καταληπτα, and Numenius in Euseb. *Praep. Ev.* XIV. 8, p. 739, who treats him throughout his notice as a renegade. (2) is evident from the *Academica* and from Sextus as quoted above. The foundation for knowledge which he substituted is more difficult to comprehend. Sextus indeed tells us that he held things to be *in their own nature* καταληπτα (ὁσον δε επι τη φυσει των πραγματων αυτων καταλ.). But Arcesilas and Carneades would not have attempted to disprove this; they never tried to show that things *in themselves* were incognisable, *but* that human faculties do not avail to give information about them. Unless therefore Philo deluded himself with words, there was nothing new to him about such a doctrine. The Stoics by their καταληπτικη φαντασια professed to be able to get at *the thing in itself*, in its real being, if then Philo did away with the καταλ. φαντ. and substituted no other mode of curing the defects alleged by Arcesilas and Carneades to reside in sense, he was fairly open to the retort of Antiochus given in the text. Numenius treats his polemic against the καταλ. φαντ. as a mere feint intended to cover his retreat towards dogmatism. A glimpse of his position is afforded in 112 of this book, where we may suppose Cic. to be expressing the views of Philo, and not those of Clitomachus as he usually does. It would seem from that passage that he defined the cognisable to be "*quod impressum esset e vero*" (φαντασια απο ῾υπαρχοντος εναπομεμαγμενη), refusing to add "*quo modo imprimi non posset a falso* (῾οια ουκ αν γενοιτο απο μη ῾υπαρχοντος), cf. my n. on the passage. Thus defined, he most likely tried to show that the cognisable was equivalent to the δηλον or πιθανον of Carneades, hence he eagerly pressed the doubtful statement of the latter that the wise man would "opine," that is, would pronounce definite judgments on phenomena. (See 78 of this book.) The scarcity of references to Philo in ancient authorities does not allow of a more exact view of his doctrine. Modern inquiry has been able to add little or nothing to the elucidation given in 1596 by Petrus Valentia in his book entitled *Academica* (pp. 313—316 of the reprint by Orelli). With regard to (3), it it not difficult to see wherein Philo's "lie" consisted. He denied the popular view of Arcesilas and Carneades, that they were apostles of doubt, to be correct (12). I may add that from the mention of Philo's ethical works at the outset of Stobaeus' *Ethica*, he would appear to have afterwards left dialectic and devoted himself to ethics. What is important for us is, that Cic. never seems to have made himself the defender of the new Philonian dialectic. By him the dialectic of Carneades is treated as genuinely Academic. *Revolvitur*: cf. *De Div.* II. 13, also 148 of this book. *Eam definitionem*: it is noteworthy that the whole war between the sceptics and the dogmatists was waged over the definition of the single sensation. Knowledge, it was thought, was a homogeneous compound of these sense atoms, if I may so call them, on all hands it was allowed that *all* knowledge ultimately rests on sense; therefore its possibility depends on the truth of the individual perception of sense.

§§19—29. Summary. If the senses are healthy and unimpaired, they give perfectly true information about external things. Not that I maintain the truth of *every* sensation, Epicurus must see to that. Things which impede the action of the senses must always be removed, in practice we always do remove them where we can (19). What power the cultivated senses of painters and musicians have! How keen is the sense of touch! (20). After the perceptions of sense come the equally clear perceptions of the mind, which are in a certain way perceptions of sense, since they come through sense, these rise in complexity till we arrive at definitions and ideas (21). If these ideas may possibly be false, logic memory, and all kinds of arts are at once rendered impossible (22). That true perception is possible, is seen from moral action. Who would act, if the things on which he takes action might prove to be false? (23) How can wisdom be wisdom if she has nothing certain to guide her? There must he some ground on which action can proceed (24). Credence must be given to the thing which impels us to action, otherwise action is impossible (25). The doctrines of the New Academy would put an end to all processes of reasoning. The fleeting and uncertain can never be discovered. Rational proof requires that something, once veiled, should be brought to light (26). Syllogisms are rendered useless, philosophy too cannot exist unless her dogmas have a sure basis (27). Hence the Academics have been urged to allow their *dogma* that perception is impossible, to be a certain perception of their minds. This, Carneades said, would be inconsistent, since the very dogma excludes the supposition that there can be *any* true perception (28). Antiochus declared that the Academics could not be held to be philosophers if they had not even confidence in their one dogma (29).

§19. *Sensibus*: it is important to observe that the word *sensus* like αισθησις means two things, (1) one of the *five* senses, (2) an individual act of sensation. *Deus*: for the supposed god cf. *T.D.* II. 67. *Non videam*: this strong statement is ridiculed in 80. *De remo inflexo et de collo columbae*: cf. 79, 82. The κωπη εναλος κεκλασμενη and περιστερας τραχηλος are frequently mentioned, along with numerous other instances of the deceptiveness of sense, by Sext. Emp., e.g. *Pyrrhon. Hypot.* I. 119-121, *Adv. Math.* VII. 244, 414. Cicero, in his speech of the day before, had probably added other examples, cf. Aug. *Cont. Ac.* III. 27. *Epicurus hoc viderit*: see 79, 80. Epic. held all sensation, *per se*, to be infallible. The chief authorities for this are given in R. and P. 343, 344, Zeller 403, footnote. *Lumen mutari*: cf. *Brut.* 261. *Intervalla ... diducimus*: for this cf. Sext. *Pyrrh.* I. 118 πεμπτος εστι λογος (i.e. the 5th sceptic τροπος for showing sense to be untrustworthy) ʻο παρα τας θεσεις (*situs*) και τα διαστηματα (*intervalla*) και τους τοπους. *Multaque facimus usque eo*: Sext. *Adv. Math.* VII. 258 παντα ποιει μεχρις αν τρανην και πληκτικην σπαση φαντασιαν. *Sui iudicii*: see for the gen. *M.D.F.* II. 27; there is an extraordinary instance in Plaut. *Persa* V. 2, 8, quoted by Goer. *Sui cuiusque*: for this use of *suus quisque* as a single word see *M.D.F.* V. 46.

§20. *Ut oculi ... cantibus*: Halm after Dav. treats this as a gloss: on the other hand I think it appropriate and almost necessary. *Quis est quin cernat*: read Madvig's strong remarks on Goerenz's note here (*D.F.* II. 27). *Umbris ... eminentia*: Pliny (see Forc.) often uses *umbra* and *lumen*, to denote background and foreground, so in Gk. σκια and σκιασμα are opposed to λαμπρα; cf. also σκιαγραφειν, *adumbrare*, and Aesch. *Agam.* 1328. Cic. often applies metaphorically to oratory the two words here used, e.g. *De Or.* III. 101, and after him Quintilian, e.g. II. 17, 21. *Inflatu*: cf. 86 (where an answer is given) and αναβολη. *Antiopam*: of Pacuvius. *Andromacham*: of Ennius, often quoted by Cic., as *De Div.* I. 23. *Interiorem*: see R. and P. 165 and Zeller's *Socrates and the Socratic Schools*, 296. *Quia sentiatur*: αισθησις being their only κριτηριον. Madv. (without necessity, as a study of the passages referred to in R. and P. and Zeller will show) conj. *cui adsentiatur*, comparing 39, 58; cf. also 76. *Inter eum ... et inter*: for the repetition of *inter* cf. *T.D.* IV. 32 and Madv. *Gram.* 470. *Nihil interesse*: if the doctrine of the Academics were true, a man might really be in pain when he fancied himself in pleasure, and *vice versa*; thus the distinction between pleasure and pain would be obscured. *Sentiet ... insaniat*: For the sequence cf. *D.F.* I. 62 and Wesenberg's fine note on *T.D.* V. 102.

§21. *Illud est album*: these are αξιωματα, judgments of the mind, in which alone truth and falsehood reside; see Zeller 107 sq. There is a passage in Sext. *Adv. Math.* VII. 344, 345 which closely resembles ours; it is too long to quote entire: αισθησεσι μεν ουν μοναις λαβειν ταληθες (which resides only in the αξιωμα) ου δυναται ανθρωπος. ... φυσει γαρ εισιν αλογοι ... δει δε εις φαντασιαν αχθηναι του τοιουτου πραγματος "τουτο λευκον εστι και τουτο γλυκυ εστιν." τωι δε τοιουτωι πραγματι ουκετι της αισθησεως εργον εστιν επιβαλλειν ... συνεσεως τε δει και μνημης. *Ille deinceps*: deinceps is really out of place; cf. 24 *quomodo primum* for pr. quom. *Ille equus est*: Cic. seems to consider that the αξιωμα, which affirms the existence of an abstract quality, is prior to that which affirms the existence of a concrete individual. I can quote no parallel to this from the Greek texts. *Expletam comprehensionem*: full knowledge. Here we rise to a definition. This one often appears in Sextus: e.g. *Adv. Math.* VII. ανθρωπος εστι ζωον λογικον θνητον, νου και επιστημης δεκτικον. The Stoic ʻοροι, and this among them, are amusingly ridiculed, *Pyrrh. Hyp.* II. 208—211. *Notitiae*: this Cic. uses as a translation both of προληψις and εννοια, for which see Zeller 79, 89. In I. 40 *notiones rerum* is given. *Sine quibus*: δια γαρ των εννοιων τα πραγματα λαμβανεται Diog. VII. 42.

§22. *Igitur*: for the anacoluthia cf. Madv. *Gram.* 480. *Consentaneum*: so Sextus constantly uses ακολουθον. *Repugnaret*: cf. I. 19 and n. *Memoriae certe*: n. on 106. *Continet*: cf. *contineant* in 40. *Quae potest esse*: Cic. nearly always writes *putat esse, potest esse* and the like, not *esse putat* etc., which form is especially rare at the end of a clause. *Memoria falsorum*: this difficulty is discussed in Plato *Sophist.* 238—239. *Ex multis animi perceptionibus*: the same definition of an art occurs in *N.D.* II. 148, *D.F.* III. 18 (see Madv.), Quint, II. 17, 41, Sext. *Pyrrh. Hyp.* III. 188 τεχνην ειναι συστημα εκ καταληψεον συγγεγυμνασμενων *ib.* III. 250. *Quam*: for the change from plural to singular (*perceptio in universum*) cf. n. on I. 38, Madv. *D.F.* II. 61, *Em.* 139. *Qui distingues*: Sext. *Adv. Math.* VIII. 280 ου διοισει της ατεχνιας ʻη τεχνη. Sextus often comments on similar complaints of the Stoics. *Aliud eiusmodi genus sit*: this distinction is as old as Plato and Arist., and is of constant occurrence in the late philosophy. Cf. Sext. *Adv. Math.* XI. 197 who adds a third class of τεχναι called αποτελεσματικαι to the usual θεωρητικαι and πρακτικαι, also Quint. II. 18, 1 and 2, where ποιητικη corresponds to the απoτ. of Sext. *Continget:* "will be the natural consequence." The notion that the verb *contingit* denotes necessarily *good* fortune is quite unfounded; see Tischer on *T.D.* III. 4. *Tractabit:* μελλει μεταχειριζεσθαι.

§23. *Cognitio:* like Germ. *lehre,* the branch of learning which concerns the virtues. Goer. is quite wrong in taking it to be a trans. of καταληψις here. *In quibus:* the antecedent is not *virtutum,* as Petrus Valentia (p. 292 ed. Orelli) supposes and gets into difficulty thereby, but *multa.* This is shown by *etiam;* not *merely* the virtues but *also* all επιστημη depends on καταληψεις; cf. I. 40, 41, with notes, Zeller 88, R. and P. 367. *Stabilem:* βεβαιον και αμεταπτωτου. *Artem vivendi:* "*tralaticium hoc apud omnes philosophos*" *M.D.F.* I. 42. Sextus constantly talks about 'η ονειροπολουμενη περι τον βιον τεχνη (*Pyrrh. Hyp.* III. 250) the existence of which he disproves to his own satisfaction (*Adv. Math.* XI. 168 sq). *Ille vir bonus:* in all ancient systems, even the Epicurean, the happiness of the *sapiens* must be proof against the rack; cf. esp. *D.F.* III. 29, 75, *T.D.* V. 73, Zeller 450, and the similar description of the σοφος in Plato's *Gorgias. Potius quam aut:* Lamb. *ut;* but I think C.F. Hermann is right in asserting after Wopkens that Cic. *never* inserts *ut* after *potius quam* with the subj. Tischer on *T.D.* II. 52 affirms that *ut* is frequently found, but gives no exx. For the meaning cf. *De Off.* I. 86, Aug. *Cont. Ac.* II. 12 who says the *sapiens* of the Academy must be *desertor officiorum omnium. Comprehensi ... constituti:* cf. the famous *abiit, evasit, excessit, crupit. Iis rebus:* note the assumption that the *sensation* corresponds to the *thing* which causes it. *Adsensus sit ... possint:* nearly all edd. before Halm read *possunt,* but the subj. expresses the possibility as present to the mind of the supposed *vir bonus.* Cf. Madv. *Gram.* 368.

§24. *Primum:* out of place, see on 21. *Agere:* the dogmatist always held that the sceptic must, if consistent, be ανενεργητος εν βιωι (Sext. *Pyrrh. Hyp.* I. 23). *Extremum:* similar attempts to translate τελος are made in D.F. I. 11, 29, V. 17. *Cum quid agere:* cf. I. 23 for the phrase *Naturae accommodatum.* a purely Stoic expression, 'ωμοιωμενον τη φυσει; cf. 38 and *D.F.* V. 17, also III. 16, Zeller 227, footnote, R. and P. 390. *Impellimur:* κινουμεθα, Sext. *Adv. Math.* VII. 391, as often.

§25. *Oportet videri:* "ought to be seen." For this use cf. 39, 81 and 122 of this book. *Videri* at the end of this section has the weak sense, "to seem." Lucretius often passes rapidly from the one use to the other; cf. I. 262 with I. 270, and Munro's n., also *M.D.F.* II. 52, *Em. Liv.* p. 42. *Non poterit:* as the Academics allege. *Naturae ... alienum:* Cic. uses this adjective with the dat, and also with the ablative preceded by *ab;* I doubt whether the phrase *maiestate alienum* (without the preposition) can be right in *De Div.* II. 102, where the best texts still keep it. *Non occurrit ... aget:* occurrit is probably the perfect. Cf. n. on 127.

§26. *Quid quod si:* Goer., outrageously reads *quid quod si, si. Tollitur:* the verb *tollere* occurs as frequently in this sense as αναιρειν does in Sextus. *Lux lumenque:* Bentl. *dux* The expression *dux vitae* is of course frequent (cf. *N.D.* I. 40, *T.D.* V. 5 and Lucretius), but there is no need to alter. *Lux* is properly natural light, *lumen* artificial, cf. *Ad Att.* XVI. 13, 1. *lumina dimiseramus, nec satis lucebat,* D.F. III. 45 *solis luce ... lumen lucernae.* There is the same difference between φως and φεγγος, the latter is used for the former (φεγγος 'ηλιου) just as *lumen* is for *lux* (*si te secundo lumine his offendere—Ad Att.* VII. 26, 1) but not often *vice versa.* Trans. "the luminary and the lamp of life," and cf. Sext. *Adv. Math.* VII. 269 where the φαντασια is called φεγγος. *Finis:* so in the beginning of the *Nicom. Eth.* Aristot. assumes that the actual existence of human exertion is a sufficient proof that there is a τελος. *Aperta:* a reminiscence of the frequently recurring Greek terms εκκαλυπτειν, εκκαλυπτικος etc., cf. Sextus *passim,* and *D.F.* I. 30. *Initium ... exitus* = αρχη ... τελος. *Tenetur:* MSS. *tenet,* the nom. to which Guietus thought to be *ratio* above. Αποδειξις: cf. the definition very often given by Sext. e.g. *Pyrrh. Hyp.* II. 143 λογος δι' 'ομολογουμενων λημματων (premisses) κατα συναγωγην επιφοραν (conclusion) εκκαλυπτων αδηλον, also Diog. VII. 45, λογον δια των μαλλον καταλαμβανομενων το ῾ηττον καταλαμβανομενον περαινοντα (if the reading be right).

§27. *Notio*: another trans. of εννοια. *Conclusisse*: although the Greeks used συμπερασμα instead of επιφορα sometimes for the conclusion of the syllogism, they did not use the verb συμπεραινειν which has been supposed to correspond to *concludere*. It is more likely to be a trans. of συναγειν, and *conclusum argumentum* of συνακτικος λογος, which terms are of frequent occurrence. *Rationibus progredi*: to a similar question Sextus answers, ουκ εστιν αναγκαιον τας εκεινον (the dogmatists) δογματολογιας προβαινειν, πλασματωδεις ῾υπαρχουσας (*Adv. Math.* VIII. 367). *Sapientiae ... futurum est*: for the dat. with *facio* and *fio* see Madv. *Gram.* 241, obs. 5, *Opusc.* I. 370, *D.F.* II. 79, and cf. 96 of this book. *Lex veri rectique*: cf. 29; the *constitutio veri* and the determination of what is *rectum* in morals are the two main tasks of philosophy. *Sapientique satis non sit*: so Manut. for the *sapientisque sit* of the MSS. Halm after Dav. reads *sapientis, neque satis sit*, which I think is wrong, for if the ellipse be supplied the construction will run *neque dubitari potest quin satis sit*, which gives the exact opposite of the sense required. *Ratum*: cf. 141.

§28. *Perceptum*: thoroughly known and grasped. Similar arguments are very frequent in Sextus, e.g. *Adv. Math.* VIII. 281, where the dogmatist argues that if proof be impossible, as the sceptic says, there must be a proof to show it impossible; the sceptic doctrine must be *provable*. Cf. 109 of this book. *Postulanti*: making it a necessity for the discussion; cf. *De Leg.* I. 21. *Consentaneum esse*: ακολουθον ειναι. *Ut alia*: although others. *Tantum abest ut—ut*: cf. Madv. *Gram.* 440 a.

§29. *Pressius*: cf. *De Fato* 31, 33, *N.D.* II. 20, *T.D.* IV. 14, *Hortensius* fragm. 46 ed. Nobbe. The word is mocked in 109. *Decretum*: of course the Academics would say they did not hold this δογμα as *stabile fixum ratum* but only as *probabile*. Sextus however *Pyrrh. Hyp.* I. 226 (and elsewhere) accuses them of making it in reality what in words they professed it not to be, a fixed dogma. *Sentitis enim*: cf. *sentis* in *D.F.* III. 26. *Fluctuare*: "to be at sea," Halm *fluctuari*, but the deponent verb is not elsewhere found in Cic. *Summa*: cf. *summa philosophiae D.F.* II. 86. *Veri falsi*: cf. n. on 92. *Quae visa*: so Halm for MSS. *quaevis*, which edd. had changed to *quae a quovis*. *Repudiari*: the selection depended on the *probabile* of course, with the Academics. *Veri falsique*: these words were used in different senses by the dogmatist and the sceptic, the former meant by them "the undestructibly true and false." This being so, the statements in the text are in no sense arguments, they are mere assertions, as Sext. says, ψιλη φασει ισον φερεται ψιλη φασις (*A.M.* VII. 315), φασει μεν φασις επισχεθησεται (*ib.* 337). *Cognoscendi initium*: cf. 26, "This I have," the Academic would reply, "in my *probabile*." *Extremum expetendi*: a rather unusual phrase for the ethical *finis*. *Ut moveri non possint*: so κινεισθαι is perpetually used in Sext. *Est ut opinor*: so Halm after Ernesti for *sit* of the MSS. I think it very likely that the MSS. reading is right, and that the whole expression is an imitation of the Greek ῾ικανος ειοησθω and the like. The subj. is supported by *D.F.* III. 20, *De Off.* I. 8, *Ad Att.* XIII. 14, 3, where *ut opinor* is thrown in as here, and by *Ac.* II. 17, *D.F.* III. 21, 24, *N.D.* I. 109, where *si placet* is appended in a similar way.

§§30—36. Summary. With respect to physical science, we might urge that nature has constructed man with great art. His mind is naturally formed for the attainment of knowledge (30). For this purpose the mind uses the senses, and so gradually arrives at virtue, which is the perfection of the reason. Those then who deny that any certainty can be attained through the senses, throw the whole of life into confusion (31). Some sceptics say "we cannot help it." Others distinguish between the absolute absence of certainty, and the denial of its absolute presence. Let us deal with these rather than with the former (32). Now they on the one hand profess to distinguish between true and false, and on the other hold that no absolutely certain method for distinguishing between true and false is possible (33). This is absurd, a thing cannot be known at all unless by such marks as can appertain to no other thing. How can a thing be said to be "evidently white," if the possibility remains that it may be really black? Again, how can a thing be "evident" at all if it may be after all a mere phantom (34)? There is no definite mark, say the sceptics, by which a thing may be known. Their "probability" then is mere random guess work (35). Even if they only profess to decide after careful pondering of the circumstances, we reply that a decision which is still possibly false is useless (36).

§30. *Physicis*: neuter not masc.; cf. I. 6. *Libertatem et licentiam*: *et* = "and even." *Libertas* = παρρησια as often in Tacitus. *Abditis rebus et obscuris*: cf. n. on I. 15, and the word συνεσκιασμενος Sext. *Adv. Math.* VII. 26. *Lucem eripere*: like *tollere* (n. on 26), cf. 38, 103 and *N.D.* I. 6. For the sense see n. on 16, also 61. *Artificio*: this word is used in Cic. as equivalent to *ars* in all its senses, cf. 114 and *De Or.* II. 83. *Fabricata esset*: the expression is sneered at in 87. *Quem ad modum primum*: so Halm rightly for MSS. *prima* or *primo*, which latter is not often followed by *deinde* in Cicero. *Primum* is out of position, as in 24. *Appetitio pulsa*: = *mota*, set in motion. For ʽορμη see 24. *Intenderemus*: as in the exx. given in 20. *Fons*: "reservoir," rather than "source" here. It will be noted that συγκαταθεσις must take place before the ʽορμη is roused. *Ipse sensus est*: an approach to this theory is made in Plat. *Theaet.* 185, 191. Cf. especially Sext. *Adv. Math.* VII. 350 και ʽοι μεν διαφερειν αυτην των αισθησεων, ʽως ʽοι πλειους, ʽοι δε αυτην ειναι τας αισθησεις ... ʽης στασεως ηρξε Στρατον. All powers of sensation with the Stoics, who are perhaps imitated here, were included in the ʽηγεμονικον, cf. n. on I. 38. *Alia quasi*: so Faber for *aliqua*. "*In vera et aperta partitione nec Cicero nec alius quisquam aliquis—alius dixit, multo minus alius—aliquis*," *M.D.F.* III. 63. Goer. on the other hand says he can produce 50 exx. of the usage, he forbears however, to produce them. *Recondit*: so the εννοιαι are called αποκειμεναι νοησεις (Plut. *De Sto. Repug.* p. 1057 a). In Sext. *Adv. Math.* VII. 373 μνημη is called θησαυρισμος φαντασιων. *Similitudinibus*: καθ' ʽομοιωσιν Sext. *Pyrr. Hyp.* II. 75. Cic. uses this word as including all processes by which the mind gets to know things not immediately perceived by sense. In *D.F.* III. 33 it receives its proper meaning, for which see Madv. there, and the passages he quotes, "analogies" will here best translate the word, which, is used in the same wide sense in *N.D.* II. 22 38. *Construit*: so MSS. Orelli gave *constituit*. *Notitiae*: cf. 22. Cic. fails to distinguish between the φυσικαι εννοιαι or κοιναι which are the προληψεις, and those εννοιαι which are the conscious product of the reason, in the Stoic system. Cf. *M.D.F.* III. 21, V. 60, for this and other inaccuracies of Cic. in treating of the same subject, also Zeller 79. *Rerumque*: "facts". *Perfecta*: *sapientia, virtus, perfecta ratio*, are almost convertible terms in the expositions of Antiocheanism found in Cic. Cf. I. 20.

§31. *Vitaeque constantiam*: which philosophy brings, see 23. *Cognitionem*: επιστημην. *Cognitio* is used to translate καταληψις in *D.F.* II. 16, III. 17, cf. n. on I. 41. *Ut dixi ... dicemus*: For the repetition cf. 135, 146, and *M.D.F.* I. 41. The future tense is odd and unlike Cic. Lamb. wrote *dicimus*, I would rather read *dicamus*; cf. n. on 29. *Per se*: καθ' αυτην, there is no need to read *propter*, as Lamb. *Ut virtutem efficiat*: note that virtue is throughout this exposition treated as the result of the exercise of the *reason*. *Evertunt*: cf. *eversio* in 99. *Animal ... animo*: Cic. allows *animus* to all animals, not merely *anima*; see Madv. *D.F.* V. 38. The rule given by Forc. s.v. *animans* is therefore wrong. *Temeritate*: προπετεια, which occurs *passim* in Sext. The word, which is constantly hurled at the dogmatists by the sceptics, is here put by way of retort. So in Sext. *Adv. Math.* VII. 260, the sceptic is called εμβροντητος for rejecting the καταληπτικη φαντασια.

§32. *Incerta*: αδηλα. *Democritus*: cf. I. 44. *Quae ... abstruserit*: "*because* she has hidden." *Alii autem*: note the ellipse of the verb, and cf. I. 2. *Etiam queruntur*: "actually complain;" "go so far as to complain." *Inter incertum*: cf. Numenius in Euseb. *Pr. Ev.* XIV. 7, 12, διαφοραν ειναι αδηλου και ακαταληπτου, και παντα μεν ειναι ακαταληπτα ου παντα δε αδηλα (quoted as from Carneades), also 54 of this book. *Docere*: "to prove," cf. n. on 121. *Qui haec distinguunt*: the followers of Carneades rather than those of Arcesilas; cf. n. on I. 45. *Stellarum numerus*: this typical uncertainty is constantly referred to in Sext. e.g. *P.H.* II. 90, 98, *A.M.* VII. 243, VIII. 147, 317; where it is reckoned among things αιωνιον εχοντα αγνωσιαν. So in the Psalms, God only "telleth the number of the stars;" cf. 110. *Aliquos*: contemptuous;

απονενοημενους τινας. Cf. *Parad.* 33 *agrestis aliquos*. *Moveri*: this probably refers to the speech of Catulus; see Introd. p. 51. Aug. *Cont. Ac.* III. 15 refers to this passage, which must have been preserved in the second edition.

§33. *Veri et falsi*: these words Lamb. considered spurious in the first clause, and Halm brackets; but surely their repetition is pointed and appropriate. "You talk about a rule for distinguishing between the true and the false while you do away with the notion of true and false altogether." The discussion here really turns on the use of terms. If it is fair to use the term "true" to denote the *probably true*, the Academics are not open to the criticism here attempted; cf. 111 *tam vera quam falsa cernimus*. *Ut inter rectum et pravum*: the sceptic would no more allow the absolute certainty of this distinction than of the other. *Communis*: the απαραλλακτος of Sextus; "in whose vision true and false are confused." Cf. κοινη φαντασια αληθους και ψευδους Sext. *A.M.* VII. 164 (R. and P. 410), also 175. *Notam*: the σημειον of Sextus; cf. esp. *P.H.* II. 97 sq. *Eodem modo falsum*: Sext. *A.M.* VII. 164 (R. and P. 410) ουδεμια εστιν αληθης φαντασια ʽοια ουκ αν γενοιτο ψευδης. *Ut si quis*: Madv. in an important n. on *D.F.* IV. 30 explains this thus; *ista ratione si quis ... privaverit, possit dicere*. I do not think our passage at all analogous to those he quotes, and still prefer to construe *quem* as a strong relative, making a pause between *quis* and *quem*. *Visionem*: Simply another trans. of φαντασια. *Ut Carneades*: see Sext. *A.M.* VII. 166 την τε πιθανην φαντασιαν και την πιθανην ʽαμα και απερισπαστον και διεξωδευμενην (R. and P. 411). As the trans. of the latter phrase in Zeller 524 "probable undisputed and tested" is imperfect, I will give Sextus' own explanation. The merely πιθανη is that sensation which at first sight, without any further inquiry, seems probably true (Sext. *A.M.* VII. 167—175). Now no sensation is perceived *alone*; the percipient subject has always other synchronous sensations which are able to turn him aside (περισπαν, περιελκειν) from the one which is the immediate object of his attention. This last is only called απερισπαστος when examination has shown all the concomitant sensations to be in harmony with it. (Sext. as above 175—181.) The word "undisputed," therefore, is a misleading trans. of the term. The διεξωδευμενη ("thoroughly explored") requires more than a mere apparent agreement of the concomitant sensations with the principal one. Circumstances quite external to the sensations themselves must be examined; the time at which they occur, or during which they continue; the condition of the space within which they occur, and the apparent intervals between the person and the objects; the state of the air; the disposition of the person's mind, and the soundness or unsoundness of his eyes (Sext. 181—189).

§34. *Communitas*: απαραλλαξια or επιμιξια των φαντασιων; Sext. *A.M.* VII. 403, *P.H.* I. 127. *Proprium*: so Sext. often uses ιδιωμα, e.g. *A. M.* IX. 410. *Signo notari*: *signo* for *nota*, merely from love of variety. The *in* before *communi*, though bracketed by Halm after Manut., Lamb. is perfectly sound; it means "within the limits of," and is so used after *notare* in *De Or.*, III. 186. *Convicio*: so Madv. *Em.* 143 corrected the corrupt MSS. readings, comparing *Orator* 160, *Ad Fam.* XV. 18. A.W. Zumpt on *Pro Murena* 13 rightly defines the Ciceronian use of the word, "*Non unum maledictum appellatur convicium sed multorum verborum quasi vociferatio.*" He is wrong however in thinking that Cic. only uses the word *once* in the plural (*Ad Att.* II. 18, 1), for it occurs *N.D.* II. 20, and elsewhere. *Perspicua*: εναργη, a term used with varying signification by all the later Greek schools. *Verum illud quidem*: "which is indeed what *they* call 'true'." *Impressum*: n. on 18. *Percipi atque comprehendi*: Halm retains the barbarous *ac* of the MSS. before the guttural. It is quite impossible that Cic. could have written it. The two verbs are both trans. of καταλαμβανεσθαι; Cic. proceeds as usual on the principle thus described in *D.F.* III. 14 *erit notius quale sit, pluribus notatum vocabulis idem declarantibus*. *Subtiliter*: Cic.'s constant trans. of ακριβως or κατʼ ακριβειαν (*passim* in Sext. e.g. *P.H.* II. 123). *Inaniterne moveatur*: MSS. agree in *ve* for *ne*, on which see *M.D.F.* IV. 76. *Inaniter* = κενως = ψευδως. Cf. n. on I. 35, also II. 47, *D.F.* V. 3 (*inaniter moveri*), *T.D.* IV. 13, *De Div.* II. 120, 126, 140 (*per se moveri*), Greek κενοπαθειν (Sext. *P.H.* II. 49), κενοπαθεια (= *inanis motus*, Sext. *A.M.* VIII. 184), κενοπαθηματα και αναπλασματα της διανοιας (*ib.* VIII. 354), διακενος ʽελκυσμος (*ib.* VII. 241), διακενος φαντασια (*ib.* VIII. 67), and the frequent phrase κινημα της διανοιας. For the meaning see n. on 47. *Relinquitur*: so in Sext. απολειπειν is constantly used as the opposite of αναιρειν (*tollere*).

§35. *Neminem* etc.: they are content to make strong statements without any mark of certainty. *Primo quasi adspectu*: the *merely* πιθανη φαντασια is here meant; see 33.

§36. *Ex circumspectione*, etc.: the διεξωδευμενη; see n. on 33. *Primum quia ... deinde*: for the slight anacoluthia, cf. *M.D.F* ed. II. p. 796. *Iis visis*, etc.: i.e. if you have a number of *things*, emitting a number of *appearances*, and you cannot be sure of uniting each *appearance* to the *thing* from which it proceeds, then you can have no faith in any *appearance* even if you have gone through the process required by Carneades' rules. *Ad verum ipsum*: cf. 40. *Quam proxime*: cf. 47, and also 7. *Insigne*: σημειον, the same as *nota* and *signum* above. *Quo obscurato*: so Lamb. for MSS. *obscuro* which Halm keeps. Cf. *quam obscurari volunt* in 42 and *quo sublato* in 33. *Argumentum*: Cic. seems to be thinking of the word τεκμηριον, which, however, the Stoics hardly use. *Id quod significatur*: το σημειωντον in Sext.

§§37—40. Summary The distinction of an animal is to act. You must either therefore deprive it of sensation, or allow it to assent to phenomena (37). Mind, memory, the arts and virtue itself, require a firm assent to be given to some phenomena, he therefore who does away with assent does away with all action in life (38, 39).

§37. *Explicabamus*: 19—21 and 30 (*quae vis esset in sensibus*). *Inanimum*: not *inanimatum*, cf. *M.D.F.* IV. 36. *Agit aliquid*: I. 23. *Quae est in nostra*: Walker's insertion of *non* before *est* is needless, cf. n. on I. 40. It is the impact of the sensation from without, not the assent given to it, that is involuntary (Sext. *A.M.* VIII. 397 το μεν γαρ φαντασιωθηναι αβουλητον ην). For *in potestate* cf. *De Fato* 9, *N.D.* I. 69

§38. *Eripitur*: cf. 30. *Neque sentire*: Christ om. *neque*; but the sceptics throughout are supposed to rob people of their senses. *Cedere*: cf. εικειν, ειξις in Sext. *P.H.* I. 193, 230, Diog. VII. 51, των δε αισθητικων μετα ειξεως και συγκαταθεσεως γινονται [ʾαι φαντασια]; also 66 of this book. Οικειον: cf. 34. *Adsentitur statim*: this really contradicts a good deal that has gone before, esp. 20. *Memoriam*: cf. 22. *In nostra potestate*: this may throw light on fragm. 15 of the *Ac. Post.*, which see.

§39. *Virtus*: even the Stoics, who were fatalists as a rule, made moral action depend on the freedom of the will; see n. on I. 40. *Ante videri aliquid* for the doctrine cf. 25, for the passive use of *videri*, n. on 25. *Adsentiatur*: the passive use is illustrated by Madv. *Em.* 131, the change of construction from infin. to subj. after *necesse est* on *D.F.* V. 25. *Tollit e vita*: so *De Fato* 29.

§§40—42. Summary. The Academics have a regular method. They first give a general definition of sensation, and then lay down the different classes of sensations. Then they put forward their two strong arguments, (1) *things* which produce *sensations* such as might have been produced in the same form by other *things*, cannot be partly capable of being perceived, partly not capable, (2) *sensations* must be assumed to be of the same form if our faculties do not enable us to distinguish between them. Then they proceed. Sensations are partly true, partly false, the false cannot of course be real *perceptions*, while the true are always of a form which the false *may* assume. Now sensations which are indistinguishable from false cannot be partly perceptions, partly not. There is therefore no sensation which is also a perception (40). Two admissions, they say, are universally made, (1) false sensations cannot be perceptions, (2) sensations which are indistinguishable from false, cannot be partly perceptions, partly not. The following two assertions they strive to prove, (1) sensations are partly true, partly false, (2) every sensation which proceeds from a reality, has a form which it might have if it proceeded from an unreality (41). To prove these propositions, they divide perceptions into those which are sensations, and those which are deduced from sensations; after which they show that credit cannot be given to either class (42). [The word "perception" is used to mean "a certainly known sensation."]

§40. *Quasi fundamenta*: a trans. probably of θεμελιος or the like; cf. ʽωσπερ θεμελιος in Sext. *A.M.* V. 50. *Artem*: method, like τεχνη, cf. *M.D.F.* III. 4, Mayor on Iuv. VII. 177. *Vim*: the general character which attaches to all φαντασιαι; *genera* the different classes of φαντασιαι. *Totidem verbis*: of course with a view to showing that nothing really corresponded to the definition. Carneades largely used the *reductio ad absurdum* method. *Contineant ... quaestionem*: cf. 22 and *T.D.* IV. 65 *una res videtur causam continere*. *Quae ita*: it is essential throughout this passage to distinguish clearly the *sensation* (*visum*) from the *thing* which causes it. Here the *things* are meant; two *things* are supposed to cause two *sensations* so similar that the person who has one of the *sensations* cannot tell from which of the two *things* it comes. Under these circumstances the sceptics urge that it is absurd to divide *things* into those which can be perceived (known with certainty) and those which cannot. *Nihil interesse autem*: the sceptic is not concerned to prove the absolute similarity of the two sensations which come from the two dissimilar things, it is enough if he can show that human faculties are not perfect enough to discern whatever difference may exist, cf. 85. *Alia vera sunt*: Numenius in Euseb. *Pr. Ev.* XIV. 8, 4 says Carneades allowed that truth and falsehood (or reality and unreality) could be affirmed of *things*, though not of *sensations*. If we could only pierce *through* a sensation and arrive at its source, we should be able to tell whether to believe the sensation or not. As we cannot do this, it is wrong to assume that *sensation* and *thing* correspond. Cf. Sext. *P.H.* I. 22 περι μεν του φαισθαι τοιον η τοιον το ʽυποκειμενον (i.e. the thing from which the appearance proceeds) ουδεις ισως αμφισβητει, περι δε του ει τοιουτον εστιν ʽοποιον φαινεται ζητειται. Neither Carneades nor Arcesilas ever denied, as some modern sceptics have done, the actual existence of things which cause sensations, they simply maintained that, granting the existence of the things, our sensations do not give us correct information about them. *Eiusdem modi*: cf. 33 *eodem modo*. *Non posse accidere*: this is a very remarkable, and, as Madv. (*D.F.* I. 30) thinks, impossible, change from *recta oratio* to *obliqua*. Halm with Manut. reads *potest*. Cf. 101.

§41. *Neque enim*: a remark of Lucullus' merely. *Quod sit a vero*: cf. Munio on Lucr. II. 51 *fulgor ab auro*. *Possit*: for the om. of *esse* cf. n. on I. 29.

§42. *Proposita*: cf. προτασεις *passim* in Sext. *In sensus*: = *in ea, quae ad sensus pertinent* cf. I. 20. *Omni consuetudine*: "general experience" εμπειρια, cf. *N.D.* I. 83. *Quam obscurari volunt*: cf. I. 33. *quod explanari volebant*; the em. of Dav. *obscurare* is against Cic.'s usage, that of Christ *quam observari nolunt* is wanton without being ingenious. *De reliquis*: i.e. *iis quae a sensibus ducuntur*. *In singulisque rebus*: the word *rebus* must mean *subjects*, not *things*, to which the words *in minima dispertiunt* would hardly apply. *Adiuncta*: Sext. *A.M.* VII. 164 (R. and P. 410) πασηι τη δοκουσηι αληθει καθεσταναι ευρισκεται τις απαραλλακτος ψευδης, also VII. 438, etc.

§§43—45. Summary. The sceptics ought not to *define*, for (1) a definition cannot be a definition of two things, (2) if the definition is applicable only to one thing, that thing must be capable of being thoroughly known and distinguished from others (43). For the purposes of reasoning their *probabile* is not enough. Reasoning can only proceed upon *certain* premises. Again to say that there are false sensations is to say that there are true ones; you acknowledge therefore a difference, then you contradict yourselves and say there is none (44). Let us discuss the matter farther. The innate clearness of *visa*, aided by reason, can lead to knowledge (45).

§43. *Horum*: Lamb. *harum*; the text however is quite right, cf. Madv. *Gram.* 214 *b*. *Luminibus*: cf. 101. *Nihilo magis*: = ουδεν μαλλον, which was constantly in the mouths of sceptics, see e.g. Sext. *P.H.* I. 14. *Num illa definitio ... transferri*: I need hardly point out that the ʽορος of the Academics was merely founded on probability, just as their "truth" was (cf. n. on 29). An Academic would say in reply to the question, "probably it cannot, but I will not affirm it." *Vel illa vera*: these words seem to me genuine, though nearly all editors attack them. *Vel* = "even" i.e. if *even* the definition is firmly known, the thing, which is more important, must also be known. In *illa vera* we have a pointed mocking repetition like that of *veri et falsi* in 33. *In falsum*: note that *falsum = aliam rem* above. For the sense cf. Sext. *P.H.* II. 209 μοχθηρους ΄ορους ειναι τους περιεχοντας τι των μη προσοντων τοις ΄οριστοις, and the schoolmen's maxim *definitio non debet latior esse definito suo*. *Minime volunt*: cf. 18. *Partibus*: Orelli after Goer. ejected this, but *omnibus* hardly ever stands for *omn. rebus*, therefore C.F. Hermann reads *pariter rebus* for *partibus*. A little closer attention to the subject matter would have shown emendation to be unnecessary, cf. 42 *dividunt in partis*, *T.D.* III. 24, where *genus* = division, *pars* = subdivision.

§44. *Impediri ... fatebuntur*: essentially the same argument as in 33 at the end. *Occurretur*: not an imitation of εναντιουσθαι as Goer. says, but of απανταν, which occurs very frequently in Sext. *Sumpta*: the two premisses are in Gk. called together λημματα, separately λημμα and προσληψις (*sumptio et adsumptio De Div* II. 108). *Orationis*: as Faber points out, Cic. does sometimes use this word like *ratio* (συλλογισμος), cf. *De Leg.* I. 48 *conclusa oratio*. Fab. refers to Gell. XV. 26. *Profiteatur*: so ΄υπισχνεισθαι is often used by Sext. e.g. *A.M.* VIII. 283. *Patefacturum*: n. on 26, εκκαλυπτειν, εκκαλυπτικος, δηλωτικος (the last in Sext. *A.M.* VIII. 277) often recur in Greek. *Primum esse ... nihil interesse*: there is no inconsistency. Carneades allowed that *visa*, in themselves, might be true or false, but affirmed that human faculties were incapable of distinguishing those *visa* which proceed from real things and give a correct representation of the things, from those which either are mere phantoms or, having a real source, do not correctly represent it. Lucullus confuses *essential* with *apparent* difference. *Non iungitur*: a supposed case of διαρτησις, which is opposed to συναρτησις and explained in Sext. *A.M.* VIII. 430.

§45. *Assentati*: here simply = *assensi*. *Praeteritis*: here used in the strong participial sense, "in the class of things passed over," cf. *in remissis Orat.* 59. *Primum igitur ... sed tamen*: for the slight anacoluthia cf. Madv. *Gram.* 480. *Iis qui videntur*: Goer. *is qui videtur*, which is severely criticised by Madv. *Em.* 150. For Epicurus' view of sensation see n. on 79, 80.

§§46—48. Summary. The refusal of people to assent to the innate clearness of some phenomena (εναργεια) is due to two causes, (1) they do not make a serious endeavour to see the light by which these phenomena are surrounded, (2) their faith is shaken by sceptic paradoxes (46). The sceptics argue thus: you allow that mere phantom sensations are often seen in dreams, why then do you not allow what is easier, that two sensations caused by two really existing things may be mistaken the one for the other? (47). Further, they urge that a phantom sensation produces very often the same effect as a real one. The dogmatists say they admit that mere phantom sensations *do* command assent. Why should they not admit that they command assent when they so closely resemble real ones as to be indistinguishable from them? (48)

§46. *Circumfusa sint*: Goer. retains the MSS. *sunt* on the ground that the clause *quanta sint* is inserted παρενθετικως! Orelli actually follows him. For the phrase cf. 122 *circumfusa tenebris*. *Interrogationibus*: cf. I. 5 where I showed that the words *interrogatio* and *conclusio* are convertible. I may add that in Sextus pure syllogisms are very frequently called ερωτησεις, and that he often introduces a new argument by ερωταται και τουτο, when there is nothing interrogatory about the argument at all. *Dissolvere*: απολυεσθαι in Sext. *Occurrere*: cf. 44.

§47. *Confuse loqui*: the mark of a bad dialectician, affirmed of Epicurus in *D.F.* II. 27. *Nulla sunt*: on the use of *nullus* for *non* in Cic. cf. Madv. *Gram.* 455 obs. 5. The usage is mostly colloquial and is very common in Plaut. and Terence, while in Cic. it occurs mostly in the Letters. *Inaniter*: cf. 34. There are two ways in which a sensation may be false, (1) it may come from one really existent thing, but be supposed by the person who feels it to be caused by a totally different thing, (2) it may be a mere φαντασμα or αναπλασμα της διανοιας, a phantom behind which there is no reality at all. *Quae in somnis videantur*: for the support given by Stoics to all forms of divination see Zeller 166, *De Div.* I. 7, etc.

Quaerunt: a slight anacoluthon from *dicatis* above. *Quonam modo ... nihil sit omnino*: this difficult passage can only be properly explained in connection with 50 and with the general plan of the Academics expounded in 41. After long consideration I elucidate it as follows. The whole is an attempt to prove the proposition announced in 41 and 42 viz. *omnibus veris visis adiuncta esse falsa*. The criticism in 50 shows that the argument is meant to be based on the assumption known to be Stoic, *omnia deum posse*. If the god can manufacture (*efficere*) sensations which are false, but probable (as the Stoics say he does in dreams), why can he not manufacture false sensations which are so probable as to closely resemble true ones, or to be only with difficulty distinguishable from the true, or finally to be utterly indistinguishable from the true (this meaning of *inter quae nihil sit omnino* is fixed by 40, where see n.)? *Probabilia*, then, denotes false sensations such as have only a slight degree of resemblance to the true, by the three succeeding stages the resemblance is made complete. The word *probabilia* is a sort of tertiary predicate after *efficere* ("to manufacture so as to be probable"). It *must not be repeated* after the second *efficere*, or the whole sense will be inverted and this section placed out of harmony with 50. *Plane proxime*: = *quam proxime* of 36.

§48. *Ipsa per sese*: simply = *inaniter* as in 34, 47, i.e. without the approach of any external object. *Cogitatione*: the only word in Latin, as διανοια is in Greek, to express our "imagination." *Non numquam*: so Madv. for MSS. *non inquam*. Goer. after Manut. wrote *non inquiunt* with an interrogation at *omnino*. *Veri simile est*: so Madv. *D.F.* III. 58 for *sit*. The argument has the same purpose as that in the last section, viz to show that phantom sensations may produce the same effect on the mind as those which proceed from realities. *Ut si qui*: the *ut* here is merely "as," "for instance," cf. n. on 33. *Nihil ut esset*: the *ut* here is a repetition of the *ut* used several times in the early part of the sentence, all of them alike depend on *sic*. Lamb. expunged *ut* before *esset* and before *quicquam*. *Intestinum et oblatum*: cf. Sext. *A.M.* VII. 241 ητοι των εκτος η των εν ʽημιν παθων, and the two classes of *falsa visa* mentioned in n. on 47. *Sin autem sunt*, etc.: if there *are* false sensations which are probable (as the Stoics allow), why should there not be false sensations so probable as to be with difficulty distinguishable from the true? The rest exactly as in 47.

§§49—53. Antiochus attacked these arguments as *soritae*, and therefore faulty (49). The admission of a certain amount of similarity between true and false sensations does not logically lead to the impossibility of distinguishing between the true and the false (50). We contend that these phantom sensations lack that self evidence which we require before giving assent. When we have wakened from the dream, we make light of the sensations we had while in it (51). But, say our opponents, while they last our dreaming sensations are as vivid as our waking ones. This we deny (52). "But," say they, "you allow that the wise man in madness withholds his assent." This proves nothing, for he will do so in many other circumstances in life. All this talk about dreamers, madmen and drunkards is unworthy our attention (53).

§49. *Antiochus*: Sext. often quotes him in the discussion of this and similar subjects. *Ipsa capita*: αυτα τα κεφαλαια. *Interrogationis*: the *sorites* was always in the form of a series of questions, cf. *De Div.* II. 11 (where Cic. says the Greek word was already naturalised, so that his proposed trans. *acervalis* is unnecessary), *Hortens.* fragm. 47, and n. on 92. *Hoc vocant*: i.e. *hoc genus*, cf. *D.F.* III. 70 *ex eo genere, quae prosunt. Vitiosum*: cf. *D.F.* IV. 50 *ille sorites, quo nihil putatis* (Stoici) *vitiosius*. Most edd. read *hos*, which indeed in 136 is a necessary em. for MSS. *hoc. Tale visum*: i.e. *falsum. Dormienti*: sc. τινι. *Ut probabile sit*, etc.: cf. 47, 48 and notes. *Primum quidque*: not *quodque* as Klotz; cf. *M.D.F.* II. 105, to whose exx. add *De Div.* II. 112, and an instance of *proximus quisque* in *De Off.* II. 75. *Vitium*: cf. *vitiosum* above.

§50. *Omnia deum posse*: this was a principle generally admitted among Stoics at least, see *De Div.* II. 86. For the line of argument here cf. *De Div.* II. 106 *fac dare deos, quod absurdum est. Eadem*: this does not mean that the two sensations are merged into one, but merely that when one of them is present, it cannot be distinguished from the other; see n. on 40. *Similes*: after this *sunt* was added by Madv. *In suo genere essent*: substitute *esse viderentur* for *essent*, and you get the real view of the Academic, who would allow that *things in their essence* are divisible into sharply-defined *genera*, but would deny that the *sensations* which proceed from or are caused by the *things*, are so divisible.

§51. *Una depulsio*: cf. 128 (*omnium rerum una est definitio comprehendendi*), *De Div.* II. 136 (*omnium somniorum una ratio est*). *In quiete*: = *in somno*, a rather poetical usage. *Narravit*: Goer., Orelli, Klotz alter into *narrat*, most wantonly. *Visus Homerus*, etc.: this famous dream of Ennius, recorded in his *Annals*, is referred to by Lucr. I. 124, Cic. *De Rep.* VI. 10 (*Somn. Scip.* c. 1), Hor. *Epist.* II. 1, 50. *Simul ut*: rare in Cic., see Madv. *D.F.* II. 33, who, however, unduly restricts the usage. In three out of the five passages where he allows it to stand, the *ut* precedes a vowel; Cic. therefore used it to avoid writing *ac* before a vowel, so that in *D.F.* II. 33 *ut* should probably be written (with Manut. and others) for *et* which Madv. ejects.

§52. *Eorumque*: MSS. om. *que*. Dav. wrote *ac* before *eorum*, this however is as impossible in Cic. as the c before a guttural condemned in n. on 34. For the argument see n. on 80 *quasi vero quaeratur quid sit non quid videatur*. *Primum interest*: for om. of *deinde* cf. 45, 46. *Imbecillius*: cf. I. 41. *Edormiverunt*: "have slept *off* the effects," cf. αποβριζειν in Homer. *Relaxentur*: cf. ανιεναι της οργης Aristoph. *Ran.* 700, *relaxare* is used in the neut. sense in *D.F.* II. 94. *Alcmaeonis*: the Alcmaeon of Ennius is often quoted by Cic., e.g. *D.F.* IV. 62.

§53. *Sustinet*: επεχει; see on 94. *Aliquando sustinere*: the point of the Academic remark lay in the fact that in the state of madness the εποχη of the *sapiens* becomes *habitual*; he gives up the attempt to distinguish between true and false *visa*. Lucullus answers that, did no distinction exist, he would give up the attempt to draw it, even in the sane condition. *Confundere*: so 58, 110, Sext. *A.M.* VIII. 56 (συγχεουσι τα πραγματα), *ib.* VIII. 157 (συγχεομεν τον βιον), VIII. 372 (῾ολην συγχεει την φιλοσοφον ζητησιν), Plut. *De Communi Notit. adv. Stoicos* p. 1077 (῾ως παντα πραγματα συγχεουσι). *Utimur*: "we have to put up with," so χρησθαι is used in Gk. *Ebriosorum*: "habitual drunkards," more invidious than *vinolenti* above. *Illud attendimus*: Goer., and Orelli write *num illud*, but the emphatic *ille* is often thus introduced by itself in questions, a good ex. occurs in 136. *Proferremus*: this must apparently be added to the exx. qu. by Madv. on *D.F.* II. 35 of the subj. used to denote "*non id quod fieret factumve esset, sed quod fieri debuerit.*" As such passages are often misunderstood, I note that they can be most rationally explained as elliptic constructions in which a *condition* is expressed without its *consequence*. We have an exact parallel in English, e.g. "*tu dictis Albane maneres*" may fairly be translated, "hadst thou but kept to thy word, Alban!" Here the condition "*if* thou hadst kept, etc." stands without the consequence "thou wouldst not have died," or something of the kind. Such a condition may be expressed without *si*, just as in Eng. without "*if*," cf. Iuv. III. 78 and Mayor's n. The use of the Greek optative to express a wish (with ει γαρ, etc., and even without ει) is susceptible of the same explanation. The Latin subj. has many such points of similarity with the Gk. optative, having absorbed most of the functions of the lost Lat. optative. [Madv. on *D.F.* II. 35 seems to imply that he prefers the hypothesis of a suppressed protasis, but as in his *Gram.* 351 *b*, obs. 4 he attempts no elucidation, I cannot be certain.]

§§54—63. Summary. The Academics fail to see that such doctrines do away with all probability even. Their talk about twins and seals is childish (54). They press into their service the old physical philosophers, though ordinarily none are so much ridiculed by them (55). Democritus may say that innumerable worlds exist in every particular similar to ours, but I appeal to more cultivated physicists, who maintain that each thing has its own peculiar marks (55, 56). The Servilii were distinguished from one another by their friends, and Delian breeders of fowls could tell from the appearance of an egg which hen had laid it (56, 57). We however, do not much care whether we are able to distinguish eggs from one another or not. Another thing that they say is absurd, viz. that there may be distinction between individual sensations, but not between classes of sensations (58). Equally absurd are those "probable and undisturbed" sensations they profess to follow. The doctrine that true and false sensations are indistinguishable logically leads to the unqualified εποχη of Arcesilas (59). What nonsense they talk about inquiring after the truth, and about the bad influence of authority! (60). Can you, Cicero, the panegyrist of philosophy, plunge us into more than Cimmerian darkness? (61) By holding that knowledge is impossible you weaken the force of your famous oath that you "knew all about" Catiline. Thus ended Lucullus, amid the continued wonder of Hortensius (62, 63). Then Catulus said that he should not be surprised if the speech of Lucullus were to induce me to change my view (63).

§54. *Ne hoc quidem*: the common trans. "not even" for "*ne quidem*" is often inappropriate. Trans. here "they do not see this *either*," cf. n. on I. 5. *Habeant*: the slight alteration *habeat* introduced by Goer. and Orelli quite destroys the point of the sentence. *Quod nolunt*: cf. 44. *An sano*: Lamb. *an ut sano*, which Halm approves, and Baiter reads. *Similitudines*: cf. 84—86. The impossibility of distinguishing between twins, eggs, the impressions of seals, etc. was a favourite theme with the sceptics, while the Stoics contended that no two things were absolutely alike. Aristo the Chian, who maintained the Stoic view, was practically refuted by his fellow pupil Persaeus, who took two twins, and made one deposit money with Aristo, while the other after a time asked for the money back and received it. On this subject cf. Sextus *A.M.* VII. 408—410. *Negat esse*: in phrases like this Cic. nearly always places *esse* second, especially at the end of a clause. *Cur eo non estis contenti*: Lucullus here ignores the question at issue, which concerned the *amount* of similarity. The dogmatists maintained that the similarity between two phenomena could never be great enough to render it impossible to guard against mistaking the one for the other, the sceptics argued that it could. *Quod rerum natura non patitur*: again Lucullus confounds *essential* with *phenomenal* difference, and so misses his mark; cf. n. on 50. *Nulla re differens*: cf. the *nihil differens* of 99, the substitution of which here would perhaps make the sentence clearer. The words are a trans. of the common Gk. term απαραλλακτος (Sext. *A.M.* VII. 252, etc.). *Ulla communitas*: I am astonished to find Bait. returning to the reading of Lamb. *nulla* after the fine note of Madv. (*Em.* 154), approved by Halm and other recent edd. The opinion maintained by the Stoics may be stated thus *suo quidque genere est tale, quale est, nec est in duobus aut pluribus nulla re differens ulla communitas* (ουδε 'υπαρχει επιμιγη απαραλλακτος). This opinion is negatived by *non patitur ut* and it will be evident at a glance that the only change required is to put the two verbs (*est*) into the subjunctive. The change of *ulla* into *nulla* is in no way needed. *Ut [sibi] sint*: *sibi* is clearly wrong here. Madv., in a note communicated privately to Halm and printed by the latter on p. 854 of Bait. and Halm's ed of the philosophical works, proposed to read *nulla re differens communitas visi? Sint et ova* etc. omitting *ulla* and *ut* and changing *visi* into *sibi* (cf. Faber's em. *novas* for *bonas* in 72). This ingenious but, as I think, improbable conj. Madv. has just repeated in the second vol. of his *Adversaria*. Lamb. reads *at tibi sint*, Dav. *at si vis, sint*, Christ *ut tibi sint*, Bait. *ut si sint* after C.F.W. Muller, I should prefer *sui* for *sibi* (SVI for SIBI). B is very frequently written for V in the MSS., and I would easily slip in. *Eosdem*: once more we have Lucullus' chronic and perhaps intentional misconception of the sceptic position; see n. on 50. Before leaving this section, I may point out that the επιμιγη or επιμιξια των φαντασιων supplies Sext. with one of the sceptic τροποι, see *Pyrrh. Hyp.* I. 124.

§55. *Irridentur*: the contradictions of physical philosophers were the constant sport of the sceptics, cf. Sext. *A.M.* IX. 1. *Absolute ita paris*: Halm as well as Bait. after Christ, brackets *ita*; if any change be needed, it would be better to place it before *undique*. For this opinion of Democr. see R. and P. 45. *Et eo quidem innumerabilis*: this is the quite untenable reading of the MSS., for which no satisfactory em. has yet been proposed, cf. 125. *Nihil differat, nihil intersit*: these two verbs often appear together in Cic., e.g.*D.F.* III. 25.

§56. *Potiusque*: this adversative use of *que* is common with *potius*, e.g.*D.F.* I. 51. Cf. *T.D.* II. 55 *ingemescere nonnum quam viro concessum est, idque raro*, also *ac potius*, *Ad Att.* I. 10, etc. *Proprietates*:

the ιδιοτητες or ιδιωματα of Sextus, the doctrine of course involves the whole question at issue between dogmatism and scepticism. *Cognoscebantur*: Dav. *dignoscebantur*, Walker *internoscebantur*. The MSS. reading is right, cf. 86. *Consuetudine*: cf. 42, "experience". *Minimum*: an adverb like *summum*.

§57. *Dinotatas*: so the MSS., probably correctly, though Forc. does not recognise the word. Most edd. change it into *denotatas*. *Artem*: τεχνην, a set of rules. *In proverbio*: so *venire in proverbium, in proverbii usum venire, proverbii locum obtinere, proverbii loco dici* are all used. *Salvis rebus*: not an uncommon phrase, e.g. *Ad Fam.* IV. 1. *Gallinas*: cf. fragm. 19 of the *Acad. Post.* The similarity of eggs was discussed *ad nauseam* by the sceptics and dogmatists. Hermagoras the Stoic actually wrote a book entitled, ωι σκοπια (egg investigation) η περι σοφιστειας προς Ακαδημαικους, mentioned by Suidas.

§58. *Contra nos*: the sense requires *nos*, but all Halm's MSS. except one read *vos*. *Non internoscere*: this is the reading of all the MSS., and is correct, though Orelli omits *non*. The sense is, "we are quite content not to be able to distinguish between the eggs, we shall not on that account be led into a mistake for our rule will prevent us from making any positive assertion about the eggs." *Adsentiri*: for the passive use of this verb cf. 39. *Par est*: so Dav. for *per*, which most MSS. have. The older edd. and Orelli have *potest*, with one MS. *Quasi*: the em. of Madv. for the *quam si* of the MSS. *Transversum digitum*: cf. 116. *Ne confundam omnia*: cf. 53, 110. *Natura tolletur*: this of course the sceptics would deny. They refused to discuss the nature of *things in themselves*, and kept to *phenomena*. *Intersit*: i.e. *inter visa*. *In animos*: Orelli with one MS. reads *animis*; if the MSS. are correct the assertion of Krebs and Allgayer (*Antibarbarus*, ed. 4) "*imprimere* wird klas sisch verbunden *in aliqua re*, nicht *in aliquam rem*," will require modification. *Species et quasdam formas*: ειδη και γενη, *quasdam* marks the fact that *formas* is a trans. I have met with no other passage where any such doctrine is assigned to a sceptic. As it stands in the text the doctrine is absurd, for surely it must always be easier to distinguish between two *genera* than between two individuals. If the *non* before *vos* were removed a better sense would be given. It has often been inserted by copyists when *sed, tamen*, or some such word, comes in the following clause, as in the famous passage of Cic *Ad Quintum Fratrem*, II. 11, discussed by Munro, Lucr. p. 313, ed. 3.

§59. *Illud vero perabsurdum*: note the omission of *est*, which often takes place after the emphatic pronoun. *Impediamini*: cf. n. on 33. *A veris*: if *visis* be supplied the statement corresponds tolerably with the Academic belief, if *rebus* be meant, it is wide of the mark. *Id est ... retentio*: supposed to be a gloss by Man., Lamb., see however nn. on I. 6, 8. *Constitit*: from *consto*, not from *consisto* cf. 63 *qui tibi constares*. *Si vera sunt*: cf. 67, 78, 112, 148. The *nonnulli* are Philo and Metrodorus, see 78. *Tollendus est adsensus*: i.e. even that qualified assent which the Academics gave to probable phenomena. *Adprobare*: this word is ambiguous, meaning either qualified or unqualified assent. Cf. n. on 104. *Id est peccaturum*: "which is equivalent to sinning," cf. I. 42. *Iam nimium etiam*: note *iam* and *etiam* in the same clause.

§60. *Pro omnibus*: note *omnibus* for *omnibus rebus*. *Ista mysteria*: Aug. *Contra Ac.* III. 37, 38 speaks of various doctrines, which were *servata et pro mysteriis custodita* by the New Academics. The notion that the Academic scepticism was merely external and polemically used, while they had an esoteric dogmatic doctrine, must have originated in the reactionary period of Metrodorus (of Stratonice), Philo, and Antiochus, and may perhaps from a passage of Augustine, *C. Ac.* III. 41 (whose authority must have been Cicero), be attributed to the first of the three (cf. Zeller 534, n.). The idea is ridiculed by Petrus Valentia (Orelli's reprint, p. 279), and all succeeding inquirers. *Auctoritate*: cf. 8, 9. *Utroque*: this neuter, referring to two fem. nouns, is noticeable, see exx. in Madv. *Gram.* 214 *c*.

§61. *Amicissimum*: "*because* you are my dear friend". *Commoveris*: a military term, cf. *De Div.* II. 26 and Forc., also Introd. p. 53. *Sequere*: either this is future, as in 109, or *sequeris*, the constant form in Cic. of the pres., must be read. *Approbatione omni*: the word *omni* is emphatic, and includes both qualified and unqualified assent, cf. 59. *Orbat sensibus*: cf. 74, and *D.F.* I. 64, where Madv. is wrong in reproving

Torquatus for using the phrase *sensus tolli*, on the ground that the Academics swept away not *sensus* but *iudicium sensuum Cimmeriis*. Goer. qu. Plin. *N.H.* III. 5, Sil. Ital. XII. 131, Festus, s.v. *Cimmerii*, to show that the town or village of Cimmerium lay close to Bauli, and probably induced this mention of the legendary people. *Deus aliquis*: so the best edd. without comment, although they write *deus aliqui* in 19. It is difficult to distinguish between *aliquis* and *aliqui*, *nescio quis* and *nescio qui*, *si quis* and *si qui* (for the latter see n. on 81). As *aliquis* is substantival, *aliqui* adjectival, *aliquis* must not be written with impersonal nouns like *terror* (*T.D.* IV. 35, V. 62), *dolor* (*T.D.* I. 82, *Ad Fam.* VII. 1, 1), *casus* (*De Off.* III. 33). In the case of personal nouns the best edd. vary, e.g. *deus aliqui* (*T.D.* I. 23, IV. 35), *deus aliquis* (*Lael.* 87, *Ad Fam.* XIV. 7, 1), *anularius aliqui* (86 of this book), *magistratus aliquis* (*In Verr.* IV. 146). With a proper name belonging to a real person *aliquis* ought to be written (*Myrmecides* in 120, see my n.). *Dispiciendum*: not *despiciendum*, cf. *M.D.F.* II. 97, IV. 64, also *De Div.* II. 81, *verum dispicere*. *Iis vinculis*, etc. this may throw light on fragm. 15 of the *Acad. Post.*, which see.

§62. *Motum animorum*: n. on 34. *Actio rerum*: here *actio* is a pure verbal noun like πραξις, cf. *De Off.* I. 83, and expressions like *actio vitae* (*N.D.* I. 2), *actio ullius rei* (108 of this book), and the similar use of *actus* in Quintilian (*Inst. Or.* X. 1, 31, with Mayor's n.) *Iuratusque*: Bait. possibly by a mere misprint reads *iratus*. *Comperisse*: this expression of Cic., used in the senate in reference to Catiline's conspiracy, had become a cant phrase at Rome, with which Cic. was often taunted. See *Ad Fam.* V. 5, 2, *Ad Att.* I. 14, 5. *Licebat*: this is the reading of the best MSS., not *liquebat*, which Goer., Kl., Or. have. For the support accorded by Lucullus to Cic. during the conspiracy see 3, and the passages quoted in Introd. p. 46 with respect to Catulus, in most of which Lucullus is also mentioned.

§63. *Quod ... fecerat, ut*: different from the constr. treated by Madv. *Gram.* 481 *b*. *Quod* refers simply to the fact of Lucullus' admiration, which the clause introduced by *ut* defines, "which admiration he had shown ... to such an extent that, etc." *Iocansne an*: this use of *ne ... an* implies, Madv. says (on *D.F.* V. 87), more doubt than the use of *ne* alone as in *vero falsone*. *Memoriter*: nearly all edd. before Madv. make this mean *e memoria* as opposed to *de scripto*; he says, "*laudem habet bonae et copiosae memoriae*" (on *D.F.* I. 34). See Krebs and Allgayer in the *Antibarbarus*, ed. 4. *Censuerim*: more modest than *censeo*, see Madv. *Gram.* 380. *Tantum enim non te modo monuit*: edd. before Madv., seeing no way of taking *modo* exc. with *non*, ejected it. Madv. (*Em.* 160) retains it, making it mean *paulo ante*. On the other hand, Halm after Christ asserts that *tantum non* = μovov ov occurs nowhere else in Cic. Bait. therefore ejects *non*, taking *tantum* as *hoc tantum, nihil praeterea*. Livy certainly has the suspected use of *tantum non*. *Tribunus*: a retort comes in 97, 144. *Antiochum*: cf. I. 13. *Destitisse*: on the difference between *memini* followed by the pres. and by the perf. inf. consult Madv. *Gram.* 408 *b*, obs. 2.

§§64—71. Summary. Cic. much moved thus begins. The strength of Lucullus argument has affected me much, yet I feel that it can be answered. First, however, I must speak something that concerns my character (64). I protest my entire sincerity in all that I say, and would confirm it by an oath, were that proper (65). I am a passionate inquirer after truth, and on that very account hold it disgraceful to assent to what is false. I do not deny that I make slips, but we must deal with the *sapiens*, whose characteristic it is never to err in giving his assent (66). Hear Arcesilas' argument: if the *sapiens* ever gives his assent he will be obliged to *opine*, but he never will *opine* therefore he never will give his assent. The Stoics and Antiochus deny the first of these statements, on the ground that it is possible to distinguish between true and false (67). Even if it be so the mere habit of assenting is full of peril. Still, our whole argument must tend to show that *perception* in the Stoic sense is impossible (68). However, a few words first with Antiochus. When he was converted, what proof had he of the doctrine he had so long denied? (69) Some think he wished to found a school called by his own name. It is more probable that he could no longer bear the opposition of all other schools to the Academy (70). His conversion gave a splendid opening for an *argumentum ad hominem* (71).

§64. *Quadam oratione*: so Halm, also Bait. after the best MSS., not *quandam orationem* as Lamb., Orelli. *De ipsa re*: cf. *de causa ipsa* above. *Respondere posse*: for the om. of *me* before the infin, which has wrongly caused many edd. either to read *respondere* (as Dav., Bait.) or to insert *me* (as Lamb.), see n. on I. 7.

§65. *Studio certandi*: = φιλονεικια. *Pertinacia ... calumnia*: n. on 14. *Iurarem*: Cic. was thinking of his own famous oath at the end of his consulship.

§66. *Turpissimum*: cf. I. 45, *N.D.* I. 1. *Opiner*: *opinio* or δοξα is judgment based on insufficient grounds. *Sed quaerimus de sapiente*: cf. 115, *T.D.* IV. 55, 59 also *De Or.* III. 75 *non quid ego sed quid orator. Magnus ... opinator*: Aug. *Contra Acad.* III. 31 qu. this passage wrongly as from the *Hortensius*. He imitates it, *ibid.* I. 15 *magnus definitor. Qua fidunt*, etc.: these lines are part of Cic.'s *Aratea*, and are quoted in *N.D.* II. 105, 106. *Phoenices*: the same fact is mentioned by Ovid, *Fasti* III. 107, *Tristia* IV. 3, 1. *Sed Helicen*: the best MSS. om. *ad*, which Orelli places before *Helicen. Elimatas*: the MSS. are divided between this and *limatas. Elimare*, though a very rare word occurs *Ad Att.* XVI. 7, 3. *Visis cedo*: cf. n. on 38. *Vim maximam*: so *summum munus* is applied to the same course of action in *D.F.* III. 31. *Cogitatione*: "idea". *Temeritate*: cf. I. 42, *De Div.* I. 7, and the charge of προπετεια constantly brought against the dogmatists by Sext. *Praepostere*: in a disorderly fashion, taking the wrong thing first.

§67. *Aliquando ... opinabitur*: this of course is only true if you grant the Academic doctrine, *nihil posse percipi. Secundum illud ... etiam opinari*: it seems at first sight as though *adsentiri* and *opinari* ought to change places in this passage, as Manut. proposes. The difficulty lies in the words *secundum illud*, which, it has been supposed, must refer back to the second premiss of Arcesilas' argument. But if the passage be translated thus, "Carneades sometimes granted *as a second premiss* the following statement, that the wise man sometimes does opine" the difficulty vanishes. The argument of Carneades would then run thus, (1) *Si ulli rei*, etc. as above, (2) *adsentietur autem aliquando*, (3) *opinabitur igitur*.

§68. *Adsentiri quicquam*: only with neuter pronouns like this could *adsentiri* be followed by an accusative case. *Sustinenda est*: εφεκτεον. *Iis quae possunt*: these words MSS. om. *Tam in praecipiti*: for the position of *in* cf. n. on I. 25. The best MSS. have here *tamen in*. Madv. altered *tamen* to *tam* in n. on *D.F.* V. 26. The two words are often confused, as in *T.D.* IV. 7, cf. also n. on I. 16. *Sin autem*, etc.: cf. the passage of Lactantius *De Falsa Sapientia* III. 3, qu. by P. Valentia (p. 278 of Orelli's reprint) *si neque sciri quicquam potest, ut Socrates docuit, neque opinari, oportet, ut Zeno, tota philosophia sublata est. Nitamur ... percipi*: "let us struggle to prove the proposition, etc." The construction is, I believe, unexampled so that I suspect *hoc*, or some such word, to have fallen out between *igitur* and *nihil*.

§69. *Non acrius*: one of the early editions omits *non* while Goer. reads *acutius* and puts a note of interrogation at *defensitaverat*. M. *Em.* 161 points out the absurdity of making Cic. say that the old arguments of Antiochus in favour of Academicism were weaker than his new arguments against it. *Quis enim*: so Lamb. for MSS. *quisquam enim. Excogitavit*: on interrogations not introduced by a particle of any kind see Madv. *Gram.* 450. *Eadem dicit*: on the subject in hand, of course. Taken without this limitation the proposition is not strictly true, see n. on 132. *Sensisse*: = *iudicasse*, n. on I. 22. *Mnesarchi ... Dardani*: see *Dict. Biogr.*

§70. *Revocata est*: Manut. here wished to read *renovata*, cf. n. on I. 14. *Nominis dignitatem*, etc.: hence Aug. *Contra Acad.* III. 41 calls him *foeneus ille Platonicus Antiochus* (that *tulchan* Platonist). *Gloriae causa*: cf. Aug. *ibid.* II. 15 *Antiochus gloriae cupidior quam veritatis. Facere dicerent*: so Camerarius for the MSS. *facerent. Sustinere*: cf. 115 *sustinuero Epicureos. Sub Novis*: Faber's brilliant em. for the MSS. *sub nubes*. The *Novae Tabernae* were in the forum, and are often mentioned by Cic. and Livy. In *De Or.* II. 266 a story is told of Caesar, who, while speaking *sub Veteribus*, points to a "*tabula*" which hangs *sub*

Novis. The excellence of Faber's em. may be felt by comparing that of Manut. *sub nube*, and that of Lamb. *nisi sub nube*. I have before remarked that *b* is frequently written in MSS. for *v. Maenianorum*: projecting eaves, according to Festus s.v. They were probably named from their inventor like *Vitelliana*, *Vatinia* etc.

§71. *Quoque ... argumento*: the sentence is anacoluthic, the broken thread is picked up by *quod argumentum* near the end. *Utrum*: the neuter pronoun, not the so called conjunction, the two alternatives are marked by *ne* and *an*. The same usage is found in *D.F.* II. 60, *T.D.* IV. 9, and must be carefully distinguished from the use of *utrum ... ne ... an*, which occurs not unfrequently in Cic., e g *De Invent.* II. 115 *utrum copiane sit agri an penuria consideratur*. On this point cf. M. *Em.* 163, *Gram.* 452, obs. 1, 2, Zumpt on Cic. *Verr.* IV. 73. *Honesti inane nomen esse*: a modern would be inclined to write *honestum*, in apposition to *nomen*, cf. *D.F.* V. 18 *voluptatis alii putant primum appetitum*. *Voluptatem* etc.: for the conversion of Dionysius (called ʽο μεταθεμενος) from Stoicism to Epicureanism cf. *T.D.* II. 60, Diog. Laert. VII. 166—7. *A vero*: "coming from a reality," cf. 41, n. *Is curavit*: Goer. reads *his*, "*solet V. D. in hoc pronomen saevire*," says Madv. The scribes often prefix *h* to parts of the pronoun *is*, and Goer. generally patronises their vulgar error.

§§72—78. Summary. You accuse me of appealing to ancient names like a revolutionist, yet Anaxagoras, Democritus, and Metrodorus, philosophers of the highest position, protest against the truth of sense knowledge, and deny the possibility of knowledge altogether (72, 73). Empedocles, Xenophanes, and Parmenides all declaim against sense knowledge. You said that Socrates and Plato must not be classed with these. Why? Socrates said he knew nothing but his own ignorance, while Plato pursued the same theme in all his works (74). Now do you see that I do not merely name, but take for my models famous men? Even Chrysippus stated many difficulties concerning the senses and general experience. You say he solved them, even if he did, which I do not believe, he admitted that it was not easy to escape being ensnared by them (75). The Cyrenaics too held that they knew nothing about things external to themselves. The sincerity of Arcesilas may be seen thus (76). Zeno held strongly that the wise man ought to keep clear from *opinion*. Arcesilas agreed but this without *knowledge* was impossible. *Knowledge* consists of *perceptions*. Arcesilas therefore demanded a definition of *perception*. This definition Arcesilas combated. This is the controversy which has lasted to our time. Do away with *opinion* and *perception*, and the εποχη of Arcesilas follows at once (77, 78).

§72. *De antiquis philosophis*: on account of the somewhat awkward constr. Lamb. read *antiquos philosophos*. *Popularis*: cf. 13. *Res non bonas*: MSS. om. *non*, which Or. added with two very early editions. Faber ingeniously supposed the true reading to be *novas*, which would be written *nobas*, and then pass into *bonas*. *Nivem nigram*: this deliverance of Anaxagoras is very often referred to by Sextus. In *P.H.* I. 33 he quotes it as an instance of the refutation of φαινομενα by means of νοουμενα, "Αναξαγορας τωι λευκην ειναι την χιονα, ανετιθει ʽοτι χιων εστιν ʽυδορ πεπηγος το δε ʽυδορ εστι μελαν και ʽη χιων αρα μελαινα." There is an obscure joke on this in *Ad Qu. Fratrem* II. 13, 1 *risi nivem atram ... teque hilari animo esse et prompto ad iocandum valde me iuvat*. *Sophistes*: here treated as the demagogue of philosophy. *Ostentationis*: = επιδειξεος.

§73. *Democrito*: Cic., as Madv. remarks on *D.F.* I. 20, always exaggerates the merits of Democr. in order to depreciate the Epicureans, cf. *T.D.* I. 22, *De Div.* I. 5, II. 139, *N.D.* I. 120, *De Or.* I. 42. *Quintae classis*: a metaphor from the Roman military order. *Qui veri esse aliquid*, etc.: cf. *N.D.* I. 12 *non enim sumus ii quibus nihil verum esse videatur, sed ii qui omnibus veris falsa quaedam adiuncta dicamus*. *Non obscuros sed tenebricosos*: "not merely dim but darkened." There is a reference here to the σκοτιη γνωσις of Democr., by which he meant that knowledge which stops at the superficial appearances of things as shown by sense. He was, however, by no means a sceptic, for he also held a γνησιη γνωσις, dealing with the realities of material existence, the atoms and the void, which exist ετεηι and not merely νομωι as appearances do. See R. and P. 51.

§74. *Furere*: cf. 14. *Orbat sensibus*: cf. 61, and for the belief of Empedocles about the possibility of επιστημη see the remarks of Sextus *A.M.* VII. 123—4 qu. R. and P. 107, who say "*patet errare eos qui scepticis adnumerandum Empedoclem putabant.*" *Sonum fundere*: similar expressions occur in *T.D.* III. 42, V. 73, *D.F.* II. 48. *Parmenides, Xenophanes*: these are the last men who ought to be charged with scepticism. They advanced indeed arguments against sense-knowledge, but held that real knowledge was attainable by the reason. Cf. Grote, *Plato* I. 54, Zeller 501, R. and P. on Xenophanes and Parmenides. *Minus bonis*: Dav. qu. Plut. *De Audit.* 45 A, μεμψαιτο δ' αν τις Παρμενιδου την στιχοποιιαν. *Quamquam*: on the proper use of *quamquam* in clauses where the verb is not expressed see *M.D.F.* V. 68 and cf. I. 5. *Quasi irati*: for the use of *quasi* = almost cf. *In Verr. Act.* I. 22, *Orat.* 41. *Aiebas removendum*: for om. of *esse* see n. on I. 43. *Perscripti sunt*: cf. n. on I. 16. *Scire se nihil se scire*: cf. I. 16, 44. The words referred to are in Plat. *Apol.* 21 εοικα γουν τουτου σμικρωι τινι αυτωι τουτωι σοφωτερος ειναι, 'οτι α μη οιδα ουδε οιομαι ειδεναι, a very different statement from the *nihil sciri posse* by which Cic. interprets it (cf. R. and P. 148). That επιστημη in the strict sense is impossible, is a doctrine which Socrates would have left to the Sophists. *De Platone*: the doctrine above mentioned is an absurd one to foist upon Plato. The dialogues of search as they are called, while exposing sham knowledge, all assume that the real επιστημη is attainable. *Ironiam*: the word was given in its Greek form in 15. *Nulla fuit ratio persequi*: n. on 17.

§75. *Videorne*: = *nonne videor*, as *videsne* = *nonne vides*. *Imitari numquam nisi*: a strange expression for which Manut. conj. *imitari? num quem*, etc., Halm *nullum unquam* in place of *numquam*. Bait. prints the reading of Man., which I think harsher than that of the MSS. *Minutos*: for the word cf. *Orat.* 94, also *De Div.* I. 62 *minuti philosophi, Brut.* 256 *minuti imperatores. Stilponem*, etc.: Megarians, see R. and P. 177—182. σοφισματα: Cic. in the second edition probably introduced here the translation *cavillationes*, to which Seneca *Ep.* 116 refers, cf. Krische, p. 65. *Fulcire porticum*: "to be the pillar of the Stoic porch". Cf. the anonymous line ει μη γαρ ην Χρυσιππος, ουκ αν ην Στοα. *Quae in consuetudine probantur*: n. on 87. *Nisi videret*: for the tense of the verb, see Madv. *Gram.* 347 *b*, obs. 2.

§76. *Quid ... philosophi*: my reading is that of Durand approved by Madv. and followed by Bait. It is strange that Halm does not mention this reading, which only requires the alteration of *Cyrenaei* into *Cyrenaici* (now made by all edd. on the ground that *Cyrenaeus* is a citizen of Cyreno, *Cyrenaicus* a follower of Aristippus) and the insertion of *tibi*. I see no difficulty in the *qui* before *negant*, at which so many edd. take offence. *Tactu intimo*: the word 'αφη I believe does not occur in ancient authorities as a term of the Cyrenaic school; their great word was παθος. From 143 (*permotiones intimas*) it might appear that Cic. is translating either παθος or κινησις. For a clear account of the school see Zeller's *Socrates*, for the illustration of the present passage pp 293—300 with the footnotes. Cf. also R. and P. 162 sq. *Quo quid colore*: cf. Sext. *A.M.* VII. 191 (qu. Zeller *Socrates* 297, R. and P. 165). *Adfici se*: = πασχειν. *Quaesieras*: note the plup. where Eng. idiom requires the perfect or aorist. *Tot saeculis*: cf. the same words in 15. *Tot ingeniis tantisque studiis*: cf. *summis ingeniis, maximis studiis* in 15. *Obtrectandi*: this invidious word had been used by Lucullus in 16; cf. also I. 44.

§77. *Expresserat*: "had put into distinct shape". Cf. 7 and I. 19. *Exprimere* and *dicere* are always sharply distinguished by Cic., the latter merely implying the mechanic exercise of utterance, the former the moulding and shaping of the utterance by conscious effort; cf. esp. *Orat.* 3, 69, and *Ad Att.* VIII. 11, 1; also *De Or.* I. 32, *De Div.* I. 79, qu. by Krebs and Allgayer. The conj. of Dav. *exposuerat* is therefore needless. *Fortasse*: "we may suppose". *Nec percipere*, etc.: cf. 68, n. *Tum illum*: a change from *ille, credo* (sc. *respondit*), the *credo* being now repeated to govern the infin. For the constr. after *ita definisse* cf. *M.D.F.* II. 13 (who quotes exx.); also the construction with *ita iudico* in 113. *Ex eo, quod esset*: cf. 18, n. *Effictum*: so Manut. for MSS. *effectum*, cf. 18. *Ab eo, quod non est*: the words *non est* include the two meanings "is non existent," and "is different from what it seems to be"—the two meanings of *falsum* indeed, see n. on 47. *Eiusdem modi*: cf. 40, 84. MSS. have *eius modi*, altered by Dav. *Recte ... additum*: the semicolon at *Arcesilas* was added by Manutius, who is followed by all edd. This involves taking *additum = additum est*, an ellipse of excessive rarity in Cic., see Madv. *Opusc.* I. 448, *D.F.* I. 43, *Gram.* 479 *a*. I think it quite possible that *recte consensit additum* should be construed together, "agreed that the addition had been rightly made." For the omission of *esse* in that case cf. Madv. *Gram.* 406, and such expressions as *dicere solebat perturbatum* in 111, also *ita scribenti exanclatum* in 108. *Recte*, which with the ordinary stopping expresses Cic.'s needless approval of Arcesilas' conduct would thus gain in point. Qy, should *concessit* be read, as in 118 *concessisse* is now read for MSS. *consensisse*? *A vero*: cf. 41.

§78. *Quae adhuc permanserit*: note the subj., "which is of such a nature as to have lasted". *Nam illud ... pertinebat*: by *illud* is meant the argument in defence of εποχη given in 67; by *nihil ... pertinebat* nothing more is intended than that there was no *immediate* or *close* connection. Cf. the use of *pertinere* in *D.F.* III. 55. *Clitomacho*: cf. n. on 59.

§§79—90. Summary You are wrong, Lucullus, in upholding your cause in spite of my arguments yesterday against the senses. You are thus acting like the Epicureans, who say that the inference only from the sensation can be false, not the sensation itself (79, 80). I wish the god of whom you spoke would ask me whether I wanted anything more than sound senses. He would have a bad time with me. For even granting that our vision is correct how marvellously circumscribed it is! But say you, *we* desire no more. No I answer, you are like the mole who desires not the light because he is blind. Yet I would not so much reproach the god because my vision is narrow, as because it deceives me (80, 81). If you want something greater than the bent oar, what can be greater than the sun? Still he seems to us a foot broad, and Epicurus thinks he may be a little broader or narrower than he seems. With all his enormous speed, too, he appears to us to stand still (82). The whole question lies in a nutshell; of four propositions which prove my point only one is disputed viz. that every true sensation has side by side with it a false one indistinguishable from it (83). A man who has mistaken P. for Q. Geminus could have no infallible mode of recognising Cotta. You say that no such indistinguishable resemblances *exist*. Never mind, they *seem* to exist and that is enough. One mistaken sensation will throw all the others into uncertainty (84). You say everything belongs to its own *genus* this I will not contest. I am not concerned to show that two sensations *are* absolutely similar, it is enough that human faculties cannot distinguish between them. How about the impressions of signet rings? (85) Can you find a ring merchant to rival your chicken rearer of Delos? But, you say, art aids the senses. So we cannot see or hear without art, which so few can have! What an idea this gives us of the art with which nature has constructed the senses! (86) But about physics I will speak afterwards. I am going now to advance against the senses arguments drawn from Chrysippus himself (87). You said that the sensations of dreamers, drunkards and madmen were feebler than those of the waking, the sober and the sane. The cases of Ennius and his Alcmaeon, of your own relative Tuditanus, of the Hercules of Euripides disprove your point (88, 89). In their case at least 'mind and eyes agreed. It is no good to talk about the saner moments of such people; the question is, what was the nature of their sensations at the time they were affected? (90)

§79. *Communi loco*: τοπω, that of blinking facts which cannot be disproved, see 19. *Quod ne [id]*: I have bracketed *id* with most edd. since Manut. If, however, *quod* be taken as the conjunction, and not as the pronoun, *id* is not altogether insupportable. *Heri*: cf. Introd. 55. *Infracto remo*: n. on 19. Tennyson seems to allude to this in his "Higher Pantheism"—"all we have power to see is a straight staff bent in a pool". *Manent illa omnia, iacet*: this is my correction of the reading of most MSS. *maneant ... lacerat*. Madv. *Em.* 176 in combating the conj. of Goer. *si maneant ... laceratis istam causam*, approves *maneant ... iaceat*, a reading with some MSS. support, adopted by Orelli. I think the whole confusion of the passage arises from the mania of the copyists for turning indicatives into subjunctives, of which in critical editions of Cic. exx. occur every few pages. If *iacet* were by error turned into *iaceret* the reading *lacerat* would arise at once. The nom. to *dicit* is, I may observe, not Epicurus, as Orelli takes it, but Lucullus. Trans. "all my arguments remain untouched; your case is overthrown, yet his senses are true quotha!" (For this use of *dicit* cf. *inquit* in 101, 109, 115). Hermann approves the odd reading of the ed. Cratandriana of 1528 *latrat*. Dav. conjectured comically *blaterat iste tamen et*, Halm *lacera est ista causa*. *Habes*: as two good MSS. have *habes et eum*, Madv. *Em.* 176 conj. *habet*. The change of person, however, (from *dicit* to *habes*) occurs also in 101. *Epicurus*: n. on 19.

§80. *Hoc est verum esse*: Madv. *Em.* 177 took *verum* as meaning fair, candid, in this explanation I concur. Madv., however, in his critical epistle to Orelli p. 139 abandoned it and proposed *virum esse*, a very strange em. Halm's conj. *certum esse* is weak and improbable. *Importune*: this is in one good MS. but the rest have *importata*, a good em. is needed, as *importune* does not suit the sense of the passage. *Negat ... torsisset*: for the tenses cf. 104 *exposuisset, adiungit*. *Cum oculum torsisset*: i.e. by placing the finger beneath the eye and pressing upwards or sideways. Cf. Aristot. *Eth. Eud.* VII. 13 (qu. by Dav.) οφθαλμους διαστρεψαντα ῾ωστε δυο το ῾εν φανηναι. Faber qu. Arist. *Problemata* XVII. 31 δια τι εις το πλαγιον κινουσι τον οφθαλμον ου (?) φαινεται δυο το ῾εν. Also *ib.* XXXI. 3 inquiring the reason why drunkards see double he says ταυτο τουτο γιγνεται και εαν τις κατωθεν πιεση τον οφθαλμον. Sextus refers to the same thing *P.H.* I. 47, *A.M.* VII. 192 (῾ο παραπιεσας τον οφθαλμον) so Cic. *De Div.* II. 120. Lucretius gives the same answer as Timagoras, *propter opinatus animi* (IV. 465), as does Sext. *A.M.* VII. 210 on behalf of Epicurus. *Sed hic*: Bait. *sit hic. Maiorum*: cf. 143. *Quasi quaeratur*: Carneades refused to discuss about things in themselves but merely dealt with the appearances they present, το γαρ αληθες και το ψευδες εν τοις πραγμασι συνεχωρει (Numen in Euseb. *Pr. Eu.* XIV. 8). Cf. also Sext. *P.H.* I. 78, 87, 144, II. 75. *Domi nascuntur*: a proverb used like γλαυκ᾽ εσ᾽ Αθηνας and "coals to Newcastle," see Lorenz on Plaut. *Miles* II. 2, 38, and cf. *Ad Att.* X. 14, 2, *Ad Fam.* IX. 3. *Deus*: cf. 19. *Audiret ... ageret*: MSS. have *audies ... agerent*. As the insertion of *n* in the imp. subj. is so common in MSS. I read *ageret* and alter *audies* to suit it. Halm has *audiret ... ageretur* with Dav., Bait. *audiet, egerit. Ex hoc loco video ... cerno*: MSS. have *loco cerno regionem video Pompeianum non cerno* whence Lipsius conj. *ex hoc loco e regione video*. Halm ejects the words *regionem video*, I prefer to eject *cerno regionem*. We are thus left with the slight change from *video* to *cerno*, which is very often found in Cic., e.g. *Orat.* 18. Cic. sometimes however joins the two verbs as in *De Or.* III. 161. *O praeclarum prospectum*: the view was a favourite one with Cic., see *Ad Att.* I. 13, 5.

§81. *Nescio qui*: Goer. is quite wrong in saying that *nescio quis* implies contempt, while *nescio qui* does not, cf. *Div. in qu. Caec.* 47, where *nescio qui* would contradict his rule. It is as difficult to define the uses of the two expressions as to define those of *aliquis* and *aliqui*, on which see 61 n. In *Paradoxa* 12 the best MSS. have *si qui* and *si quis* almost in the same line with identically the same meaning Dav. quotes Solinus and Plin. *N.H.* VII. 21, to show that the man mentioned here was called Strabo—a misnomer surely. *Octingenta*: so the best MSS., not *octoginta*, which however agrees better with Pliny. *Quod abesset*: "whatever might be 1800 stadia distant," *aberat* would have implied that Cic. had some particular thing in mind, cf. Madv. *Gram.* 364, obs. 1. *Acrius*: οξυτερον, Lamb. without need read *acutius* as Goer. did in 69. *Illos pisces*: so some MSS., but the best have *ullos*, whence Klotz conj. *multos*, Orelli *multos illos*, omitting *pisces*. For the allusion to the fish, cf. *Acad. Post.* fragm. 13. *Videntur*: n. on 25. *Amplius*: cf. 19 *non video cur quaerat amplius. Desideramus*: Halm, failing to understand the passage, follows Christ in reading *desiderant* (i.e. *pisces*). To paraphrase the sense is this "But say my opponents, the Stoics and Antiocheans, we desire no better senses than we have." Well you are like the mole, which does not yearn for the light because it does not know what light is. Of course all the ancients thought the mole blind. A glance will show the insipidity of the sense given by Halm's reading. *Quererer cum deo*: would enter into an altercation with the god. The phrase, like λοιδορεσθαι τινι as opposed to λοιδορειν τινα implies mutual recrimination, cf. *Pro Deiotaro* 9 *querellae cum Deiotaro*. The reading *tam quererer* for the *tamen quaereretur* of the MSS. is due to Manut. *Navem*: Sextus often uses the same illustration, as in *P.H.* I. 107, *A.M.* VII. 414. *Non tu verum testem*, etc.: cf. 105. For the om. of *te* before *habere*, which has strangely troubled edd. and induced them to alter the text, see n. on I. 6.

§82. *Quid ego*: Bait. has *sed quid* after Ernesti. *Nave*: so the best MSS., not *navi*, cf. Madv. *Gram.* 42. *Duodeviginti*: so in 128. Goer. and Roeper qu. by Halm wished to read *duodetriginta*. The reff. of Goer. at least do not prove his point that the ancients commonly estimated the sun at 28 times the size of the earth. *Quasi pedalis*: cf. *D.F.* I. 20 *pedalis fortasse*. For *quasi = circiter* cf. note on 74. Madv. on *D.F.* I. 20 quotes Diog. Laert. X. 91, who preserves the very words of Epicurus, in which however no mention of a foot occurs, also Lucr. V. 590, who copies Epicurus, and Seneca *Quaest. Nat.* I. 3, 10 (*solem sapientes viri pedalem esse contenderunt*). Madv. points out from Plut. *De Plac. Phil.* II. 21, p. 890 E, that Heraclitus asserted the sun to be a foot wide, he does not however quote Stob. *Phys.* I. 24, 1 ʽηλιον μεγεθος εχειν ευρος ποδος ανθρωπειου, which is affirmed to be the opinion of Heraclitus and Hecataeus. *Ne maiorem quidem*: so the MSS., but Goer. and Orelli read *nec* for *ne*, incurring the reprehension of Madv. *D.F.* p. 814, ed 2. *Nihil aut non multum*: so in *D.F.* V. 59, the correction of Orelli, therefore, *aut non multum mentiantur aut nihil*, is rash. *Semel*: see 79. *Qui ne nunc quidem*: sc. *mentiri sensus putat*. Halm prints *quin*, and is followed by Baiter, neither has observed that *quin ne ... quidem* is bad Latin (see *M.D.F.* V. 56). Nor can *quin ne* go together even without *quidem*, cf. Krebs and Allgayer, *Antibarbarus* ed. 4 on *quin*.

§83. *In parvo lis sit*: Durand's em. for the *in parvulis sitis* of the MSS., which Goer. alone defends. *Quattuor capita*: these were given in 40 by Lucullus, cf. also 77. *Epicurus*: as above in 19, 79 etc.

§84. *Geminum*: cf. 56. *Nota*: cf. 58 and the speech of Lucullus *passim*. *Ne sit ... potest*: cf. 80 *quasi quaeratur quid sit, non quid videatur*. *Si ipse erit* for *ipse* apparently = *is ipse* cf. *M.D.F.* II. 93.

§85. *Quod non est*: = qu. n. e. *id quod esse videtur*. *Sui generis*: cf. 50, 54, 56. *Nullum esse pilum*, etc.: a strong expression of this belief is found in Seneca *Ep.*. 113, 13, qu. R. and P. 380. Note the word *Stoicum*; Lucullus is of course not Stoic, but Antiochean. *Nihil interest*: the same opinion is expressed in 40, where see my note. *Visa res*: Halm writes *res a re*, it is not necessary, however, either in Gk. or Lat. to express *both* of two related things when a word is inserted like *differat* here, which shows that they *are* related. Cf. the elliptic constructions in Gk. with ʽομοιον, μεταξυ, μεσος, and such words. *Eodem caelo atque*: a difficult passage. MSS. have *aqua*, an error easy, as Halm notes, to a scribe who understood *caelum* to be the heaven, and not γλυφειον, a graving tool. Faber and other old edd. defend the MSS. reading, adducing passages to show that sky and water were important in the making of statues. For *aqua* Orelli conj. *acu* = *schraffirnadel*, C.F. Hermann *caelatura*, which does not seem to be a Ciceronian word. Halm's *aeque* introduces a construction with *ceteris omnibus* which is not only not Ciceronian, but not Latin at all. I read *atque*, taking *ceteris omnibus* to be the abl. neut. "all the other implements." Formerly I conj. *ascra*, or *atque in*, which last leading would make *omnibus = om. statuis*. *Alexandros*: Lysippus alone was privileged to make statues of Alexander, as Apelles alone was allowed to paint the conqueror, cf. *Ad Fam.* V. 12, 7.

§86. *Anulo*: cf. 54. *Aliqui*: n. on 61. *Gallinarium*: cf. 57. *Adhibes artem*: cf. 20 *adhibita arte*. *Pictor ... tibicen*: so in 20. *Simul inflavit*: note *simul* for *simul atque*, cf. *T.D.* IV. 12. *Nostri quidem*: i.e. *Romani*. *Admodum*: i.e. adm. *pauci* cf. *De Leg.* III. 32 *pauci enim atque admodum pauci*. *Praeclara*: evidently a fem. adj. agreeing with *natura*. Dav. and Ern. made the adj. neuter, and understanding *sunt* interpreted "these arguments I am going to urge are grand, viz. *quanto art.* etc."

§87. *Scilicet*: Germ. "naturlich." *Fabricata sit*: cf. 30, 119, 121 and N.D. I. 19. *Ne modo*: for *modo ne*, a noticeable use. *Physicis*: probably neut. *Contra sensus*: he wrote both for and against συνηθεια; cf. R. and P. 360 and 368. *Carneadem*: Plut. *Sto. Rep.* 1036 B relates that Carneades in reading the arguments of Chrysippus against the senses, quoted the address of Andromache to Hector: δαιμονιε φθισει σε το σον μενος. From Diog. IV. 62 we learn that he thus parodied the line qu. in n. on 75, ει μη γαρ ην Χρυσιππος ουκ αν ην εγω.

§88. *Diligentissime*: in 48—53. *Dicebas*: in 52 *imbecillius adsentiuntur. Siccorum*: cf. Cic. *Contra Rullum* I. 1 *consilia siccorum. Madere* is common with the meaning "to be drunk," as in Plaut. *Mostellaria* I. 4, 6. *Non diceret*: Orelli was induced by Goer. to omit the verb, with one MS., cf. 15 and I. 13. The omission of a verb in the subjunctive is, Madv. says on *D.F.* I. 9, impossible; for other ellipses of the verb see *M.D.F.* V. 63. *Alcmaeo autem*: i.e. Ennius' own Alcmaeon; cf. 52. *Somnia reri*: the best MSS. have *somniare*. Goer. reads *somnia*, supplying *non fuisse vera*. I have already remarked on his extraordinary power of *supplying*. Halm conj. *somnia reprobare*, forgetting that the verb *reprobare* belongs to third century Latinity, also *sua visa putare*, which Bait. adopts. Thinking this too large a departure from the MSS., I read *reri*, which verb occurred in I. 26, 39. Possibly *putare*, a little farther on, has got misplaced. *Non id agitur*: these difficulties supply Sextus with one of his τροποι, i.e. ʿο περι τας περιστασεις; cf. *P.H.* I. 100, also for the treatment of dreams, *ib.* I. 104. *Si modo*, etc.: "if only he dreamed it," i.e. "merely because he dreamed it." *Aeque ac vigilanti*: = *aeque ac si vigilaret*. Dav. missing the sense, and pointing out that *when awake* Ennius did not assent to his sensations at all, conj. *vigilantis*. Two participles used in very different ways not unfrequently occur together, see Madv. *Em. Liv.* p. 442. *Ita credit*: MSS. have *illa*, which Dav. altered. Halm would prefer *credidit. Itera dum*, etc.: from the *Iliona* of Pacuvius; a favourite quotation with Cic.; see *Ad Att.* XIV. 14, and *T.D.* II. 44.

§89. *Quisquam*: for the use of this pronoun in interrogative sentences cf. Virg. *Aen.* I. 48 with the FileOutputStreams of Wagner and Conington. *Tam certa putat*: so Sextus *A.M.* VII. 61 points out that Protagoras must in accordance with his doctrine παντων μετρον ανθρωπος hold that the μεμηνως is the κριτηριον των εν μανιαι φαινομενων. *Video, video te*: evidently from a tragedy whose subject was Αιας μαινομενος, see Ribbeck *Trag. Lat. rel.* p. 205. Cic. in *De Or.* III. 162 thus continues the quotation, "*oculis postremum lumen radiatum rape.*" So in Soph. *Aiax* 100 the hero, after killing, as he thinks, the Atridae, keeps Odysseus alive awhile in order to torture him. *Hercules*: cf. Eur. *Herc. Fur.* 921—1015. The mad visions of this hero, like those of Orestes, are often referred to for a similar purpose by Sext., e.g. *A.M.* VII. 405 ʿο γουν ʿΕρακλης μανεις και λαβων φαντασιαν απο των ιδιων παιδων ʿως Ευρυσθεος, την ακολουθον πραξιν ταυτηι τη φαντασιαι συνηψεν. ακολουθον δε ην το τους του εχθρου παιδας ανελειν, ʿοπερ και εποιησεν. Cf. also *A.M.* VII. 249. *Moveretur*: imperf. for plup. as in 90. *Alcmaeo tuus*: cf. 52. *Incitato furore*: Dav. reads *incitatus*. Halm qu. from Wesenberg *Observ. Crit. ad Or. p. Sestio* p. 51 this explanation, "*cum furor eius initio remissior paulatim incitatior et vehementior factus esset,*" he also refers to Wopkens *Lect. Tull.* p. 55 ed. Hand. *Incedunt* etc.: the MSS. have *incede*, which Lamb. corrected. The subject of the verb is evidently *Furiae. Adsunt*: is only given once by MSS., while Ribbeck repeats it thrice, on Halm's suggestion I have written it twice. *Caerulea ... angui*: *anguis* fem is not uncommon in the old poetry. MSS. here have *igni. Crinitus*: ακερσεκομης, "never shorn," as Milton translates it. *Luna innixus*: the separate mention in the next line of *Diana*, usually identified with the moon, has led edd. to emend this line. Some old edd. have *lunat*, while Lamb. reads *genu* for *luna*, cf. Ov. *Am.* I. 1, 25 (qu. by Goer.) *lunavitque genu sinuosum fortiter arcum.* Wakefield on Lucr. III. 1013 puts a stop at *auratum*, and goes on with *Luna innixans*. Taber strangely explains *luna* as = *arcu ipso lunato*, Dav. says we ought not to expect the passage to make sense, as it is the utterance of a maniac. For my part, I do not see why the poet should not regard *luna* and *Diana* as distinct.

§90. *Illa falsa*: sc. *visa*, which governs the two genitives. Goer. perversely insists on taking *somniantium recordatione ipsorum* closely together. *Non enim id quaeritur*: cf. 80 n. Sext. very often uses very similar language, as in *P.H.* I. 22, qu. in n. on 40. *Tum cum movebantur*: so Halm for MSS. *tum commovebantur*, the em. is supported by 88.

§§91—98. Summary: Dialectic cannot lead to stable knowledge, its processes are not applicable to a large number of philosophical questions (91). You value the art, but remember that it gave rise to fallacies like the *sorites*, which you say is faulty (92). If it is so, refute it. The plan of Chrysippus to refrain from answering, will avail you nothing (93). If you refrain because you *cannot* answer, your knowledge fails you, if you *can* answer and yet refrain, you are unfair (94). The art you admire really undoes itself, as Penelope did her web, witness the *Mentiens*, (95). You assent to arguments which are identical in form with the *Mentiens*, and yet refuse to assent to it Why so? (96) You demand that these sophisms should be made exceptions to the rules of Dialectic. You must go to a tribune for that exception. I just remind you that Epicurus would not allow the very first postulate of your Dialectic (97). In my opinion, and I learned Dialectic from Antiochus, the *Mentiens* and the arguments identical with it in form must stand or fall together (98).

§91. *Inventam esse*: cf. 26, 27. *In geometriane*: with this inquiry into the special function of Dialectic cf. the inquiry about Rhetoric in Plato *Gorg.* 453 D, 454 C. *Sol quantus sit*: this of course is a problem for φυσικη, not for διαλεκτικη. *Quod sit summum bonum*: not διαλεκτικη but ηθικη must decide this. *Quae coniunctio*: etc. so Sext. often opposes συμπλοκη or συνημμενον to διεζευγμενον, cf. esp *P.H.* II. 201, and Zeller 109 sq. with footnotes. An instance of a *coniunctio* (hypothetical judgment) is "*si lucet, lucet*" below, of a *disiunctio* (disjunctive judgment) "*aut vivet cras Hermarchus aut non vivet*". *Ambigue dictum*: αμφιβολον, on which see *P.H.* II. 256, Diog VII. 62. *Quid sequatur*: το ακολουθον, cf. I. 19 n. *Quid repugnet*: cf. I. 19, n. *De se ipsa*: the *ipsa*, according to Cic.'s usage, is nom. and not abl. Petrus Valentia (p. 301, ed Orelli) justly remarks that an art is not to be condemned as useless merely because it is unable to solve every problem presented to it. He quotes Plato's remarks (in *Rep.* II.) that the Expert is the man who knows exactly what his art can do and what it cannot. Very similar arguments to this of Cic. occur in Sext., cf. esp. *P.H.* II. 175 and the words εαυτου εσται εκκαλυπτικον. For the mode in which Carneades dealt with Dialectic cf. Zeller 510, 511. The true ground of attack is that Logic always *assumes* the truth of phenomena, and cannot *prove* it. This was clearly seen by Aristotle alone of the ancients; see Grote's essay on the Origin of Knowledge, now reprinted in Vol II. of his *Aristotle*.

§92. *Nata sit*: cf. 28, 59. *Loquendi*: the Stoic λογικη, it must be remembered, included ῾ρητορικη. *Concludendi*: του συμπεραινειν or συλλογιζεσθαι. *Locum*: τοπον in the philosophical sense. *Vitiosum*: 49, n. *Num nostra culpa est*: cf. 32. *Finium*: absolute limits; the fallacy of the *sorites* and other such sophisms lies entirely in the treatment of purely *relative* terms as though they were *absolute*. *Quatenus*: the same ellipse occurs in *Orator* 73. *In acervo tritici*: this is the false *sorites*, which may be briefly described thus: A asks B whether one grain makes a heap, B answers "No." A goes on asking whether two, three, four, etc. grains make a heap. B cannot always reply "No." When he begins to answer "Yes," there will be a difference of one grain between heap and no heap. One grain therefore *does* make a heap. The true *sorites* or chain inference is still treated in books on logic, cf. Thomson's *Laws of Thought*, pp 201—203, ed 8. *Minutatim*: cf. Heindorf's note on κατα σμικρον in *Sophistes* 217 D. *Interrogati*: cf. 104. In 94 we have *interroganti*, which some edd. read here. *Dives pauper*, etc.: it will be easily seen that the process of questioning above described can be applied to any relative term such as these are. For the omission of any connecting particle between the members of each pair, cf. 29, 125, *T.D.* I. 64, V. 73, 114, Zumpt *Gram.* 782. *Quanto addito aut dempto*: after this there is a strange ellipse of some such words as *id efficiatur, quod interrogatur*. [*Non*] *habemus*: I bracket *non* in deference to Halm, Madv. however (*Opusc.* I. 508) treats it as a superabundance of negation arising from a sort of anacoluthon, comparing *In Vatin.* 3, *Ad Fam.* XII. 24. The scribes insert and omit negatives very recklessly, so that the point may remain doubtful.

§93. *Frangite*: in later Gk. generally απολυειν. *Erunt ... cavetis*: this form of the conditional sentence is illustrated in Madv. *D.F.* III. 70, *Em. Liv.* p. 422, *Gram.* 340, obs. 1. Goer. qu. Terence *Heaut.* V. 1, 59 *quot incommoda tibi in hac re capies nisi caves*, cf. also 127, 140 of this book. The present is of course required by the instantaneous nature of the action. *Chrysippo*: he spent so much time in trying to solve the sophism that it is called peculiarly his by Persius VI. 80. *inventus, Chrysippe, tui finitor acervi*. The titles of numerous distinct works of his on the *Sorites* and *Mentiens* are given by Diog. *Tria pauca sint*: cf. the instances in Sext. *A.M.* VII. 418 τα πεντηκοντα ολιγα εστιν, τα μυρια ολιγα εστιν, also Diog. VII. 82

ʽησυχαζειν the advice is quoted in Sext. *P.H.* II. 253 (δειν ʽιστασθαι και επεχειν), *A.M.* VII. 416 (ʽο σοφος στησεται και ʽησυχασει). The same terms seem to have been used by the Cynics, see Sext. *P.H.* II. 244, III. 66. *Stertas*: imitated by Aug. *Contra Ac.* III. 25 *ter terna novem esse ... vel genere humano stertente verum sit*, also *ib.* III. 22. *Proficit*: Dav. *proficis*, but Madv. rightly understands το ʽησυχαζειν (*Em.* 184), cf. *N.D.* II. 58. *Ultimum ... respondere*: "to put in as your answer" cf. the use of *defendere* with an accus. "to put in as a plea". Kayser suggests *paucorum quid sit*.

§94. *Ut agitator*: see the amusing letter to Atticus XIII. 21, in which Cic. discusses different translations for the word επεχειν, and quotes a line of Lucilius *sustineat currum ut bonu' saepe agitator equosque*, adding *semperque Carneades* προβολην *pugilis et retentionem aurigae similem facit* εποχη. Aug. *Contra Ac.* trans. εποχη by *refrenatio* cf. also *Lael.* 63. *Superbus es*: I have thus corrected the MSS. *responde superbe*; Halm writes *facis superbe*, Orelli *superbis*, which verb is hardly found in prose. The phrase *superbe resistere* in Aug. *Contra Ac.* III. 14 may be a reminiscence. *Illustribus*: Bait. with some probability adds *in*, comparing *in decimo* below, and 107, cf. however Munro on Lucr. I. 420. *Irretiat*: parallel expressions occur in *T.D.* V. 76, *De Or.* I. 43, *De Fato* 7. *Facere non sinis*: Sext. *P.H.* II. 253 points the moral in the same way. *Augentis nec minuentis*: so Halm for MSS. *augendi nec minuendi*, which Bait. retains. I cannot believe the phrase *primum augendi* to be Latin.

§95. *Tollit ... superiora*: cf. *Hortensius* fragm. 19 (Orelli) *sed ad extremum pollicetur prolaturum qui se ipse comest quod efficit dialecticorum ratio*. *Vestra an nostra*: Bait. after Christ needlessly writes *nostra an vestra*. αξιωμα: "a judgment expressed in language"; cf. Zeller 107, who gives the Stoic refinements on this subject. *Effatum*: Halm gives the spelling *ecfatum*. It is probable that this spelling was antique in Cic.'s time and only used in connection with religious and legal formulae as in *De Div.* I. 81, *De Leg.* II. 20, see Corss. *Ausspr.* I. 155 For the word cf. Sen. *Ep.* 117 *enuntiativum quiddam de corpore quod alii effatum vocant, alii enuntiatum, alii edictum*, in *T.D.* I. 14 *pronuntiatum* is found, in *De Fato* 26 *pronuntiatio*, in Gellius XVI. 8 (from Varro) *prologium*. *Aut verum esse aut falsum*: the constant Stoic definition of αξιωμα, see Diog. VII. 65 and other passages in Zeller 107. *Mentiris an verum dicis*: the *an* was added by Schutz on a comparison of Gellius XVIII. 10 *cum mentior et mentiri me dico, mentior an verum dico?* The sophism is given in a more formally complete shape in *De Div.* II. 11 where the following words are added, *dicis autem te mentiri verumque dicis, mentiris igitur*. The fallacy is thus hit by Petrus Valentia (p. 301, ed Orelli), *quis unquam dixit "ego mentior" quum hoc ipsum pronuntiatum falsum vellet declarare? Inexplicabilia*: απορα in the Greek writers. *Odiosius*: this adj. has not the strong meaning of the Eng. "hateful," but simply means "tiresome," "annoying." *Non comprehensa*: as in 99, the opposite of *comprehendibilia* III. 1, 41. The past partic. in Cic. often has the same meaning as an adj. in -*bilis*. Faber points out that in the *Timaeus* Cic. translates αλυτος by *indissolutus* and *indissolubilis* indifferently. *Imperceptus*, which one would expect, is found in Ovid.

§96. *Si dicis*: etc. the words in italics are needed, and were given by Manut. with the exception of *nunc* which was added by Dav. The idea of Orelli, that Cic. clipped these trite sophisms as he does verses from the comic writers is untenable. *In docendo*: *docere* is not to *expound* but to *prove*, cf. n. on 121. *Primum ... modum*: the word *modus* is technical in this sense cf. *Top.* 57. The πρωτος λογος αναποδεικτος of the Stoic logic ran thus ει ʽημερα εστι, φως εστιν ... αλλα μην ʽημερα εστιν φως αρα εστιν (Sext. *P.H.* II. 157, and other passages qu. Zeller 114). This bears a semblance of inference and is not so utterly tautological as Cic.'s translation, which merges φως and ʽημερα into one word, or that of Zeller (114, note). These arguments are called μονολημματοι (involving only one premise) in Sext. *P.H.* I. 152, 159, II. 167. *Si dicis te mentiri*, etc.: it is absurd to assume, as this sophism does, that when a man *truly* states that he *has* told a lie, he establishes against himself not merely that he *has* told a lie, but also that he *is* telling a lie at the moment when he makes the *true* statement. The root of the sophism lies in the confusion of past and present time in the one infinitive *mentiri*. *Eiusdem generis*: the phrase *te mentiri* had been substituted for *nunc lucere*. *Chrysippea*: n. on 93. *Conclusioni*: on *facere* with the dat. see n. on 27. *Cederet*: some edd.

crederet, but the word is a trans. of Gk. εικειν; n. on 66. *Conexi*: = συνημμενον, cf. Zeller 109. This was the proper term for the hypothetical judgment. *Superius*: the συνημμενον consists of two parts, the hypothetical part and the affirmative—called in Greek ʽηγουμενον and ληγον; if one is admitted the other follows of course.

§97. *Excipiantur*: the legal *formula* of the Romans generally directed the *iudex* to condemn the defendant if certain facts were proved, unless certain other facts were proved; the latter portion went by the name of *exceptio*. See *Dict. Ant. Tribunum ... adeant*: a retort upon Lucullus; cf. 13. The MSS. have *videant* or *adeant*; Halm conj. *adhibeant*, comparing 86 and *Pro Rabirio* 20. *Contemnit*: the usual trans. "to despise" for *contemnere* is too strong; it means, like ολιγωρειν, merely to neglect or pass by. *Effabimur*; cf. *effatum* above. *Hermarchus*: not *Hermachus*, as most edd.; see *M.D.F.* II. 96. *Diiunctum*: διεζευγμενον, for which see Zeller 112. *Necessarium*: the reason why Epicurus refused to admit this is given in *De Fato* 21 *Epicurus veretur ne si hoc concesserit, concedendum sit fato fieri quaecumque fiant*. The context of that passage should be carefully read, along with *N.D.* I. 69, 70. Aug. *Contra Ac.* III. 29 lays great stress on the necessary truth of disjunctive propositions. *Catus*: so Lamb. for MSS. *cautus*. *Tardum*: *De Div.* II. 103 *Epicurum quem hebetem et rudem dicere solent Stoici*; cf. also *ib.* II. 116, and the frequent use of βραδυς in Sext., e.g. *A.M.* VII. 325. *Cum hoc igitur*: the word *igitur*, as usual, picks up the broken thread of the sentence. *Id est*: n. on I. 8. *Evertit*: for the Epicurean view of Dialectic see R. and P. 343. Zeller 399 sq., *M.D.F.* I. 22. *E contrariis diiunctio*: = διεζευγμενον εξ εναντιων.

§98. *Sequor*: as in 95, 96, where the *Dialectici* refused to allow the consequences of their own principles, according to Cic. *Ludere*: this reminds one of the famous controversy between Corax and Tisias, for which see Cope in the old *Journal of Philology*. No. 7. *Iudicem ... non iudicem*: this construction, which in Greek would be marked by μεν and δε, has been a great crux of edd.; Dav. here wished to insert *cum* before *iudicem*, but is conclusively refuted by Madv. *Em.* 31. The same construction occurs in 103. *Esse conexum*: with great probability Christ supposes the infinitive to be an addition of the copyists.

§§98—105. Summary. In order to overthrow at once the case of Antiochus, I proceed to explain, after Clitomachus, the whole of Carneades' system (98). Carneades laid down two divisions of *visa*, one into those capable of being perceived and those not so capable, the other into probable and improbable. Arguments aimed at the senses concern the first division only; the sapiens will follow probability, as in many instances the Stoic sapiens confessedly does (99, 100). Our sapiens is not made of stone; many things *seem* to him true; yet he always feels that there is a possibility of their being false. The Stoics themselves admit that the senses are often deceived. Put this admission together with the tenet of Epicurus, and perception becomes impossible (101). It is strange that our *Probables* do not seem sufficient to you. Hear the account given by Clitomachus (102). He condemns those who say that sensation is swept away by the Academy; nothing is swept away but its *necessary* certainty (103). There are two modes of withholding assent; withholding it absolutely and withholding it merely so far as to deny the *certainty* of phenomena. The latter mode leaves all that is required for ordinary life (104).

98. *Tortuosum*: similar expressions are in *T.D.* II. 42, III. 22, *D.F.* IV. 7. *Ut Poenus*: "as might be expected from a Carthaginian;" cf. *D.F.* IV. 56, *tuus ille Poenulus, homo acutus*. A different meaning is given by the *ut* in passages like *De Div.* II. 30 *Democritus non inscite nugatur, ut physicus, quo genere nihil arrogantius*; "for a physical philosopher."

§99. *Genera*: here = classifications of, modes of dividing *visa*. This way of taking the passage will defend Cic. against the strong censure of Madv. (Pref. to *D.F.* p. lxiii.) who holds him convicted of ignorance, for representing Carneades as dividing *visa* into those which can be perceived and those which cannot. Is it possible that any one should read the *Academica* up to this point, and still believe that Cic. is capable of supposing, even for a moment, that Carneades in any way upheld καταληψις? *Dicantur*: i.e. *ab*

Academicis. Si probabile: the *si* is not in MSS. Halm and also Bait. follow Christ in reading *est, probabile nihil esse. Commemorabas*: in 53, 58. *Eversio*: cf. *D.F.* III. 50 (the same words), Plat. *Gorg.* 481 C ʿημων ʿο βιος ανατετραμμενος αν ειη, Sext. *A.M.* VIII. 157 συγχεομεν τον βιον. *Et sensibus*: no second *et* corresponds to this; *sic* below replaces it. See Madv. *D.F.* p. 790, ed. 2. *Quicquam tale* etc.: cf. 40, 41. *Nihil ab eo differens*: n. on 54. *Non comprehensa*: n. on 96.

§100. *Si iam*: "if, for example;" so *iam* is often used in Lucretius. *Probo ... bono*: it would have seemed more natural to transpose these epithets. *Facilior ... ut probet*: the usual construction is with *ad* and the gerund; cf. *De Div.* II. 107, *Brut.* 180. *Anaxagoras*: he made no ʿομοιομερειαι of snow, but only of water, which, when pure and deep, is dark in colour. *Concreta*: so Manut. for MSS. *congregata*. In 121 the MSS. give *concreta* without variation, as in *N.D.* II. 101, *De Div.* I. 130, *T.D.* I. 66, 71.

§101. *Impeditum*: cf. 33, n. *Movebitur*: cf. *moveri* in 24. *Non enim est*: Cic. in the vast majority of cases writes *est enim*, the two words falling under one accent like *sed enim, et enim* (cf. Corss. *Ausspr.* II. 851); Beier on *De Off.* I. p. 157 (qu. by Halm) wishes therefore to read *est enim*, but the MSS. both of the *Lucullus* and of Nonius agree in the other form, which Madv. allows to stand in *D.F.* I. 43, and many other places (see his note). Cf. fragm. 22 of the *Acad. Post. E robore*: so Nonius, but the MSS. of Cic. give here *ebore. Dolatus*: an evident imitation of Hom. *Od.* T 163 ου γαρ απο δρυος εσσι παλαιφατου ουδʹ απο πετρης. *Neque tamen habere*: i.e. *se putat*. For the sudden change from *oratio recta* to *obliqua* cf. 40 with n. *Percipiendi notam*: = χαρακτηρα της συγκταθεσεως in Sext. *P.H.* I. 191. For the use of the gerund cf. n. on 26, with Madv. *Gram.* 418, Munro on Lucr. I. 313; for *propriam* 34. *Exsistere.* cf. 36. *Qui neget*: see 79. *Caput*: a legal term. *Conclusio loquitur*: cf. *historiae loquantur* (5), *consuetudo loquitur* (*D.F.* II. 48), *hominis institutio si loqueretur* (ib. IV. 41), *vites si loqui possint* (ib. V. 39), *patria loquitur* (*In Cat.* I. 18, 27); the last use Cic. condemns himself in *Orat.* 85. *Inquit*: "quotha," indefinitely, as in 109, 115; cf. also *dicit* in 79.

§102. *Reprehensio est ... satis esse vobis*: Bait. follows Madv. in placing a comma after *est*, and a full stop at *probabilia. Tamen* ought in that case to follow *dicimus*, and it is noteworthy that in his communication to Halm (printed on p. 854 of Bait., and Hahn's ed. of the philosophical works, 1861) Madv. omits the word *tamen* altogether, nor does Bait. in adopting the suggestion notice the omission. *Ista diceret*: "stated the opinions you asked for." *Poetam*: this both Halm and Bait. treat as a gloss.

§103. For this section cf. Lucullus' speech, passim, and Sext. *P.H.* I. 227 sq. *Academia ... quibus*: a number of exx. of this change from sing. to plural are given by Madv. on *D.F.* V. 16. *Nullum*: on the favourite Ciceronian use of *nullus* for *non* see 47, 141, and Madv. *Gram.* 455, obs. 5. *Illud sit disputatum*: for the construction cf. 98; *autem* is omitted with the same constr. in *D.F.* V. 79, 80. *Nusquam alibi*: cf. 50.

§104. *Exposuisset adiungit*: Madv. on *D.F.* III. 67 notices a certain looseness in the use of tenses, which Cic. displays in narrating the opinions of philosophers, but no ex. so strong as this is produced. *Ut aut approbet quid aut improbet*: this Halm rejects. I have noticed among recent editors of Cic. a strong tendency to reject explanatory clauses introduced by *ut*. Halm brackets a similar clause in 20, and is followed in both instances by Bait. Kayser, who is perhaps the most extensive *bracketer* of modern times, rejects very many clauses of the kind in the Oratorical works. In our passage, the difficulty vanishes when we reflect that *approbare* and *improbare* may mean either to render an *absolute* approval or disapproval, or to render an approval or disapproval merely based on *probability*. For example, in 29 the words have the first meaning, in 66 the second. The same is the case with *nego* and *aio*. I trace the whole difficulty of the passage to the absence of terms to express distinctly the difference between the two kinds of assent. The general sense will be as follows. "There are two kinds of εποχη, one which prevents a man from expressing any assent or disagreement (in either of the two senses above noticed), another which does not

119

prevent him from giving an answer to questions, provided his answer be not taken to imply absolute approval or absolute disapproval; the result of which will be that he will neither absolutely deny nor absolutely affirm anything, but will merely give a qualified 'yes' or 'no,' dependent on probability." My defence of the clause impugned is substantially the same as that of Hermann in the *Philologus* (vol. VII.), which I had not read when this note was first written. *Alterum placere ... alterum tenere*: "the one is his formal dogma, the other is his actual practice." For the force of this see my note on *non probans* in 148, which passage is very similar to this. *Neget ... aiat*: cf. 97. *Nec ut placeat*: this, the MSS. reading, gives exactly the wrong sense, for Clitomachus *did* allow such *visa* to stand as were sufficient to serve as a basis for action. Hermann's *neu cui* labours under the same defect. Various emendations are *nam cum* (Lamb., accepted by Zeller 522), *hic ut* (Manut.), *et cum* (Dav. followed by Bait.), *sed cum* (Halm). The most probable of these seems to me that of Manut. I should prefer *sic ut*, taking *ut* in the sense of "although." *Respondere*: "to put in as an answer," as in 93 and often. *Approbari*: sc. *putavit*. Such changes of construction are common in Cic., and I cannot follow Halm in altering the reading to *approbavit*.

§105. *Lucem eripimus*: cf. 30.

§§105—111. Summary. You must see, Lucullus, by this time, that your defence of dogmatism is overthrown (105). You asked how memory was possible on my principles. Why, did not Siron remember the dogmas of Epicurus? If nothing can be remembered which is not absolutely true, then these will be true (106). Probability is quite sufficient basis for the arts. One strong point of yours is that nature compels us to *assent*. But Panaetius doubted even some of the Stoic dogmas, and you yourself refuse assent to the *sorites*, why then should not the Academic doubt about other things? (107) Your other strong point is that without assent action is impossible (108). But surely many actions of the dogmatist proceed upon mere probability. Nor do you gain by the use of the hackneyed argument of Antiochus (109). Where probability is, there the Academic has all the knowledge he wants (110). The argument of Antiochus that the Academics first admit that there are true and false *visa* and then contradict themselves by denying that there is any difference between true and false, is absurd. We do not deny that the difference *exists*; we do deny that human faculties are capable of perceiving the difference (111).

105. *Inducto ... prob.*: so Aug. *Cont Ac.* II. 12 *Soluto, libero*: cf. n. on 8. *Implicato*: = *impedito* cf. 101. *Iacere*: cf. 79. *Isdem oculis*: an answer to the question *nihil cernis?* in 102. *Purpureum*: cf. fragm. 7 of the *Acad. Post. Modo caeruleum ... sole*: Nonius (cf. fragm. 23) quotes *tum caeruleum tum lavum* (the MSS. in our passage have *flavum*) *videtur, quodque nunc a sole*. C.F. Hermann would place *mane ravum* after *quodque* and take *quod* as a proper relative pronoun, not as = "because." This transposition certainly gives increased clearness. Hermann further wishes to remove *a*, quoting exx. of *collucere* without the prep., which are not at all parallel, i.e. *Verr.* I. 58, IV. 71. *Vibrat*: with the ανηριθμον γελασμα of Aeschylus. *Dissimileque*: Halm, followed by Bait., om. *que*. *Proximo et*: MSS. have *ei*, rightly altered by Lamb., cf. e.g. *De Fato* 44. *Non possis ... defendere*: a similar line is taken in 81.

§106. *Memoria*: cf. 22. *Polyaenus*: named *D.F.* I. 20, Diog. X. 18, as one of the chief friends of Epicurus. *Falsum quod est*: Greek and Latin do not distinguish accurately between the *true* and the *existent*, the *false* and the *non existent*, hence the present difficulty; in Plato the confusion is frequent, notably in the *Sophistes* and *Theaetetus*. *Si igitur*: "if then recollection is recollection only of things perceived and known." The dogmatist theory of μνημη and νοησις is dealt with in exactly the same way by Sext. *P.H.* II. 5, 10 and elsewhere, cf. also Plat *Theaet.* 191 sq. *Siron*: thus Madv. on *D.F.* II. 119 writes the name, not *Sciron*, as Halm. *Fateare*: the em. of Dav. for *facile, facere, facias* of MSS. Christ defends *facere*, thinking that the constr. is varied from the subj. to the inf. after *oportet*, as after *necesse est* in 39. For *facere* followed by an inf. cf. *M.D.F.* IV. 8. *Nulla*: for *non*, cf. 47, 103.

§107. *Fiet artibus*: n. on 27 for the constr., for the matter see 22. *Lumina*: "strong points." Bentl. boldly read *columina*, while Dav. proposed *vimina* or *vincula*. That an em. is not needed may be seen from *D.F.* II. 70. *negat Epicurus (hoc enim vestrum lumen est) N.D.* I. 79, and 43 of this book. *Responsa*: added by Ernesti. Faber supplies *haruspicia*, Orelli after Ern. *haruspicinam*, but, as Halm says, some noun in the plur. is needed. *Quod is non potest*: this is the MSS. reading, but most edd. read *si is*, to cure a wrong punctuation, by which a colon is placed at *perspicuum est* above, and a full stop at *sustineat*. Halm restored the passage. *Habuerint*: the subj. seems due to the attraction exercised by *sustineat*. Bait. after Kayser has *habuerunt*. *Positum*: "when laid down" or "assumed."

§108. *Alterum est quod*: this is substituted for *deinde*, which ought to correspond to *primum* above. *Actio ullius rei*: n. on *actio rerum* in 62, cf. also 148. *Adsensu comprobet*: almost the same phrase often occurs in Livy, Sueton., etc. see Forc. *Sit etiam*: the *etiam* is a little strange and was thought spurious by Ernesti. It seems to have the force of Eng. "indeed", "in what indeed assent consists." *Sensus ipsos adsensus*: so in I. 41 *sensus* is defined to be *id quod est sensu comprehensum*, i.e. κατάληψις, cf. also Stobaeus I. 41, 25 αισθητικη γαρ φαντασια συγκαταθεσις εστι. *Appetitio*: for all this cf. 30. *Et dicta ... multa*: Manut. ejected these words as a gloss, after *multa* the MSS. curiously add *vide superiora*. *Lubricos sustinere*: cf. 68 and 94. *Ita scribenti ... exanclatum*: for the om. of *esse* cf. 77, 113 with notes. *Herculi*: for this form of the gen. cf. Madv. on *D.F.* I. 14, who doubts whether Cic. ever wrote *-is* in the gen. of the Greek names in -*es*. When we consider how difficult it was for copyists *not* to change the rarer form into the commoner, also that even Priscian (see *M.D.F.* V. 12) made gross blunders about them, the supposition of Madv. becomes almost irresistible. *Temeritatem*: προπετειαν, εικαιοτητα.

§109. *In navigando*: cf. 100. *In conserendo*: Guretus interprets "εν τω φυτυεσθαι τον αγρον," and is followed by most commentators, though it seems at least possible that *manum* is to be understood. For the suppressed accus. *agrum* cf. n. on *tollendum* in 148. *Sequere*: the fut. not the pres. ind., cf. 61. *Pressius*: cf. 28. *Reprehensum*: sc. *narrasti*. *Id ipsum*: = *nihil posse comprehendi*. *Saltem*: so in 29. *Pingue*: cf. *Pro Archia* 10. *Sibi ipsum*: note that Cic. does not generally make *ipse* agree in case with the reflexive, but writes *se ipse*, etc. *Convenienter*: "consistently". *Esse possit*: Bait. *posset* on the suggestion of Halm, but Cic. states the doctrine as a living one, not throwing it back to Antiochus time and to this particular speech of Ant. *Ut hoc ipsum*: the *ut* follows on *illo modo urguendum* above. *Decretum quod*: Halm followed by Bait. gives *quo*, referring to *altero quo neget* in 111, which however does not justify the reading. The best MSS. have *qui*. *Et sine decretis*: Lamb. gave *nec* for *et*, but Dav. correctly explains, "*multa decreta habent Academici, non tamen percepta sed tantum probabilia.*"

§110. *Ut illa*: i.e. the *decreta* implied in the last sentence. Some MSS. have *ille*, while Dav. without necessity gives *alia*. *Sic hoc ipsum*: Sext. then is wrong is saying (*P.H.* I. 226) that the Academics διαβεβαιουνται τα πραγματα ειναι ακαταληπτα, i.e. state the doctrine dogmatically, while the sceptics do not. *Cognitionis notam*: like *nota percipiendi, veri et falsi*, etc. which we have already had. *Ne confundere omnia*: a mocking repetition of Lucullus phrase, cf. 58. *Incerta reddere*: cf. 54. *Stellarum numerus*: another echo of Lucullus; see 32. *Quem ad modum ... item*: see Madv. on *D.F.* III. 48, who quotes an exact parallel from *Topica* 46, and *sicut ... item* from *N.D.* I. 3, noting at the same time that in such exx. neither *ita* nor *idem*, which MSS. sometimes give for *item*, is correct.

§111. *Dicere ... perturbatum*: for om. of *esse* cf. 108, etc. *Antiochus*: this Bait. brackets. *Unum ... alterum*: cf. 44. *Esse quaedam in visis*: it was not the *esse* but the *videri*, not the actual existence of a difference, but the possibility of that difference being infallibly perceived by human sense, that the Academic denied. *Cernimus*: i.e. the *probably* true and false. *Probandi species*: a phenomenal appearance which belongs to, or properly leads to qualified approval.

§§112—115. Summary. If I had to deal with a Peripatetic, whose definitions are not so exacting, my course would be easier; I should not much oppose him even if he maintained that the wise man sometimes *opines* (112). The definitions of the real Old Academy are more reasonable than those of Antiochus. How, holding the opinions he does, can he profess to belong to the Old Academy? (113) I cannot tolerate your assumption that it is possible to keep an elaborate dogmatic system like yours free from mistakes (114). You wish me to join your school. What am I to do then with my dear friend Diodotus, who thinks so poorly of Antiochus? Let us consider however what system not I, but the *sapiens* is to adopt (115).

§112. *Campis ... exsultare ... oratio*: expressions like this are common in Cic., e.g. *D.F.* I. 54, *De Off.* I. 61, *Orat.* 26; cf. also Aug. *Cont. Ac.* III. 5 *ne in quaestionis campis tua eqitaret oratio. Cum Peripatetico*: nothing that Cic. states here is at discord with what is known of the tenets of the later Peripatetics; cf. esp. Sext. *A.M.* VII. 216—226. All that Cic. says is that he could accept the Peripatetic formula, putting upon it his own meaning of course. Doubtless a Peripatetic would have wondered how a sceptic *could* accept his formulae; but the spectacle of men of the most irreconcilable opinions clinging on to the same formulae is common enough to prevent us from being surprised at Cicero's acceptance. I have already suggested (n. on 18) that we have here a trace of Philo's teaching, as distinct from that of Carneades. I see absolutely no reason for the very severe remarks of Madvig on *D.F.* V. 76, a passage which very closely resembles ours. *Dumeta*: same use in *N.D.* I. 68, Aug. *Cont. Ac.* II. 6; the *spinae* of the Stoics are often mentioned, e.g. *D.F.* IV. 6. *E vero ... a falso*: note the change of prep. *Adhiberet*: the MSS. are confused here, and go Halm reads *adderet*, and Bait. follows, while Kayser proposes *adhaereret*, which is indeed nearer the MSS.; cf. however I. 39 *adhiberet. Accessionem*: for this cf. 18 and 77. *Simpliciter*: the opposite of *subtiliter*; cf. *simpliciter—subtilitas* in I. 6. *Ne Carneade quidem*: cf. 59, 67, 78, 148.

§113. *Sed qui his minor est*: given by Halm as the em. of Io. Clericus for MSS. *sed mihi minores*. Guietus gave *sed his minores*, Durand *sed minutior*, while Halm suggests *sed minutiores*. I conj. *nimio minares*, which would be much nearer the MSS.; cf. Lucr. I. 734 *inferiores partibus egregie multis multoque minores. Tale verum: visum* omitted as in *D.F.* V. 76. *Incognito*: cf. 133. *Amavi hominem*: cf. Introd. p. 6. *Ita iudico, politissimum*; it is a mistake to suppose this sentence incomplete, like Halm, who wishes to add *eum esse*, or like Bait., who with Kayser prints *esse* after *politissimum*. Cf. 108 *ita scribenti, exanclatum*, and the examples given from Cic. by Madv. on *D.F.* II. 13. *Horum neutrum*: cf. 77 *nemo. Utrumque verum*: Cic. of course only accepts the propositions as Arcesilas did; see 77.

§114. *Illud ferre*: cf. 136. *Constituas*: this verb is often used in connection with the ethical *finis*; cf. 129 and I. 19. *Idemque etiam*: Krebs and Allgayer (*Antibarbarus*, ed. 4) deny that the expression *idem etiam* is Latin. One good MS. here has *atque etiam*, which Dav. reads; cf. however *Orat.* 117. *Artificium*: = *ars*, as in 30. *Nusquam labar*: cf. 138 *ne labar. Subadroganter*: cf. 126.

§115. *Qui sibi cum oratoribus ... rexisse*: so Cic. vary often speaks of the Peripatetics, as in *D.F.* IV. 5, V. 7. *Sustinuero*: cf. 70. *Tam bonos*: Cic. often speaks of them and of Epicurus in this patronising way; see e.g. *T.D.* II. 44, III. 50, *D.F.* I. 25, II. 81. For the Epicurean friendships cf. esp. *D.F.* I. 65. *Diodoto*: cf. Introd. p. 2. *Nolumus*: Halm and Bait., give *nolimus*; so fine a line divides the subjunctive from the indicative in clauses like these that the choice often depends on mere individual taste. *De sapiente loquamur*: n. on 66.

§§116—128. Summary. Of the three parts of philosophy take Physics first. Would your *sapiens* swear to the truth of any geometrical result whatever? (116) Let us see which one of actual physical systems the *sapiens* we are seeking will select (117). He must choose *one* teacher from among the conflicting schools of Thales, Anaximander, Anaximenos, Anaxagoras, Xenophanes, Leucippus, Democritus, Empedocles, Heraclitus, Melissus, Plato and Pythagoras. The remaining teachers, great men though they be, he must reject (118). Whatever system he selects he must know absolutely; if the Stoic, he must believe as strongly in the Stoic theology as he does in the sunlight. If he holds this, Aristotle will pronounce him mad; you, however, Lucullus, must defend the Stoics and spurn Aristotle from you, while you will not allow me even to doubt (119). How much better to be free, as I am and not compelled to find an answer to all the riddles of the universe! (120) Nothing can exist, say you, apart from the deity. Strato, however, says he does not need the deity to construct the universe. His mode of construction again differs from that of Democritus. I see some good in Strato, yet I will not assent absolutely either to his system or to yours (121). All these matters lie far beyond our ken. We know nothing of our bodies, which we can dissect, while we have not the advantage of being able to dissect the constitution of things or of the earth to see whether she is firmly fixed or hovers in mid air (122). Xenophanes, Hicetas, Plato and Epicurus tell strange things of the heavenly bodies. How much better to side with Socrates and Aristo, who hold that nothing can be known about them! (123) Who knows the nature of mind? Numberless opinions clash, as do those of Dicaearchus, Plato and Xenocrates. Our *sapiens* will be unable to decide (124). If you say it is better to choose any system rather than none, I choose Democritus. You at once upbraid me for believing such monstrous falsehoods (125). The Stoics differ among themselves about physical subjects, why will they not allow me to differ from them? (126) Not that I deprecate the study of Physics, for moral good results from it (127). Our *sapiens* will be delighted if he attains to anything which seems to resemble truth. Before I proceed to Ethics, I note your weakness in placing all perceptions on the same level. You must be prepared to asseverate no less strongly that the sun is eighteen times as large as the earth, than that yon statue is six feet high. When you admit that all things can be perceived no more and no less clearly than the size of the sun, I am almost content (128).

§116. *Tres partes*: cf. I. 19. *Et a vobismet*: "and especially by you". The threefold division was peculiarly Stoic, though used by other schools, cf. Sext. *P.H.* II. 13 (on the same subject) ʽοι Στωικοι και αλλοι τινες. For other modes of dividing philosophy see Sext. *A.M.* VII. 2. *At illud ante*: this is my em. for the MSS. *velut illud ante*, which probably arose from a marginal variant "vel ut" taking the place of *at*; cf. a similar break in 40 *sed prius*, also in 128 *at paulum ante*. Such breaks often occur in Cic., as in *Orator* 87 *sed nunc aliud*, also *T.D.* IV. 47 *repenam fortasse, sed illud ante*. For *velut* Halm writes *vel* (which Bait. takes), Dav. *verum*. *Inflatus tumore*: cf. *De Off.* I. 91 *inflati opinionibus*. Bentl. read *errore*. *Cogere*: this word like αναγκαζειν and βιαζεσθαι often means simply to argue irresistibly. *Initia*: as in 118, bases of proof, themselves naturally incapable of proof, so αρχαι in Gk. *Digitum*: cf. 58, 143. *Punctum esse* etc.: σημειον εστιν ου μερος ουθεν (Sext. *P.H.* III. 39), στιγμη = το αμερες (*A.M.* IX. 283, 377). *Extremitatem*: = επιφανειαν. *Libramentum*: so this word is used by Pliny (see Forc.) for the slope of a hill. *Nulla crassitudo*: in Sext. the επιφανεια is usually described not negatively as here, but positively as μηκος μετα πλατους (*P.H.* III. 39), περας (*extremitas*) σωματος δυο εχον διαστασεις, μηκος και πλατος (*A.M.* III. 77). *Liniamentum ... carentem*: a difficult passage. Note (1) that the line is defined in Greek as μηκος απλατες. (Sext. as above), (2) that Cic. has by preference described the point and surface negatively. This latter fact seems to me strong against the introduction of *longitudinem* which Ursinus, Dav., Orelli, Baiter and others propose by conjecture. If anything is to be introduced, I would rather add *et crassitudine* before *carentem*, comparing I. 27 *sine ulla specie et carentem omni illa qualitate*. I have merely bracketed *carentem*, though I feel Halm's remark that a verb is wanted in this clause as in the other two, he suggests *quod sit sine*. Hermann takes *esse* after *punctum* as strongly predicative ("there *is* a point," etc.), then adds *similiter* after *liniamentum* and ejects *sine ulla*. Observe the awkwardness of having the *line* treated of after the *superficies*, which has induced some edd. to transpose. For *liniamentum* = *lineam* cf. *De Or.* I. 187. *Si adigam*: the fine em. of Manut. for *si adiiciamus* of MSS. The construction *adigere aliquem ius iurandum* will be found in Caes. *Bell. Civ.* I. 76, II. 18, qu. by Dav., cf. also Virg. *Aen.* III. 56 *quid non mortalia pectora cogis auri sacra fames? Sapientem nec prius*: this is the "*egregia lectio*" of three of Halm's MSS. Before Halm *sapientemne* was read, thus was destroyed the whole point of the sentence, which is *not* that the *sapiens* will swear to the size of the sun after he has seen Archimedes go through his calculations, *but* that the *sapiens*, however true he admits the bases of proof to be which Archimedes uses, will *not* swear to the truth of the elaborate conclusions which that geometer rears upon them. Cicero is arguing as in 128 against the absurdity of attaching one and the same degree of certainty to the simplest and the most complex truths, and tries to condemn the Stoic *sapiens* out of his own mouth, cf. esp. *nec ille iurare posset* in 123. *Multis partibus*: for this expression see Munro on Lucr. I. 734, for the sense cf. 82, 123, 126, 128. *Deum*: see 126.

§117. *Vim*: = αναγκην, cf. *cogere* in 116. *Ne ille*: this asseverative *ne* is thus always closely joined with pronouns in Cic. *Sententiam eliget et*: MSS. have (by *dittographia* of *m, eli*) added *melius* after *sententiam*, and have also dropped *et*. Dav. wished to read *elegerit*, comparing the beginning of 119. *Insipiens eliget*: cf. 115 *quale est a non sapiente explicari sapientiam?* and 9 *statuere qui sit sapiens vel maxime videtur esse sapientis. Infinitae quaestiones*: θεσεις, general propositions, opposed to *finitae quaestiones*, limited propositions, Gk. ὑποθεσεις. Quintal III. 5, 5 gives as an ex. of the former *An uxor ducenda*, of the latter *An Catoni ducenda*. These *quaestiones* are very often alluded to by Cic. as in *D.F.* I. 12, IV. 6, *De Or.* I. 138, II. 65—67, *Topica* 79, *Orat.* 46, cf. also Quint. X. 5, II. *E quibus omnia constant*: this sounds like Lucretius, *omnia* = το παν.

§118. For these *physici* the student must in general be referred to R. and P., Schwegler, and Grote's *Plato* Vol. I. A more complete enumeration of schools will be found in Sext. *P.H.* III. 30 sq. Our passage is imitated by Aug *De Civ. Dei* XVIII. 37. *Concessisse primas*: Cic. always considers Thales to be *sapientissimus e septem* (*De Leg.* II. 26). Hence Markland on Cic. *Ad Brutum* II. 15, 3 argued that that letter cannot be genuine, since in it the supremacy among the seven is assigned to Solon. *Infinitatem naturae*: το απειρον, *naturae* here = ουσιας. *Definita*: this is opposed to *infinita* in *Topica* 79, so *definire* is used for *finire* in *Orat.* 65, where Jahn qu. *Verr.* IV. 115. *Similis inter se*: an attempt to translate ὁμοιομερειας. *Eas primum*, etc.: cf. the exordium of Anaxagoras given from Diog. II. 6 in R. and P. 29 παντα χρηματα ην ὁμου ειτα νους ελθων αυτα διεκοσμησε. *Xenophanes ... deum*: Eleaticism was in the hands of Xenoph. mainly theological. *Neque natum unquam*: cf. *neque ortum unquam* in 119. *Parmenides ignem*: cf. Arist. *Met. A.* 5 qu. R. and P. 94. He only hypothetically allowed the existence of the phenomenal world, after which he made two αρχαι, θερμον και ψυχρον τουτων δε το μεν κατα μεν το ὁν θερμον ταττει, θατερον δε κατα το μη ον. *Heraclitus*: n. on I. 39. *Melissus*: see Simplicius qu. R. and P. 101, and esp. το εον αιει αρα ην τε και εσται. *Plato*: n. on I. 27. *Discedent*: a word often used of those vanquished in a fight, cf. Hor. *Sat.* I. 7, 17.

§119. *Sic animo ... sensibus*: knowledge according to the Stoics was homogeneous throughout, no one thing could be more or less known than another. *Nunc lucere*: cf. 98, also 128 *non enim magis adsentiuntur*, etc. *Mundum sapientem*: for this Stoic doctrine see *N.D.* I. 84, II. 32, etc. *Fabricata sit*: see 87 n. *Solem*: 126. *Animalis intellegentia*: reason is the essence of the universe with the Stoics, cf. Zeller 138—9, also 28, 29 of Book I. *Permanet*: the deity is to the Stoic πνευμα ενδιηκον δι ὁλου του κοσμου (Plut. *De Plac. Phil.* I. 7 qu. R. and P. 375), *spiritus per omnia maxima ac minima aequali intentione diffusus.* (Seneca, *Consol. ad Helvid.* 8, 3 qu. Zeller 147). *Deflagret*: the Stoics considered the κοσμος φθαρτος, cf. Diog. VII. 141, Zeller 156—7. *Fateri*: cf. *tam vera quam falsa cernimus* in 111. *Flumen aureum*: Plut. *Vita Cic.* 24 alludes to this (ὁτι χρυσιου ποταμος ειη ρεοντος). This is the constant judgment of Cic. about Aristotle's style. Grote, *Aristot.* Vol I. p. 43, quotes *Topica* 3, *De Or.* I. 49, *Brut.* 121, *N.D.* II. 93, *De Inv.* II. 6, *D.F.* I. 14, *Ad Att.* II. 1, and discusses the difficulty of applying this criticism to the works of Aristotle which we possess. *Nulla vis*: cf. I. 28. *Exsistere*: Walker conj. *efficere*, "*recte ut videtur*" says Halm. Bait. adopts it. *Ornatus*: = κοσμος.

§120. *Libertas ... non esse*: a remarkable construction. For the Academic liberty see Introd. p. 18. *Quod tibi est*: after these words Halm puts merely a comma, and inserting *respondere* makes *cur deus*, etc. part of the same sentence. Bait. follows. *Nostra causa*: Cic. always writes *mea, tua, vestra, nostra causa*, not *mei, tui, nostri, vestri*, just as he writes *sua sponte*, but not *sponte alicuius*. For the Stoic opinion that men are the chief care of Providence, see *N.D.* I. 23, II. 37, *D.F.* III. 67, *Ac.* I. 29 etc., also Zeller. The difficulties surrounding the opinion are treated of in Zeller 175, *N.D.* II. 91—127. They supply in Sext.

P.H. I. 32, III. 9—12 an example of the refutation of νοουμενα by means of νοουμενα. *Tam multa ac*: MSS. om. *ac*, which I insert. Lactantius qu. the passage without *perniciosa*. *Myrmecides*: an actual Athenian artist, famed for minute work in ivory, and especially for a chariot which a fly covered with its wings, and a ship which the wings of a bee concealed. See Plin. *Nat. Hist.* VII. 21, XXXVI. 5.

§121. *Posse*: n. on I. 29. *Strato*: R. and P. 331. *Sed cum*: *sed* often marks a very slight contrast, there is no need to read *et*, as Halm. *Asperis ... corporibus*: cf. fragm. 28 of the *Ac. Post.*, also *N.D.* I. 66. *Somnia*: so *N.D.* I. 18 *miracula non disserentium philosophorum sed somniantium*, ib. I. 42 *non philosophorum iudicia sed delirantium somnia*, also ib. I. 66 *flagitia Democriti*. *Docentis*: giving *proof*. *Optantis*: Guietus humorously conj. *potantis*, Durand *oscitantis* (cf. *N.D.* I. 72), others *opinantis*. That the text is sound however may be seen from *T.D.* II. 30 *optare hoc quidem est non docere, De Fato* 46, *N.D.* I. 19 *optata magis quam inventa*, ib. III. 12 *doceas oportet nec proferas*; cf. also *Orat.* 59 *vocis bonitas optanda est, non est enim in nobis*, i.e. a good voice is a thing to be prayed for, and not to be got by exertion. There is a similar Greek proverb, ευχη μαλλον η αληθεια, in Sext. *P.H.* VIII. 353. *Magno opere*: Hermann wishes to read *onere*. The phrase *magnum onus* is indeed common (cf. *De Or.* I. 116), but *magnum opus*, in the sense of "a great task," is equally so, cf. *T.D.* III. 79, 84, *Orat.* 75. *Modo hoc modo illud*: 134.

§122. *Latent ista*: see n. on fragm. 29 of the *Ac. Post.*; for *latent* cf. I. 45. Aug. *Cont. Ac.* II. 12, III. 1 imitates this passage. *Circumfusa*: cf. I. 44, and 46 of this book. *Medici*: cf. *T.D.* I. 46 *Viderentur*: a genuine passive, cf. 25, 39, 81. *Empirici*: a school of physicians so called. *Ut ... mutentur*: exactly the same answer was made recently to Prof. Huxley's speculations on protoplasm; he was said to have assumed that the living protoplasm would have the same properties as the dead. *Media pendeat*: cf. *N.D.* II. 98, *De Or.* III. 178.

§123. *Habitari ait*: for this edd. qu. Lactant. *Inst.* III. 23, 12. *Portenta*: "monstrosities these," cf. *D.F.* IV. 70. *Iurare*: cf. 116. *Neque ego*, etc.: see fragm. 30 of *Ac. Post.* Αντιποδας: this doctrine appears in Philolaus (see Plut. *Plac. Phil.* III. 11 qu. R. and P. 75), who give the name of αντιχθων to the opposite side of the world. Diog. VIII. 26 (with which passage cf. Stob. *Phys.* XV. 7) mentions the theory as Pythagorean, but in another passage (III. 24) says that Plato first invented the name. The word αντιπους seems to occur first in Plat. *Tim.* 63 A. The existence of αντιποδες; was of course bound up with the doctrine that the universe or the world is a globe (which is held by Plat. in the *Tim.* and by the Stoics, see Stob. *Phys.* XV. 6, Diog. VII. 140), hence the early Christian writers attack the two ideas together as unscriptural. Cf. esp Aug. *De Civ. Dei* XVI. 9. *Hicetas*: he was followed by Heraclides Ponticus and some Pythagoreans. Sext. *A.M.* X. 174 speaks of the followers of Aristarchus the mathematician as holding the same doctrine. It seems also to be found in Philolaus, see R. and P. 75. *Theophrastus*: who wrote much on the history of philosophy, see R. and P. 328. *Platonem*: the words of Plato (*Tim.* 40 B) are γην δε τροφον μεν 'ημετεραν, ειλλομενην δε περι τον δια παντος πολον τεταμενον. *Quid tu, Epicure*: the connection is that Cic., having given the crotchets of other philosophers about φυσικη, proceeds to give the peculiar crotchet of Epic. *Putas solem ... tantum*: a hard passage. *Egone? ne bis* is the em. of Lamb. for MSS. *egone vobis*, and is approved by Madv., who thus explains it (*Em.* 185) "*cum interrogatum esset num tantulum (quasi pedalem 82) solem esse putaret, Epic. non praecise definit (tantum enim esse censebat quantus videretur vel paulo aut maiorem aut minorem) sed latius circumscribit, ne bis quidem tantum esse, sed inter pedalem magnitudinem et bipedalem*". (*D.F.* I. 20) This explanation though not quite satisfactory is the best yet given. Epicurus' absurdity is by Cic. brought into strong relief by stating the outside limit to which Epic. was prepared to go in estimating the sun's size, i.e. twice the apparent size. *Ne ... quidem* may possibly appear strange, cf. however *ne maiorem quidem* in 82. *Aristo Chius*: for this doctrine of his see R. and P. 358.

§124. *Quid sit animus*: an enumeration of the different ancient theories is given in *T.D.* I. 18—22, and by Sext. *A.M.* VII. 113, who also speaks in *P.H.* II. 31 of the πολλη και ανηνυτος μαχη concerning the soul.

In *P.H.* II. 57 he says Γοργιας ουδε διανοιαν ειναι φησι. *Dicaearcho*: *T.D.* I. 21. *Tres partis*: in Plato's *Republic*. *Ignis*: Zeno's opinion, *T.D.* I. 19. *Animam*: *ib.* I. 19. *Sanguis*: Empodocles, as in *T.D.* I. 19 where his famous line ʾαιμα γαρ ανθρωποις περικαρδιον εστι νοημα is translated, see R. and P. 124. *Ut Xenocrates*: some edd. read *Xenocrati*, but cf. I. 44, *D.F.* II. 18, *T.D.* III. 76. *Numerus*: so Bentl. for *mens* of MSS., cf. I. 39, *T.D.* I. 20, 41. An explanation of this Pythagorean doctrine of Xenocrates is given in R. and P. 244. *Quod intellegi* etc.: so in *T.D.* I. 41 *quod subtiliter magis quam dilucide dicitur. Momenta* n. on I. 45.

§125. *Verecundius*: cf. 114 *subadroganter*. *Vincam animum*: a common phrase in Cic., cf. *Philipp.* XII. 21. *Queru potissimum? quem?*: In repeated questions of this kind Cic. usually puts the corresponding case of *quisnam*, not *quis*, in the second question, as in *Verr.* IV. 5. The mutation of Augustine *Contra Ac.* III. 33 makes it probable that *quemnam* was the original reading here. Zumpt on *Verr.* qu. Quint. IX. 2, 61, Plin. *Epist.* I. 20, who both mention this trick of style, and laud it for its likeness to impromptu. *Nobilitatis*: this is to be explained by referring to 73—75 (*imitari numquam nisi clarum, nisi nobilem*), where Cic. protests against being compared to a demagogue, and claims to follow the aristocracy of philosophy. The attempts of the commentators to show that Democr. was literally an aristocrat have failed. *Convicio*: cf. 34. *Completa et conferta*: n. on I. 27. *Quod movebitur ... cedat*: this is the theory of motion disproved by Lucr. I. 370 sq., cf. also *N.D.* II. 83. Halm writes *quo quid* for *quod* (with Christ), and inserts *corpus* before *cedat*, Baiter following him. The text is sound. Trans. "whatever body is pushed, gives way." *Tam sit mirabilis*: n. on I. 25. *Innumerabilis*: 55. *Supra infra*: n. on 92. *Ut nos nunc simus*, etc.: n. on fragm. 13 of *Ac. Post. Disputantis*: 55. *Animo videre*: cf. 22. *Imagines*: ειδωλα, which Catius translated (*Ad Fam.* XV. 16) by *spectra*, Zeller 432. *Tu vero*: etc. this is all part of the personal *convicium* supposed to be directly addressed to Cic. by the Antiocheans, and beginning at *Tune aut inane* above. *Commenticiis*: a favourite word of Cic., cf. *De Div.* II. 113.

§126. *Quae tu*: elliptic for *ut comprobem quae tu comprobas* cf. 125. *Impudenter*: 115. *Atque haud scio*: *atque* here = καιτοι, "and yet," n. on 5 *ac vereor*. *Invidiam*: cf. 144. *Cum his*: i.e. *aliis cum his*. *Summus deus*: "the highest form of the deity" who was of course one in the Stoic system. Ether is the finest fire, and πυρ τεχνικον is one of the definitions of the Stoic deity, cf. I. 29, Zeller 161 sq. *Solem*: as of course being the chief seat of fire. *Solis autem ... nego credere*: Faber first gave *ac monet* for MSS. *admonens*, which Halm retains, Manut. then restored to its place *permensi refertis*, which MSS. have after *nego*. *Hic*, which MSS. have after *decempeda*, Madv. turns into *hunc*, while *hoc*, which stands immediately after *nego*, he ejects (*Em.* 187). *Ergo* after *vos* is of course analeptic. Halm departs somewhat from this arrangement. *Leniter*: Halm and Hermann *leviter*; the former reads *inverecundior* after Morgenstern, for what reason it is difficult to see.

§127. *Pabulum*: similar language in *D.F.* II. 46. *Consideratio contemplatioque*: Cic. is fond of this combination, as *De Off.* I. 153; cf. Wesenberg on *T.D.* V. 9, who qu. similar combinations from *D.F.* V. 11, 58. *Elatiores*: MSS. mostly have *latiores*. Halm with Lamb. reads *altiores*, in support of which reading Dav. qu. *D.F.* II. 51, Val. Flaccus *Argon.* II. 547, add Virg. *Aen.* VI. 49, Cic. *Orat.* 119. *Exigua et minima*: σμικρα και ελαχιστα. Madv. on *D.F.* V. 78 notes that except here Cic. always writes *exigua et paene minima* or something of the kind. *Occultissimarum*: n. on I. 15. *Occurit ... completur*: MSS. have *occuret* mostly, if that is retained *complebitur* must be read. Madv. *Opusc.* II. 282 takes *occurit*, explaining it as a perfect, and giving numerous exx. of this sequence of tenses, cf. also Wesenb. on *T.D.* IV. 35.

§128. *Agi secum*: cf. *nobiscum ageret* in 80. *Simile veri*: cf. 66. *Notionem*: = *cognitionem*, επιστημην. *At paulum*: MSS. *et* Halm *sed.*; cf. *at illud ante* in 116. *Si quae*: Halm and many edd. have *se, quae*. But the *se* comes in very awkwardly, and is not needed before the infinitive. Madv. indeed (*Em.* 114), after producing many exx. of the reflexive pronoun omitted, says that he doubts about this passage because *considero* does not belong to the class of verbs with which this usage is found, but he produces many instances with *puto*, which surely stands on the same level. *Non magis*: so in 119 *nec magis approbabit nunc lucere*, etc. The sunlight was the stock example of a most completely cognisable phenomenon; hence the Academics showed their hostility to absolute knowledge by refusing τον ῾ηλιον ῾ομολογειν ειναι καταληπτον (Galen *De Opt. Gen. Dicendi* 497 B qu. P. Valentia 304 ed. Or.). *Cornix*: for the Stoic belief in divination see Zeller 349—358. *Signum illud*: the *xystus* (9) was adorned with statues; edd. qu. Plin. *Nat. Hist.* XXXIV. 8. *Duodeviginti*: 82, I just note that *octodecim* is not used by Cic. *Sol quantus sit*: 91. *Omnium rerum ... comprehendendi*: not a case of a plural noun with a singular gerund like *spe rerum potiendi*, etc., but of two genitives depending in different ways on the same word (*definitio*). M. *Em.* 197 qu. Plat. *Leg.* 648 E την παντων ῾ητταν φοβουμενος ανθρωπον τοι πωματος, *Brut.* 163 *Scaevolae dicendi elegantia, De Or.* III. 156. Other exx. in *M.D.F.* I. 14. For the turn of expression cf. *T.D.* IV. 62 *omnium philosophorum una est ratio medendi, Lael.* 78 *omnium horum vitiorum una cautio est*, also 51 of this book.

§§129—141. Summary. What contention is there among philosophers about the ethical standard! I pass by many abandoned systems like that of Herillus but consider the discrepancies between Xenophanes, Parmenides, Zeno of Elea, Euclides, Menedemus, Aristo, Pyrrho, Aristippus, Epicurus, Callipho, Hieronymus, Diodorus, Polemo, Antiochus, Carneades (129-131). If I desire to follow the Stoics, Antiochus will not allow me, while if I follow Polemo, the Stoics are irate (132). I must be careful not to assent to the unknown, which is a dogma common to both you, Lucullus, and myself (133). Zeno thinks virtue gives happiness. "Yes," says Antiochus, "but not the greatest possible." How am I to choose among such conflicting theories? (134) Nor can I accept those points in which Antiochus and Zeno agree. For instance, they regard emotion as harmful, which the ancients thought natural and useful (135). How absurd are the Stoic Paradoxes! (136) Albinus joking said to Carneades "You do not think me a praetor because I am not a *sapiens*." "That," said Carneades, "is Diogenes' view, not mine" (137). Chrysippus thinks only three ethical systems can with plausibility be defended (138). I gravitate then towards one of them, that of pleasure. Virtue calls me back, nor will she even allow me to join pleasure to herself (139). When I hear the several pleadings of pleasure and virtue, I cannot avoid being moved by both, and so I find it impossible to choose (141, 142).

§129. *Quod coeperam*: in 128 at *veniamus nunc ad boni maique notionem. Constituendi*: n. on 114. *Bonorum summa*: cf. *D.F.* V. 21 and Madv. *Est igitur*: so in *De Div.* II. 8, *igitur* comes fourth word in the clause; this is not uncommon in Cic., as in Lucretius. *Omitto*: MSS. *et omitto*, but cf. Madv. *Em.* 201 *certe contra Ciceronis usum est 'et omitto' pro simplici 'omitto,' in initio huius modi orationis ubi universae sententiae exempla subiciuntur per figuram omissionis. Relicta*: cf. 130 *abiectos.* Cic. generally classes Herillus (or Erillus as Madv. on *D.F.* II. 35 spells the name), Pyrrho and Aristo together as authors of exploded systems, cf. *D.F.* II. 43, *De Off.* I. 6, *T.D.* V. 85. *Ut Herillum.* MSS. have either *Erillum* or *et illum*, one would expect *ut Herilli. Cognitione et scientia*: double translation of επιστημη. For the *finis* of Herillus see Madv. on *D.F.* II. 43. *Megaricorum: Xenophanes.* Cic considers the Eleatic and Megarian schools to be so closely related as to have, like the schools of Democritus and Epicurus, a continuous history. The Megarian system was indeed an ethical development of Eleatic doctrine. Zeller, *Socrates* 211. *Unum et simile*: for this see Zell. *Socr.* 222 sq, with footnotes, R. and P. 174 sq. *Simile* ought perhaps to be *sui simile* as in *Tim.* c. 7, already quoted on I. 30, see my note there and cf. I. 35. *Menedemo*: see Zeller *Socr.* 238, R. and P. 182. The *Erctrian* school was closely connected with the Megarian. *Fuit*: = *natus est*, as often. *Herilli*: so Madv. for *ulli* of MSS.

§130. *Aristonem*: this is Aristo of Chios, not Aristo of Ceos, who was a Peripatetic; for the difference see R. and P. 332, and for the doctrines of Aristo the Chian *ib.* 358, Zeller 58 sq. *In mediis*: cf. I. 36, 37. *Momenta* = *aestimationes*, αξιαι in 36, where *momenti* is used in a different way. *Pyrrho autem*: one would expect Pyrrhoni as Dav. conj., but in 124 there is just the same change from *Pyrrhoni* to

Xenocrates. Απαθεια: Diog. IX. 108 affirms this as well as πραιοτης to be a name for the sceptic τελος, but the name scarcely occurs if at all in Sext. who generally uses αταραξια, but occasionally μετριοπαθεια; cf. Zeller 496, R. and P. 338. Απαθεια was also a Stoic term. *Diu multumque*: n. on I. 4.

§131. *Nec tamen consentiens*: cf. R. and P. 352 where the differences between the two schools are clearly drawn out, also Zeller 447, 448. *Callipho*: as the genitive is *Calliphontis*, Cic. ought according to rule to write *Calliphon* in the nom; for this see Madv. on *D.F.* II. 19, who also gives the chief authorities concerning this philosopher. *Hieronymus*: mentioned *D.F.* II. 19, 35, 41, V. 14, in which last place Cic. says of him *quem iam cur Peripateticum appellem nescio. Diodorus*: see Madv. on *D.F.* II. 19. *Honeste vivere*, etc.: in *D.F.* IV. 14 the *finis* of Polemo is stated to be *secundum naturam vivere*, and three Stoic interpretations of it are given, the last of which resembles the present passage—*omnibus aut maximis rebus iis quae secundum naturam sint fruentem vivere*. This interpretation Antiochus adopted, and from him it is attributed to the *vetus Academia* in I. 22, where the words *aut omnia aut maxima*, seem to correspond to words used by Polemo; cf. Clemens Alex. qu. by Madv. on *D.F.* IV. 15. See n. below on Carneades. *Antiochus probat*: the germs of many Stoic and Antiochean doctrines were to be found in Polemo; see I. 34, n. *Eiusque amici*: Bentl. *aemuli*, but Halm refers to *D.F.* II. 44. The later Peripatetics were to a great degree Stoicised. *Nunc*: Halm *huc* after Jo. Scala. *Carneades*: this *finis* is given in *D.F.* II. 35 (*frui principiis naturalibus*), II. 42 (*Carneadeum illud quod is non tam ut probaret protulit, quam ut Stoicis quibuscum bellum gerebat opponeret*), V. 20 (*fruendi rebus iis, quas primas secundum naturam esse diximus, Carneades non ille quidem auctor sed defensor disserendi causa fuit*), *T.D.* V. 84 (*naturae primus aut omnibus aut maximis frui, ut Carneades contra Stoicos disserebat*). The *finis* therefore, thus stated, is not different from that of Polemo, but it is clear that Carneades intended it to be different, as he did not include *virtus* in it (see *D.F.* II. 38, 42, V. 22) while Polemo did (I. 22). See more on 139. *Zeno*: cf. *D.F.* IV. 15 *Inventor et princeps*: same expression in *T.D.* I. 48, *De Or.* I. 91, *De Inv.* II. 6; *inv.* = οικιστης.

§132. *Quemlibet*: cf. 125, 126. *Prope singularem*: cf. *T.D.* I. 22 *Aristoteles longe omnibus—Platonem semper excipio—praestans*; also *D.F.* V. 7, *De Leg.* I. 15. *Per ipsum Antiochum*: a similar line of argument is taken in Sext. *P.H.* I. 88, II. 32, etc. *Terminis ... possessione*: there is a similar play on the legal words *finis terminus possessio* in *De Leg.* I. 55, 56, a noteworthy passage. *Omnis ratio* etc.: this is the constant language of the later Greek philosophy; cf. Aug. *De Civ. Dei* XIX. 1 *neque enim existimat* (Varro) *ullam philosophiae sectam esse dicendam, quae non eo distat a ceteris, quod diversos habeat fines bonorum et malorum*, etc. *Si Polemoneus*: i.e. *sapiens fuerit. Peccat*: a Stoic term turned on the Stoics, see I. 37. *Academicos et*: MSS. om. *et* as in I. 16, and *que* in 52 of this book. *Dicenda*: for the omission of the verb with the gerundive (which occurs chiefly in emphatic clauses) cf. I. 7, and Madv. on *D.F.* I. 43, who how ever unduly limits the usage. *Hic igitur ... prudentior*: MSS. generally have *assentiens*, but one good one (Halm's E) has *assentientes*. I venture to read *adsentietur*, thinking that the last two letters were first dropt, as in 26 (*tenetur*) and that then *adsentiet*, under the attraction of the *s* following, passed into *adsentiens*, as in 147 *intellegat se* passed into *intelligentes*. N, I may remark, is frequently inserted in MSS. (as in I. 7 *appellant*, 16 *disputant*, 24 *efficerentur*), and all the changes involved in my conj. are of frequent occurrence. I also read *sin, inquam* (sc. *adsentietur*) for *si numquam* of MSS. The question *uter est prudentior* is intended to press home the dilemma in which Cicero has placed the supposed *sapiens*. All the other emendations I have seen are too unsatisfactory to be enumerated.

§133. *Non posse ... esse*: this seems to me sound; Bait. however reads *non esse illa probanda sap.* after Lamb., who also conj. *non posse illa probata esse. Paria*: *D.F.* III. 48, *Paradoxa* 20 sq., Zeller 250. *Praecide*: συντομος or συνελων ειπε, cf. *Cat. Mai.* 57, *Ad Att.* VIII. 4, X. 16. *Inquit*: n. on 79. *Quid quod quae*: so Guietus with the approval of Madv. (*Em.* 203) reads for MSS. *quid quae* or *quid quaeque*, Halm and Bait., follow Moser in writing *Quid? si quae* removing the stop at *paria*, and make *in utramque* *partem* follow *dicantur*, on Orelli's suggestion. When several relative pronouns come together the MSS. often omit one. *Dicebas*: in 27. *Incognito*: 133.

§134. *Etiam*: = "yes," Madv. *Gram.* 454. *Non beatissimam*: I. 22, n. *Deus ille*: i.e. more than man (of Aristotle's η θεος η θηριον), if he can do without other advantages. For the omission of *est* after the emphatic *ille* cf. 59, n. *Theophrasto*, etc.: n. on I. 33, 35. *Dicente*: before this Halm after Lamb., followed by Bait., inserts *contra*, the need for which I fail to see. *Et hic*: i.e. Antiochus. *Ne sibi constet*: Cic. argues in *T.D.* V. that there cannot be degrees in happiness. *Tum hoc ... tum illud*: cf. 121. *Iacere*: 79. *In his discrepant*: I. 42 *in his constitit*.

§135. *Moveri*: κινεισθαι, 29. *Laetitia efferri*: I. 38. *Probabilia*: the removal of passion and delight is easier than that of fear and pain. *Sapiensne ... deleta sit*: see Madv. *D.F.* p. 806, ed. 2, who is severe upon the reading of Orelli (still kept by Klotz), *non timeat? nec si patria deleatur? non doleat? nec, si deleta sit?* which involves the use of *nec* for *ne ... quidem*. I have followed the reading of Madv. in his *Em.*, not the one he gives (after Davies) in *D.F. ne patria deleatur*, which Halm takes, as does Baiter. Mine is rather nearer the MSS. *Decreta*: some MSS. *durata*; Halm conj. *dictata*. *Mediocritates*: μεσοπετες, as in Aristotle; cf. *T.D.* III. 11, 22, 74. *Permotione*: κινεσει. *Naturalem ... modum*: so *T.D.* III. 74. *Crantoris*: sc. *librum*, for the omission of which see n. on I. 13; add Quint. IX. 4, 18, where Spalding wished to read *in Herodoti*, supplying *libro*. *Aureolus ... libellus*: it is not often that two diminutives come together in Cic., and the usage is rather colloquial; cf. *T.D.* III. 2, *N.D.* III. 43, also for *aureolus* 119 *flumen aureum*. *Panaetius*: he had addressed to Tubero a work *de dolore*; see *D.F.* IV. 23. *Cotem*: *T.D.* IV. 43, 48, Seneca *De Ira* III. 3, where the saying is attributed to Aristotle (*iram calcar esse virtutis*). *Dicebant*: for the repetition of this word cf. 146, I. 33.

§136. *Sunt enim Socratica*: the Socratic origin of the Stoic paradoxes is affirmed in *Parad.* 4, *T.D.* III. 10. *Mirabilia*: Cic. generally translates παραδοξα by *admirabilia* as in *D.F.* IV. 74, or *admiranda*, under which title he seems to have published a work different from the *Paradoxa*, which we possess: see Bait., and Halm's ed. of the Phil. works (1861), p. 994. *Quasi*: = almost, ΄ως επος ειπειν. *Voltis*: cf. the Antiochean opinion in I. 18, 22. *Solos reges*: for all this see Zeller 253 sq. *Solos divites*: ΄οτι μονος ΄ο σοφος πλουσιος, *Parad.* VI. *Liberum*: *Parad.* V. ΄οτι μονος ΄ο σοφος ελευθερος και πας αφρον δουλος. *Furiosus*: *Parad.* IV. ΄οτι πας αφρον μαινεται.

§137. *Tam sunt defendenda*: cf. 8, 120. *Bono modo*: a colloquial and Plautine expression; see Forc. *Ad senatum starent*: "were in waiting on the senate;" cf. such phrases as *stare ad cyathum*, etc. *Carneade*: the vocative is *Carneades* in *De Div.* I. 23. *Huic Stoico*: i.e. *Diogeni*; cf. *D.F.* II. 24. Halm brackets *Stoico*, and after him Bait. *Sequi volebat*: "professed to follow;" cf. *D.F.* V. 13 *Strato physicum se voluit* "gave himself out to be a physical philosopher:" also Madv. on *D.F.* II. 102. *Ille noster*: Dav. *vester*, as in 143 *noster Antiochus*. But in both places Cic. speaks as a friend of Antiochus; cf. 113. *Balbutiens*: "giving an uncertain sound;" cf. *De Div.* I. 5, *T.D.* V. 75.

§138. *Mihi veremini*: cf. Caes. *Bell. Gall.* V. 9 *veritus navibus*. Halm and Bait. follow Christ's conj. *verenti*, removing the stop at *voltis*. *Opinationem*: the οιησιν of Sext., e.g. *P.H.* III. 280. *Quod minime voltis*: cf. I. 18. *De finibus*: not "concerning," but "from among" the different *fines*; otherwise *fine* would have been written. Cf. I. 4 *si qui de nostris*. *Circumcidit et amputat*: these two verbs often come together, as in *D.F.* I. 44; cf. also *D.F.* III. 31. *Si vacemus omni molestia*: which Epicurus held to be the highest pleasure. *Cum honestate*: Callipho in 131. *Prima naturae commoda*: Cic. here as in *D.F.* IV. 59, V. 58 confuses the Stoic πρωτα κατα φυσιν with τα του σωματος αγαθα και τα εκτος of the Peripatetics, for which see I. 19. More on the subject in Madvig's fourth Excursus to the *D.F. Relinquit*: Orelli *relinqui* against the MSS.

§139. *Polemonis ... finibus*: all these were composite *fines*. *Adhuc*: I need scarcely point out that this goes with *habeo* and not with *probabilius*; *adhuc* for *etiam* with the comparative does not occur till the silver writers. *Labor eo*: cf. Horace's *nunc in Aristippi furtim praecepta relabor*, also *D.F.* V. 6 *rapior illuc: revocat autem Antiochus. Reprehendit manu*: *M.D.F.* II. 3. *Pecudum*: I. 6, *Parad.* 14 *voluptatem esse summum bonum, quae mihi vox pecudum videtur esse non hominum*; similar expressions occur with a reference to Epicurus in *De Off.* I. 105, *Lael.* 20, 32. *T.D.* V. 73, *D.F.* II. 18; cf. also Aristoph. *Plut.* 922 προβατιου βιον λεγεις and βοσκηματων βιος in Aristotle. The meaning of *pecus* is well shown in *T.D.* I. 69. *Iungit deo*: Zeller 176 sq. *Animum solum*: the same criticism is applied to Zeno's *finis* in *D.F.* IV. 17, 25. *Ut ... sequar*: for the repeated *ut* see *D.F.* V. 10, Madv. *Gram.* 480, obs. 2. Bait. brackets the second *ut* with Lamb. *Carneades ... defensitabat*: this is quite a different view from that in 131; yet another of Carneades is given in *T.D.* V. 83. *Istum finem*: MSS. *ipsum*; the two words are often confused, as in I. 2. *Ipsa veritas*: MSS. *severitas*, a frequent error; cf. *In Verr. Act.* I. 3, III. 162, *De Leg.* I. 4, also Madv. on *D.F.* IV. 55. *Obversetur*: Halm takes the conj. of Lamb., *adversetur*. The MSS. reading gives excellent sense; cf. *T.D.* II. 52 *obversentur honestae species viro*. Bait. follows Halm. *Tu ... copulabis*: this is the feigned expostulation of *veritas* (cf. 34 *convicio veritatis*), for which style see 125.

§140. *Voluptas cum honestate*: this whole expression is in apposition to *par*, so that *cum* must not be taken closely with *depugnet*; cf. Hor. *Sat.* I. 7, 19 *Rupili et Persi par pugnat uti non compositum melius* (sc. *par*) *cum Bitho Bacchius. Si sequare, ruunt*: for constr. cf. I. 7. *Communitas*: for Stoic philanthropy see Zeller 297. *Nulla potest nisi erit*: Madv. *D.F.* III. 70 "*in hac coniunctione—hoc fieri non potest nisi—fere semper coniunctivus subicitur praesentis—futuri et perfecti indicativus ponitur.*" *Gratuita*: "disinterested." *Ne intellegi quidem*: n. on I. 7, cf. also *T.D.* V. 73, 119. *Gloriosum in vulgus*: cf. *D.F.* II. 44 *populus cum illis facit* (i.e. Epicureis). *Normam ... regulam*: n. on *Ac. Post.* fragm. 8. *Praescriptionem*: I. 23, n.

§141. *Adquiescis*: MSS. are confused here, Halm reads *adsciscis*, comparing 138. Add *D.F.* I. 23 (*sciscat et probet*), III. 17 (*adsciscendas esse*), III. 70 (*adsciscet probari*) Bait. follows Halm. *Ratum ... fixum*: cf. 27 and n. on *Ac. Post.* fragm. 17. *Falso*: like *incognito* in 133. *Nullo discrimine*: for this see the explanation of *nihil interesse* in 40, n. *Iudicia*: κριτηρια as usual.

§§142—146. Summary. To pass to Dialectic, note how Protagoras, the Cyrenaics, Epicurus, and Plato disagree (142). Does Antiochus follow any of these? Why, he never even follows the *vetus Academia*, and never stirs a step from Chrysippus. Dialecticians themselves cannot agree about the very elements of their art (143). Why then, Lucullus, do you rouse the mob against me like a seditious tribune by telling them I do away with the arts altogether? When you have got the crowd together, I will point out to them that according to Zeno all of them are slaves, exiles, and lunatics, and that you yourself, not being *sapiens*, know nothing whatever (144). This last point Zeno used to illustrate by action Yet his whole school cannot point to any actual *sapiens* (145). Now as there is no knowledge there can be no art. How would Zeuxis and Polycletus like this conclusion? They would prefer mine, to which our ancestors bear testimony.

§142. *Venio iam*: Dialectic had been already dealt with in 91—98 here it is merely considered with a view to the choice of the supposed *sapiens*, as was Ethical Science in 129—141 and Physics in 116—128. With the enumeration of conflicting schools here given compare the one Sextus gives in *A.M.* VII. 48 sq. *Protagorae*: R. and P. 132 sq. *Qui putet*: so MSS., Halm and Bait. *putat* after Lamb. Trans. "inasmuch as he thinks". *Permotiones intimas*: cf. 20 *tactus interior*, also 76. *Epicuri*: nn. on 19, 79, 80. *Iudicium*: κριτηριον as usual. *Rerum notitiis*: προληψεσι, Zeller 403 sq. *Constituit*: note the constr. with *in*, like *ponere in. Cogitationis*: cf. I. 30. Several MSS. have *cognitionis*, the two words are frequently confused. See Wesenberg *Em.* to *T.D.* III. p. 17, who says, *multo tamen saepius "cogitatio" pro "cognitio" substituitur quam contra*, also *M.D.F* III. 21.

§143. *Ne maiorum quidem suorum*: sc. *aliquid probat*. For *maiorum* cf. 80. Here Plato is almost excluded from the so-called *vetus Academia*, cf. I. 33. *Libri*: titles of some are preserved in Diog. Laert. IV. 11—14. *Nihil politius*: cf. 119, n. *Pedem nusquam*: for the ellipse cf. 58, 116, *Pro Deiot.* 42 and *pedem latum* in Plaut. *Abutimur*: this verb in the rhetorical writers means to use words in metaphorical or unnatural senses, see Quint. X. 1, 12. This is probably the meaning here; "do we use the name Academic in a non natural fashion?" *Si dies est lucet*: a better trans of ει φως εστιν, ΄ημερα εστιν than was given in 96, where see n. *Aliter Philoni*: not Philo of Larissa, but a noted dialectician, pupil of Diodorus the Megarian, mentioned also in 75. The dispute between Diodorus and Philo is mentioned in Sext. *A.M.* VIII. 115—117 with the same purpose as here, see also Zeller 39. *Antipater*: the Stoic of Tarsus, who succeeded Diogenes Babylonius in the headship of the school. *Archidemus*: several times mentioned with Antipater in Diog., as VII. 68, 84. *Opiniosissimi*: so the MSS. I cannot think that the word is wrong, though all edd. condemn it. Halm is certainly mistaken in saying that a laudatory epithet such as *ingeniosissimi* is necessary. I believe that the word *opiniosissimi* (an adj. not elsewhere used by Cic.) was manufactured on the spur of the moment, in order to ridicule these two philosophers, who are playfully described as men full of *opinio* or δοξα—just the imputation which, as Stoics, they would most repel. Hermann's *spinosissimi* is ingenious, and if an em. were needed, would not be so utterly improbable as Halm thinks.

§144. *In contionem vocas*: a retort, having reference to 14, cf. also 63, 72. For these *contiones* see Lange, *Romische Alterthumer* II. 663, ed 2. They were called by and held under the presidency of magistrates, all of whom had the right to summon them, the right of the tribune being under fewer restrictions than the right of the others. *Occludi tabernas* in order of course that the artisans might all be at the meeting, for this see Liv. III. 27, IV. 31, IX. 7, and compare the cry "to your tents, O Israel" in the Bible. *Artificia*: n. on 30. *Tolli*: n. on 26. *Ut opifices concitentur*: cf. *Pro Flacc.* 18 *opifices et tabernarios quid neqoti est concitare? Expromam*: Cic. was probably thinking of the use to which he himself had put these Stoic paradoxes in *Pro Murena* 61, a use of which he half confesses himself ashamed in *D.F.* IV. 74. *Exsules* etc.: 136.

§145. *Scire negatis*: cf. Sext. *A.M.* VII. 153, who says that even καταληψις when it arises in the mind of a φαυλος is mere δοξα and not επιστημη; also *P.H.* II. 83, where it is said that the φαυλος is capable of το αληθες but not of αληθεια, which the σοφος alone has. *Visum ... adsensus*: the Stoics as we saw (II. 38, etc.) analysed sensations into two parts; with the Academic and other schools each sensation was an ultimate unanalysable unit, a ψιλον παθος. For this symbolic action of Zeno cf. *D.F.* II. 18, *Orat.* 113, Sextus *A.M.* II. 7, Quint. II. 20, 7, Zeller 84. *Contraxerat*: so Halm who qu. Plin. *Nat. Hist.* XI. 26, 94 *digitum contrahens aut remittens*; Orelli *construxerat*; MSS. mostly *contexerat*. *Quod ante non fuerat*: καταλαμβανειν however is frequent in Plato in the sense "to seize firmly with the mind." *Adverterat*: the best MSS. give merely *adverat*, but on the margin *admoverat* which Halm takes, and after him Bait.; one good MS. has *adverterat*. *Ne ipsi quidem*: even Socrates, Antisthenes and Diogenes were not σοφοι according to the Stoics, but merely were εν προκοπηι; see Diog. VII. 91, Zeller 257, and cf. Plut. *Sto. Rep.* 1056 (qu. by P. Valentia p. 295, ed Orelli) εστι δε ουτος (i.e. ΄ο σοφος) ουδαμου γης ουδε γεγονε. *Nec tu*: sc. *scis*; Goer. has a strange note here.

§146. *Illa*: cf. *illa invidiosa* above (144). *Dicebas*: in 22. *Refero*: "retort," as in Ovid. *Metam.* I. 758 *pudet haec opprobria nobis Et dici potuisse et non potuisse referri*; cf. also *par pari referre dicto. Ne nobis quidem*: "nor would they be angry;" cf. n. on. I. 5. *Arbitrari*: the original meaning of this was "to be a bystander," or "to be an eye-witness," see Corssen I. 238. *Ea non ut*: MSS. have *ut ea non aut*. Halm reads *ut ea non* merely, but I prefer the reading I have given because of Cicero's fondness for making the *ut* follow closely on the negative: for this see Madv. *Gram.* 465 *b*, obs.

§147. *Obscuritate*: cf. I. 44, n. on I. 15. *Plus uno*: 115. *Iacere*: cf. 79. *Plagas*: cf. n. on 112.

§148. *Ad patris revolvor sententiam*: for this see Introd. 50, and for the expression 18. *Opinaturum*: see 59, 67, 78, 112. *Intellegat se*: MSS. *intellegentes*, cf. n. on 132. *Qua re*: so Manut. for *per* of MSS. Επoχην *illam omnium rerum*: an odd expression; cf. *actio rerum* in 62. *Non probans*: so Madv. *Em.* 204 for MSS. *comprobans*. Dav. conj. *improbans* and is followed by Bait. I am not sure that the MSS. reading is wrong. The difficulty is essentially the same as that involved in 104, which should be closely compared. A contrast is drawn between a theoretical dogma and a practical belief. The dogma is that *assent* (meaning absolute assent) is not to be given to phenomena. This dogma Catulus might well describe himself as formally approving (*comprobans*). The *practice* is to give assent (meaning modified assent). There is the same contrast in 104 between *placere* and *tenere*. I may note that the word *alteri* (cf. *altero* in 104) need not imply that the dogma and the practice are irreconcilable; a misconception on this point has considerably confirmed edd. in their introduction of the negative. *Nec eam admodum*: cf. *non repugnarem* in 112. *Tollendum*: many edd. have gone far astray in interpreting this passage. The word is used with a double reference to *adsensus* and *ancora*; in the first way we have had *tollere* used a score of times in this book; with regard to the second meaning, cf. Caes. *Bell. Gall.* IV. 23, *Bell. Civ.* I. 31, where *tollere* is used of weighing anchor, and Varro *De Re Rust.* III. 17, 1, where it occurs in the sense "to get on," "to proceed," without any reference to the sea. (The exx. are from Forc.) This passage I believe and this alone is referred to in *Ad Att.* XIII. 21, 3. If my conjecture is correct, Cic. tried at first to manage a joke by using the word *inhibendum*, which had also a nautical signification, but finding that he had mistaken the meaning of the word, substituted *tollendum*.

[1] *De Leg.* II. §3.

[2] Cf. *De Or.* II. §1 with II. §5.

[3] *Ad Fam.* XIII. 1, Phaedrus nobis,... cum pueri essemus, valde ut philosophus probabatur.

[4] *N.D.* I. §93, Phaedro nihil elegantius, nihil humanius.

[5] *Ad Fam.* XIII. 1.

[6] *Brutus*, §309.

[7] *Ad Att.* II. 20, §6.

[8] *Ad Fam.* XIII. 16. *T.D.* V. §113. *Acad.* II. §115.

[9] *Brutus*, §306.

[10] *Ibid.*

[11] *Rep.* I. §7. *T.D.* V. §5. *De Off.* II. §§3,4. *De Fato*, §2.

[12] Cf. *Brutus*, §§312, 322.

[13] Cf. *Brutus*, §§312, 314, 316.

[14] *Brutus*, §315.

[15] *N.D.* I. §59.

[16] VII. I. §35.

[17] Cf. *N.D.* I. §93 with *Ad Fam.* XIII. 1, §1.

[18] *Ac.* I. §46.

[19] *D.F.* V. §3.

[20] *D.F.* I. §16.

[21] *D.F.* V. §6, etc.

[22] *D.F.* V. §8.

[23] *Ac.* II. §4.

[24] *Ib.* §69.

[25] *Ad Att.* XIII. 19, §5.

[26] *Ac.* II. §113.

[27] *Ac.* II. §113. *De Leg.* I. §54.

[28] II. §12.

[29] *Brutus,* §316.

[30] *Hortensius,* fragm. 18, ed. Nobbe.

[31] *T.D.* II. §61.

[32] *De Div.* I. §130.

[33] *D.F.* I. §6.

[34] *Ad Att.* I. 10 and 11.

[35] *Ibid.* II. 1, §3. *N.D.* I. §6.

[36] *Ad Att.* II. 2.

[37] *Ibid.* I. 20. Cf. II. 1, §12.

[38] II. 6.

[39] *Ad Att.* II. 7 and 16.

[40] *Ibid.* II. 6, §2.

[41] Cf. *Ad Att.* IV. 11 with IV. 8 a.

[42] *Ibid.* IV. 10.

[43] *Ibid.* IV. 16, §2.

[44] *Ibid.* IV. 16 c, §10, ed. Nobbe.

[45] *Ad Qu. Fr.* II. 14.

[46] *Ad Qu. Fr.* III. 5 and 6.

[47] §332.

[48] *Ad Fam.* XIII. 1. *Ad Att.* V. 11, §6.

[49] *Ad Att.* V. 10, §5.

[50] *De Off.* I. §1.

[51] *Tim.* c. 1.

[52] Cf. *Tim.* c. 1 with *De Div.* I. §5. *Brutus*, §250.

[53] *Ad Att.* VI. 1, §26.

[54] *Ibid.* VI. 2, §3.

[55] *Ibid.* VI. 6, §2.

[56] *Ibid.* VI. 7, §2. *Ad Fam.* II. 17, §1.

[57] *T.D.* V. §22.

[58] *Ad Att.* VII. 1, §1.

[59] *Ibid.* VII. 3, VIII. 11.

[60] *Ad Att.* X. 8, §6.

[61] *Ibid.* VIII. 2, §4.

[62] περι 'ομονοιας, *Ad Att.* IX. 9, §2, etc.

[63] *Ibid.* IX. 4, §2; 9, §1.

[64] *Ibid.* IX. 10, §2.

[65] *Ad Fam.* IX. 1.

[66] *Ibid.* IX. 3.

[67] *Ibid.* IV. 3 and 4.

[68] *De Rep.* I. §7. *T.D.* V. §5, etc.

[69] Cf. *N.D.* I. §6.

[70] Esp. I. §§26, 37.

[71] Cf. *Ac.* II. §29.

[72] *Ac.* II. §70.

[73] *De Div.* II. §1. *Ac.* I. §45, etc.

[74] *N.D.* I. §1.

[75] Cf. esp. *N.D.* I. §5. *T.D.* II. §5.

[76] *De Div.* II. §1. *N.D.* I. §7, etc.

[77] *T.D.* II. §4.

[78] *N.D.* I. §10.

[79] Cf. *Ac.* II. §8. *N.D.* I. §§10, 66.

[80] *T.D.* II. §9.

[81] *N.D.* I. §10.

[82] *Ibid.* I. §17. *Ac.* II. §§120, 137.

[83] *T.D.* V. §33.

[84] *Ac.* II. §121.

[85] *T.D.* V. §82, *libas ex omnibus.*

[86] *Ac.* II. §143.

[87] *T.D.* V. §11.

[88] *Ac.* II. §10.

[89] *N.D.* I. §12.

[90] *Parad.* §2. *De Fato*, §3. *T.D.* I. §7. *De Off.* I. §3.

[91] *D.F.* IV. §5.

[92] *Paradoxa*, §2.

[93] *T.D.* I. §55. *De Div.* II. §62.

[94] *T.D.* V. §11. *D.F.* II. §§1 and 2, etc.

[95] §13.

[96] Cf. esp. *N.D.* i. §6. *Ac.* ii. §§11 and 17.

[97] *De Leg.* I. §39.

[98] *Ibid.* I. §§55, 56.

[99] *N.D.* I. §4.

[100] *T.D.* IV. §53.

[101] Cf. *De Off.* III. §20.

[102] *T.D.* V. §§21-31, esp. §23.

[103] *Ibid.* V. §75.

[104] *De Off.* II. §35.

[105] *T.D.* V. §34.

[106] *Ac.* I. §16.

[107] *Paradoxa*, §4. *Ac.* II. §§136, 137. *T.D.* III. §10.

[108] *Ac.* II. §135.

[109] See esp. *N.D.* I. §§3, 4.

[110] *Ibid.*, also *T.D.* V. §83.

[111] Grote's *Aristotle*, vol. I. ch. 11.

[112] *T.D.* IV. §9. *D.F.* III. §41.

[113] I. §6.

[114] *T.D.* IV. §7.

[115] *Ibid.* IV. §7. Cf. *D.F.* II. §44, *populus cum illis facit.*

[116] *Ac.* I. §6. *T.D.* IV. 6, 7; II. §7; III. §33. *D.F.* III. §40.

[117] *T.D.* IV. §3.

[118] *D.F.* I. §§4-6. *Ac.* I. §10. *D.F.* III. §5.

[119] *De Div.* I. §§4, 5.

[120] *D.F.* III. §5. *N.D.* I. §8. *T.D.* III. §§10, 16.

[121] *T.D.* I. §5.

[122] *T.D.* II. §5.

[123] *De Div.* II. §1. *De Off.* II. §4.

[124] *De Div.* II. §6. *De Off.* II. §2.

[125] See esp. *De Consolatione*, fragm. 7, ed. Nobbe. *T.D.* V. §5. *Ac.* I. §11.

[126] *N.D.* I. §6.

[127] *T.D.* II. §§1, 4. *De Off.* II. §3. *D.F.* I. §1.

[128] *T.D.* II. §1. *D.F.* I. §§1, 3.

[129] *D.F.* I. §§1, 11.

[130] *De Div.* II. §5. *De Off.* II. §2. *T.D.* IV. §1.

[131] *De Div.* II. §4.

[132] *N.D.* I. §9. *T.D.* II. §1.

[133] *De Div.* II. §4.

[134] *Ad Att.* XII. 19, §1.

[135] *Ibid.* XII. 14, §3.

[136] *Ibid.* XII. 15, 16.

[137] *Ibid.* XII. 21, §5.

[138] *Ibid.* XII. 23, §2.

[139] *Ut scias me ita dolere ut non iaceam.*

[140] *De Or.* III. §109.

[141] *Ad Att.* XII. 28, §2.

[142] Cf. esp. *Ad Att.* XII. 40, §2 with 38, §3.

[143] *Ibid.* XII. 40, §2.

[144] *Ibid.* XII. 40, §5.

[145] *Ibid.* XIII. 26.

[146] *Ibid.* XII. 41, §1, also 42, 43; XIII. 26.

[147] *Ibid.* XII. 46.

[148] *Ad Att.* XII. 45, §1.

[149] *Über Cicero's Akademika,* p. 4.

[150] Cf. *Ad Att.* XII. 12, §2, where there is a distinct mention of the first two books.

[151] *Ibid.* XIII. 12, §3.

[152] *Ibid.* XIII. 19, §4.

[153] *Ibid.* XIII. 21, §§4, 5; 22, §3.

[154] II. §2.

[155] *De Fin.* Praef. p. lvii. ed. 2.

[156] *Ad Att.* XIII. 12, §3; 16, §1.

[157] *Ibid.* XVI. 3, §1.

[158] *Ibid.* XVI. 6, §4.

[159] *Ac.* II. §61.

[160] *D.F.* I. §2.

[161] *T.D.* II. §4. *De Div.* II. §1.

[162] Cf. Krische, p. 5.

[163] *Ac.* II. §61.

[164] *Ad Att.* XIII. 5, §1.

[165] *Ibid.* XIII. 32, §3.

[166] *Ad Att.* XIII. 33, §4.

[167] *Ibid.* XIII. II. §1.

[168] *Ibid.* XII. 42.

[169] *Ibid.* XIII. 16, §1.

[170] *Ibid.* XIII. 12, §3.

[171] *Ibid.* IV. 16a, §2.

[172] *Ibid.* XIII. 12, §3; also IV. 16a, §2.

[173] *Ad Att.* XIII. 12, §3.

[174] *Ibid.* XIII. 19, §4.

[175] *Ibid.* XIII. 12, §3.

[176] *Ibid.* XIII. 19, §4.

[177] *Ibid.* XIII. 12, §3; 19, §4; 16, §1.

[178] *Ibid.* XIII. 19, §3.

[179] *Ad Att.* XIII. 22, §1.

[180] *Ibid.* XIII. 19, §5.

[181] Cf. *Ibid.* XIII. 14, §3; 16, §2; 18; 19, §5.

[182] *Ibid.* XIII. 19, §5.

[183] *Ibid.* XIII. 25, §3.

[184] *Ad Att.* XIII. 24.

[185] *Ibid.* XIII. 13, §1; 18.

[186] *Ibid.* XIII. 13, §1; 18; 19, §4.

[187] *Ibid.* XIII. 12, §3. I may here remark on the absurdity of the dates Schütz assigns to these letters. He makes Cicero execute the second edition of the *Academica* in a single day. Cf. XIII. 12 with 13.

[188] *Ad Att.* XIII. 13, §1.

[189] *Ibid.* XIII. 19, §5.

[190] *Ibid.* XIII. 19, §3.

[191] *Ibid.* XIII. 25, §3.

[192] *Ibid.* XIII. 25, §3.

[193] *Ibid.* XIII. 21, §4.

[194] *Ibid.* XIII. 21, §5.

[195] *Ad Att.* XIII. 22, §3.

[196] *Ibid.* XIII. 24.

[197] *Ibid.* XIII. 35, 36, §2.

[198] *Ibid.* XIII. 38, §1.

[199] *Ibid.* XIII. 21, §§3, 4.

[200] *T.D.* II. §4. Cf. Quintil. *Inst. Or.* III. 6, §64.

[201] *Ad Att.* XVI. 6, §4. *N.D.* I. §11. *De Div.* II. §1.

[202] *De Off.* II. §8, *Timæus*, c. 1. *Ad Att.* XIII. 13, §1; 19, §5.

[203] *Ad Att.* XIII. 12; 16; 13; 19.

[204] *Ibid.* XVI. 6, §4. *T.D.* II. §4. *N.D.* I. §11. *De Div.* II. §1.

[205] *Nat. Hist.* XXXI. c. 2.

[206] *Inst. Or.* III. 6, §64.

[207] Plut. *Lucullus*, c. 42.

[208] §§12, 18, 148.

[209] Cf. *Att.* XIII. 19, §4.

[210] *Lucullus*, §12.

[211] *Ad Att.* XIII. 16, §1.

[212] Lactant. *Inst.* VI 2.

[213] Cf. esp. *De Off.* I. §133 with *Brutus*, §§133, 134.

[214] Esp. *Pro Lege Manilia*, §51.

[215] *Brutus*, §222.

[216] *In Verrem*, II. 3, §210.

[217] *Pro Lege Manilia*, §59.

[218] *Pro Sestio*, §122.

[219] *Pro Sestio*, §101.

[220] *Philipp.* II. §12.

[221] *Ad Att.* II. 24, §4.

[222] *Pis.* §6. *Pro Sestio*, §121. *Pro Domo*, §113. *Post Reditum in Senatu*, §9. *Philipp.* II. §12.

[223] *Ad Fam.* IX. 15, §3.

[224] Cf. *Post Reditum in Senatu*, §9. *Pro Domo*, §113.

[225] *Pro Archia*, §§6, 28.

[226] Cf. *Ac.* II. §9 with §80.

[227] §62.

[228] *Pro Plancio*, §12. *Pro Murena*, §36. *Pro Rabirio*, §26. *Pro Cornelia* II. fragm. 4, ed. Nobbe.

[229] *T.D.* V. §56. Cf. *De Or.* III. §9. *N.D.* III. §80.

[230] Cf. esp. III. §173.

[231] *Ibid.* II. §28.

[232] *Ibid.* II. §§13, 20, 21.

[233] *Ibid.* II. §51.

[234] Cf. *ibid.* II. §74 with III. §127.

[235] Cf. II. §152 with III. §187.

[236] *Ibid.* II. §154.

[237] *Brutus*, §§132, 133, 134, 259. *De Or.* III. §29.

[238] *Brutus*, §132.

[239] *De Or.* II. §244. *N.D.* I. §79. Cf. Gellius, XIX. 9.

[240] *De Or.* II. §155.

[241] *Ibid.* III. §194.

[242] Cf. *De Or.* II. §68 with III. §§182, 187.

[243] *De Or.* I. §82 sq.; II. §360.

[244] *Ibid.* I. §45; II. §365; III. §§68, 75.

[245] §12, *commemoravit a patre suo dicta Philoni.*

[246] Cf. *De Or.* III. §110.

[247] *Ac.* II. §148.

[248] Cf. *Ac.* II. §11.

[249] *Ibid.*

[250] *Ibid.* §§12, 18, with my notes.

[251] *Ac.* II. §12: *ista quae heri defensa sunt* compared with the words *ad Arcesilam Carneademque veniamus.*

[252] See below.

[253] *Ac.* II. §§33—36 inclusive; §54.

[254] *Ac.* II. §28.

[255] Cf. *Ac.* II. §§59, 67, 78, 112, 148, with my notes.

[256] *Ibid.* II. §10.

[257] *Ibid.* II. §28.

[258] Cf. II. §61 with the fragments of the *Hortensius*; also *T.D.* II. §4; III. §6; *D.F.* I. §2.

[259] Lactant. III. 16.

[260] Cf. *Ac.* II. §10.

[261] *Ib.* II. §61.

[262] §§44—46.

[263] §13.

[264] Cf. II. §14 with I. §44, and II. §§55, 56.

[265] II. §§17, 18, 22.

[266] Cf. II. §31 with I. §45.

[267] II. §§17, 24, 26, 27, 29, 38, 54, 59.

[268] II. §79.

[269] Cf. the words *tam multa* in II. §79.

[270] See II. §42, where there is a reference to the "*hesternus sermo.*"

[271] II. §10.

[272] Cf. II. §10: *id quod quaerebatur paene explicatum est, ut tota fere quaestio tractata videatur.*

[273] What these were will appear from my notes on the *Lucullus*.

[274] II. §12.

[275] *Ad Fam.* IX. 8.

[276] Cf. *Ad Att.* XIII. 25, §3: *Ad Brutum transeamus.*

[277] This is not, as Krische supposes, the villa Cicero wished to buy after Hortensius' death. That lay at Puteoli: see *Ad Att.* VII. 3, §9.

[278] II. §9.

[279] Cf. II. §61.

[280] II. §80: *O praeclarum prospectum*!

[281] Cf. II. §9 with §128 (*signum illud*), also §§80, 81, 100, 105, 125.

[282] II. §115.

[283] II. §63.

[284] II. §§147, 148.

[285] II. §135.

[286] Cf. II. §§11, 12 with the words *quae erant contra* ακαταληψιαν *praeclare collecta ab Antiocho: Ad Att.* XIII. 19, §3.

[287] Varro, *De Re Rust.* III. 17.

[288] II. §11.

[289] *Paradoxa*, §1. *D.F.* III. §8. *Brutus*, §119.

[290] *Ac.* I. §12. *D.F.* V. §8.

[291] Cf. II. §80.

[292] Cf. Aug. *Adv. Acad.* III. §35. Nonius, sub v. *exultare*.

[293] Cf. the word *nuper* in §1.

[294] §11.

[295] §§3, 18.

[296] *Ad Fam.* IX. 8, §1.

[297] *Ad Att.* II. 25, §1.

[298] *Ibid.* III. 8, §3.

[299] *Ibid.* III. 15, §3; 18, §1.

[300] *Ad Fam.* IX. 1—8. They are the only letters from Cicero to Varro preserved in our collections.

[301] Above, pp. xxxvii—xlii.

[302] *De Civ. Dei*, XIX. cc. 1—3.

[303] See Madvig, *De Fin.* ed. 2, p. 824; also Krische, pp. 49, 50. Brückner, *Leben des Cicero*, I. p. 655, follows Müller.

[304] Cf. Krische, p. 58.